OSCAR WILDE
AND THE YELLOW 'NINETIES

OSCAR WILDE IN AMERICA, 1882

From a photograph

OSCAR WILDE and the YELLOW 'NINETIES

By Frances Winwar

BLUE RIBBON BOOKS, GARDEN CITY, NEW YORK

CONTENTS

FOREWORD
By Lord Alfred Douglas

A S I HAVE BEEN INVITED to defend myself against the accusations
brought against me in this book I feel that it would be impossible for me to decline that invitation and to refuse to shoulder the
burden of all the unpleasantness it implies.

It will not be disputed that this book of Miss Frances Winwar's
(though I entirely acquit her of malice and deliberate unfairness)
is of such a character, so libelous in fact, that it could never have
been published in England. I could have prevented its publication
in Great Britain as easily and as effectively as I prevented the sale
of Frank Harris' *Oscar Wilde, His Life and Confessions* from the
time it was published without a publisher's imprimatur in the U.S.A.
till, after Harris' death, I was persuaded by my friend, Mr. Bernard
Shaw, to consent to its reissue in London on his undertaking to
remove or rewrite all the passages which contained aspersions on
me.

Harris himself had already written a complete retraction of and
apology for those aspersions in a book called *A New Preface to the
Life and Confessions of Oscar Wilde,* published in London by The
Fortune Press in 1925 (second edition 1927). It is no exaggeration to say that in this *New Preface,* which he wrote in Nice and
personally handed to me in manuscript, Harris admitted that prac-
tically everything he had written against me in his life of Wilde was
untrue, and he explained that he had been deceived and misled by

the malice of Robert Ross and by Oscar Wilde himself into making statements which he now bitterly regretted and of which he was ashamed.

Here are a few extracts from Harris' *New Preface*.

Now when I review the whole case, I have to admit that in many essentials I misjudged Lord Alfred Douglas again and again and did him grave injustice. . . . As the editor of *Pearson's Magazine* in the United States during the war years, I compared him with the greatest: as a writer of sonnets he can stand with Shakespeare. . . . That I should have misjudged the foremost poet of this time is my keenest regret.

I naturally supposed that Mr. Bernard Shaw, having read this *New Preface,* would make use of Harris' own words in correcting the libels on me contained in Harris' book. Unfortunately it appears Mr. Bernard Shaw had forgotten all about the book, and when I asked him why he had not taken it as the basis for his rewriting or revising of Harris' text he told me he had never read or seen the *New Preface.* As it happened, I had and have still in my possession a long letter which Mr. Shaw wrote to me about the *New Preface* at the time it came out, and I was thus able to convince Mr. Shaw that he *had* read it. He had simply forgotten it, and though he carried out his promise of removing Harris' aspersions and rewriting some of the most offensive passages, by the time Mr. Shaw's reissue of Harris came out it was still not altogether free from libels and misstatements. However, after the removal of about half of one chapter I was satisfied, and the brilliant preface which Mr. Shaw wrote for the reissue of Harris' book, for which he made himself responsible, contained such kind and flattering references to myself (he exalted me as a poet, compared me favourably to Shelley, defended my moral character, and vindicated the nature of my relations with and treatment of Oscar Wilde in the strongest and most generous terms) that it would ill become me to cherish any grievance about his lapse of memory in the case of Harris' admissions of error in regard to me. On the contrary, I owe him a deep debt of gratitude. I think it is fairly obvious that Miss Winwar has not seen this reissue of Frank Harris' *Life and Confessions of Oscar Wilde* with a preface by Bernard Shaw (published in London by Constable in 1938), just as it is also fairly obvious that she has relied, to a great extent, on the uncorrected version of Harris' book for her story of the events in which I am concerned. If she had read either Harris' retraction or Mr. Shaw's defense of me she would surely not have ignored both the one and the other.

I do not propose to bore my readers by going into elaborate details or by entering into meticulous arguments, but I would like to point out that Harris' book has been exposed as grossly inaccurate, to say the least of it, not only by Mr. Shaw and myself, but by Mr. Robert Harborough Sherard in his latest book. It is unlucky that Miss Winwar, who includes in her bibliography of works studied for the purposes of her narrative all the books about Wilde by Mr. Sherard except the last one published in 1937, *George Bernard Shaw, Frank Harris and Oscar Wilde,* in which Mr. Sherard admits that he completely misjudged me, misled again by Robert Ross, and makes me a most generous *amende,* should have missed just that one book out of Sherard's collection. Because if she had read it she would surely have felt it right to mention that Mr. Sherard, who was one of the first after Wilde's death to attack me, has now admitted that he was completely wrong, that he did me great injustice, and that he has completely revised his opinion of Robert Ross, whose appalling character I exposed at the Central Criminal Court in London in 1914.

I think I have said enough to convince any impartial person (not excluding Miss Winwar herself) that the sources from which *Oscar Wilde and the Yellow Nineties* is derived are not sufficiently authenticated to serve, as she has made them serve, for an attack on my character and on my whole attitude to Wilde.

Many things related about me in Miss Winwar's book are utterly false, and there is also a continual suppression (I do not for a moment suggest deliberate) of facts which tell in my favour. For example, how comes it that Miss Winwar, in her description of Wilde's last days in Paris, does not mention that I was at that time supplying him with what were, for a very poor man like myself, very large sums of money? In the Appendix to my *Autobiography* (London, 1929, published later in the U.S.A. as *My Friendship with Oscar Wilde*) there is a list of my cheques payable to Wilde which was supplied to me by my bankers. This list shows that in one year I gave him nearly four hundred pounds. I explained in my book that this sum only represented a part, probably not the larger part, of what I gave him, because I frequently handed him bank notes for a thousand francs when he came to lunch or dine with me (in those days a thousand francs was forty pounds) and that, in fact, during the whole of the time between the death of my father, when I came into a small amount of money, and that of Wilde himself, I scarcely ever saw him without giving him ready money, and when I did not see him I sent him cheques whose record fortunately survives. It is true that Miss Winwar does not in so many words say that I "left Wilde penniless," which was the generally accepted story before the publication of my *Autobiography,* but she certainly leaves her readers free to infer that I was not a good friend to him either then or at any other time. Surely this is not fair dealing.

Again when she relates the story of my separation from Wilde at Naples caused by the threat of my mother to stop my allowance, she dismisses as worthless my own account of the matter, which is simply that I got two hundred pounds from my mother to give him because I could not bear to leave him without money. She declares that this two hundred pounds was merely a part of a much larger sum (five hundred pounds she says) which I "owed" him and that this mythical (for it is mythical) five hundred pounds was "a debt of honour." She declares that Wilde himself is her authority for this story and that he wrote it in a letter. I have never seen any such letter, though I am quite prepared to believe in its existence; there are hundreds of letters of Wilde's which I have never seen. Most of them are now, I believe, in the hands of my friend, Mr. A. J. A. Symons, who is writing a full length "official" biography of Wilde and who has been entrusted by Oscar Wilde's only surviving son with all the documents available. Mr. Symons has assured me that when his book is finished it will result in my complete and final vindication and in the establishing of the exact truth of my story as related in my *Autobiography* and that this result will be reached largely on the strength of Wilde's own letters which I have not seen. Mr. Symons told me he was amazed at the way letters and documents turned up to endorse my version of the facts. He has even, almost miraculously, got hold of the original manuscript of an article I wrote in *La Revue Blanche* in 1896 while Wilde was still in prison.

Surely Miss Winwar should have known that Wilde's letters can hardly be accepted as conclusive proofs against anyone, for it can be shown, and will be shown in Mr. Symons' book, that he frequently flatly contradicted himself in consecutive letters and that when he was annoyed or had a grievance, real or imaginary, his statements were apt to be utterly reckless and venomously regardless of truth. In his *De Profundis* letter written in prison, to which Miss Winwar frequently refers, he makes the astonishing statement that I interfered with his art and prevented him from writing, whereas the truth, which is susceptible of complete proof, is that from the time he met me till the day of his death the only thing he wrote when I was not with him (generally sitting in the same room) was precisely this *De Profundis* screed which is a letter to me! He wrote *The Importance of Being Earnest* at a house in Worthing when I was staying with him and while I was sitting in the room with him. The same applies to *A Woman of no Importance,* written at Babbacombe in a house lent to him by Lady Mount Temple, where I stayed with him; he wrote *The Ideal Husband* partly in a house he took at Goring, where we lived together for two or three months, and partly in rooms in St. James's Place in London, where I visited him regularly every day; he wrote *A Florentine Tragedy* when we were together at Florence, and finally he wrote *The Ballad of Reading Gaol* in my villa at Naples, and from the day when we were separated till the hour of his death he never wrote another line.

I think I am entitled to say that a man who is capable, in the face of these facts, of brazenly declaring that I interfered with his art and prevented him from writing is so utterly discredited as a truthful witness that no reasonable being would accept his bare word for anything if it conflicted with any respectable evidence. All this recapitulation of events, repeated for the hundredth time, is wearisomely repugnant to me. I fondly hoped that having, at great violence to my own feelings, told the whole truth about myself in my *Autobiography* and other books, having never spared myself, and having even gone out of my way, against the advice of my friends, to make damaging admissions about facts or states of mind which could never have been otherwise substantiated, I was entitled to think that my word and my *bona fides* were established and that I would be believed, as in fact I have been believed till now by every biographer of Wilde who has written since I published my *Autobiography* in 1929.

There are a number of statements about me in Miss Winwar's book which are incorrect, but I really feel that I am not concerned to answer them one by one. I have never denied that I was in many respects "a bad boy" in my early youth. I have admitted it and expressed the deepest contrition for it over and over again, publicly, in my books, and in the witness box in open court. Those who are sufficiently interested in me to want to know the exact truth about me personally will find it in my books. I owed no money at all to Oscar Wilde at the time I left him in Naples: the boot was very much on the other leg; there was never any such thing as any "debt of honour" between him and me, and, on the contrary, if I were now to do what (to do us both justice) we never did—that is, make up a strict account of all money transactions between us—the result would show a large balance in my favour. Just for one instance, I gave him three hundred and sixty pounds after he had started the action against my father. He started the prosecution without my knowledge and upon the advice of Robert Ross and then told me *after* the warrant for my father had been issued that he found he had not enough money to pay the demands of his solicitors and carry on the case. I thereupon, without a word of remonstrance, gave him the amount required, and I never dreamed of asking him to give it back. At the trial of my action for libel against Arthur Ransome in 1913 this episode was used against me, on the production of my banking account, in a very virulent cross-examination, the object being to make out that I was actuated by unnatural and unfilial feelings toward my father.

As I pointed out in one of my books, if I had not given him the three hundred and sixty pounds no doubt Counsel in the Ransome case would have brought this up against me as an example of my mean refusal to help a friend in distress! With my persistent detractors and calumniators it has always been axiomatic in connection with the Wilde affair that whatever I did or said I was sure to be wrong and actuated by the most ignoble motives, and I suppose I must resign myself to the inevitable. I know too much about history and how it gets written to hope that the real truth about anything is ever certain to be accepted. The most one can hope is that it will prevail with people of good will, who are, however, unfortunately not usually in a majority.

There would be no object in pinning down all the minor errors in Miss Winwar's book; e.g., Wilde was not reading *The Yellow Book* when he was arrested in my sitting room at the Cadogan Hotel; neither he nor I could stand *The Yellow Book* at any price. He refused to write for it, chiefly because he was at that time on very bad terms with his publisher, John Lane. It is quite untrue that he was chagrined at not being asked to write for the publication. He *was* asked and he refused. Again, my father's whiskers were not red but very dark brown, almost black, as was his hair. Not that it matters. I merely mention it and *The Yellow Book* story (which was originally invented by an enterprising reporter in a London evening paper) to give specimens of what might be done in the way of picking holes in Miss Winwar's book. I deliberately refrain from doing more in this direction because I wish to put it on record that I consider Miss Winwar's book to be very well written and highly dramatic and because, as I have already said, I do not wish to accuse her of deliberate unfairness to me. I merely suggest that she has been rash in making accusations against me on flimsy and easily discredited evidence. She accepts, for example, without question the malicious story for whose inception Frank Harris is responsible (a man who cheated me out of two thousand pounds, as related in my

xiii

Autobiography, and who, after I had forgiven him for this, years later tried to blackmail me at the time when he was editing *Vanity Fair* and I was editing *The Academy*); namely, that it was I who forced the reluctant Wilde to attack my father simply because I hated my father. I have never denied that I urged Wilde to take legal proceedings against my father from the first moment that he started his insane and brutal attack on Wilde and his own son. But if Wilde had taken my advice at the time I first gave it to him my father would never have had a leg to stand upon, and my motives for advising Wilde as I did were not in any way affected by my dislike for my father. All I wanted to do was to protect Wilde and prevent my father from finally breaking the heart of my mother by causing the hideous scandal for which he was responsible.

How can Miss Winwar or any reasonable being believe that if my father's object had been, as he hypocritically pretended, to "save his son from a dangerous friendship" (to use Carson's words in the Wilde-Queensberry trial) he would have acted as he did?

If Sir Edward Clarke had not gone back on his solemn undertaking and promise (given to me and Wilde in his chambers in consultation in the presence of our solicitors) that he would call me as a witness, I am convinced that my father would have lost his case and been convicted, in which case he would of course merely have been "bound over." No jury would have given my father a verdict once they had realized that his object in libeling Wilde was, mainly, to ruin his own son and to break the heart of his already deeply injured wife.

As for the ravings against me of Wilde in his *De Profundis* letter, I have already shown how much credence can be attached to his evidence. Wilde wrote that letter when he was half mad and nearly starving in prison and under the entirely erroneous impression that I had abandoned him. Directly he got out of prison and realized how utterly mistaken he had been about my attitude to him he started writing me letters "in the old adoring strain," as Harris puts it in his *New Preface,* and, quite obviously, he very quickly completely got over all his absurd prison-fostered delusions about me. The accusations which he brings against me in the letter (including the comic episode of my alleged "cruel" refusal to obtain lemonade for him when he was ill at Brighton) are either so fantastic or so childishly idiotic that when I first read the letter, withheld from me by Robert Ross till twelve years after Wilde's death, I took it for granted that their undignified absurdity was such that no reasonable person could possibly be found to believe them. It was I that insisted on the letter being read in court at the trial of my action against Arthur Ransome in 1913. I said to my counsel, "People have only got to listen to all this wild nonsense to see how ridiculous it is." I was quite wrong of course. To this day this farrago of malignant imbecility is taken quite seriously by many people and is sometimes referred to as a "terrible indictment," a "damning exposure," and so forth. All I can say is that I decline to argue with anyone who is stupid enough to be taken in by such twaddle which Wilde himself would, I am perfectly certain, have blushed for if he had realized that it would ever be taken seriously. In fact, he did blush for it and told me that he was "mad and starving" when he wrote it. Only, unfortunately, at that time, as I had never read the letter which he entrusted to Ross to give to me and which Ross withheld from my knowledge till twelve years after his death, I did not in the least know what he was talking about, and to what letter he was referring. All this is explained at length in my *Autobiography,* and it would be intolerable to go into it all again at length.

Miss Winwar also adopts Frank Harris' story that I (a poor little undergraduate "kid" of twenty, very young for my age and looking about fifteen at the time when I first met Wilde) immediately proceeded to take possession, body and soul, of this man of genius of thirty-nine and to dominate him completely and turn him into a helpless puppet. It is no use arguing with people who can swallow such drivel, so I say no more about it.

There is one more point, the literary one which I would have expected Miss Winwar, as herself a woman of letters, to appreciate better than she has done. She quotes my two poems, *Two Loves* and *In Praise of Shame* (a sonnet), which originally appeared in *The Chameleon* and were read in court during the Queensberry trial at the Old Bailey and at the subsequent trials of Wilde, and she solemnly reproduces the absurd comments made by the judge, Mr. Justice Wills, and by Counsel about them. Both these poems appear in the latest edition of my poetry (published in two volumes, *Lyrics* and *Sonnets,* by Rich and Cowan, London, 1935).

To the sonnet *In Praise of Shame* I have, in this edition, added the following footnote:

As this sonnet was entirely misrepresented in the Law Courts by wooden-headed lawyers on at least two occasions, I take this opportunity of referring enquirers about its meaning to the last verse of the second chapter of the Book of Genesis.

The sonnet, which happens, though I say it, to be a pretty good one, and which obviously is influenced in its style by Swinburne, has nothing on earth to do with the vice which was the subject of Wilde's trials. It has not the remotest connection with or reference to homosexuality. Anyone who is not, artistically speaking, ignorant and illiterate (as I venture to suggest was the case with Mr. Justice Wills) could not fail to appreciate this. What, then, is the point of rehashing up the foolish remarks made about it at the time by a judge who was under the influence of the mass hysteria which overwhelmed the country at the time of the Wilde trials?

As to the other poem, I do not deny that it contains an allusion to homosexuality, but it is really very harmless and decorous, and if it had been printed for the first time within the last ten years as the work of one of our "modern poets" no one would have turned a hair over it.

In my Rich and Cowan 1935 edition I have the following footnote to it:

This poem was used against me in the Law Courts in cross-examination at the instigation of that stern moralist, the late Robert Ross, in a court presided over by another moralist, Mr. Justice Darling. As I tried to explain then (unsuccessfully), it is merely the outcome of a classical education and a passion for the sonnets of Shakespeare. Its morality or immorality is "in the eye of the beholder" or, I should say more properly, "the mind of the reader."

Counsel opposed to me in the case referred to (1913) was of

course quite entitled to put any of my own writings to me in cross-examination, but the reading of these two poems at the Wilde trials in 1895 was grossly unfair to Wilde, who was not responsible for them, and to me, who was not represented in the case and unable to go into the witness box in my own defense. A just judge would have recognized this. Equally, a just judge would have dealt very differently with the juryman who, in the course of the Wilde trial, as recorded by Miss Winwar on pages 316 to 317 of her book, wanted to know why I had not been "arrested" and said, "If we are to consider these letters [that is, Wilde's two letters to me read in court] as evidence of guilt, and if we adduce any guilt from these letters, it applies as much to Lord Alfred Douglas as to the defendant." Instead of pointing out, as any fair judge would have done, that I could not possibly be tried, much less convicted, in my absence in a case in which I was not represented and unable to go into the witness box, and that it was his (the judge's) duty to protect me against such gross and ignorant unfairness, this precious representative of the "great tradition of the English Bench" proceeded to go as far as he dared to join in this cowardly and oblique attack on an absent man. Pandering to the same mass hysteria to which I have already referred, he gave no rebuke to the juryman and merely explained that "no prosecution would be possible on the mere production of Wilde's letters to Lord Alfred Douglas." I should think not indeed! And on another page Miss Winwar quotes the judge's description of these letters from Wilde to me as "disgusting letters." I really think I am entitled to ask her to explain what she means and why she thought it right to reproduce Mr. Justice Wills's vapourings after a lapse of nearly fifty years. On page 190 of her book she quotes in full one of these letters (the other, equally innocuous, also appears on page 274), and this is what she says about it:

It was a lovely letter, worthy of being sent by a poet to a poet.

Quite so, Miss Winwar, but would it not have been fairer to me and even to your own readers to enter a little more deeply into the question of these letters written to me by Wilde, described by the judge as "disgusting" and by you as "lovely"? Which is it to be, please, Miss Winwar?

Even in 1895 a man in England could not very well be "arrested" and tried because someone had written him a letter, whether it was a "lovely" letter or a "disgusting" letter. That being so (and is there one single man or woman in the world who will dispute it?), can Miss Winwar lay her hand on her heart and conscientiously declare that she has been fair to me?

I am quite aware that my claim to rank as a major poet, which has not been seriously disputed in this country (England) for at least twenty years, may not have penetrated to America, where my poetry has been persistently boycotted by publishers, but even if I am not a great poet I am surely entitled to common fair play, and even if I behaved foolishly and rashly (and even, perhaps, sometimes wickedly) between forty and fifty years ago am I therefore condemned to be the perpetual scapegoat of all the Pharisees in the world in this year of Grace, 1941? Is there never to be an end of this mudslinging? At any rate, perhaps I may be allowed to plead that as I am now over seventy years of age people, who still feel an irresistible "urge" to throw mud at me might decently bring themselves to wait a few years till I am dead.

Part One

OSCAR WILDE

Chapter I: Speranza

J ANE FRANCESCA ELGEE could no longer have been reckoned
young by Victorian standards when in 1851 she became the
wife of Dr. William Robert Wills Wilde. For she had already turned the quarter-century mark, a time of life which the
women of her day usually commemorated by bestowing another
increase on the kingdom. Her Majesty herself, by her twenty-
fifth year, had insured succession by providing the throne with
a baby Prince of Wales, her second child, and made assurance
almost foolproof by a staggering sequence of births. Indeed,
some of the peers of the realm who knew what demands and
petitions followed each royal blessing, were beginning to show
their consternation whenever Victoria, addressing the people
after the term of her lying-in, announced that the latest event
had "filled the measure of the Queen's domestic happiness."
Since Her Majesty had not entered the period of her literary
activity and since therefore concentration on the establishment
of her line suffered no distraction, it seemed to the irreverent
that the measure of the Queen's happiness had much in common with the magic cup of that other happy pair, Philemon and
Baucis, blessed of the gods.

There is no doubt that Jane Francesca Elgee counted herself
among the irreverent. Three years earlier in fact she had
come out boldly in the public prints as an Irish nationalist
seeking to stir up her compatriots to the storming of Dublin
Castle, the seat of British power in Ireland. "Jacta Alea Est."
Under that forbidding title the Dublin *Nation*, a weekly magazine, printed an appeal that made young patriots rush to their
guns and tried old fighters shake their heads. "The Irish nation
has at last decided," it began. "England has done us one good
service at least. Her recent acts have taken away the last miserable pretext for passive submission . . . Oh! for a hundred
thousand muskets glittering brightly in the light of heaven,"

3

it exhorted, "and the monumental barricades stretching across each of our noble streets, made desolate by England—circling round the doomed Castle, made infamous by England . . . Gather round the standard of your chiefs . . . One bold, one decisive move. One instant to take breath, and then a rising; a rush, a charge from north, south, east and west upon the English garrison, and *the land is ours*."

Unfortunately the bold decisive move was taken by the authorities against the editor of the *Nation*, and the paper was suppressed.

From her eighteenth year when after a studious girlhood Jane Francesca Elgee burst into poetry she had been inflaming the readers of the Irish magazines with intensely patriotic verse, kindled at the oratory of the leader O'Brien and flaring with her own pent-up ardor. Speranza was the name she adopted as the nationalist muse, Speranza, the bringer of hope to a people whose glories and sorrows had yet to find tongue. As John Fenshawe Ellis she abandoned the heights for pedestrian prose, to enable those to reach her who could not otherwise follow. The names fulfilled the two sides of her nature. In the romantic Speranza she saw herself beautiful, inspiring, feminine, a Dantean Beatrice guiding to regions of bliss her people condemned to the Inferno of poverty, hunger and oppression. In John Fenshawe Ellis she beheld the Irish patriot whose

> thunder words
> Are like lifted swords
> To war against man or devil.

The person she saw in the mirror had more of John Fenshawe Ellis than of the ethereal Speranza. There was little of the feminine in her great tall body and her large hands and feet. The massive head with its heavy features was set on square, masculine shoulders. The bold nose might have jutted from the face of a Roman senator; the mouth, though well cut, was thick of lip. The eyes, however, wide apart under the straight brows, had depth and thoughtfulness, and the expanse

4

of forehead above them gave the handsome face an expression
of placidity that was immediately dispelled by the irrelevant
motions of those huge hands arranging a stray wisp of hair
or some bit of frippery. For to compensate for nature's defi-
ciency Speranza resorted to art in creating the figure which
she presented to the world. In a day when crinolines were the
fashion she would wear two instead of one under the vo-
luminous crimson silk skirt flounced with Limerick lace. Her
bodice, draped with a scarf of Oriental splendor, was further
adorned with brooches and other jewelry that jangled as she
walked. To emphasize her sensibility she had always within
reach a fan and a scent bottle. On state occasions she wore
on her straight black hair, parted in the middle and brushed
to frame her face in the Grecian manner, a wreath of false
laurels in gilt. As Speranza Apollo's crown, even if imitation,
was no more than her due.

  She had moreover found for herself a poet ancestor who had
also been a fighter for freedom. Though she was born in
Wexford into the family of the conservative Protestant Irish
Elgees—her grandfather had been Archdeacon Elgee—she preferred to trace her lineage to Dante Alighieri. The name Elgee,
she informed one with an aplomb that cast some doubt on her
knowledge of Italian, was merely a corruption of Alighieri.
None came forward to dispute her claim and she was happy in
the dream that set her apart from the dull people and the hum-
drum of daily life.

  For her descent from another famous personage Speranza
did not have to resort to invention, for the Rev. Charles Maturin, author of *Melmoth the Wanderer*, was her uncle. He
died two years before her birth, therefore she had never seen
him in the flesh. Nevertheless she felt a close kinship with him
and was proud of the relation, though not so proud as of the
fictive strain from the medieval poet. Still Maturin too had
won some distinction. Since 1820 when his strange novel of
a combined Faust and Wandering Jew made its readers shiver
with pleasant horror, Maturin's fame had spread. Byron, impressed by what he thought genius in Melmoth's creator, had

5

helped him to gain a public. Thackeray had been so struck by the description of the dark compelling gaze of Melmoth that he was immediately reminded of it on seeing Goethe's eyes. The Rossetti children for a long time made *Melmoth* their bedtime reading, Dante Gabriel especially falling under the spell of the eternal wanderer seeking in vain a substitute who of his own free will would release him from the fatal barter of his soul for youth. In France fifteen years after the book's appearance, Balzac paid it the compliment of writing its sequel in *Melmoth Réconcilié*. Speranza herself had felt the fascination of the Gothic hero doomed by his unquenchable desire for knowledge to eternal disenchantment.

Dr. William Robert Wills Wilde pretended to no exalted strain in his ancestry, but as far as he could remember there was nothing in it to be ashamed of. Long ago his great-grandfather, a Durham business man, had settled in Ireland, married the daughter of an old Irish family and himself become as Irish as his Saxon blood would permit. In the succeeding generation the Irish almost wholly obliterated the Saxon, so that in William Robert Wills Wilde the Irish prevailed except in the matter of religion; for like the Elgees the Wildes were Protestant. At the age of thirty-six William Wilde, well known as an ear and eye specialist, found himself sufficiently established to marry. What prompted his choice of Jane Francesca Elgee there is no record to tell us. It may be that the reputation of Speranza attracted in him the amateur of Ireland's traditions; it may be too that he saw in Speranza the perfect hostess for the salon which as a married man he was expected to have. At any rate Dublin approved the match.

Some few had misgivings for Speranza's sake. Although an excellent surgeon Dr. Wilde left something to be desired as a man. Far from handsome physically—indeed he was to attain a dubious fame by appearing in a volume devoted to the signally ugly—he salved his self-esteem by an irregular private life. It was bruited about that he had a number of illegitimate children. He was known besides to be a heavy drinker. Dr. Wilde denied neither rumor and in the case of drink he

6

even defended it staunchly. In early youth he had been so ill that the doctors had given him up. One of them, however, more wise than the rest, prescribed a glass of strong ale every hour, a prescription, Dr. Wilde would laugh, that saved his life.

To his skill as a surgeon nothing but praise was ever given. It was still told how as a student he had saved a man's eyesight by extracting a needle imbedded in the eyeball; and there was that other operation which he had performed with a common pair of scissors on a child who had swallowed a pin. Both times he had been called in a hurry and without warning, and in each case he had been successful. More orthodox practitioners frowned upon such slipshod methods. Dr. Wilde merely shrugged his shoulders, knowing that if he had not brought immediate help the man might have lost his eye and the child have choked to death. To the people who had witnessed his performances they seemed nothing short of miraculous and his practice grew. With the years he was to gain a European reputation, receive the Order of the Polar Star from Oscar I, King of Sweden, and the knighthood from Lord Carlisle, Viceroy of Ireland.

In the meantime with his statuesque bride he took a house at 21 Westland Row, Dublin. Speranza was happy, whatever the gossip that reached her ears. Men, she knew, had never been angels, nor had women either. "There has never been a woman yet in the world," she was fond of saying in such prose as one never expected from a Speranza, "who wouldn't have given the top of the milk-jug to some man, if she had met the right one." Had she met the right one in Dr. Wilde? As far as she would confide in the world, she had. Not a word of complaint or resentment ever passed her lips even when she was confronted with situations that would have brought less forbearing women to the divorce courts. Something perplexed in her complete acceptance of her husband's straying, making one wonder whether its source were indifference, blind faith or an astounding amorality.

Toward the close of 1864, nine months after Dr. Wilde was knighted, one of his private intrigues reached the proportions

7

of a public scandal. A Miss Travers, it appeared, the daughter of a professor of medical jurisprudence at Dublin's Trinity College, involved Sir William Wilde in a lawsuit in which she alleged that she had been violated after the administration of chloroform. Such cases had been fairly common in the courts since the introduction of anesthesia. But Miss Travers's suit had other complicated threads which the jury was asked to disentangle, among them a claim for two thousand pounds damages against Lady Wilde for a libelous letter which she had written to the girl's father. The letter was presented and read. In terms that left no room for doubt Lady Wilde informed Professor Travers that his daughter had been trying to blackmail Sir William after carrying on an intrigue with him. "The wages of disgrace she had so basely treated for and demanded shall never be given her," were Lady Wilde's amazing closing words. For days the Dublin press enjoyed an increased circulation while the pot houses did excellent business.

Dramatic and more imposing than ever in her recently acquired ladyship, Speranza invoked her libertarian past to gain sympathy for her case and her husband's although there were simple souls in court who were left gaping by some of her answers.

"Why did you not answer Miss Travers," she was asked, "when she wrote telling you of your husband's attempt on her virtue?"

"I took no interest in the matter," Speranza retorted shortly. Was hers a newer, loftier morality, or no morality at all?

At the summing up Chief Justice Monahan made a concise speech and then addressed the jury to draw its own conclusions from the evidence. The verdict when it came had wit if not justice: for the loss of her honor Miss Travers was awarded a farthing damages, which farthing was also to carry costs.

How much of the scandal reached the ears of the two sons who had been born to the Wildes? William the elder was now twelve, and Oscar who had come into the world on the 16th of October, 1854, had passed his tenth birthday. Both children from the time they were able to keep awake at night had been

8

admitted to the parties and *conversazioni* in the parlor of the handsome mansion at 1 Merrion Square, the fashionable part of Dublin to which the family had moved a year after Oscar's birth in Westland Row. They were amorphous gatherings at which Speranza in her wreath and crinolines, with the miniatures of her children and relations like badges of honor on her broad bosom, swept from guest to guest, endeavoring by her social tact to bring order out of chaos. Her white kid gloves moved restlessly as she talked. Now and then her lace handkerchief was raised to her face where powder and make-up, heavily applied, called attention to the first few wrinkles which she ardently essayed to conceal. She had a horror of old age. With tightly shuttered windows she tried to keep it out, and with lamps so shaded that her rooms appeared always in a glowing dusk, she dimmed her sight to its intrusion.

The two boys, early accustomed to her, found nothing unusual in her eccentricity. They also accepted their father whom they often accompanied on antiquarian jaunts. The writers, artists, critics, revolutionaries, bohemians and charlatans who swarmed to the Wilde "at homes" they took for granted as representatives of the outside world, and from them learned wisdom orthodox and unorthodox. Conviviality and brilliant talk were the order of the day, and if epigrams came fastest when their speakers staggered, the two lads reasoned philosophically that no body can carry lightly a burden of wit. They knew besides another side of household life—the hours when their mother withdrew to her room in her appointed office of patriotic muse, and when their father, his visiting hours over, sat at his desk to compile statistics for the Irish Census or put down some curious fact of Ireland's past. Whatever his personal indulgences he was a serious scholar, a merit recognized by the Royal Irish Academy when it awarded him the Cunningham Medal.

To Speranza with her ultramundane view of things life had not been unkind except in one respect. She had wanted her second child to be a girl. On finding herself pregnant after the birth of Willie she was so certain her wish would be fulfilled that she talked of the unborn baby as if it were a girl and made her plans accordingly. When the time came her disappointment in the birth of another boy proved all the more bitter in that it found her completely unprepared. As if to atone for her lack of enthusiasm she gave the infant a string of resounding names: Oscar Fingal O'Flahertie Wills Wilde, betraying in them the keenness of her unfulfilled hope. Since the child was not what she had most wanted he must at least be destined to greatness. His names would lead him to distinction. The first, therefore, honored the King of Sweden; Fingal stood for the Gaelic hero, father of Ossian, Macpherson's gigantic hoax which, though exposed, the fervent Speranza still accepted. As for O'Flahertie, it perpetuated the memory of Ireland's first historian who claimed descent from her earliest kings. Wills, a name borne by a distinguished Celtic family and already carried by Dr. Wilde, was given to the child for the father's sake.

Nationalism together with a peculiar regard for royalty marked Speranza's choice. It is curious that in her reverence for her antecedents she should have omitted Dante, for neither her first nor her second son received the least godfatherly augury from the Florentine poet. Perhaps the name would have seemed unfamiliar to the public. And yet it was becoming more and more known through Dante Gabriel Rossetti, a young man who had been making himself greatly talked about. Since 1848 he and the rest of the Pre-Raphaelites had been coming to the fore and in a quiet revolution had been gradually taking over Philistine strongholds. Dublin had buzzed about them after their exhibition in 1849—the year of the terrible famine that left Ireland weak and depopulated, many of her sons, the strongest and bravest, abandoning her for the more promising soil of America. Yet in spite of pain and hunger the people still could raise their heads to see what was happening in the England that kept them slaves and wonder whether hope might not come to them through the leaven of revolt that was working in her youth. So far it seemed only an aesthetic uprising. But art had a way of shaping life.

Those who could read, therefore, pored over the articles that had been getting into the papers about the writings and paintings of the new school. The very year of Oscar's birth none other than Ruskin had taken up his pen in defense of Holman Hunt's "The Light of the World" at the Royal Academy exhibition. In some circles that group of earnest young men made more stir than the opening of Sir Joseph Paxton's Crystal Palace, sponsored by the Queen's consort to encourage industry.

Balked of her desire, Speranza would not be wholly cheated, and to heal her discontent entered into an elaborate game of pretense. Oscar was not a boy but a girl. She dressed the little one in girl's clothes, let his hair grow long and in all ways treated him as she would have the delicate girl baby she had dreamed of through the months of her pregnancy. A want in her nature had sought to fulfill itself vicariously and fate intervened. She had longed to bring into the world a beautiful feminine Speranza and she had perpetuated John Fenshawe Ellis. She verged on the abnormal in her rage for femininity. People who came to her house saw something very wrong in the spectacle of the little boy in ribbons and laces and hung all over with jewels till he looked, as someone remarked, like a tiny Hindoo idol.

When the boy reached the age at which other lads are being photographed in manly suits on their hobby horses, Speranza took him to have his picture taken. She dressed him in his best clothes for the occasion and posed him before the camera. The portrait is still in existence. On a rug patterned in squares Oscar, a sturdy youngster of four or five, stands self-assuredly in long white stockings and dancing slippers. His dress made of some sumptuous heavy material exposes his chest and shoulders giving him the look of a diminutive primadonna. The full skirt stands out fold on fold like a ballerina's, its hem as well as the bodice, edged with a ruffle of wide embroidered scallops. Along the front parades a row of buttons, and a great sash of plaid ribbon crosses his chest, falling from a knot on the right sleeve. The little face over this extraordinary regalia

11

looks out earnestly from within its frame of long, light brown hair, formalized into curls. The eyes gazing into the lens seem aware that the occasion is more than of a moment. With his left hand grasping the back of a chair, Oscar is consciously profiting from the circumstances that are making him the central figure in the solemn masquerade. Even as a child he knew the value of a pose.

Fortunately the time came for Oscar to be sent away to school. Without too much pain Speranza took leave of him for fate had finally made her the mother of a little girl whom she named Isola. The lad was very fond of his sister, much more than of Willie who, abusing the prerogative of elder brother, was over-inclined to exercise his fists on him with true Irish proficiency. Like Speranza, whose constant companionship had colored his consciousness, Oscar doted on the delicate grace of Isola who used to dance like a ray of sunshine about the house.

He was a little over nine when in 1864 he was sent to the Portora Royal School at Enniskillen whither Willie had preceded him. All sorts of exciting things happened that year. On St. Patrick's Day Dr. Wilde had been knighted. Then Speranza had brought out a book of poems. And then—but of the Travers scandal the two boys would not have talked even if they had known about it. There is no doubt, however, that like Speranza they took pleasure in mentioning the name of Sir William with just the slightest emphasis on the *Sir*. In the parlor of the mansion at Merrion Square titles of nobility had been respected and the society of gentility sought after, however lustily over the brave glasses many an inspired patriot might extol the life republican.

At Portora Oscar at first made little impression. The too tall boy—he had inherited Speranza's physique—with his lazy walk and his dislike for games, was nobody's favorite. Willie in fact was considered the brighter of the two and was held up to Oscar by the headmaster as a model to follow. But Oscar would not study. Knowledge came to him only through pleasure. While the other boys were hard at their tasks or at their

12

particular sports, Oscar was reading poetry, novels, or dreaming away his time. He loved to talk whenever he could get a group about him, and his fantastic adventures kept the boys entranced until Willie came along to cap them with absurder stories of his own. Willie was distinctly the wittier and the better talker according to the boys' tastes, and therefore the more popular. Besides, he joined them at their games and was not so finical as Oscar about his clothes. Instinctively the boys betrayed mistrust of the youngster who liked to mope by himself and who blushed like a girl at their rough talk. Even in a school as free from vice as Portora Oscar's purity seemed unnatural. "Grey-crow," they nicknamed him for some mysterious reason.

He loved to be the center of everything. Once when a group of boys were discussing a notorious prosecution that was then making a great stir, Oscar who had been listening broke forth with, "I'd like nothing better than to go down to posterity in such a case. *Regina versus Wilde!*" Years later Sir Edward Sullivan who had been one of the group recalled the words. What evil genius had overheard? "I am not afraid of things, but I am afraid of words," Wilde was to write in *The Picture of Dorian Gray*, expressing his Celtic regard for superstition. "I cannot understand how it is that no prophecy has ever been fulfilled. None has, I know. And yet it seems to me that to say a thing, is to bring it to pass." As if in dread of his challenge of destiny he crossed out the words he had just written.[1]

Suddenly in his final year, with his discovery of the wonder and beauty of the life of ancient Greece, Oscar made such remarkable progress that he easily carried away the most coveted prizes. At the award of the Carpenter Greek Testament medal on presentation day he was summoned to the dais by Dr. Steele. "Oscar Fingal O'Flahertie Wills Wilde," the sounding names echoed down the hall. As the result of the chaff that followed, Wilde determined to make as little use as possible of the Fingal and the O'Flahertie. At seventeen, minus the Celtic appendages, he started out with the exhibition he had won for

[1] Holograph MS. *The Picture of Dorian Gray*, page 24. The Morgan Library.

Trinity College, Dublin, where he was elected to a Queen's scholarship.

A great grief had come to him during one of his vacations with his family when little Isola died. The doctor who watched the boy haunting the sickroom was struck by the intensity of his sorrow. After the child was buried, Oscar, inconsolable, spent hours at her graveside. For the first time the boy had encountered death, the death of a bright young being made for the radiance of life, and he was filled with the horror of it. It was only years afterward that, at the sight of other beauty, he thought of Isola and transmuted the memory of his earlier sorrow to such music as he was not often to sing.

Chapter II: The Student

AFTER the examination for Honors in the classics held at Trinity College on the 31st of January 1872, there were two students at least who were keenly interested in the results. Oscar Wilde saw with some disappointment that he had come out third of the eight in the First Rank. But he would do better the following term. Already his teachers were beginning to regard him as a classical scholar of exceptional talent which they recognized by awarding him a prize of two pounds for Greek verse and a premium for composition at the term lectures. His zeal for the classics, especially for all that pertained to the culture of ancient Greece, amounted almost to a passion. For the sake of that zeal the school authorities were inclined to close an eye to Wilde's apathy toward sports and his complete lack of interest in the sciences. In his utter disregard of the workings of the universe about him Wilde might have exclaimed with Rossetti: "What is it to me whether the world revolves around the sun or the sun around the earth?" Enough for him that he could admire a sunset without searching into the causes of its hues and mists; enough for him indeed that he could go into even greater raptures before a Turner dusk on canvas, for in the matter of painting he was already assuming a pose. The boys who used to be admitted to his untidy rooms on the north side of one of the less elegant squares known as Botany Bay, were to grow familiar with the unfinished landscape on the sprawling easel, the first thing one saw on entering the sitting room. They learned also to expect the invariable gesture of his hand toward it and his engaging roguish apologia: "I have just put in the butterfly." His friend Sullivan who remembered Wilde's daubs in the drawing class at Portora took the boast for what it was worth, but some, less sympathetic, disliked him for his pretense.

Edward Carson, the other student interested in the examinations, was among those who did not know how to take this newcomer in the college lists. So far he had managed to hold his own and his name appeared toward the top in the Second Rank. In the next examinations, however, Oscar Wilde came out first in his class and carried off the Michaelmas prize. The following year it fell to Carson in the Second Rank. It was a neck-to-neck race, but after that term it was Wilde who made the greater headway, capturing in 1874 the coveted Berkeley Gold Medal for Greek. The good Bishop Berkeley who had established so material a prize in contradiction to his philosophy of the nonexistence of matter had never before adopted so unlikely a protégé.

Wilde and Carson never became friends. They were too dissimilar, the one gay and indolent, the other studious, earnest, and in spite of his ready wit, lacking in humor. A thorough classicist, Carson inclined to the laws of Sparta rather than to the graces of Athens, making for himself a rule of conduct from the wisdom of Greece where Wilde found warranty for a full and joyous life. Not that he stood out from the rest of his fellows by his way of living. Sir William believed in keeping his sons on short leash for the avoiding of mischief, and the allowance he sent permitted of no extravagance. Oscar, however, had managed even at Portora to afford himself luxuries in editions of the classics with wide margins and clear print. Now at Trinity, with the addition of twenty pounds a year to his income on his election to a University Scholarship, he could also indulge in flowers and—an elegance new and therefore overdone—in perfumes that raised an odorous cloud when he burned them in his room.

All this was softness and nonsense to the Spartan Edward Carson. His nostrils sniffed ominously at the scented air, and though he and Wilde chatted cordially enough on occasion, he kept himself aloof, drawing a protective mantle about his spiritual self, just as he drew his coat about his tall, spare figure against the evil blast. "Rawbones" Carson the boys had dubbed him at Arlington House school. He still looked his nickname.

On this lean pillar of a son his father rested all his hopes. Himself an architect, descended of an Italian family of architects, the Carsoni, who had settled first in Scotland, then in Ireland in the latter part of the eighteenth century, he had resolved that his son should distinguish himself at the bar. There were enough examples of the family's decorative art in the dwellings and public buildings of Dublin; it was time the name asserted itself within those buildings, perhaps finally in Parliament. Edward, the favorite of his six children, would do it, he knew. No less certain was Edward's mother, a Lambert of the "Middle Nation" and a descendant of one of Cromwell's major-generals.

From the beginning the Carsoni had married wisely, mingling their Italian blood so well with the Irish that the two streams flowed as one. For final proof that they had been wholly assimilated they shortened their patronymic to the common Ulster name of Carson. More, they acquired a brogue that the most fervent of nationalists might have envied. It did not stand in the way of the senior Carson's election to the Vice-Presidency of the Royal Institution of Irish Architects, or of his sitting in the Dublin Corporation as a "Liberal-Conservative," a paradoxical yet an accurate designation. Neither did it interfere with young Edward's scholarship. Still, he envied the perfectly enunciated English of Wilde, his quick repartee like the crack of a whip and as stinging, his wonderful command of words which at his bidding carried out the least intention of his thought. What an asset they would be at the bar! To what use would Wilde put his wonderful gifts? In his instinctive dislike of him Carson was inclined to be unkind. He had no precise reason for his aversion but he trusted it, and condemned. It was Wilde's excessive purity in the midst of the drinking, barmaid-wooing life of Trinity that Carson found suspicious. He himself was a Galahad. But there are shades and degrees in chastity as in everything else. Wilde's purity was physical only. Carson, indeed, would hardly have been surprised had he overheard Wilde saying to a schoolfellow: "Come home with me. I want to introduce you to my mother. We have founded a Society for the Suppression of Virtue." Words—but they revealed much. During their years at school together, therefore, the two young men, despite their common interests, kept each other at a distance as if warned by some preternatural sense of the roles life had reserved for them.

Meanwhile Wilde drank deep of the fountain that for him was the source of life. It was but a step from Hellenic paganism to the hedonism of Swinburne whose *Poems and Ballads*, a strong wine, had gained in potency with the years. One draught tempered the other but the effect was still staggering. Wilde kept his balance as best he could, and when he stumbled Professor Mahaffy was there to steady him.

The Rev. John Pentland Mahaffy had newly become a fellow when Wilde entered Trinity, and with Tyrrell he took the promising classicist under his wing. Wilde basked in the light they brought from Greece till he, the unathletic, felt himself one of a band of fleet-footed youths, "noble and nude and antique" with only the yellow sun for covering, their shadows a purple glow in the palaestra. Both men fostered his love of bygone splendor. It was Mahaffy who made it real.

A less profound scholar than Tyrrell, Mahaffy who had stood in the very traces of the past came back with some of their golden dust still clinging. He was young, moreover, only thirty-four or five, with an eye for beauty and the gift to express it. In his talks beauty was the dominant note, the beauty of white statues in the blue dusk of the temples, of time-mellowed columns against the sky, of poppies bursting to flame from the crevices of a ruin; of emerald lizards on the warmed stones, of olive trees on the slopes, their very roots striving toward the sun as their branches turned now green, now silver. Like another Keats with his Grecian urn Mahaffy re-evoked from those flowering ruins the reality of what was now a dream to be recaptured by the imagination. To Wilde, however, the dream alone was real, more real than the daily life of classes, examinations and cricket which he refused to play because, he said, its postures were indecent.

18

Unlike Mahaffy who was steadied in his classical ecstasy by the hard truths of philosophy—he had but recently made an annotated translation of Kuno Fischer's *Commentary on Kant*—Wilde would not realize that the fate of those who follow in the steps of vanished glory holds in it something of tragedy. In the world of the now widowed Victoria with its decent pleasures and its ritualistic griefs, where greatness was frowned upon and bigness was all, its shadow was especially threatening. Wilde, dazzled by the splendid sun upon which he gazed so steadily, saw nothing but its image reproduced everywhere.

The gold medal won in his last year was like a material counterfeit of that orb; the scholarship with its annual income of nearly a hundred pounds seemed a gift of the gods, Zeus himself descended like another golden shower upon his favorite. Glowing with his triumphs which he saw with delight were announced in the *Oxford University Gazette*, he entered Magdalen College. He was just one day past twenty, but except for his intellectual curiosity, still a boy.

His development was not long retarded in the atmosphere of Oxford whose name alone breathed life, poetry, spiritual expansion. In Magdalen, the fairest of Oxford's fair colleges, beauty's self seemed to linger, deepening the green of the ivy, softening the hue of the stone, leaving the traces of her feet in the near-by meadow glinting with cowslip and crown imperial, healing with moss the marks bitten by time on the gray walls. Here time itself had come to a pause at that aspect of Magdalen which seemed to have captured forever the vision in the mind of the architects. In the city of Florence, Brunelleschi in stone sits in a corner of the square, his eyes lifted toward the cathedral dome, his creation and his true monument. By Cherwell's banks and along the hushed walks dim figures pass one another in the twilight, scholars in flowing gowns of the time of Wolsey whose name still sings in the bell tower he designed, Puritans of John Hampden's day in rusty black, dainty eighteenth-century gallants in slashed sleeves, with lace at throat and knee. In the laughter of renewed generations, in youth's strivings and ideals, they lived forever.

Wilde installed himself in a suite of three rooms in the most coveted part of the college called quaintly enough the Kitchen Staircase. From his window he could look out upon the Cherwell spanned by the arches of Magdalen Bridge and reflecting with tree and cloud and sky the flock of white ducks paddling forward with scarcely a ripple of the water. The great willow near the bridge towered above it, cascading its branches in pale green sprays of shade. On the lawns youths sat reading or sketching or lay back lazily shading their eyes against the sun as they pondered Plato's ideal republic, Walter Pater's new green silk tie, the Slade Professor's recent lecture, or merely the exploits of the previous night.

Aestheticism was beginning to flourish in Oxford. Through John Ruskin who had been appointed Slade Professor of Art in 1869, the link was immediate with the Pre-Raphaelites. From the beginning he it was who had defended the young rebels, first when Dickens, setting himself up as the champion of Victorian art, betrayed by his ranting that he knew nothing about the subject; and later when John Bull, rearing before the unfamiliar phenomenon, protected himself with kicks and insults. When Holman Hunt's religious paintings failed to carry their message it was Ruskin who had interpreted them; and when John Millais, the darling of the Academy school, received rough treatment from the critics, Ruskin had come to the rescue, taking him on vacations to Scotland, commissioning paintings, and finally losing his wife to him. In the hard days of struggle he had bought the water colors of Dante Gabriel Rossetti who alone of modern artists he considered the equal of Turner; and when he saw that poverty stood in the way of his marrying Elizabeth Siddal, the beautiful frail girl whose face appeared on all his canvases, Ruskin gave her an allowance for the pale, poetic drawings in which, expressing her devotion to her straying lover, she faithfully copied his defects. Overriding the girl's proud rejection of his money because she thought he was helping her for Rossetti's sake, Ruskin had pleaded: "I should simply do what I do as I should try to save a beautiful tree from being cut down." The tree had not been saved. Two years after a marriage that had come too late Elizabeth died, by her own hand.

Now, however, the Pre-Raphaelites, though no longer united in a school, were a force in the life of the day. A few years earlier, at Exeter in Oxford itself, William Morris and his friend Edward Burne-Jones under the influence of Rossetti, indeed, under his personal guidance, had engaged in an undertaking as ambitious as it proved disastrous, when with the cooperation of a group of enthusiastic volunteers, they frescoed the Debating Room of the Oxford Union. Too fervent for common precautions the impatient artists had dashed paint fast and furiously on the fresh walls in wonderful visions from the medieval past. Here Sir Palomides manifested his jealousy of Sir Tristram. There Merlin languished in the toils of the Damsel of the Lake. On another wall Rossetti depicted Launcelot after his sin, dreaming of the Holy Grail from which Guinevere evermore will keep him. Elsewhere, in the foreground of one of the murals, Morris painted a whole palisade of sunflowers on lofty stalks.

"Clever but not right," Ruskin criticized at the time. But that had been in 1857. Meanwhile of the once brilliant murals nothing remained but curled flakes of color on a peeling wall while the sunflowers, so vividly alive with the energy which the indefatigable Morris had imparted, showed faint as the ghosts of blooms in another world. The sunflower as a symbol of aestheticism, however, had come to stay. That very moment in the Kitchen Staircase of Magdalen its future prophet was decking his rooms with it.

"Fessie" Ruskin spread the gospel of the good, the true and the beautiful in his lectures held at the Sheldonian theatre, as none of the rooms was large enough to hold his disciples. The Slade professorship had come to him as a godsend in the most tragic period of his life when Rose La Touche, the young girl in whom he had seen embodied his concept of all that was pure and noble in womanhood, was sinking before his eyes in the darkness of insanity. Her very virtues killed her. Knowing herself dying she had reproached him for loving her more than he loved God, and in the face of death he had not been able to lie. He had loved her more than God; her death had been his punishment. For a time the loss of her had robbed him of physical and intellectual power. Now, however, with the first cruel **pangs** deadened by the force of his mind, he betrayed his secret grief only in the troubled look of his eyes and in the paroxysm of joy and sorrow with which he welcomed the first wildrose of spring—her flower.

At the Sheldonian theatre, however, Ruskin rebecame the author of *Modern Painters*, preaching the function of art in life and, because he was Ruskin, linking art with ethics. He never tired of reiterating his message, the first he had formed with infant lips when, using a chair in the Herne Hill sitting room as a pulpit, he had exhorted: "People, be good." That same message had appeared over and over in *Modern Painters* and in the books that had followed. "Painting is nothing but a noble and expressive language, invaluable as a vehicle of thought, but by itself nothing." To him the conception was all. In the Pre-Raphaelites he had admired more than the painting the complicated symbolism of its content which enabled him from the mere representation of a stone to point a moral for the edification of mankind. The good and the true were to him of vaster importance than the beautiful. "The picture which has the nobler and more numerous ideas, however awkwardly expressed," he affirmed, "is a greater and a better picture than that which has the less noble and less numerous ideas, however beautifully expressed." Little did he realize that in his ethical theory he was confounding the very principles of aesthetics by judging art on the merits of its poetry. In France, and now in England through the fiery American, Whistler, another point of view was being advanced, a little too raucously perhaps, and with no regard for the established sanctities. But then it was new, and all newness is at first uncouth. Painting, Whistler maintained, should be judged not by its intellectual import but by the sensuous pleasure derived from the management of the pigments on the canvas. The rousing of that pleasurable sensation was the end of art.

While at Oxford Oscar Wilde attended Ruskin's lectures, but he veered also toward the opposite camp. He was an ardent Pre-Raphaelite—all of Oxford had succumbed to their lure— yet what he and his generation saw in their paintings and heard in the poetry of Rossetti and Swinburne was as far removed from Ruskin's beatitudes as Ruskin himself was removed from the stirring sensuous world. To the eyes of youth the men whom Ruskin extolled as apostles of good seemed rather the exponents of Walter Pater's new Hellenism. As for Swinburne whose shrill voice still echoed in the halls of Balliol, not all the whitewashing of a Ruskin could dull a hair of his daemonic halo. Allegiance, therefore, was balanced between "Fessie" Ruskin, adored, cajoled and sometimes secretly laughed at, and Walter Pater who in exquisite prose modeled on the best of Ruskin, expounded a dangerous credo.

He was in his middle thirties, twenty years younger than Ruskin. As a boy he had fallen upon a copy of *Modern Painters* and from that moment discovered his career. Yet how different was the disciple from the master, and how wide the gap that divided Ruskin's ascetic cult from Pater's hedonistic, live-for-the-moment philosophy of life! A shy, retiring little man with close-set eyes and an aggressive mustache, he was hardly the embodiment of his daring paganism, the interpretation of which came as a surprise even to himself. For some ten years he had been publishing essays in the *Fortnightly Review* on various figures of the Renaissance. When in 1873 the studies came out in book form, he was shocked at the meaning put upon his philosophy. What he had intended as an exposition of a full rich view of life became to unthinking youth a sanction for license. In 1877 while Wilde was still at Magdalen, Pater reissued his book with a modified conclusion. The truth lay deeper than the words. In spite of the care with which he chose them, his followers could read one message and one only. Wilde with the rest found in it the plea for his fulfillment. How else in the hunger of his young manhood could he have interpreted it?

"Every moment some form grows perfect in hand or face; some tone on the hills or the sea is choicer than the rest; some mood of passion or insight or intellectual excitement is irresistibly real and attractive for us—for that moment only. Not the fruit of experience but experience itself is the end. A counted number of pulses only is given to us of a variegated, dramatic life. How may we see in them all that is to be seen in them by the finest senses? How shall we pass most swiftly from point to point, and be present always at the focus where the greatest number of vital forces unite in their purest energy? To burn always with this hard, gemlike flame, to maintain this ecstasy, is success in life."

In those words which like a charm overthrew the rose-bowered cot of English domesticity that Victoria had so carefully built up, Oscar Wilde found himself. The learning he acquired, the honors he won in an extraordinarily brilliant career were nothing to the effect of that message flashing upon his spirit with the light of revelation.

He went frequently to Ruskin's study, with its Turners and Rossetti water colors, its geological specimens on cotton wool under glass, and bits of his drawings of flowers and architectural details strewn upon the writing table. Wilde, susceptible to suggestion, sent home letters from a trip to Italy enclosing with them sketches of monuments and funerary urns for the delectation of the antiquarians at Merrion Square. To capture the exquisite moment he also burst into poetry which began to appear in the Trinity College magazine *Kottabos*, in the *Irish Monthly* and the *Dublin University Magazine*.

He was living the complete life between his two preceptors. Even physically. But that owed more to Ruskin's persuasiveness than to any natural inclination on the part of the overgrown, overtall youth who "flopped about ponderously." During the famous winter when Ruskin stirred up the civic pride of Oxford's undergraduates whom he enlisted as navvies to mend a bad stretch of the Hincksey Road, his eloquence

24

on the nobility of manual labor so moved the indolent aesthete that he came round one morning ready for work. Under the supervision of Downes, Ruskin's gardener at Denmark Hill, Wilde broke stones with the rest in the gray November dawns while "Fessie" Ruskin, more pink-faced than ever in the chill morning air, set them the rhythm of their labor. Wilde was especially favored; his was the task of filling the Professor's wheelbarrow. It is the only time in his life that he ever volunteered to do any rough work with his hands, though he was later to boast to an audience of astonished Americans: "I always loved lilies. At Oxford I kept my room filled with them, and I had a garden of them, where I used to work very often." Where the garden was that nurtured the flower of Mary Virgin and the Blessed Damozel no one ever knew, for none ever saw him tending it. Like Rossetti perhaps he also gathered his lilies in the artificial flower shop on Wigmore Street.

As the aesthetic cloud encompassed Oxford not everyone was happy about it. Over the tea and crumpets of his entertainments "Fessie" Ruskin apostrophized his faithful, only to gaze after them in dismay when, the teacups empty, they made a beeline from his threshold to Pater's. Jowett, startled out of composure when his nest of Balliol owls hatched a flamingo, had recovered during the intervening years from the shock of Swinburne whom he had chastised, spoiled and adored. Then the redheaded poet had been an anomaly; but now there were many anomalies. The whole university teemed with them— long-haired youths who wore flowers in their buttonholes and burned incense in their rooms. Pater's chambers at Brasenose were the temple of their worship. There where the rose jar exhaled the breath of dying petals, the followers of the new cult seemed to find the air they needed. On the walls hung round with the bloodless, half-sensual, half-mystical drawings of Simeon Solomon, they beheld the beauty they sought. In the slow words of the master, weighed and measured like the most precious jewels and set in sentences like glowing reliquaries, they found their spiritual host. There, too, as in Solomon's drawings, the sensuous mingled with the mystical in a novel paganism.

Wilde absorbed those words as meaningful to him as if sprung from his own soul. In his room he too enshrined the rose jar and burned the incense, carrying on the ritual of aestheticism. He did it so thoroughly that he soon began to be looked upon as the leading exponent of Pater's philosophy. Pictures as allusive as the master's hung on the paneled walls; he piled the mantels high with blue china collected in out-of-the-way London shops. Was it not Rossetti who had established the fashion? If like him he could have kept a wombat he would have done so. Perhaps he did in the mythical garden of the lily.

In Pater's rooms he seemed to hold communion with the Pre-Raphaelites. Sometimes Simeon Solomon himself, their close disciple and the bosom friend of Swinburne, visited Pater. A small graceful man with a face deep-eyed with reverie like one of his own drawings, Solomon would sit before a hushed group and read to them his poetical allegory, *A Vision of Love Revealed in Sleep*. It was a disturbing tale, the account of a pagan calvary wherein Love, beautiful as Eros yet like Christ cognizant of pain, walked the stages of his passion— Hellenism borrowing the mysteries of the Church.

Wilde was strongly attracted to the artist-poet with his eccentricities and his fondness for the society of adolescents. The scandal had not yet broken that brought Solomon to a prison cell. Meanwhile at Oxford Pater sat to him for his portrait, and the unwitting man basked in the glory that was so soon to slip from him in the squalor of Whitechapel and Houndsditch.

Chapter III: The Aesthete Tries His Wings

At Merrion Square in April, 1876 the doctors were in attendance. Sir William Wilde was mortally ill. Throughout the weeks that he lay on his deathbed a veiled woman would come to the house in the early morning and sit silently in the sickroom till nightfall. No one knew who she was or why she watched there, and none questioned her, least of all Speranza. With the loftiness of spirit which she had cultivated, it would have been beneath her to show curiosity toward the stranger who for reasons of her own felt that her place was by Sir William's side. As she once declared in court, Speranza took no interest in the matter. Other women might have said it out of bravado. The extraordinary thing about Speranza was that she meant it. Sir William had had too great an admixture of Adam's clay. Hence with admirable serenity she left him on his plane while she concerned herself with eternalities. From her altitude she could face with composure the final scene with its incongruous tinge of melodrama.

Gossip, reported by no less a witness than Bernard Shaw, said that Sir William left a family in every farmhouse. As a boy Shaw had seen the Wildes at a concert in the Antient Concert Rooms in Dublin. "Wilde was dressed in snuffy brown; and as he had the sort of skin that never looks clean, he produced a dramatic effect beside Lady Wilde (in full fig) of being, like Frederick the Great, Beyond Soap and Water." Earlier Sir William had exercised his skill on the elder Shaw to correct a squint, "and overdid the correction so much that my father squinted the other way all the rest of his life." Shavian exaggeration, but with its grain of truth.

To Lady Wilde the death of her husband brought real grief. There were many things shared together whose absence left a blank in her life—the antiquarian researches, his literary work, his passion for the folklore of Ireland. Before his death

27

he had been occupied in writing a life of Béranger. Speranza dedicated herself to its completion and to massing together his archaeological discoveries. Whatever he may have been as a man, in his interests at least he had sometimes attained to the heights where Speranza roamed. As she looked back upon Sir William's achievements for his obituary notice she had enough to record to make her proud of him. The Royal Victoria Eye and Ear Hospital which he had founded alone sufficed to outweigh the veiled mourner at his bedside.

Willie and Oscar Wilde each acquired a modest inheritance. For Oscar it came just in time to realize a cherished dream. From the moment Mahaffy had opened out to him the vistas of the ancient world he had yearned for the day when he too would stand on the summit of the Acropolis and look out on the birthplace of the civilization that claimed him. Now Mahaffy came with an invitation to escort him to Greece the following spring. Wilde accepted at once. But the lingering Puseyite mysticism of Oxford still hung like a mist of incense to dim the Hellenic sun. Wilde would go to Greece—via Rome. Before he bathed in the golden radiance of the pagan world he must stand in the apostolic grandeur of St. Peter's. Mahaffy to whom Wilde confessed his Catholic leanings grew solicitous for his Arcadian lamb. What was all this rubbish about burning candles in the shrine of Our Lady? "Stop this nonsense!" he wrote him. "Come with me to Greece. I am going to make an honest pagan out of you."

Wilde clung to his desire to see Rome. In the turmoil of his emotions he was sure he was undergoing a crisis, and with Speranza's instinct for drama he saw himself the center of a conflict between Zeus and Christ. "I start for Rome on Sunday . . ." he wrote to "Kitten," a young friend at Oxford. "I hope to see the golden dome of St. Peter's and the Eternal City by Tuesday night. This is an era in my life . . . I wish I could look into the seeds of time and see what is coming."

The seeds of time which were to have such consequence had hardly begun to germinate when he wrote. They took root when his too enlightened guide carried him off to Greece.

Wilde was twenty-three. He had grown a handsome giant, over six feet in height and proportionately broad—John Fenshawe Ellis. Following the fashion of Oxford, or rather, setting it by his exaggeration of it, he wore his hair parted in the middle and falling in loose waves almost to the shoulders, in the manner of the pages of the Pre-Raphaelites' medieval period. His face, rid of the plumpness of adolescence, had attained a fine oval dominated by the broad, high forehead and magnificent eyes, soulful in repose but ready to twinkle with merriment. The slight lack of alignment in their setting, scarcely noticeable except when the play of expression ceased, seemed to give him an added charm. He had also a faint asymmetry in the development of his countenance which occasioned an odd conflict between the right and the left side of his face. It was as if in him two natures were united, a phenomenon which the ancients in their allegorical simplification, portrayed in their numerous nature deities. His mouth was perfect. Only in the statues of Greece could one find that bold curve of the lip united to the delicate modeling of the corners, turning upward with the tremulous suggestion of a smile. "His mouth was vowed always to pure beauty," Frank Harris, not always generous, said of him. It was a remarkable thing in Wilde, this almost virginal purity of speech.[1]

He had also advanced in dress since his first year at Oxford. No more the tweeds in checks and squares that used to emphasize his massive frame and the student's slope of the right shoulder. Gone was the ridiculous bowler hat. He had begun to experiment in style and soon he was to adopt the aesthetic garb that was to make him the most talked-of man on both sides of the Atlantic. As it was he had attracted attention by his collection of "blue" and his quip, "Would that I could live up to my blue china!" It found echo in the parlors of Philistia, creating something of a storm in the ironstone teacups. In the Oxford University Church it became the text for a sermon, the preacher weighing the words with dire meaning: "When a

[1] See Havelock Ellis, *Sexual Inversion*, for the commonness of this trait among inverts.

young man says, not in polished banter, but in sober earnestness that he finds it difficult to live up to the level of his blue china, there has crept into the cloistered shades a form of heathenism which it is our bounden duty to fight against and to crush out if possible."

Wilde evolved no special costume for Greece, although with his page's haircut and his peculiar impulsive stride, he was the observed of all observers. Did he find in Greece the things he sought? Did it fulfill the concepts he had formed from his reading of Plato in whose pages a new world was revealed? With the indefatigable Mahaffy he climbed the rock of the Acropolis, roamed the sites where once the gods had walked, "did" museums like the veriest tourist, bought souvenirs and felt a Greek among the Greeks. Vaguely the impressions of Italy mingled with the cold purity of the Hellenic marbles, the naked body of a martyred saint in the museum of Genoa fusing with the statues of those Adonises, those slim eidolons which the Athenian sculptors hewed with such love out of the stone. There was no content in those representations; beauty alone embodied the Idea. Art existed for its own sake, and everywhere its presence was manifest. The humblest funeral jars marking the graves of the poor outside the city gates were shaped to beauty no less than the columns of the temples in their faultless proportion and majesty. Wilde thrilled to it, knowing that here was his world, the world to which by all his natural inclinations he belonged. "All culture culminated in Greece," he wrote when those confused first impressions crystallized to a point of view, "all Greece in Athens . . ." And he was an Athenian.

At that time, however, only beauty in the abstract, the Platonic ideal, possessed him. It was the stuff from which to make a philosophy for the mind, not a rule of living. The fascination of the Catholic mysteries still lured him, so that when he returned to Oxford—later than the appointed day, incurring a fine of forty-five pounds—he still continued going to the Oratory of St. Philip Neri at Brompton to interview the priests. One of his close friends had become a Catholic in 1875. In his abnormal impressibility he would have followed his example had not fate, or perhaps the keenness of the priests who detected the goat's foot in their devotee, prevented it. He was never to be out of the shadow of the basilica, however, even when his true pagan nature finally asserted itself. In his dualism he was akin to those children of a fairy father and a mortal mother of whom Speranza wrote in her *Ancient Legends of Ireland*—fateful beings who grow up to be beautiful and strong but with evil and dangerous natures.

For the present Greece and Holy Rome were united under the generous sky of Wilde's acceptance. He saw no discrepancy in his double fealty. When he harvested the fruit of his experience the duality persisted, Hera's golden apples lying on the altar of art together with the Christian vine. That July the *Irish Monthly* contained an article and a poem by Wilde, "The Tomb of Keats," the result of his visit to the Roman cemetery where the singer of the "Ode on a Grecian Urn" lay buried.

"As I stood beside the mean grave of this divine boy," wrote Wilde, "I thought of him as a Priest of Beauty slain before his time, and the vision of Guido's St. Sebastian came before my eyes as I saw him at Genoa, a lovely brown boy, with crisp, clustering hair and red lips, bound by his evil enemies to a tree, and though pierced by arrows, raising his eyes with divine, impassioned gaze towards the Eternal Beauty of the opening heavens." Thus Keats, the Priest of Beauty, was converted to the Christian martyr of Wilde's sonnet—a youth "fair as Sebastian, and as early slain."

His description of Guido's saint like those that were to follow of the Dorians and other gilded youths of imagination and of life contained the first version of what was to become almost a formula in Wilde's writing. The naked young martyr of the canvas haunted him as no Grecian marble ever did, recurring to him again and again in later periods of his life. Manly beauty, rather, the comeliness of boys like those of whom the Athenians made a cult, stirred him more than Pheidias's goddesses. Feminine loveliness he was seldom moved to celebrate in verse, and when he did describe some woman or girl, the attributes most often at the point of his pen were of white lilies, cool ivory, the shadow of a white rose in a mirror of silver—everything that was removed from the warmth of life. Or he endowed women with characteristics which to the as yet unawakened pagan spelled the ideal of beauty.

> She had a belt of amber beads
> Around her little boyish hips,

he said of a girl on a page of his unpublished early notebooks; and again, elsewhere:

> He rose and took his polished crook;
> She hid her face in boyish laughter.

Insistently the adjective recurred—"boyish petulance," "boyish lips." It was the clue, still ignored, in the mazes of his personality, that was to lead to the inevitable.

Back from his classical tour Wilde plunged eagerly into his chosen life. He became widely known as a wit, his fame spreading from Magdalen throughout Oxford and from Oxford to London where Willie Wilde, forgetting his early rivalry with Oscar, and recognizing in him the spark which he himself lacked, lost no opportunity in giving him helpful publicity in the society paper, *The World*, where as a journalist he found exercise for his easy Irish style.

Speranza, now the widowed Lady Wilde, also made her home in London. After the death of little Isola and of Sir William, the Merrion Square mansion held too many unhappy memories. At Oakley Street, a wide quiet roadway leading to the Embankment, she took root again in one of a row of old-fashioned houses bowered with ivy, that made up with quaintness for their lack of elegance. It was the best she could afford. Sir William's prodigality had eaten into his income; at his death the family was aghast to find only seven thousand pounds willed to Lady Wilde besides some small holdings of houses and land. Even if she had wished to remain in Dublin she would have had to live on a much lower scale than that to which Sir William had accustomed his cronies. Her pride would not permit it. In London she could start anew and throw dust in the eyes of her circle who would be seeing only good taste in her genteel poverty. Soon, what with Willie's literary connections and her own passion for social climbing, Lady Wilde filled her parlor—she called it a salon—with the Bohemia and near-great of London.

Brighter than ever the new renaissance glowed in the air. Oscar who stayed up late at night and therefore was among the first to see the dawn, became its lark, no very melodious lark, as yet, but a herald nonetheless. More frequently his poems appeared in the Dublin university magazines and other limited organs. Willie found space for them in *The World*. Oscar became a man about town. He visited galleries, attended first nights and insinuated himself into the salons of upper Philistia. They were by no means the goal of his ambition, but in the meantime they would serve. The day was coming when Mayfair itself would woo one who with his inherited cult of republicanism still found room for a love of high-sounding, aristocratical titles. It was the regret of his life that he had not been better born.

Aesthetically his link was still with the Pre-Raphaelites, his spiritual fathers. As their self-constituted son he would carry on the traditions; he might even perhaps found a new school. He gained encouragement from the opening of the Grosvenor Gallery in May, 1877.

All London was in a flutter that spring day. Bond Street overflowed with the equipages of polite society eager to be the first to enter the gallery which the banker, Sir Coutts Lindsay, had founded for the artists who had rebelled against the Royal Academy. It was a highly fashionable event. Within, the exhibition rooms were arranged tastefully with palms and festoons, the walls decorated to enhance the prevailing Pre-Raphaelite colors —the golds and sage greens which were to make W. S. Gilbert sing of the "Greenery-yallery, Grosvenor Gallery, je ne-sais-quoi young man" who was in a very short time to form the vanguard of the aesthetic movement. But not all the Pre-Raphaelites were represented. Though Millais, Holman Hunt and Burne-

33

Jones showed their works, Rossetti was conspicuously absent. Robert Buchanan's deadly attack, "The Fleshly School of Poetry," had done its work. Alone in his huge house possessed by ghosts real and imagined, the poet and painter of the Blessed Damozel lived out his tortured life seeking companionship only in the animals in his back garden—the only creatures that could not hurt him.

But if the almost legendary Rossetti was absent on varnishing day, his absence was more than made up for by the sprightly James Abbott McNeill Whistler in his cutaway, top hat, monocle and tall gold-headed cane. With his lined, parchment-like face a palimpsest of intellect and emotion, the single white lock in awful frost against the youthful black of his hair, with his hands, long-nailed like an Oriental's, conducting the tempo of his speech and his eyes fixing his listeners like the Ancient Mariner's, he was a figure to make propriety stare and the cockney snicker, but not with impunity. The wit of the little American was as redoubtable as his temper, and both had already been exercised in the building of a reputation that made the wise approach him with the wariness of a cat before the unfamiliar snake—a tempting, brilliant object, but how safe? Many, as it was, were nursing the bruises of his verbal lashings, and the hurt rankled in a desire for vengeance. Whistler, however, lost not a jot of his aggressiveness in the midst of his enemies. Carefree as the butterfly whose symbol he adopted for his signature, he danced into the sunlight of publicity flashing his brilliance for friend and foe alike. But let the incautious person beware who sought to make a thrust at him! Then the Butterfly found both a voice and a sting that spared no one. His satanic "Ha! Ha!" so sinister that Irving imitated it for his most chilling effects, paralyzed the victim; his sting gave him the *coup de grace*.

That season Whistler displayed his talents to the utmost, as he had good cause to do when puzzled critics and outraged Academicians, agape before the seven canvases he exhibited, had not the good sense to hold their tongues. Oscar Wilde who visited the Grosvenor at every opportunity and championed it

34

in the *Dublin University Magazine* listened, all admiration. Here was such repartee as he would have loved to make; here was a man to study. Whistler, it is true, was not a Pre-Raphaelite —he scorned all schools, for his originality could fit in none— but he had what the serious brethren lacked, a sense of humor. In him it amounted almost to genius.

The receptive Wilde, folding his vast limbs, sat at his feet and learned. To the sanctities of Ruskin and the hedonism of Pater he added the spice of Whistler, undisturbed by the fact that his divinities were at odds with one another. That very July when he was writing so appreciatively of the Grosvenor Gallery, John Ruskin fulminated against Whistler's "Nocturne in Black and Gold." "I have seen and heard much of cockney impudence before now," he blasted, "but never expected to hear a coxcomb ask two hundred guineas for flinging a pot of paint in the public's face." And this from the Ruskin who had been known to pay a thousand pounds an inch for a favorite canvas! His hasty words were to precipitate a lawsuit, Whistler bristling at last against all who were conspiring to deprive him of his livelihood. The court of law in England, however, resembled that other gathering of bigwigs in Dublin when a certain Miss Travers sought compensation against Sir William Wilde for the loss of her honor. With the same sardonic wit it arrived at a similar judgment: one farthing damages for the plaintiff's artistic reputation.

No wonder his sting grew sharper against the whetstone of public contempt! A critic demurred against the title of a painting, "Symphony in White," in which, he complained, one lady wore a yellowish dress and a bit of blue ribbon, while another carried a red fan. *"Bon Dieu!"* cried the exacerbated Butterfly. "Did this wise person expect white hair and chalked faces? . . . And does he then believe . . . that a Symphony in F contains no other note but F.F.F. . . . Fool!"

Wilde was ecstatic. Somehow he contrived to get an invitation to Whistler's charming White House in Tite Street and they struck up an acquaintance. Friendship was out of the question. Whistler had too much of the primadonna in him to tolerate competition, whereas Wilde, newly come before the limelight, liked it so well that he would not be put in the shade. For the present the disciple hung upon the Butterfly's words and gave him the admiration he demanded, provided the laughter was loud and long for his own quips. Amid the wonderful "blue" collection of Whistler, the Japanese paintings, the smell of oils of the studio, the fan and peacock feather decorations, the exciting atmosphere of an artist's life, the aspirant found his true milieu. Some day perhaps he would come to live in Tite Street and have just such a house and such a salon as Whistler's where disciples of his own would come to worship at his feet.

At Oxford his reputation grew by leaps and bounds as he carried off honor after honor in a final year that climaxed even the distinguished careers of former graduates. He had determined to conquer and he did. Arnold, with his faith in culture, must have seen it exemplified in the wonderful undergraduate who spoke with the tongue of men and of angels. What if on closer analysis the context could not win the master's approval? It had beauty and the quality of imagination. Pater was entranced. According to Harris, Wilde told him that one day as the two were sitting together under the trees at Oxford watching the students bathing in the Cherwell, "the beautiful white figures all grace and ease and virile strength," Wilde spoke of how Christianity had flowered into romance, how the pale Christ had been outlived and the world was moving toward a synthesis of art in the ideals of a new paganism which would combine romantic beauty and classicism. "I really talked as if inspired, and when I paused, Pater—the stiff, quiet silent Pater—suddenly slipped from his seat and knelt down by me and kissed my hand."

In spite of his reputation or perhaps because of it, he was looked upon with suspicion by his more ordinary fellow students. He was too brilliant, which to the bore is always a crime, and he affected to worship beauty, surely one of the devil's disguises. The root of the mistrust lay deeper than that, however. Beneath the mysticism of the aesthetic coterie there were suspected refinements of eroticism such as those mentioned in

36

Plato's *Symposium*. Wilde's affectations lent credence to the rumors. They were more than the Oxford bloods could tolerate. It was one thing to indulge in sexual license—and Oxford was notorious for the profligacy beneath its towers and spires—it was quite another to make a cult of paganism. The bric-a-brac, the fine editions, the drawings in Wilde's rooms were a challenge to normal masculinity that could see decorative beauty only in a pair of stag's antlers.

A group of the heftiest, therefore, determined to teach the "blue china cove" a lesson. But they underestimated the strength of their victim. When four stalwarts burst into Wilde's rooms while a mob stood below to enjoy the sport, a scene ensued which none of them had expected. Instead of a shower of broken china and the pinioning of the aesthete whom they had hoped to see crowned with the broken frame of one of his Solomons, they saw hurled down the stairs in quick succession three of the assailants. A moment later Wilde stood at the door holding the fourth and toughest of the gang in his arms like a baby. Marching down the stairs like a giant with his struggling burden, he carried him through the crowd of gapers to his own rooms where he left him under a pile of furniture.

The opposite camp insisted on victory, however, and once they succeeded. One day as Wilde was out walking, eight of the braves fell upon him, bound him and dragged him along the road and up a hill. Wilde could do nothing to defend himself, but although he was cut and bruised by the stones he would not give his tormentors the satisfaction of uttering a single word. At the top of the hill they untied the cords. With remarkable self-possession Wilde brushed the dust off his coat and looking round him said, "Yes, the view from this hill is really very charming." With one sentence he deprived them of the better part of their triumph.

He was to enjoy his own on the 26th of June, 1878, upon an occasion of great solemnity. Toward half-past seven o'clock that evening the noblemen, heads of houses and the proctors and gentlemen who partook of Lord Crewe's benefaction to the University met the Rev. James Edwards Sewell, the Vice Chancellor, in the hall of New College. When they were all convened they marched in procession to the Sheldonian theatre, already crowded, and took their seats. The ceremony opened with an oration by the Professor of Poetry and then various speakers were called upon. Finally Oscar O'Flahertie Wills Wilde, winner of the Newdigate Prize, recited portions of his poem *Ravenna*.

> A year ago I breathed the Italian air,—
> And yet, methinks this northern Spring is fair—
> These fields made golden with the flower of March,
> The throstle singing on the feathered larch,
> The cawing rooks, like wood-doves fluttering by.
> The little clouds that race across the sky . . .
> The crocus-bed, (that seems a moon of fire
> Round-girdled with a purple marriage-ring);
> And all the flowers of our English Spring,
> Fond snowdrops, and the bright-starred daffodil . . .

The resonant tenor voice filled the theatre, caressing the ears of the listeners as it caressed each syllable of the opening verses. How Edward Carson, aspirant to the bar, would have envied that delivery, that masterly poise! And how annoyed he would have been at the much too long hair which the languid hand tossed off the face with that over-graceful backward motion! The audience listened with admiring attention as couplet followed couplet in the long musing on the glory that was Ravenna. Those with keen ears might have detected in the opening a startling plagiarism of Wilde's own earlier poem, "Magdalen Walks," almost word for word and image for image, even to the crocus-bed enclosed in its ring; and later in his account of Gaston de Foix. fallen on Ravenna's plain, the wholesale lifting of a couplet from his sonnet on Keats' grave:

> He rests at last beneath God's veil of blue:
> Taken from life when life and love were new.

In *Ravenna* he had merely transposed the lines and made God's

38

veil of blue "seamless." Otherwise the lord of war supplanted Sebastian—Keats whose martyrdom Wilde had sung with such pathos. Had he been in too great a hurry to finish the poem for the competition? Or with total absence of artistic conscience had he snipped purple patches to deck the more promising fabric? In that case the Peter-Paul sleight of hand had proved profitable. Besides the honor and the twenty-one pound annual value of the Newdigate Prize he would have easy access to the publishers when he left the university for London.

In his lonely brooding Ruskin must have thought back on his own youth at this triumph of Wilde's. Long ago he too had competed for the Newdigate Prize. Twice he submitted his entry without success. At the third attempt he won with his *Salsette and Elephanta.* The victory at that time had healed his hurt over an early disappointed love. How many years had passed since then! And how little joy yet how much suffering they had contained!

Pater who had his doubts of his disciple's poetic gifts took Wilde's success in the light of that eternity which he was always contemplating. There had been beautiful apostrophes to Hellas and the fond Hellenic dream in *Ravenna* with here and there a happy verse. But again he would have asked Wilde, as once before, with a smile to remove the sting: "Why do you always write poetry? Why do you not write prose?—Prose is so much more difficult."

Speranza and Willie Wilde were unreservedly proud as they awaited the arrival in London of Oscar, described in Foster's *Alumni Oxonienses* as "Professor of Aesthetics and Art Critic." Surely he would conquer the metropolis as he had conquered the university town. Like Speranza he too adopted the great Florentine. With that example of noble martyrdom before him, he could overcome any fate.

> Alas! my Dante! thou hast known the pain
> Of meaner lives,—the exile's galling chain,
> How steep the stairs within kings' houses are,
> And all the petty miseries which mar

Man's nobler nature with the sense of wrong.
Yet this dull world is grateful for thy song . . .

He had chosen better than he knew even though not so long since he had exclaimed to a companion walking with him through the choir-filled lanes of Magdalen: "I want to eat of the fruit of all the trees in the garden of the world."

Chapter IV: Lily of Love, Pure and Inviolate

LILY LANGTRY was the rage of London. Langtry hoods, Langtry shoes, the Langtry coiffure and the Langtry fan were featured in the shops, tempting women to propitiate nature by the imitative magic of art. At a Marlborough House ball it was said she had worn a yellow tulle gown draped with gold fish net in which were imprisoned mounted butterflies of every size and sheen for the Prince of Wales to pick up the morning after from the ballroom floor.

Everywhere pictures of the reigning fair in some fascinating pose and costume threatened to displace in popularity the touching presentment of the widowed Queen seated with resigned folded hands and gazing for guidance on a bust of the departed Albert. Ever since the Prince Consort's death there had been scarcely a house in England without its effigy of the bereaved Queen in her mourning pose. More than anything it had helped to restore her to the hearts of her people, estranged by her early concentration in her grief.

But now Hecuba was being dispossessed by the New Helen. In her amazement at the superior power of beauty over virtue, it is said that Her Majesty once stood up the better to inspect Mrs. Langtry as she made one of her annihilating entrances. The Queen was more than a little concerned. Everyone, even the royal household, was bewitched by the woman. Pictures of her found their way to Buckingham Palace itself. Only recently when Her Majesty had gone to see her youngest, Prince Leopold, who was ill at the palace, she had had to climb up on a chair to take down a pencil drawing of Mrs. Langtry which the young man had hung at the head of his bed. What is more, well-founded rumor had it that the too susceptible Prince of Wales stood very close to the throne of the rival queen of beauty.

There was a Mr. Langtry but he was almost mythical, cast in the shade by the splendor of his wife. A Belfast widower, Edward Langtry had met the sixteen-year-old Emilie Charlotte Le Breton, daughter of the dean of the Isle of Jersey, and finding her face more valuable than a dowry, married her in 1874. Edward Langtry was old enough to be her father but that disturbed neither Lily, as she was called, whose vision extended beyond the marital threshold, nor Mr. Langtry who was satisfied to shine as a satellite in whatever glory chanced to fall his way. Provided he could sail his yachts and go on fishing expeditions he not too unwillingly submitted, during the season, to being his wife's tactful chaperon in the splendid houses to which her beauty gained him entrance. No great effulgence of his own was possible on an income of twelve hundred pounds a year, especially when Lily soon required that and more for her toilettes and the entertainment of royalty.

Her meeting with the Prince of Wales had had in it an element of fate. Sir Allen Young, the arctic explorer and a friend of Wales, was on a yachting cruise when he came upon the siren. As if to make up for his failure to discover the North Pole, he presented to his friend the Jersey Aphrodite. A lover of the beautiful, the Prince of Wales responded with enthusiasm. Though Her Majesty his mother might have preferred a stretch of arctic ice on which to plant the flag of empire, he found Mrs. Langtry much more to his liking and was not slow, in his communicative transports, to fill the best houses with her praises. Inevitably Mrs. Langtry was sought after by the hostesses in the highest society who moved heaven and earth to disappoint their competitors.

Leaving his lands in Ireland Mr. Langtry established his wife in London, the better soil for her growth. It was no violet by a mossy stone that he had found in the Isle of Jersey, but rather a gorgeous native lily to adorn the drawing-rooms of the elite. As "The Jersey Lily" John Millais painted her, and the Jersey Lily she became, a name and a flower to conjure up romance in the drab middle-classness of the Queen's England.

The young Professor of Aesthetics and Art Critic newly

down from Oxford with a vast ambition and a microscopic income had been a worshiper of the Lily long before he took a modest set of rooms in Salisbury Street off the Strand. Magdalen Walks had heard his sighs many a night when he came up from London, and the midnight oil had burned in the student room where the scratching of his pen alone gave voice to the tumult in his heart. For Wilde was in love, desperately in love with Lily Langtry. He had met her one night after the theatre at the studio of Frank Miles who had abandoned his passion for gardening to make innumerable sketches of her from all possible angles. From that first meeting Wilde joined her court. Ruskin, whom he still came to see, smiled his rueful smile at the stories Wilde told him of his London adventures. Once he broke into delighted laughter when Oscar narrated how while he was waiting for a hansom with an armful of great orange lilies for Mrs. Langtry, a street arab staring at him and his flowers cried: "How rich you must be!' Wilde did not say, but his luncheon and supper had probably been sacrificed to that Covent Garden bouquet.

And how did the Jersey Lily whose name re-echoed throughout Europe, look upon this most fervent of her followers? She was too much the woman not to be flattered by his gigantic posies and the doglike devotion that made him sleep upon her doorstep, to the annoyance of Mr. Langtry who grumbled at stumbling over him on returning late from the club. She was also too prudent to risk a sure favor for a penniless Professor of Aesthetics whose only claim to fame was a pile of the Newdigate poem published by the Shrimptons at Oxford. At twenty-seven a woman, however beautiful, bestows her favors judiciously, knowing that a Helen too grows old.

Nevertheless Lily Langtry found her admirer "remarkably fascinating and compelling." Though she was repelled by his pallor and a certain sensuality about his face, she succumbed to the appeal of his eyes, his brilliance "and one of the most alluring voices I ever heard, round and soft and full of variety." Besides, it is touching to have one's flower worn like the pledge which the medieval knight carried with him to death, and to be

43

regarded as pure and stainless, the Madonna Mia of a nineteenth-century troubadour. For Wilde besides gifts of flowers brought her gifts of song. Artists as famous as Watts, Millais and Burne-Jones had set her down on canvas and all the scribes of Britannia had been lavish in publishing her praise. Only Wilde had written of her as all women, even the Aspasias of the world, wish to remember themselves best:

> A lily-girl, not made for this world's pain,
>   With brown, soft hair close braided by her ears
>   And longing eyes half veiled by slumberous tears
> Like bluest water seen through mists of rain:
> Pale cheeks whereon no love hath left its stain,
>   Red underlip drawn in for fear of love,
>   And white throat, whiter than the silver dove,
> Through whose wan marble creeps one purple vein.
> Yet, though my lips shall praise her without cease,
>   Even to kiss her feet I am not bold,
>   Being o'ershadowed by the wings of awe . . .[1]

The regions wherein Wilde placed his love were certainly empyrean. Even when with classical passion he addressed Lily Langtry as "The New Helen" the sphere of his adoration remained ultra-terrestrial. While in the throes of inspiration, he would prowl about the neighborhood of her house with the persistence of the ghosts left over from the days when Tyburn Tree had stood in the very site of the Langtry shrine. London became ancient Troy, the red-faced, undistinguished little house a temple housing divinity. In the exigence of his tardily awakened love he desired more than Mrs. Langtry was willing to give, but her denial caused no deep affliction.

For a season she encouraged the vagaries of the cumbersome youth and enjoyed the scandal he was creating by the strange turns which his passion took. Now he was seen as the apostle of

---

[1] Originally the inspiration for the sonnet had been the picture of a boy. In 1877 the poem had appeared in *Kottabos* under the title "Wasted Days," and began, "A fair slim boy, not made for this world's pain." The transference was significant.

44

beauty, his hair half covering his collar, as he strolled through the astonished thoroughfares with an amaryllis in his hand. Again he brought new worshipers, poetical like himself. One day he led thither none other than Ruskin whose name he whispered with such awed humility that Lily scarcely dared lift her eyes to the great brow and the patriarchal hirsuteness of the Slade Professor. Then Wilde, aware perhaps of some lack in the New Helen and wishing her classic perfection lighted by some intellectual beam, persuaded her to attend with him Newton's lectures on Greek art—to the disruption of all discipline among the students who had eyes and ears only for her. To encourage her studies he varied the lectures with visits to the coin section of the British Museum where from the glorious ancient specimens he gave her proof of the eternity of her beauty. Wherever she went he was sure to trail her, a large, too substantial shadow, sometimes inconvenient, but always eloquently flattering.

For one who like Mrs. Langtry thrived on the breath of publicity, Oscar Wilde was a valuable asset. Not everyone could have been as conspicuous as he, and none had that ability to carry off his pose. His repartee was as formidable as Whistler's. Sometimes it could even sting.

"Where is your lily?" a tactless hostess asked him when he appeared at a reception without his amaryllis.

"At home, madam, with your manners," he thrust back. The anecdote, repeated in other drawing-rooms, served both himself and Mrs. Langtry.

As a reward she granted him some little intimacies by an ivied seat where they met in the summer days. For an hour they chatted and laughed. She allowed him to tie back her hair that always ran riot; she let him gaze into her gray-green eyes which, he said, "lit like an amethyst." Sometimes as he stood above her, bowed and worshipful, she let him kiss her. Then suddenly in the fickle summer weather, the rain would come, and she would run for shelter, fleet and graceful, with Wilde striding on behind her. He never could catch her, she was so swift. "You had wonderful, luminous fleet little wings to your feet . . ." In her room where the lilac beat against the dripping pane, they had moments

45

of delicious seclusion. He drank in everything with his passionate eyes, the amber-brown of her dress with its yellow satin bows at the shoulders, the tiny square of lace with which she wiped the raindrops from her cheeks, her hand with its faint tracery of blue veins under the ivory whiteness. She took the homage, especially when the world was included in the worship of her beauty.

> Where hast thou been since round the walls of Troy
> The sons of god fought in that great emprise?
> Why dost thou walk our common earth again?

The readers of Edmund Yates's magazine learned by heart Wilde's Poem in which he likened Lily to the most beautiful woman that had ever been. What did it matter if carping pedants heard echoes in it of other poets' voices? The praise of her was there, to be repeated by languishing admirers who could not have found words for the

> Lily of love, pure and inviolate!
> Tower of ivory! red rose of fire!

"O Helen! Helen! Helen!" The triple invocation for a season panted behind her whenever she appeared in public.

The poem was published in July of 1879. But by that time all intimacy between Wilde and the New Helen had ceased. "You have only wasted your life," she said to him one day in that same rain-cloistered room, waving him adieu with the little handkerchief of French lace which she had held to her flushed, wet cheeks.

> Had a small tear left a stain?
> Or was it the rain?

Wilde went away in despair, and, as he thought, with a fractured heart. The wound quickly healed, however, for the goddess did not banish him from her presence. She liked him but she

46

did not love him. Like the sensible woman she was, she merely told him that under the circumstances he was losing his time. He appreciated the common sense in her frankness and respected her for it. Still, he reproached her,

> . . . hadst thou liked me less and loved me more,
>   Through all these summer days of joy and rain,
> I had not now been sorrow's heritor.

Yet long before the break, sorrow's heritor had had his eyes open for other constellations. There was Ellen Terry, whose performances with Irving had brought Wilde through the wings of the Lyceum for a nearer glimpse. Indeed, the printer's ink had scarcely dried on "The New Helen" when Oscar was sending off to brother Willie's periodical "Queen Henrietta Maria," a sonnet dedicated to Miss Terry, which he had written at the theatre in the heat of inspiration, a fact which to the scandalized Lily must have accounted for the confusion of his emotions. "O hair of gold! O crimson lips! O face made for the luring and the love of man!" he rhapsodized. With her, he said, he forgot toil and stress, time and the soul's dread weariness, indeed, even "my freedom and my life republican!" It was a great deal for Speranza's son to forget.

The only thing that condoned his easy consolation was his laudation of "my friend Henry Irving" who also became the recipient of Wilde's sonnets. No doubt Irving was pleased to be called a "trumpet set for Shakespeare's lips to blow," but it must have been embarrassing to have his legs the subject of parlor conversation. Wilde, it was told, had pronounced: "Irving's legs are limpid and utter. Both are delicately intellectual, but his left leg is a poem." The pronouncement had spread like wildfire from drawing-room to club, from club to street, till even John Bull raised his brows, not knowing whether to laugh or explode in a good round "Damn!"

One thing was obvious. Whether for praise or ridicule Oscar Wilde compelled notice. Who was this young man who vied with the wits, affected clothes that eclipsed the extremest dandy,

47

and released coveys of languorous poems to whatever little magazines would harbor them? Wilde's ark still tossed at high water, his flights of poetic doves unlike Noah's bringing him meager promise of immediate terra firma. After a few months in furnished apartments he set up bachelor quarters in Charles Street, Grosvenor Square, an address more in keeping with the life to which he aspired. He decorated the sitting room à la Whistler with flights of Japanese fans and bouquets of peacock feathers spreading out of some rare bit of "blue." He carried out the color scheme of the Pre-Raphaelites in dado and wall. The Oxford incense and the Brasenose rose jar found their place on the tabouret, and the Simeon Solomons a suitable background in sage green. Literary hack work thrown his way by brother Willie helped to keep the hearth warm; the mortgaging of the small property willed him by Sir William sent the creditors from the door.

At every first night Wilde was certain to be seen, very dapper in boutonnière and gloves. He had a passion for the theatre and everyone connected with it. When Sarah Bernhardt landed at Folkestone, among the actors and journalists gathered there to meet her stood Wilde, bearing in his arms a huge spray of lilies, though it had been in May of 1879, at the peak of his adoration for the Jersey Lily. They were even her flowers that he was holding. But Wilde was never the man to resist a dramatic effect. When, amid the cheering of the crowd a voice was heard promising Sarah a carpet of flowers for her feet in England Wilde, impulsive, threw his lilies before her, crying, "Here is one!"

Sarah Bernhardt was touched. The keen eyes lighted up surveying the gallant donor with his noble brow and classic lips. She was to see him again and again in the coming weeks and to receive her tribute of flower and sonnet, published, as usual, in faithful Willie's *The World*. What if she could not quite make out what that fluent admirer wished to convey? It was *"une grande honnœur pour la patrie"* for her to be celebrated in verse. And patiently she puzzled over:

Ah! surely once some urn of Attic clay
　　Held thy wan dust, and thou hast come again
　　Back to this common world so dull and vain,
For thou wert weary of the sunless day
　　The heavy fields of scentless asphodel,
　　The loveless lips with which men kiss in Hell.

She did not remain long in the ascendant. Rather, in the wide heaven of Wilde's enthusiasms she had to share her glory with other stars, the latest Helena Modjeska shining with so great a luster that for a time she eclipsed everyone else. For Madame Modjeska besides interpreting other men's emotions was herself a poet. True, no one could understand what she wrote in her native tongue; but England was not to remain unenlightened. The enterprising young man showed still another facet of his genius by coming forward as a translator from the Polish. Where he had acquired the language is still one of the problems to keep the curious wakeful. It is indubitable, however, that in *Routledge's Christmas Annual* for 1880 appeared "*Sen Artysty*, or The Artist's Dream," a long poem by Madame Helena Modjeska, translated from the Polish into blank verse by Oscar Wilde.

No penetrating psychologist was required to see that the Professor of Aesthetics and Art Critic was having a difficult time of it in London or he would not have been put to so many shifts. The metropolis was daily proving a harder school of life than he had expected. Spoiled by the easy honors at the university he had imagined himself striding carelessly from triumph to triumph. But the pavements of the city were harder to the feet than the larch-shaded walks of Magdalen and more destructive to shoe leather. Moreover, London was unprepared for the message he felt he had to bring—perhaps antagonistic was the truer word.

Still there was consolation in philosophy. The Pre-Raphaelites too had had their struggles. Now their school was recognized and one of their founders, Millais, had received the *Medaille d'Honnœur* at the Paris Exposition the very year Wilde came down from Oxford. Reality, however, showed the other side of the medal when Whistler's little White House in Tite Street fell under the auctioneer's hammer. Japanese prints and soaring fans, screens and embroideries, everything was knocked down to the highest bidder in the artist's effort to retrieve a straw from the consequences of his disastrous lawsuit against Ruskin. What a melancholy commentary! Ruskin who had once stood as the champion of a flock of young rebels now caused the ruin of a greater innovator to whose merits time and life's bitterness had blinded him. In vain the defiant Butterfly twiddled the court's farthing on his watch chain and hurled flying squibs against his enemies in *Art and Art Critics*. London would have none of him. Defiantly he embarked for Venice. He still had confidence in his art, though no one else did, and he vindicated his faith. On his return he had mastered a new technique, witnessed by a portfolio bulging with etchings that captured the very spirit of art in their small dimensions. Without the aid of paint or brush the vivid sunlight of Venice throbbed in the black and white of the prints, her very character set down forever in a few, swift, sapient strokes. The economy of art could go no further.

Wilde learned much from him. Shocked at first by Whistler's theories which went counter to everything he had learned from the Slade Professor, he came to realize that in painting it is what the eye beholds and not what the mind perceives that is its true function; that poetry is out of place on a canvas; that, finally, it is better to suggest than to say all. Whistler practiced what he preached in his painting as well as in his wit. As previously at Oxford before his other masters, Wilde sat at his feet and learned—so quickly that Whistler lifted his brows and dropped his monocle. What! the pupil better than the teacher? That would never do! And he pointed his sting.

Once at an exhibition of Whistler's "arrangements" an art critic, seeking to impress the painter, flung the words *good* and *bad* at the canvases with a temerity that made the wiser gasp. Whistler did not fail them.

"My dear fellow," he flashed upon the hapless Humphry Ward. "You must never say this painting's good or that bad!

Good and bad are not terms to be used by you. Say I like this and I don't like that and you'll be within your right. And now come and have some whisky. You're sure to like that."

Wilde who was standing by rashly exclaimed: "I wish I had said that."

"You will, Oscar, you will!" darted the Butterfly, exploding into his triumphant "Ha! Ha!" He felled his victims with the prowess of the little tailor in the story. Only they were men, not flies, and they could come back at him.

Oscar enjoyed these encounters which caused him to be talked about, although he preferred it when he had the last word. Forbes-Robertson who had stood with him at the gangplank to welcome Sarah Bernhardt and, less extravagant, had given her a gardenia, loved to tell one of Wilde's retorts. A squib in one of the papers had it that Whistler and Wilde had been seen at Brighton talking as usual about themselves. Whistler, seizing the opportunity, sent Wilde the cutting with the comment: "I wish these reporters would be accurate; if you remember, Oscar, we were talking about me." Immediately Wilde rejoined with the wire: "It is true, Jimmie, we were talking about you, but I was thinking about myself."

It was typical of Wilde to answer with a telegram. He felt his retort was worth the expense. What if he could ill afford it? "Give me the luxuries and anyone can have the necessaries," early became his rule of living. He knew, furthermore, that unless one is wealthy there is no use in being a charming fellow. Hence, without the wealth, he endeavored to create the illusion of wealth.

The pretense worked. If the kettle in Charles Street failed to boil, he had no lack of tea in the parlors of fashionable ladies eager to drink in their turn from the aesthetic fount. For Philistia had discovered Wilde—at second hand, as it were, since it was *Punch* that managed his debut; and as a bar sinister celebrity, since he came heralded by ridicule. To a young man impressed with his own importance, it was no matter whether the rungs of his ladder were of wood or of gold provided they led him to his ambition. Ridicule was as good a way of arriving as any, and ridicule Wilde accepted with his usual gay good grace, whatever the feelings that stung him in the privacy of his heart. The important thing for the present was that he should be talked about.

And talked about he was, not as a professor of aesthetics nor yet as a critic of art but as the chief of the sunflower-and-the-lily clan. He came, however, like the man of fate of a certain school of history which believes that past events shape their forerunner—a paradox which had he thought of it, would have pleased Wilde. He did not make the aesthetic movement; the aesthetic movement created him for its own ends.

For nearly five years *Punch* had been wielding its stick over the pates of the novel brood fathered by the young revolutionaries of 1848. But they were so unlike the early blessed and precious crew that they would have been the first to disown these changelings who claimed descent from the fountainhead. The line admitted to one grave deviation, however, in an alliance with the daemonic Swinburne, young Swinburne, the singer of "the raptures and roses of vice" who in 1866 had made the British lion jump out of its overstuffed cage—not the clipwinged, molting flamingo whom Theodore Watts, the literary solicitor, had recently carried off to Putney for purposes of reformation.

As it was, the present generation combined both strains, adding an originality of their own: intensity, the key word of Pater's philosophy of living beautifully in the moment. They did nothing but with intensity. They gazed at a flower intensely. They chanted poetry with intensity. Nothing was beautiful unless it was intense—a color, a face, an emotion. To be intense was to be of the elect, and to be of the elect one had to be aesthetic. Since the intensity of one's personality had to be expressed by the outward man, they yearned after velveteen instead of honest serge, and after knee breeches to replace the modest trouser. The aesthetic uniform had become so well defined that two years before Wilde left Oxford, George Du Maurier had been making it ridiculous in his drawings for *Punch*. Thus even the costume which he was to make notorious Wilde had found ready-made.

52

Not that the aesthetic brotherhood walked down Piccadilly with a poppy or a lily in their medieval hand, as the fleshly poet Bunthorne was to sing. Indeed, the breeches and velveteens had probably originated as a jest by the fertile Du Maurier who felt that the intense fraternity might just as well set themselves apart by their garb as by their ideas. On the hint thus given it by art, life, establishing a theory which Wilde was later to propound, proceeded at once to put it into effect by imitation. His legs encased in black silk stockings that met his breeches at the knee, and his great torso in a velvet jacket edged with braid, with a flowing cravat and a silk handkerchief of a matching color bursting from his coat pocket, Wilde astonished the honest burghers on his evening exits. For it was as a *tenue de soirée* that the aesthetic uniform was worn. Doubtless he had imitators rash enough to appear in public, but like the small fry that are cast back in favor of the large fish, they were neglected by the satirists who found the leviathan Wilde more to their purpose.

Du Maurier introduced him in *Punch* in the issue of February 4, 1880. He did it tentatively, feeling his way with the public to see how far he might go in his satire of the set which the women adored and their husbands despised. Indeed, the series of cartoons which he initiated was aimed against the whole movement in general rather than at Wilde in particular, so that at first *Punch*'s devotees could not tell whether Maudle the painter or Jellaby Postlethwaite the poet was meant for him. As for Mrs. Cimabue Brown, she was obviously the artistic woman who was throwing out her Staffordshire for precious "blue," her crinolines for clinging aesthetic gowns, her heavy Victorian furniture for Morris's, and her ideals of virtue, learned at the example of Her Most Virtuous Majesty, for the new, unpredicted, intense life. Du Maurier knew the type, impressionable but well-meaning; thus by intimation rather than by the more direct method of *Punch*'s stick he warned her of danger.

As he continued his weekly cartoons Du Maurier grew bolder in his attack, now using some mot of Wilde's as the theme of his illustration, now drawing him unmistakably as either Maudle or Postlethwaite. The text under the picture made its point.

53

"Shall I bring you anything else, sir?" asks a waiter who has just brought the poet his order of a bowlful of lilies before which he is seated with hands folded in rapture and eyes ecstatic.

"Thanks, no!" says Postlethwaite. "I have all I require, and shall soon have done."

There was nothing here but a genial taunt at the cult of the lily. The dart had a sharper point in *Postlethwaite on "Refraction."*

"Hello, my Jellaby, *you* here!" cries Grigsby, a stocky Briton with sidewhiskers who has just met the poet in front of Brill's swimming baths. "Come and take a dip in the briny, old man. I am sure you look as if you *wanted* it!"

"Thanks, no," answers the languid poet, drooping aesthetically. "I never bathe. I always see myself so dreadfully *foreshortened* in the water, you know!"

There was not a Grigsby in the whole of England who would not have sworn it was Wilde who had said the words. People were ready to believe anything, the more absurd the better.

Innuendo entered into the joke, *Maudle on the Choice of a Profession,* the more significantly directed against Wilde for the precaution Du Maurier took to deceive by his label. Never before had he drawn so close a caricature of Wilde, from the recognizable features to the body, lounging heavy-hipped on the sofa.

"How *consummately* lovely your son is, Mrs. Brown!" exclaims the artist to an ingenuous Philistine just down from the country.

"What? He's a *nice, manly* boy, if you mean *that*, Mr. Maudle. He has just left school, you know, and wishes to be an artist."

"Why should he be an artist?"

"Well, he must be *something!*"

"Why should he *be* anything?" inquires Maudle. "Why not let him remain for ever content to *exist beautifully?*"

The voice like the body was Wilde's. To the alert the parenthetical comment at the bottom of the illustration meant more than met the eye: "Mrs. Brown determines that at all events her son shall not study under Maudle."

54

Chapter V: A Most Intense Young Man

FOR some time W. S. Gilbert with his musical coadjutor Arthur Sullivan had been casting about for a new subject. Since 1875 when their irreverent skit on the law courts, *Trial by Jury,* had made all England burst into a slightly shocked guffaw, the public had been going wild over their comic operettas, till now they had become almost the favorite form of entertainment. Peers and plebs, the cultivated and those who had not yet overcome their puzzlement over the use of the aspirate, were united by Gilbert and Sullivan in a camaraderie of fun. In the parks as in the slums, in the houses of Parliament as in the factories, the clever lines of Gilbert flashed back and forth, accompanied by Sullivan's lively, easily remembered tunes. A comic Verdi, he composed with his tongue in his cheek, letting his music frisk and gambol in ways to which outside the music halls it had never been accustomed. Sullivan was no artificial strummer, however. As a child in the scarlet cloak and gold braid of the Chapel Royal choristers, he had sung solos so sweetly that royalty had noticed him with shillings. Thus encouraged he took to studying seriously in the Leipzig Conservatory under Moscheles and attained his reward when in 1862 his music for *The Tempest* was performed at the Crystal Palace. He was then just a youth of twenty, but like Byron, he awoke the next morning to find himself famous. No less a person than Dickens whose hearing proved more percipient than his sight had been in 1848, stopped to congratulate him.

"I don't pretend to know much about music," he said in a way that strangely foreshadowed Zuleika Dobson, "but I do know that I have been listening to a very great work."

Sullivan's skill had advanced with the years. Just as Gilbert availed himself of the prosodic arts of a Tennyson to achieve effects that made his listeners roll in their seats, Sullivan employed the lyric line, counterpoint and the subtlest orchestration in ways which, with the effectiveness of St. Cecelia's organ, brought down not an angel but Polyhymnia herself, a little horrified, yet amused. Words and music of the Gilbert and Sullivan operas were on every tongue. One had only to sing, "For I am a judge," quoting the susceptible judiciary of *Trial by Jury*, for the answer to come, sung to the appropriate tune: "And a good judge too." Even in Windsor the two merrymen had made their entry, to the music room of Queen Victoria who, with the high, flutelike voice which she never failed to remind one had been listened to by Mendelssohn, piped the arias of the maid Angelina whose breach of promise of marriage suit was to have such an unexpected outcome.

The Sorcerer had followed upon the success of *Trial by Jury*; both were eclipsed by the unprecedented furore of *Pinafore* in 1878 after a few months of languor when it seemed that any day the Comedy Theatre might close. Everywhere the new songs were sung, the Queen adding to her repertory "I'm called little Buttercup," and her subjects singing at the top of their hilarity the success story of the ruler of the Queen's Navee. And not only Her Majesty's subjects. Prince William and Prince Henry of Prussia, both musical enthusiasts, knew the *Pinafore* lyrics by heart and would sing them in and out of season. Once the astonished Sullivan was to have the experience of an impromptu rendering of "He polished up the handle of the big front door" by Prince William himself, not yet burdened with the tragic title of Kaiser Wilhelm II.

In the realm, W. H. Smith who had risen from a newsboy to the Admiralty, saw much matter for umbrage in the caricature of himself which he detected in the Rt. Hon. Sir Joseph Porter, K.C.B. The mischievous Gilbert had drawn very close to life— one of the reasons for the appeal of his operas. England, tired of the blanket of respectability under which it had been smothering during its phenomenal growth under the Queen's motherly care, was beginning to kick it off, and therefore seized eagerly any encouragement toward its liberation. Gilbert and Sullivan gave that blanket its first hearty tug.

Soon the strains of *Pinafore* echoed across the Atlantic. As no adequate international copyright laws existed, the opera's success began to tempt the unscrupulous. In no time eight theatres in New York alone were giving *Pinafore* before uproarious houses, to the dismay of Richard D'Oyly Carte, the manager of Gilbert and Sullivan, who saw thousands of dollars diverted from his pocket to the box offices of pirate competitors. That was not the worst of it. The very art which he felt he had in a sense created by bringing librettist and composer together was becoming bastardized in America. In their desire to make the most of this gift of the British dioscuri, the New York managers tricked out their productions to the most popular, rather, the most vulgar taste. In one version a song on a new style of trouser which had been perplexing the arbiters of elegance was introduced as part of the original *Pinafore*. In another, a patter song celebrated a supper dish that Gilbert had never heard of, but which now became poison to his palate. To obtain their share in that free for all, music publishers brought out pirated editions of the opera, including the sartorial and epicurean innovations, while barrel organs at the street corners churned out the spurious music and churned in pennies with a democratic indifference to false or true.

Incensed as well as alarmed D'Oyly Carte hurried to New York to see things for himself. He found matters worse than he expected. Not only were the theatres within the radius of fashionable Fifth Avenue doing a thriving business, but all sorts of local companies, with talents hardly above the amateur, were presenting garbled versions of the London success. Even in the Negro quarter Gilbert and Sullivan had found their way, an ebony Sir Joseph Porter doing his patter amid a bevy of sisters and cousins and aunts of varying shades of brown, the gleaming teeth and flashing eyes full of the contagion of the rollicking music. There was no stopping the plague of *Pinafores*.

After consulting with his lawyers about the copyright laws and losing his temper most un-Britishly as Dickens had done in the same fight, D'Oyly Carte returned to London in worse spirits than when he had left it. Gilbert did nothing to soothe him. "I will not have another libretto of mine produced," he threatened, "if the Americans are going to steal it. It's not that I need the money so much, but it upsets my digestion."

There was only one way of counteracting the mischief in America and that way D'Oyly Carte proposed. On his suggestion Gilbert and Sullivan crossed the ocean to present the one and only *Pinafore* at the Fifth Avenue Theatre in time for the Christmas season of 1879. On December 31 they followed it with the première of their new opera, the *Pirates of Penzance* which only twenty-four hours later opened in a little theatre in South Devon, to assure it the protection of copyright. The *Pirates* nearly caused a riot at the initial matinee performance. "The laughter and applause continued through the whole piece until the very end," Sullivan wrote his "Dearest Mum," and the delighted Americans called thunderously for librettist and composer at the end of each act, cheering them madly at every appearance.

Never had there been such an opening and such a success. Carefully, after each performance the music sheets were collected and locked up to prevent pirating. Futile precaution! The booty was too enticing. In spite of the companies which Gilbert and Sullivan sent on the road, the illegal *Pinafores* continued, while in the West, emboldened by distance, managers defied prosecution and set to pirating the *Pirates*. Their exploits in that direction were certainly lucrative, and it was with an added chuckle that these brave profiteers heard the brawny Richard sing: "For I am a Pirate King. . . . And it is, it is a glorious thing to be a Pirate King!"

Thousands of dollars the richer for their American sojourn the wanderers returned to England. D'Oyly Carte, with two successes running simultaneously before capacity houses, importuned his talented team for something new with which to whet the appetite of the public should its edge be dulled by too long a diet of them. Gilbert got busy, going as usual for the jolt of inspiration to the author of *Bab Ballads* from whom, he avowed at a public dinner, he unblushingly cribbed. Bab, the alter ego, had written a ballad, "The Rival Curates," a satire on two

58

clergymen who sought to outdo each other in mildness. Hooper, one of them,

> . . . lived on curds and whey,
> And daily sang their praises,
> And then he'd go and play
> With buttercups and daisies.

The other, Porter, played the airy flute, looked poetically depressed, did worsted work and framed it, and labeled seaweed for old maids' albums. There was nothing very inviting about the theme of the conversion of Porter to a worldly, cigar-smoking dandy, but with the doggedness of genius in carrying through an idea, Gilbert worked all of a summer to shape the plot while at the same time helping Sullivan with the libretto of a serious opera, *The Martyr of Antioch.* He was not happy with the rival curates. Do what he would, he made little progress. "I mistrust the clerical element," he confessed to Sullivan at the close of the year. "I want to return to my old idea of rivalry between two aesthetic fanatics."

He could not have hit upon a livelier subject. Even while he was wrestling with the difficult Porter and Hooper the news columns, the cartoons, the air of London had been filled with ridicule of the Maudles and Postlethwaites of the new aesthetic creed. The name of Wilde was on every tongue. His sayings were repeated, enriched by exaggeration. His breeches provided a never-ending topic for laughter. His very poems were parodied, the latest on his villanelle "Pan" rousing gales of laughter wherever it was read. Indeed, Mrs. Frankau writing under the name of Frank Danby, could not have carried cleverness farther than in her "Pan—A Villanee."

> Commissioner of Luna*cee!*

she exhorted with mock pathos,

> An inquirendo come and hold;
> For Oscar Wilde hath need of thee!

59

Flings to the world in wild fren*zee*
A poem on "a wattled fold,"
Commissioner of Luna*cee.*

In his strange verse none sense can see:
He raves of "limbs and beards of gold,"
He really hath great need of thee!

Gilbert made the most of what he found. It was not Wilde, however, whom he was ridiculing in the "fleshly" poet Reginald Bunthorne who was to have such ludicrous misadventures in the opera *Patience*. His butt, as he betrayed by his caricature of the aesthete in *Bab Ballads* was a far greater man, Swinburne himself. None who saw Gilbert's conception of Bunthorne could have been mistaken: there was the tiny frail body topped by its vast head with its aureole of upstanding hair; there was the thin neck, scarcely able to hold that weight of cranium. The features also, the pointed nose, the large eyes and ears were undeniably Swinburne's. If these were not enough there was Patience's declaration to Bunthorne whereby she sought to prove that she loved him with unselfish love:

For you are hideous—undersized,
And everything that I've despised . . .

Wilde could under no circumstances be described as undersized. Moreover there was a sly dig at Theodore Watts, Swinburne's solicitor-nursemaid, when the anguished Bunthorne cries in the raffle scene:

By the advice of my solicitor
In aid—in aid of a deserving charity,
I've put myself up to be raffled for!

Alas, Gilbert's satire came too late. The splendid poet of *Atalanta* was soon to drool of patriotism and babies in his plush-lined Putney cage.

But if the regenerate poet could not be made to serve as the laughingstock of a public eager for fun, there were plenty of youths of his sinister line who answered the description of Bunthorne:

> A most intense young man,
> A soulful eyed young man,
> An ultra poetical, super aesthetical
> Out-of-the-way young man.

Oscar Wilde embodied the type. Du Maurier had made it familiar to every reader of *Punch*—in other words, to the average Briton who like the average man everywhere had the greatest power in the world, that of molding public opinion.

Catering to that powerful body the directors of the new opera sought to give it what it wanted. Accordingly, George Grossmith junior who took the part of Bunthorne, was made up to look as much like Wilde as possible, an exigent task, for he was short where the apostle of the lily was tall, and of a frank commonplace countenance where the other, influenced more and more by the public notion of what he should be, wore his face in a permanent ecstasy—at least whenever there was anyone to look at him.

The knee breeches were of course *de rigueur*. Early in the transformation of the two mild curates into the rival aesthetes the original canonicals had been discarded for the velveteen uniform. By the time *Patience* arrived at the Opera Comique on the 23rd of April, 1881 there remained nothing but a passing reference here and there to betray Gilbert's original incentive.

The public was rapturous. Eight encores were called for during the exciting first night. The applause seemed never to end. Glowing but exhausted, the composer retired to Fielding's after the performance to cool off with a lemon and soda. "Went splendidly," he noted in his diary. "Seemed a great success."

Indeed *Patience* soon became so popular that the Opera Comique had to turn away the crowds eager to laugh at Bunthorne and his court of amorous damozels. Oscar Wilde, they knew, attended many of the performances; his presence was an added attraction. For the man in the street Bunthorne and

61

Wilde were one and the same. D'Oyly Carte observed and pondered how to turn that interest to his advantage.

Like the earlier operas *Patience* made a conquest of every
honest Briton who enjoyed a vicarious virtue at the comical pil-
lorying of what he thought ridiculous and unmanly. The catch-
words of the aesthetic crew as pronounced by the Gilbertian
poets and damozels became part of common speech. "How Bot-
ticellian! How Fra Angelican!" exclaimed the London house-
wife at the sight of some well-dressed rival. "How consummately
utter!" sputtered her husband. "Oh, are they not quite too all-
but?" asked a wag, and the retort was immediate: "They are
indeed jolly utter!" In the streets the urchins called out "Bunthorne" at any one who ventured to stray from the pattern of
his neighbor, and contorted themselves to stained-glass attitudes
singing:

> You hold yourself like this
> You hold yourself like that
> By hook or crook you try to look both angular and flat.

On young and old the "immortal fire" of aestheticism descended
with as much effect as on the officers of the Dragoon Guards
who every night, before the packed Opera Comique, went
through their irresistibly comical antics. At Windsor Her
Majesty added one more song to her repertory. With the embarrassed assistance of some male volunteer who took the part
of Archibald Grosvenor, Bunthorne's rival, Queen Victoria
piped the coy response of Patience the dairy maid in the love
duet:

> Gentle sir, my heart is frolicsome and free—
> (Hey but he's doleful, willow willow waly!)
> Nobody I care for comes a-courting me—
> Hey willow waly O!
> Nobody I care for
> Comes a-courting—therefore,
> Hey willow waly O!

Bunthorne had "come over" majesty itself.

In the meantime after setting his wonder geese brooding over another golden egg, D'Oyly Carte supervised the building of a theatre that was henceforth to house the Gilbert and Sullivan operas. The Savoy should be as perfect for stage performances as the Grosvenor Gallery had been for the exhibition of paintings. Nothing was to be omitted for the comfort of the patrons, no luxury stinted for their delight. In America both D'Oyly Carte and his team had heard of the work Thomas Edison had been doing toward harnessing lightning for common use. A thousand electric bulbs a day were even then issuing from his factories. Encouraged by the practical demonstrations of illumination by electricity, Carte had the theatre wired and the new-fangled lamps installed. Nonetheless he did not wholly trust them, and to prevent any unforeseen disaster, he made sure of an alternative set of old-fashioned lights.

On October 10, 1881 *Patience*, which for six months had been playing to clamorous houses, had another opening at the Savoy Theatre. Knowing the value of advertisement, the managers had charged no fees for the inaugural night. As a result the new theatre was packed to the rafters with a society audience that spared neither tails nor trains in its scramble for seats. Disarrayed but happy, it watched Sullivan conducting the orchestra in strains that had become as familiar as "God save the Queen." Royalty graced the opening in the person of the Prince of Wales who was taken backstage at curtainfall and introduced to the company.

Like D'Oyly Carte, Oscar Wilde had been making hay while the sun of public favor was shining upon the movement which willy-nilly he represented. Journalism at which brother Willie was such an adept earned him little or nothing; the money from the Irish property was rapidly dwindling. It was growing increasingly difficult to put up the right aesthetic front. Even at Covent Garden flowers could be had only with the coin of the realm. But purchased they had to be, no matter what the sacrifice, for he could no more have gone out without his boutonnière than without his flowing tie, symbol of the free artistic spirit. The theatre had always lured him. Ellen Terry,

Irving, Sarah Bernhardt, Madame Modjeska, all the wonderful beings to whom he gave the full measure of his worship belonged to the stage. Lily Langtry, the adored of royalty, was even then planning to make her debut upon it to retrieve her husband's fortunes. That very summer her possessions had been sold at auction. Wilde would perhaps have liked to appear upon the boards. Instead he thought of writing a play. If it proved successful he could make enough to keep him in luxuries for a while and help provide the necessities in the Oakley Street household where Speranza was beginning to learn the meaning of economy.

The subject of *Vera* was, if anything, timely. For years the press had been full of the revolutionary activities of the Nihilists in Russia. Wilde, knowing nothing of the Russian character and less of Russian history, concocted a plot, nevertheless, confident that the son of Speranza could do justice to man's desire for freedom. Of dramatic technique he had had experience both from his wide reading and from his frequent visits to the theatre. Emboldened, therefore, he produced with his customary speed a four-act melodrama which, with the interest of the people awakened to its theme by current reports, he already visualized on the stage. In September of 1880 he published it at his expense. He might as well have thrown his money into the Thames; it would at least have created a ripple.

Perhaps in moments of self-exploration he had his misgivings about the play. There is confession of inadequacy in the magniloquent description of *Vera* with which he sought to entice a prospective producer. "I have tried in it to express within the limits of art that Titan cry of the peoples for liberty. . . ." Speranza's son knew the jargon. "But it is a play not of politics but of passion," he truthfully amended. "It deals with no theories of government, but with men and women simply; the modern Nihilistic Russia, with all the terror of its tyranny and the marvel of its martyrdoms, is merely the fiery and fervent background in front of which the persons of my dream live and love." In short, the Titan cry of the people was only the effective

64

counterpoint to the cooings in the alcove. But even there the tyro betrayed his inexperience.

In March of 1881, as if the gods would have made sardonic jest of the epilogue in *Vera*, Europe was shaken by the news of the assassination of Czar Alexander II. Wilde found a producer for his play and the opening date was set for December, with Mrs. Bernard Beere in the title role. Willie Wilde, self-appointed press agent for his brother, kept the public informed of the doings at the Adelphi where the passionate Nihilist was to make her bow. He welcomed the prospect of possible affluence that might help lighten his financial burden.

Riding on the crest of his luck Oscar Wilde exhumed his sheaf of poems which had been making the rounds of the publishers' offices and this time came to an agreement with David Bogue of St. Martin's Lane. Late in June of that year the first edition came out, and a rare sight it was for those who had been wondering when Bunthorne in the flesh would bring his offering to the expectant world. A handsome octavo in full parchment with a design of plum blossoms stamped in gold on the covers, the book would have lent an elegant touch to the most fastidious boudoir. The print on the Dutch handmade paper was as artistically disposed as one of Whistler's designs; the wide margins almost invited one to hang the poems on the walls. The ultimate had here been achieved from the foreshadowing of Sheridan who envisioned the poet's dream, "a beautiful quarto page, where a neat rivulet of text shall murmur through a meadow of margin." With commendable restraint Wilde called his volume *Poems*. With less wisdom he set the price at half a guinea.

"I see that Oscar Wilde, the *utterly utter* is bringing out 10s. 6d worth of poems," wrote the Jesuit Gerard Manley Hopkins somewhat wryly to his friend Robert Bridges.

From earliest adolescence the thirty-seven-year-old ascetic had been writing poetry so extraordinary that the few friends to whom he reluctantly showed it hardly knew what standards to apply in their judgment of its merits. Bridges read the painfully wrought verses in which an almost pagan sensuousness was

65

kept within bounds by an armor of form—as Hopkins' own love of beauty in man and nature was restrained by cruel acts of self-denial—and offered him criticism to bring him nearer the comprehension of his contemporaries. His own verse, however, unconsciously suffered the influence of Hopkins'; sometimes he frankly adopted forms which surpassed in their intricacy any verse scheme yet known. Hopkins saw his experiments carried out in his friend's published work and had no fear. He knew his own public had yet to be born and was content to bide his time. Here and there in some Jesuit journal, a poem or an essay of his might find publication. He was otherwise unknown to the Victorian reader.

"If some one in authority," he confided to Bridges, "knew of my having some poems printable and suggested my doing it I should not refuse; I should be partly, though not altogether, glad. But that is very unlikely. All therefore that I think of doing is to keep my verses together in one place . . . that, if anyone should like, they might be published after my death." It was not till 1918 that the first volume of his poems appeared, and then it took ten years for an edition of seven hundred and fifty copies to be exhausted.

Oddly enough the converted Jesuit Hopkins and the aesthete Wilde had much in common, though Hopkins knew of Wilde only from the slighting references in the press, and Wilde, perhaps, was not even acquainted with his name. The censer-filtered air of Oxford had stirred the mystical yearnings of the diminutive youth with the meditative, intellectual face. Nearer by ten years to the source of the Catholic revival, Hopkins yielded to Newman where Wilde hesitated—at least in the matter of formal conversion to the Catholic Church. He too had listened to the voice of Pater, but where the younger man heard the call to a full life of the senses, Hopkins hearkened to the warning of its pitfalls. Yet more even than Wilde he had been imbued with the Greek spirit. For him the sunlight of Greece shone in the very austerity of Stonyhurst where he was sent to teach; he sought to shut his eyes to it. The glory of manhood filled him with ecstatic delight; he inflicted punishment on himself to

66

still the conflict between his senses and his asceticism. Only in his poetry and in spite of himself the rebellious senses broke in riotous description tortured into the mold of form. His adjectives could be felt, seen, smelled, tasted; his intensity burned through the pages splashed with his large handwriting. Everything in his written landscapes became vitalized till, from the mere tone-color of his poems one could summon

> This darksome burn, horseback brown,
> His rollrock highroad roaring down,
> In coop and in comb the fleece of his foam
> Flutes and low to the lake falls home.

Something which he could not altogether confine to Christian purpose betrayed itself in his work, containing more of Pater's concentration of feeling in a single verse than Wilde's whole volume. Nevertheless two years before Wilde's *Poems* appeared, Hopkins was intimating his renunciation of poetry as he struggled toward the bleak heights where in the darkness of doubt he wrestled with his God. "I cannot in conscience spend time on poetry," he wrote to Bridges, "neither have I the inducements and inspirations that make others compose. Feeling, love in particular, is the great moving power and spring of verse and the only person that I am in love with seldom, especially now, stirs my heart sensibly and when he does I cannot always 'make capital' of it; it would be sacrilege to do so." Even here the ascetic and the pagan met, although Hopkins was never to put into practice, as Wilde did, the dangerous precept: "Nothing can cure the soul like the senses."

First among the heralds of Wilde's poetic advent came *Punch*, impatient for the occasion to make a thrust at him without benefit of anonymity. Thus, hardly had the gilt dried on the decorative plum blossoms of Wilde's firstling, when *Punch* devoted a fancy portrait—by the hand of Linley Sambourne—to book and author. Set within the heart of a sunflower the head of Wilde rose from a vase and gazed down upon a sheet labeled *Ode*. A basket marked *Waste* stood on one side of the vase.

On the other an inkwell with a quill in it awaited the call of the muse while an open cigarette case invited the poet to while away in smoke the delay of her coming. "O, I feel just as happy as a bright sunflower!" read the legend under the illustration. Beneath came four lines of terse criticism:

> Aesthete of Aesthetes!
> What's in a name?
> The poet is *Wilde*,
> But his poetry's tame.

As if that were not enough *Punch's* more serious literary critic contributed his comments on the book. "The cover is consummate, the paper is distinctly precious, the binding is beautiful, and the type is utterly too . . . There is a certain amount of originality about the binding, but that is more than can be said for the inside of the volume . . . It is Swinburne and Water."

The *Athenaeum*, that pillar of criticism, offered no support whatever to the frailest tendril of encouragement. "Work of this nature has no element of endurance," it thundered four weeks after publication when the book had already gone through as many editions, "and Mr. Wilde's poems . . . will, when their temporary notoriety is exhausted, find a place on the shelves of those only who hunt after the curious in literature." The article occupied the front page of the issue, a dubious honor to a gospel which the critic accused of coming after, instead of before, the cult it would establish.

Everywhere Wilde was belabored with the critical yardstick: he was imitative, unoriginal, full of echoes of Rossetti, Swinburne, Mrs. Browning—even Thomas Hood in the rhythm of his dirge for Isola, "Requiescat," the sole perfect poem of the volume. That Wilde had made full use of his reading there was no doubt. He had plucked his flowers in all gardens, but the arrangement he made of them was distinctly his own. It is enough to turn to Tennyson's *Poems, Chiefly Lyrical,* the product of assiduous imitation, and then to Wilde's volume, to see what a different world each one inhabited. And yet the re-action of the critics had been the same despite the lapse of time, in Tennyson's case with such disastrous effect that it had taken the poet ten years to break his silence. Wilde, inured to buffetings, had developed a thicker skin. Besides, he had paid Bogue out of borrowed money for the printing. He could not afford to take to his tent and luxuriate in brooding. Fortunately, regardless of the rabid press which Willie offset with prepos-terous praise, the book—in small editions—was selling rapidly. With the jingle of money once more in his pocket, Wilde re-newed his courage, as well as his audacity. And the society papers made holiday. Only in America where Roberts Brothers risked the publication of the poems was there a good word said for them. "In Wilde," wrote the *New York Times*, "England has a new poet who, if not of the first order of power, is so true a poet underneath whatever eccentricity of conduct or cant of school that his further persecution in the press must be held contemptible." A desire for fair play gave the poet a larger laurel than he deserved.

At Oxford the undergraduates showed no such forbearance. The Union, to which Wilde belonged, refused to accept the copy which he presented to the library. As for his own college which had become identified with the aesthetic cult and con-tained a large number of disciples, it became the scene of an-other *Patience*. With no such accompaniment of flowers and music as Bunthorne enjoyed on being raffled for, a hapless Magdalen scapegoat was put under the pump amid yells and jeers and reform showed its proper aspect in shorn hair and stand-up collar.

But only temporarily. The cause lay deeper than its effect in absurdity of clothes and behavior. Frenzy, even divine, has its ludicrous side, and prophets have always seemed uncouth to their neighbors. In spite of itself the empire on which the sun never set, the stronghold of industry and material comfort, was undergoing a revolution that had flowers for ensigns, poetry for propaganda, velveteen Bunthorne suits for uniforms, and one whom the world tolerated as an amusing mountebank for its leader. The fate of the vanguard, as history shows, has never been a happy one, his position in the forefront leaving him unprotected to the onslaught as to the floral offering of the admirer. At the present stage Wilde caught only at the flowers, mingled, it is true with the darnels of the critic, and turned upon all alike his ingratiating smile.

Yet the gods had already given warning. James Rennell Rodd, a friend of his at Oxford, like him a winner of the Newdigate Prize, had recently published his first book of verse, *Songs in the South,* reminiscent of a summer they had spent together at Amboise. In the copy he gave to Oscar he inscribed a verse in Italian, the strangest dedication ever made by one friend to another on the threshold of success:

> *Al tuo martirio cupida e feroce*
> *Questa turba cui parli accorrerà;*
> *Ti verranno a veder sulla tua croce*
> *Tutti, e nessuno ti compiangerà.*[1]

[1] Unto thy martyrdom, eager and bold
That crowd will gather to thine agony;
Thee on thy cross they'll hasten to behold
And of them all, not one will pity thee.

Tr. by the author.

Chapter VI: The Sunflower Comes
to America

Ushered in by a host of circumstances, inspiration came to D'Oyly Carte. Why should he not make use of this man Oscar Wilde whom everyone was identifying with the sublimely ridiculous protagonist of *Patience*? Like Bunthorne that absurd young man wrote very precious verses; like him Wilde made a cult of the ineffable and had his circle of adoring ladies eager to be etherealized. The accidental resemblances were so many that from the earliest rehearsals they had been accentuated by the actor Grossmith in mannerisms and make-up. The publicity resulting from the identification worked both ways. It packed the theatre and it kept Wilde in the public eye which, after all, was what he wanted.

With the success of *Patience* the problem of piracy in America again reared its head. D'Oyly Carte stayed up nights worrying about it. Perhaps because of the subject the American public would not take to the new opera as readily as to the previous ones. D'Oyly Carte did not know, however, that the most biting of the *Punch* lampoons had been reproduced in the American papers which improved on the originals by ruder slaps of their own; that Wilde's poems were enjoying as wide a notoriety there as in England; that New York belles and Boston matrons were beginning to adopt the sinuous lines of the aesthetic damozels, and that the Yankee vocabulary had already been enriched by the *too toos* and the *utterly utters* of the ineffable lingo.

Helen Lenoir, the capable young business woman whom he had sent earlier in the summer to establish the Carte Bureau on Broadway and to keep an eye on American piratical enterprise, began to enlighten him on the true state of affairs. So did Colonel W. F. Morse, manager and publicity agent, recruited by the Carte Bureau. Not only was America ripe for *Patience*; it was ready to throw itself upon it in a gust of enthusiasm. The important thing was to concentrate interest on the authentic *Patience* so that the public would not be diverted to the inferior versions that would be cropping up throughout the States.

The idea took shape and that shape was Wilde's. How clever if he could be got to go to America and in a series of lectures act as a sort of advance poster for *Patience*! The disbursal would be small compared with the benefits. The Carte Bureau, D'Oyly Carte himself, could even make a tidy profit from the venture. It was all in the matter of approach.

Whether D'Oyly Carte originated the scheme, or whether inspiration winged its way across the Atlantic from the Carte Bureau, the result came in the form of a material cable to Oscar Wilde at No. 1 Ovington Square, London, from a "responsible agent in New York." Would Wilde be willing to consider an offer of fifty readings in America? The cable arrived on the last day of September. The following morning the dumbfounded young man answered: "Yes, if offer good."

But any offer that gave promise of money would have been good. The success of his volume in spite of its lively sale had been one of notoriety rather than of cash, and though he maintained that credit is a form of capital enabling one to live charmingly on it, he had found that charm difficult to sustain when he had had to practice it on next to nothing a year. There was, of course, the prospect of *Vera*. And he could keep on writing. But the fate of the fair Nihilist lay in the lap of the gods, and as for the muse—smoking an expensive brand of cigarette Wilde found that unlike the women who had been showering him with attentions since he had stepped into the limelight, the muse needed more than a cloud of tobacco to entice her.

Willie faithfully beat the drum for his brother. Because of the astonishing success of Mr. Wilde's *Poems*, he announced in *The World*, the poet had been invited to lecture in America. Meanwhile the weeks passed and October gave way to No-

72

vember with *Vera* no closer to the footlights than before. There was some difficulty in getting a suitable cast, Oscar told Willie and Willie told the world. Again, feeling in England at the moment was not sympathetic to Nihilists, for, after all, the Czarina was the sister-in-law of the Prince of Wales and one could not offend public sentiment. Whatever the reason, *Vera* was tossed off the lap of divinity to the mercies of *Punch* which, taking up an inconspicuous notice in Willie's paper, treated the theme with inimitable variations in the issue of December 10, 1881: "The production of Mr. Oscar Wilde's play 'Vera' is deferred . . . 'Vera' is about Nihilism; this looks as if there was nothing in it . . . Why did he not select the Savoy? . . . Surely where there's a Donkey Cart—we should say D'Oyly Carte—there ought to be an opportunity for an 'os-car?"

John Bull laughed from a million mouths. In his room where he could be himself Wilde looked uncommonly serious at this jest of the gods. But there was still America. It is true he had never lectured before an audience. He was confident of sufficient showmanship, however. So far in London the women had all been with him, and where the women are, the men, willingly or not, are sure to follow. In America, moreover, they wielded a power that made Englishwomen sigh for American husbands and indignant clergymen fulminate from the pulpit. Before the year was over Wilde had come to an understanding with the Carte Bureau. He was to have all expenses paid and a return of one-third of the box-office receipts.

Even if there had been any consideration to make an aristocrat hesitate before entering upon such a public career, he had a shining example before him of what aristocracy can do. Lily Langtry the beautiful, Lily Langtry the envied of all women and the desired of men, the tower of ivory and the red rose of fire, had made her professional bow in *She Stoops to Conquer* at the Haymarket Theatre. The critics devoted columns to her. They spoke of her faultless profile, her glorious eyes, her majestic carriage that was like a poem of motion, her gowns and the dovelike feet that peeped beneath them, her lily-white hands trained to eloquent gesture by Mrs. Labouchère,

73

the former Henrietta Hodson who had been on the stage till W. S. Gilbert shooed her off. They described the distinguished audience that honored her debut, mentioning particularly the Prince of Wales, accompanied for the occasion by Princess Alexandra his wife and the best known names of the Almanach de Gotha. They had little or nothing to say, however, of Lily Langtry the actress. It was enough that she was beautiful.

In America Lily Langtry's debut created a sensation as if it had been a national event. Everyone talked of it and of the amateur performances that had preceded it at Twickenham, the turreted villa which had once belonged to Pope and was now the residence of the Labouchères. They also talked of Wilde who had come to see his summer's flame burn again not for him but for the world. It was said he wore a handkerchief of tiger-lily hue in his white waistcoat in honor of the event. Taking the hint, American tradesmen put by a supply of them for the demand that was sure to set in with the coming of aestheticism to Western shores.

It arrived with the new year—on the 2nd of January, 1882. The steamship *Arizona*, unaware of the unique passenger it was carrying, made no distinction in its rolling between him and the immigrants in steerage, the Italians, Jews and Poles who brought no formula for the life beautiful, indeed, who knew nothing of it. But for years those who had come before them had sent back word that there was a good life to be had in America for men willing to work for it. They were therefore bringing their hands, horny from unprofitable toil, and a hope as great as that of the rich-looking youth in his fur-lined coat and round sealskin cap who amused himself by wandering among them from his cabin on the top deck.

The reporters who met the *Arizona* to interview the man whose arrival had been announced in the papers for nearly a fortnight did not know what to think. They had expected a wilting Bunthorne, folded hands to cheek in a gesture of rapture, and found instead an athletic looking giant whose fist could have knocked down the heftiest of them in an encounter. They had hoped to see him clad in the famous breeches, but

74

noted the long legs of the poet modestly covered by a conventional pair of trousers. The green overcoat with its fur collar and cuffs, however, was sufficiently unusual to make much of in the news story. And, thank heavens, his hair was long enough to please the most exacting. It was unfortunate that he did not carry a sunflower, even an artificial one. Probably he had a store of them in his luggage.

The interview proved a most unsatisfactory affair. Bunthorne did not scintillate; he hardly glowed. To the reporters' questions on the message he brought the American people, he replied with highfalutin jargon about the science of the beautiful, the correlation of the arts and all that sort of thing, mentioning impossible literary names that they had to ask him to spell. They fared no better when they questioned him on his breakfast food and the perfumes he used in his tub. Wilde, apparently, had been imbued with the seriousness of his mission during the long nights of the crossing, and looked upon himself as a lecturer whereas he was expected to be a buffoon.

Dismayed with their game, the reporters stalked the passengers. Surely they had heard Wilde say funny things, had seen him behave in an odd way? Well, no, not exactly, the wary voyagers answered. Then suddenly, just as the newspapermen were about to go away dejected, they got their scoop. Wilde had been disappointed in the Atlantic! He himself had said not a word of that disappointment, but the story was too good to question. In due time the papers screamed with it, rousing a storm which the Atlantic at its best could not have equaled. Bunthorne had found the ocean tame and monotonous. Where were its vaunted terrors, the waves that tore away bridge and mariner, the roars of its fury that shamed the lion in the jungle? The disobliging monster had not acted up to Bunthorne and Bunthorne sulked. The laughter rang loud and long, its echoes reverberating in England where it was taken up anew. No one but Wilde could have been so preposterous.

And yet a poet of wider fame had earlier failed to respond to the majesty of nature, with no more serious consequence than a shocked comment from Elizabeth Barrett to Robert Browning.

75

Tennyson, it seemed, had gone to look at the Swiss Alps and unlike the rest of his generation had remained unimpressed. In fact he had said it in so many words: "I was satisfied with the size of the crags, but mountains, great mountains, disappointed me."

"Is it not strange?" Elizabeth Barrett asked. "Is it a good or bad sign when people are disappointed with miracles of nature? I am accustomed to think it a bad sign . . . A man sees with his mind, and mind is at fault when he does not see greatly, I think."

Elizabeth Barrett was still too close to the Byronic romanticism of emotional identity with nature to countenance Tennyson's heresy. In America the expanse of the continent, the grandeur of its canyons and mountain chains, the unbelievable majesty of its forests attuned the mind of the people to awe for God's works. To deny their glory was to deny divinity. In vain had Emerson preached his allegory of the mountain and the squirrel in which he made the one as important as the other in its ordained sphere. At the reporters' story of Wilde's disappointment every reader, like Elizabeth Barrett, found at fault the mind that did not see greatly.

However, that mind suffered from no sense of inferiority. Wilde had scarcely set foot on American soil when with admirable impudence, to make up, perhaps, for his inadequacy with the reporters, he let the world know what he thought of himself.

"Have you anything to declare?" asked the custom's officer in the routine examination of Wilde's luggage.

"Nothing," answered Wilde. "I have nothing to declare," he repeated, smiling blandly at the curious who hoped to catch a glimpse of the Bunthorne costume tucked away somewhere. Then, after a slight hesitation as if in search of the right phrase, he added swiftly, "Except my genius."

There was an audible gasp, repeated wherever the story was told. Wilde had reached the perfection of his repartee: the innocent smiling opening, the aposiopesis for effect, the closing dart. Whistler in England fixed his monocle in his eye and glared. What! The pupil more deft than the master? Ha! Ha! Dipping his pen in his mixture of spleen and vitriol he wrote letters to the papers on the new Ossian lecturing in America. What did Wilde know of art that he had not learned from him? The embittered American, no prophet in his own or any other country, saw everywhere like Coleridge the ostrich eggs of his genius hatched by others, and the plumes of his birds feathering the caps of plagiarism.

As soon as Wilde landed Colonel Morse took him in charge. First they went to a fashionable hotel.

"A room and bath," Colonel Morse ordered at the desk.

"Sorry, there are no more rooms, sir," said the clerk.

Wilde and the colonel looked at each other in consternation.

"But I want a room for *Mr. Oscar Wilde*," insisted Colonel Morse.

"Sorry, sir, but there is no room even for *Mr. Oscar Wilde*," the clerk replied, giving Wilde his first taste of American democracy.

Bag and baggage, with the dismayed aesthete in tow, Colonel Morse rode with him through the crowded thoroughfares of a busy Tuesday morning. In the streets the horse cars clanged. Overhead clattered the wooden trains of the elevated which had begun adding to the city's noise in 1878. The counting houses in the downtown district opened their doors to white-collared young men who filed swiftly within and were lost to view. Farther uptown, from Fourteenth to Twenty-third Street, the shops raised their blinds to another business day. At the corner of Twenty-third the theatre which Edwin Booth had built in 1869 stood dark and still, sleeping late, for theatre life began at night when the money-making of the day was done.

Colonel Morse settled his charge at the Grand Hotel at Broadway and Twenty-first Street and the round of exciting life began. America's lion hunters immediately followed the spoor of the aesthete's low-water shoes and tracked him down at his hotel in the midst of New York's theatre district. Invitations poured in upon him with gushing letters from desiccated spinsters eager to expand to sunflowery luxury in the light of those godlike blue-gray eyes which the *Tribune* reporter described so feelingly. Miniature pasteboard lilies found ready buyers. Those who could afford them bought hothouse blooms, offered by the florists at exorbitant prices. Japoneries in the shape of embroidered screens and painted umbrellas decorated hitherto sober drawing-rooms. The dado came once more into its own.

Women who had until then found the gowns of Worth the last word in style sent their couturiers to *Patience* for inspiration. "I wish to see Clara Morris dressed all in white brocaded satin," Wilde announced through the newspapers to the gifted actress whom he visualized as his Vera. And behold! she appeared as he had desired at the home of one of his New York hostesses. Alas, though she took his sartorial hint, she remained deaf to his pleas for his drama. How hardhearted her millions of sisters would have found her had they known!

The men, always more conservative, studied the aesthete's day and evening costumes and kept to their own. What self-respecting man would have been caught strolling in the street in that greenery-yallery overcoat, those braided trousers, that atrocious silk hat the color of English fog and those absurd pointed shoes with so high a shine that he could have mirrored himself in them? As for the apple-green Chinese silk tie and the turned-down collar—the less said of them the better. Decidedly, masculine America was not with Wilde. Let Uncle Sam Ward and the artistic young Augustus Hayes who had nothing to lose make much of him. The venerables of the Century Club would have none of him—at any rate not the gruff old poet who, the *Tribune* gossip reported, on hearing that Wilde was expected there broke out: "Where is she? Well, why not say *she*? I understand she's a Charlotte-Ann." The pun was not the less caustic for being amusing.

Rumor, as in England, spread fanciful stories. "It appears," Wilde wrote to Sarah Bernhardt, "that some of the numerous imaginative ones who are at work to make me famous had spread the story that I slept in gorgeous lace nightgowns."

If Wilde was not fabricating to amuse the actress, the tale indicated suspicion on the part of the public. As it was, men raised incredulous brows on learning that Wilde, so proficient a trencherman and so doughty a drinker, had been offended when some gay New York blades had offered to take him out to "see the girls." Such reticence on the part of a vigorous bachelor was assuredly odd. Quips flew, making fun of the queer young man and his philosophy. The *Tribune* gossip reported the latest squib:

"Who was the first aesthete?" asked a cynic, answering in the next breath: "Balaam's ass, because the Lord made him to(o) utter."

However amused the public might be by this novel kind of merryman, general opinion was against him. The *New York Times* which had defended him against the lampooning of the British press now adopted a censorious tone. "The feeling against this young man who has foolishly taken advantage of his chances as a successful *poseur* is . . . a feeling of contempt . . . The honest literary man loves fame and dreads noise." If Wilde insisted on posing as an aesthetic sham he had only himself to blame if he was taken at his own worth. "An American Girl" interviewed by the *Daily Graphic* showed even sharper insight. "Wilde is in his pin feathers," she said. "That young man is posing for the present in borrowed plumage and the queerness of it is it's not his best plumage. He dawdles now as the drawing-room aesthete. It has given him name, fame and notoriety—and it pays. Some day he may get up and shake it all off in disgust."

It was a very serious young man, however, who appeared on the stage of Chickering Hall the night of January 9, 1882. For an hour the carriages had been arriving at the Fifth Avenue entrance and turning up Eighteenth Street. As the steps of the coaches were let down women, rustling with silks and furred luxuriously, burst from the dim interiors and leaning upon their escorts, swept through the lane of those who can only vicariously afford their pleasures. Ladies of fashion came mobled in draperies of colors never seen on sea or land. Others in their choice

79

of subtle tones revealed that they had borne in mind Lady
Jane's suggestion to the dragoons in *Patience*: "Still there *is*
a cobwebby grey velvet, with a tender bloom like cold gravy
. . ." Occasionally, a more brilliant burst of light amid that
subtlety, shone Wilde's favorite yellow satin. The ladies wore
flowers, mostly roses, although, one reporter noted, an occasional distressed lily could be seen. Not a sunflower made its
appearance.

With a sigh of relief the men marked that very few of the
ladies were wearing Gainsborough hats. Instead, dark hair and
fair flowed over the shoulders in the style of the rapturous
damozels, or hung in bangs over the brow, an effect which
gave the less beautiful the look of French poodles.

As there were few ushers in attendance it took the audience
a long time to be seated. The doors were jammed with the
arrivals and still people kept on coming. At eight o'clock a
placard announcing standing-room only was displayed at the
entrance. Nothing daunted, late comers procured tickets and
squeezed their way in. The *Tribune* man took another note:
"Leaning in mediaeval attitudes against the wall back of the
parquette were many aesthetic and pallid young men in dress
suits and banged hair."

Toward eight-fifteen a susurrous impatience awaited the entrance of the man who had been commanding more newspaper
space than the latest political scandal. Those who knew him
only through Napoleon Sarony's photographs fixed their eyes
on the stage entrance. "Will he wear a sunflower?" "Will he
carry a lily?" The questions flew back and forth in the gaslight.
To stay their impatience, women fixed their opera glasses upon
the stage setting, so aesthetic that it must surely have been arranged by some lovely female disciple. In the rear, furnishing a
background, a screen in two shades of brown like the heart of a
sunflower set the aesthetic key. The two chairs before it pursued
the motif in cushions and shoulder rests of a deeper tone of
brown. "Why two chairs?" the question arose. And why, oh,
why, wailed the communicants, had not the management pro-

vided a reading stand in keeping with the occasion instead of that cross between a muffin stand and a clothes rack?

At last the stage lights flashed on full and in their glare entered Colonel Morse followed by the attraction of the evening. Ah! Oscar Wilde! The whisper of recognition washed like a wave over the auditorium and broke against the stage. Wilde, a second before "almond white"—the adjective of Mrs. Frank Leslie— turned crimson with embarrassment. "He's blushing," the women confided to one another, finding it a miracle of nature that Wilde could blush like ordinary mortals. The next moment they were too busy studying his extraordinary costume to do more than stare.

There, surely enough, were the black velvet breeches encasing the well-rounded legs to the knee, and the silk stockings that caught the highlights at the calves. A white waistcoat, cut low, was held by two buttons over the diaphragm above which an expanse of shirt front, broad as a lake, shed the starry glimmer of a single huge stud in some colored stone. The collar, wide and Byronic, was held together by the large stiff knot of a conventional white muslin tie. A handsome gold watchfob hung from his waistcoat. Molding his torso a dress coat met his breeches at the waist in front and hung down in tails to the proper length behind. In the flare of the gas lamps his poetic *chevelure*, parted in the center and curled so that it stood out full and bushy, showed golden glints where the light struck it. What remarkably long lashes he had! Those who saw him in profile were certain that he had accentuated their thickness with the contents of a make-up box.

But oh, dear! Where was the sunflower? Bunthorne's lapels were as bare as any clergyman's.

Colonel Morse did not give them time to conjecture. Rising from the chair which he had taken upon entering the stage, he walked to the edge of the platform. "I have the honor," he said in a loud voice, "to introduce to you Oscar Wilde, the poet, who will deliver his lecture upon the *English Renaissance*." With a businesslike bow he retired.

Wilde who had been staring at the audience, recognized a

lady in the parquet and nodded. Envious opera glasses were immediately pointed at her, only to turn toward him as he rose and walked toward the lectern with stooping shoulders and long steps. The aesthetic feet planted themselves firmly on the rug placed there to receive them.

"Looks like he's toeing in," a young lady remarked audibly to her mother. The *Daily Graphic* and the *Tribune* took down her words.

Still flushing Wilde put his open manuscript on the reading stand, held it down with white gloved hands then, raising his eyes ceilingward in a rapt, ecstatic gaze communed with some unseen spirit for so long an interval that people began to stare at one another. He looked down at last. His hands shuffled the manuscript nervously, but he did not touch the carafe of water on the lower shelf of the lectern. He would not admit stage fright. The audience keyed itself for the expected merriment. Bunthorne no doubt had a whole bag of tricks to spring upon them.

"Among the debts which we owe to the supreme aesthetic faculty of Goethe," Wilde began in a forced voice that rang sepulchrally through the hall, "is that he was the first to teach us how to define beauty in terms the most complete possible . . . So, in the lecture which I have the honor to deliver before you, I will not try to give you any abstract definition of beauty . . . still less to communicate to you that which in its essence is incommunicable, the virtue by which a particular picture or poem affects us with a unique and special joy."

Astonished, the people looked at one another. Good heavens! Were they really going to be lectured to? Incredulous, they turned back to stare at Wilde. There he was, standing on the patterned rug, one hand between vest and dress coat, the other on the distressingly bulky manuscript. The voice, pleasanter now, was rolling on, unconcerned by the audience's evident discomfiture.

"It is really from the union of Hellenism, in its breadth, its sanity of purpose, its calm possession of beauty, with the adventive, the intensified individualism, the passionate colour of

82

the romantic spirit, that springs the art of the nineteenth century in England, as from the marriage of Faust and Helen of Troy sprang the beautiful boy Euphorion. . . ."

Colonel Morse in the wings paced to and fro. The box office, he estimated, must have taken in at least a thousand dollars. Not bad, in fact, very good indeed. If the public liked him he might persuade D'Oyly Carte, who would soon be arriving from England, to send their lecturing Bunthorne across the continent, maybe also to Canada. He cocked his ear for the reaction of the audience. Only silence. A cold silence. He listened to Wilde's rotund periods. How many names the man mentioned! How did he expect an American audience to know what he was talking about? Shelley, William Blake, Michelangelo, Albert Dürer, Homer, Dante, Keats, William Morris, Chaucer, Theocritus . . . He would bore the people to death. What was that? A rustle of approval? Colonel Morse breathed freely once more. If only that exasperating young man wouldn't take his mission so seriously! When was he going to mention *Patience*, by the way? There were two companies in Chicago piling up pirate profits.

"For the poet all times and places are one," Wilde was saying. "The stuff he deals with is eternal and eternally the same: no theme is inept, no past or present preferable. The steam whistle will not affright him nor the flutes of Arcadia weary him: for him there is but one time, the artistic moment; but one law, the law of form; but one land, the land of Beauty—a land removed indeed from the real world and yet more sensuous because more enduring; calm yet with the calm which dwells in the faces of the Greek statues, the calm which comes not from the rejection but from the absorption of passion, the calm which despair and sorrow cannot disturb but intensify only."

He had not sat in vain at the feet of Pater. With the optimism of his twenty-eight years—he had told the reporters he was twenty-six—he was throwing fullhanded his pearls of knowledge before men and women who would rather have seen him draw rabbits out of a hat. He read now with assurance, himself carried away by the rapture of the beauty which he strove to make

83

others see. Here and there among the many auditors one nodded in acquiescence as the message struck home; eyes brightened, kindled by the fire which Wilde had wrested from the godly great to light a bleak industrial world that could see beauty only in the gleam of gold. He rose to sublime heights, no longer Bunthorne but the prophet of a new way of living wherein the senses as well as the soul found food for the development of the perfect man. In their section the reporters kept their pencils flying, wondering how the editors would like their Balaam turn-face. But who could mock the flawless expression of such passages as were even then tingling on the air in that rich, enchanting voice?

"Those strange, wild-eyed sibyls fixed eternally in the whirl-wind of ecstasy, those mighty-limbed and Titan prophets labour-ing with the secret of the earth and the burden of mystery, that guard and glorify the chapel of Pope Sixtus at Rome—do they not tell us more of the real spirit of the Italian Renaissance, of the dream of Savonarola and the sin of Borgia, than all the brawling boors and cooking women of Dutch art can teach us of the real spirit of the history of Holland? . . . Whatever spiritual message an artist brings to his aid is a matter for his own soul. He may bring judgment like Michelangelo or peace like Angelico: he may come with mourning like the great Athenian or with mirth like the singer of Sicily; nor is it for us to do aught but accept his teaching, knowing that we can-not smite the bitter lips of Leopardi into laughter or burden with our discontent Goethe's serene calm . . . You have most of you seen, probably, the great masterpiece of Rubens which hangs in the gallery of Brussels, that swift and wonderful pag-eant of horse and rider arrested in its most exquisite and fiery moment when the winds are caught in crimson banner and the air is lit by the gleam of armour and the flash of plume. Well, that is joy in art, though that golden hillside be trodden by the wounded feet of Christ and it is for the death of the Son of Man that that gorgeous cavalcade is passing."

Joy in art, though the subject be death . . . The good people who sat there listening to a sermon when they had come to hear a few well-turned jokes were now endeavoring, while stifling their yawns, to make sense out of that oratory which floated so far above their heads. Their anticipation had indeed become the pain that is all but a pleasure and the pleasure that is all but a pain. How could they know that in those words was announced the credo of another way of life? Joy in art, joy in the fiery moment, even though it held within it the ashes of humiliation, perchance of martyrdom. For the first time, before the largest audience he had ever addressed, Wilde gave expression to the rule of joyous creation, of intense living, of the delightful moment, new and unpredictable as life itself. Alas, before the century was over a disillusioned generation that had striven for untried ways was to discover that it had never lived.

> We cannot understand
> Laughter or tears, for we have only known
> Surpassing vanity.

But Ernest Dowson who was to write the elegy of that generation was still so young that he had yet to discover life.

There were only two or three sheets left of Wilde's lecture and hardly a ripple of laughter had broken over the auditorium. Yes, only one when reluctantly Wilde had dragged in a reference to *Patience*. "You must not judge of aestheticism by the satire of Mr. Gilbert," he advised. "As little should you judge of the strength and splendour of the sun or sea by the dust that dances in the beam, or the bubble that breaks on the wave, as take your critic for any sane test of art. For the artists, like the Greek gods, are revealed only to one another." Humph! Like Colonel Morse many another released the syllable of exasperation.

Finally while with one hand he played with the tails at the small of his back, Wilde took up the last sheet of his manuscript. There was an audible sigh of relief. "You have heard, I think, a few of you," he seemed to extemporize, "of two flowers connected with the aesthetic movement in England, and said (I assure you, erroneously) to be the food of some aesthetic young men." The house for the first time broke into hearty laughter, succeeded by vigorous applause. "Well," smiled Wilde, "let me tell you that the reason why we love the lily and the sunflower, in spite of what Mr. Gilbert may tell you, is not for any vegetable fashion at all. It is because these two lovely flowers are in England the two most perfect models of design . . . the gaudy leonine beauty of the one and the precious loveliness of the other giving to the artist the most entire and perfect joy." Followed an exhortation to the Americans to let the leaves of their forests and the curving sprays of their wild-roses live in carven arch and marble—and the lecture was over.

Gathering up his manuscript Wilde bowed and walked toward the exit in the same embarrassed stoop-shouldered way that had brought him in. To Colonel Morse's surprise the audience, that is, what remained of it, applauded heartily, whereupon Wilde came out and bowed again. When he returned to the wings no further applause availed to bring him back.

"How did you like it?" a reporter heard a lady ask her daughter.

"I didn't understand a word of it," said the candid young person.

Little by little, but for the usual crowd that lingers at stage entrances, the neighborhood of Chickering Hall was left to the contemplative policeman.

The following day the criticisms appeared, almost all favorable, much to the astonishment of the Carte Bureau. Despite the fact that on the lecture platform Bunthorne had donned the invisible gown of the clergyman over his plush breeches, he had managed to win over the intelligent audience. The critic of the *World*, rhapsodic, indulged in stylistic flourishes of his own. "Long melodious sentences, seldom involved, always clear, unfolded his meaning as graceful curves reveal a beautiful figure," he indited. Those who read his appreciation, even though they had been bored to extinction during the mortal hour of the lecture, agreed that "not description was the method of the treatment, but revelation," and that they had

86

been partakers of the mystery. Perhaps Wilde after all was not so ridiculous as he was painted.

Only the *Daily Graphic* refused to be charmed. "To be just to Mr. Wilde," it wrote, "would be cruel. He is the most prosy of poets, at least while speaking his own lines with elevated chin, elongated stockings, dilapidated hair and simpering voice."

Nor would the comic artists be deprived of their legitimate prey. New York, generous, gullible New York, had taken kindly to the preposterous young man. But would Boston? In anticipation the *Graphic* artist drew a cartoon in the manner of *Punch*, labeling it "Boston Aestheticism Versus Oscar Wilde."

"No, sir," says the Cabot-faced Old Lady of Beacon Hill in plumed bonnet and straight-lined vestments as she waves away the aesthete with his offering of a sunflower. "Shoddy New York may receive you with open arms, but we have an aestheticism of our own."

The *Boston Transcript* was more direct when in a parody of *Peter Bell* it jingled:

> A lily by the river's brim
> An advertising dodge to him
> It was, and nothing more.

Pocketing the percentages from his lecture Wilde discounted the insults.

Chapter VII: The Lecturing Ossian

IN HIS brown silk dressing gown and red-braided trousers Oscar Wilde was turning over the pages of the newspapers on the morning of January 18 in the city of Brotherly Love. He found nothing in them to dispel the chill of his reception the previous night at Horticultural Hall. Never had he been faced with so cold an audience. One might have thought those people had come there to freeze him out. During the interminable hour that he had read his lecture there had been scarcely a murmur, hardly a flutter of applause. It seemed like a gathering of snow men and women—except that at one point, when he reached for his glass to fortify his failing composure, they broke into mock enthusiasm. He could still hear the cackle of their laughter. Several times he had been on the verge of laying down his manuscript and saying, "You don't like this, and there is no use in my going on," but his pride restrained him. Not all the drinking at the home of his publisher, J. M. Stoddart, after the lecture, had been able to thaw the coldness of that reception. As he read the studied insults in the papers he bore little resemblance to the Wilde whom the *Philadelphia Press* reporter had described the previous day, leaving the New York ferry. "His eye sparkled and his face was flushed with pleasure as, with a long stride which kept him far in advance of the eager rush . . . and which left his valet struggling hopelessly in the rear with a burden of baggage, he entered the Pennsylvania station. . . ." Alas, the city of Brotherly Love had had no love for him.

Later that day it was with a certain humility that, escorted by Stoddart, he crossed the Delaware to visit Walt Whitman at Camden. Breakfast at the home of Professor S. H. Grosse had somewhat lifted his spirits. Communion with a poet who had himself suffered the slings and arrows of prejudice would restore his self-assurance, for however bland the face he turned

88

to the mockers, it was not always the true witness of an inner peace.

A little after noon he walked up Stevens Street and entered the cottage which the good gray bard had been occupying since a paralytic stroke, nearly ten years earlier, had given him warning that he could no longer be an active participant "of life immense in passion, pulse and power." He was now in his early sixties, a striking figure of a man with eyes of a childlike clearness contrasting with his patriarchal beard. He did not look the invalid. Sometimes when the old vigor stirred the blood in him he would take long jaunts amid the nature that he loved, recapturing once again the sense of oneness with all created things that made him the trumpet of the universe.

People had held their ears when he had first shouted his immense song. Too dull to pierce its meaning, too small to embrace its largeness, they tried to shout down the singer by calling him names. They might as well have sought to silence the thunder. The reverberant song encompassed the earth till it was heard in England. The Rossettis were the first to hear it and rejoice. Not content to keep the discovery at home, William Michael Rossetti published a selection of Whitman's poems. The name was taken up by a widening circle, some like Anne Gilchrist, making a Bible of *Leaves of Grass*, others finding in it only a "barbaric yawp."

When Wilde entered the modest parlor of the Camden cottage he did not know that for nearly three years the widowed Mrs. Gilchrist had often sat there, darning the socks of her Beloved or soothing him with airs on the piano which she had brought from England. In a romantic dedication she had offered herself as the mate of the poet, hoping that from their union would spring another Euphorion. Too late. Anne was past the age when women may bear children, even to the gods. As for the bard, desire in him was spent for everything but nature and the book to which more than to any woman he was wedded. Mrs. Gilchrist had returned to England.

Whitman greeted his visitor with bluff good nature. He saw nothing out of the way in the long hair—he had always let his

89

grow—and in the brown velvet suit which the aesthete affected as his daytime garb, more, doubtless, because it was expected than out of choice. Whitman had suffered too much from the unkindness of man whom he still persisted in hailing as brother not to understand that the gayest front is often the mask of a hidden failure.

He made the young man immediately at home over a bottle of wine. There is nothing like wine to put one at one's ease even when like Whitman's homemade elderberry it was a little hard to swallow. As they drank together the tough old poet studied the youth before him. He liked him because he downed his glass like a man. He admired his bigness, his health, enthusiasm and buoyancy. All necessity for pretense dispelled by Whitman's simplicity, Wilde was glad to be himself.

"I have come to you," he said to the old man who sat there stroking his white beard, "I have come to you as to one with whom I have been acquainted almost from the cradle." Speranza had been one of Whitman's early admirers, and Speranza's son had first heard the clarion voice in the fluted tones of the Irish Muse. Later, at Oxford, he had read Whitman aloud on his rambles.

For nearly an hour they talked together, Wilde entertaining Whitman with stories of William Morris, Rossetti, Swinburne and Tennyson. The bottle showed an empty bottom, but still they talked on with a growing fullness of heart.

"Come up with me and I will show you my den," Whitman invited.

And up the two flights of stairs they went to the room that was Whitman's study. From the window one could glimpse over the rooftops the masts of the ships in the river. The rattle of trains from the near-by railroad sounded farther away from that height; their whistle seemed less nostalgic. Wilde looked about him. There appeared not the least attempt at interior decoration. A stool, an armchair and a bed occupied space at random. Near the window stood a plain pine table strewn with newspaper clippings. A volume of Dante and one of Shakespeare betrayed the literary man—if that magnificent graybeard, craggy as a mountainside, could have been called anything so limited. Wilde was all worship. When Whitman sat down in the armchair he drew up the stool and curled his long limbs about it.

"I should like to call you Oscar," said Whitman on whom Wilde's charm had acted as potently as the wine.

"I like that so much," responded Wilde, laying his hand on the old man's knee. As Whitman looked down upon the countenance that lifted toward him the adoration of its frank blue eyes, he saw him as a great, big, splendid boy. Why did the newspapers write such mocking things of him? He was so outspoken and manly in his speech with him. He had so many pithy things to say, and moreover he said them so well.

For nearly another hour they went on talking, rather, Wilde talked while Whitman, still stroking his beard, received the unabashed tributes. There were only two men in America who were considered true poets by the English, Wilde told him— Whitman and Emerson. He put Whitman first. Deep within him Whitman concurred.

Many years earlier he had sent a copy of *Leaves of Grass* to Emerson. Alone of the intellectuals of his day Emerson had found something to praise in the poems. He had gone to see Whitman in Brooklyn, and later in Boston he had helped to supervise the printing of the book. Yes, Emerson had been very kind, like all truly great men. But the visitor from England was right in putting him before Emerson. A larger intellect Whitman allowed the Concord sage, but the poetic gift was his own; the true voice of America sang through himself alone. Now even Emerson's intellect was failing through the ironic pranks of age. Since 1880 the brilliant memory that had reflected the rays of world cultures had been as dulled as a buried mirror. Only occasional flashes came from it when, by great effort, the dust of ordinary living was rubbed away. "My naughty memory," Emerson would smile ruefully.

During their talk Wilde of course launched upon the subject of aestheticism. Carried away by his own enthusiasm he waxed more eloquent every minute, unconscious of the incongruity of the surroundings—the plain little room, the homely denims of his host. Whitman was uncommonly sympathetic.

"I wish well to you, Oscar," he said, "and as to the aesthetes, I can only say that you are young and ardent, and the field is wide, and if you want my advice, I say, go ahead." Only once he disagreed with his guest when Wilde said, "I can't listen to anyone unless he attracts me by a charming style or by beauty of theme."

"Why, Oscar," said Whitman, "it always seems to me that the fellow who makes a dead set at beauty by itself is in a bad way. My idea is that beauty is a result, not an abstraction."

Wilde looked up quickly. He had little expected to have such a truth brought home clad in such inelegant Americanisms. "Yes," he was compelled to admit. "I remember you have said 'All beauty comes from beautiful blood and a beautiful brain.' And, after all, I think so, too." It would have been well for him had he always remembered it.

The afternoon was drawing to a close and the effects of the elderberry had long been dissipated. "Oscar, you must be thirsty," said Whitman.

"Yes, I am thirsty."

"I'll give you some punch."

Suiting the action to the word Whitman produced a tall glass of milk punch which Wilde tossed off with excellent grace. The interview was over. As the tall figure of the aesthete disappeared down the street Whitman called after him, "Good-bye, Oscar. God bless you."

In London, meanwhile, David Bogue was putting through the press another edition of Wilde's volume, interest in it and its author sustained by publicity and, unwittingly, by *Punch* that missed no opportunity to shower the lecturing Ossian with dubious attentions. To the mock poems by "Oscuro Wildgoose" were added ballads by "Brother Jonathan" Wilde. In some issues no fewer than four or five items were devoted to the wanderer. Never had man before him been so be-rhymed and so caricatured. If it was not fame it was something very near it.

With the fervor of the imitator America followed the fashion in its extremes. Parodies of Wilde appeared everywhere, some of the verses so like those which he obligingly sent to the papers that not a few mistook them for his authentic expression. Wilde had "come over" American versifiers. If the hillocks at the foot of Parnassus flowered only with weeds, they were still a joyous sight to those who would never have climbed high enough to seek the asphodel. For that matter Wilde often clung to the back gardens of Ruralia in his poetic excursions. Despite the device of the French title no one could have mistaken the locale of *"Le Jardin"* which appeared in a Philadelphia magazine. The aesthete wrote from deep dejection:

> The withered lily's chalice falls . . .
>
> The gaudy leonine sunflower
>   Hangs black and barren on its stalk,
>   And down the windy garden walk
> The dead leaves scatter,—hour by hour.

Boston, contrary to New York's prediction, invited him. Not only did the Old Lady of Beacon Hill open her door to him but Beacon Hill itself came to Wilde when he arrived to read his lecture at the Boston Music Hall. There was something electric in the air. Outside, a heavy snowstorm had whitened the streets. Within, the rows of seats glistened with brocades and ermine and all the finery that the Brahmin shipmasters had brought from voyages to the Orient. Yes, they were going to Wilde, but they were bringing to him cultural wealth as great, if not greater, than he brought to them.

Gradually the hall began to fill, except for the front rows which remained suspiciously empty. Had they been reserved by some Transcendentalist society? As the time for the lecturer's appearance drew nigh, heads turned toward the lobby and lorgnettes were raised to questioning eyes. Who was going to occupy those front seats?

The answer came in a sudden commotion as the doors burst open and a weird procession marched down the center aisle. The ladies of Beacon Hill smothered their voices to a gasp. The women of the rest of Boston shrilled their surprise. Some unmannerly men who had no business there roared with laughter and clapped their hands.

It was those Harvard students again. They could always be counted upon to do a bit of "acting up" of their own. But not the wildest imagination could have prophesied the manner of their welcome to the guest of the evening. Two by two, some sixty undergraduates filed down the length of the aisle. Their muscular legs were breeched, their calves sheathed in silk. From their collars flowed silk ties of unimaginable tints. Wigs of all shades and all states of curliness covered their heads. In the lapels of their coats some wore the lily or the sunflower. Others held the tall stalks in their hands as they gazed intensely into the center of inspiration. In languorous motion or in stained-glass attitudes they took their places, but by that time most of the house was on its feet, the ladies forgetting their dignity to the extent of risking their trains by standing on the seats. Finally order was restored and all eyes looked expectantly toward the curtain through which Wilde would come.

He appeared. As he walked toward the lectern a burst of localized clapping in the front rows was taken up by the rest of the audience. There was mockery in it, as polite as Boston could make it, but there it was. Wilde seemed not to notice. Staring down at the Harvard lads, he pretended to be pleased with what he saw, for when he turned his head toward the audience at large a broad smile covered it.

"I see about me the signs of an aesthetic movement," he said coolly, the smile spreading as the audiences responded with more genial laughter. "As I look about me I am impelled for the first time to breathe a fervent prayer, 'Save me from my disciples.'"

Wonder of wonders, Wilde himself had discarded the Bunthorne uniform. Instead, there he was in dress coat and trousers, the colorful flow of tie alone betokening the aesthete. What had happened? Who had given him warning? The masquerading boys reddened with confusion. Their wigs lay heavy on their

94

heads. Parents who recognized their sons among them fervently wished their neighbors had not noticed.

The first tumult over, Wilde read his already worn script. Brahmin Boston nodded approval. It knew a good thing when it heard it. Although there was nothing their visitor could teach them, they could admire his style with no loss of prestige. Thus when the young rapscallions in the front rows made a half-hearted attempt at roughhouse they forgot their breeding for a moment to hiss them down.

That night Wilde had his first real triumph—"by right of conquest," the *Transcript* magnanimously admitted. "It was a lovely though sad sight," it continued, elegiac, "to see those dear silly youths go out of the Music Hall in slow procession, hanging their heads meekly, and trying to avoid observation." And well might they have gone home in contrition. Not only had the conquering hero heaped the coals of conscience upon their heads, but he had further burdened them with the gift of a Greek statue in plaster to reprove them forever in their gymnasium.

The following evening, February 1, at the same hour when at Chickering Hall the citizens of New York were holding a mass meeting protesting the persecution of Jews in Russia, the Yale students attempted to stage a demonstration of a different nature at Peck's Opera House in New Haven where Wilde was scheduled to lecture. Two hundred strong they marched through the streets displaying sunflowers and flaunting red ties. Then, led by a tall Negro in aesthetic costume, they took possession of the gallery. For the benefit of Wilde a huge sunflower fan was left to occupy a conspicuous front seat. After the Boston furore, however, the New Haven coup passed unnoticed, to the discouragement of future jackanaperies. Thenceforth Wilde was free to cover America with his ubiquitous low-waters.

And cover it he did, albeit the *Daily Graphic* showed him on the front page on February 14 reading a valentine from Columbia: "Ta-ta, Oscar dear. . . . Good for one steerage passage for Europe."

With the circulation of the story of Wilde's Boston conquest, the Carte Bureau was besieged with communications from all over the country demanding a sight of its lucrative piece of property. Wherever *Patience* had been heard of, and also where it was unknown, curiosity turned like Moore's sunflower toward her god. Wilde was nothing loth. He enjoyed traveling in those fine fast American trains, and he had now learned to feel the pulse of his audience—a variable patient that needed personal treatment. Accordingly he began to follow the script a little less and extemporize a little more. He busied himself moreover with the preparation of another lecture, announced under the formidable title of "The Practical Application of the Principles of the Aesthetic Theory to Exterior and Interior House Decoration, With Observations Upon Dress and Personal Ornaments."

Oddly, it became very popular in the West where horses were being named Oscar Wilde and Lily Langtry in honor of the visiting celebrity and of the professional beauty who would soon vouchsafe America a sight of herself on the stage. Gossip had it that with other professional London beauties the fair Lily had been waging a war against the incursion of lovely Americans whom the Prince of Wales took pleasure in discovering as assiduously as Wilde was discovering America. Was the charm of the Lily fading? And had the public been too hasty in selecting her as the Cleopatra of her time when they placed her photograph with other wonders of the day in the foundation of the obelisk on the Thames Embankment? But that had been in 1878, four years earlier, and many suns had made their sequences since then. For the present Wilde held the fore undisputed, as he was sped on his way to the tune of the *Jolly Utter Galop* and the *Oscar Schottische* which an enterprising music publisher had brought out by special arrangement with Sarony who furnished Wilde's photograph for the cover. *The Dream of the Lily Waltz* soothed his pensive moods.

And America laughed. He had a way of raising people's risibilities with his expectedly unexpected reactions. There was nothing of which they thought him incapable, and because he bettered their anticipations they could not contain their wonder. There was the matter of Niagara Falls. Now Niagara is to

96

America what Mont Blanc is to Europe. The proper behavior for puny man is to hold his breath and then exhale it in a prolonged Oh-h-h of awe. Did Wilde do anything of the sort? Of course not!

"When I first saw Niagara Falls," he said, "I was disappointed in the outline." Not only did he express his displeasure, but when some zealous soul tried to impress him with the magnitude of the power generated by those millions of gallons of water, he merely shrugged his shoulders and said that the beauty of bulk alone did not in the least interest him. He could only see, he said, a vast amount of water going the wrong way and then tumbling over unnecessary rocks. The colors, he granted, were beautiful, and the sight seemed a sort of embodiment of Pantheism. But he could not force himself to higher praise. Later he expatiated upon his prejudices. "Every American bride is taken there, and the sight of this stupendous waterfall must be one of the earliest, if not the keenest, disappointments in American married life." Guffaws mingled with snorts of contempt. "The Falls, so far as we know, kept on falling," tersely commented a New York *Tribune* editorial.

From Buffalo to Chicago, from Chicago to Detroit, thence to Cleveland and on to Louisville, Wilde traveled, sometimes with his Negro boy, sometimes alone. Briefly he would stop in each city, meet its notables after the lecture, and away he would go from state to state—Illinois, Iowa, Minnesota, Nebraska, California, Colorado, Missouri, Kansas. The beautiful strange names of a young civilization rang no echo in a mind that appreciated no culture more recent than Rome's. Texas, Louisiana, Alabama, Georgia, Virginia, Rhode Island, Massachusetts: they were but places in a railroad itinerary. It was not his to propound as Coleridge had done, a whole Utopia on the mere sound of the word Susquehanna.

But if he was unresponsive to places he reacted sympathetically to people. In Leadville, a hell-roaring mining camp in Colorado where lawlessness was the law and money the measure of morality, he revealed himself so much the man by carrying his liquor better than the best and by showing not the least fear of personal assaults, that the bold bad men of the West accepted him as one of themselves, as indeed he appeared in the slouch hat and corduroy trousers which he adopted as his western costume. He might puzzle the miners by advising them to have their workmen in gold draw out the ore "in those magic threads of sunlight that are called gold wire." But he made up for his nonsense by going down the Matchless Mine shaft with the most hardened. And triumph of triumphs, before leaving the West he acknowledged the grandeur of the Rockies! Walt Whitman and the Rockies: America should rest content.

In Chicago he befriended John Donoghue, an unknown young artist who had had to beg for the materials for his work. Not only did Wilde buy from him a bas-relief illustrating his poem "Requiescat" but he went out of his way to praise him in his lectures and in interviews with the reporters. The youth's "Sophocles" he found the equal to the best in sculpture, and belatedly the Chicago Institute confirmed his opinion by acquiring the statuette.

On the long railway journeys and in hotel rooms Wilde, meanwhile, was engaged on another act of kindness or, more truly, a labor of love. While in Philadelphia he had talked so effusively of his friend Rodd's poems that Stoddart agreed to publish the book in America—if Wilde launched it on its way with an appropriate *envoi*. So it was settled. The volume, besides introducing another poet to America was to establish forever the type of the book beautiful.

At first Mr. Stoddart demurred at the expense but later, catching the Wildean fire, he was consumed by his own enthusiasm. No ordinary paper would do for the aesthetic book. Black ink was out of the question. Ransacking the Philadelphia warehouses, Stoddart finally came upon an extraordinary veined paper that had been lying desuete since the Revolution. Authorities said the stock had been manufactured in David Rittenhouse's mill for the first paper currency of the new United States. Stoddart was elate. Here was the very paper for the book beautiful—*Rose Leaf and Apple Leaf,* as Wilde retitled it without waiting for its author's consent. The name was suggestive of an innovation: between the printed pages there would be an interleaving of Japanese tissue in the predilected color of the lovers of beauty, green. James Edward Kelly made the wood blocks for the designs, one of them, on the title page, drawn from the seal of a ring which Speranza had given her son. A brown ink was chosen for the printing, and the poems were then set. All that was needed was Wilde's *Envoi*. He sent it on to Stoddart together with a dedication ostensibly from Rodd to himself, and the little book was printed in a luxurious edition of two hundred copies.

To
Oscar Wilde
"Heart's Brother"—
These Few Songs and Many Songs to Come,

read the astounded author on the dedicatory page.

If such effusiveness displeased Rodd, he had less cause for pleasure when he turned to the opening paragraph of the *Envoi* which described him as one of the young warriors of the romantic banner who were perfecting the English renaissance. "There is none whose love of art is more flawless . . . none indeed who is dearer to myself." Rennell Rodd read the sentence over. He was a level-headed ambitious young man who had every intention of going far in life in some respectable post. An eventual baronetcy was not beyond his dreams. He was worried. The more he read Wilde's encomium, the more worried he became. How wise was it for him to be identified with a movement not altogether approved by respectability? Then those personal references, that unmasculine enthusiasm—they could not possibly do him any good. There was no sense trying to explain to Oscar Wilde in detail. He would ask him to omit the dedication and let it go at that.

With Stoddart he was more explicit. "There is one thing that has annoyed me excessively. . . . The dedication is too effusive. I want to have it removed from all copies that go out

99

for the future." It was not to be the only time that Wilde would be misjudged for his kindness.

He took great pride in the little book. He had a genuine admiration for the tenuous, often sentimental, poems of Rodd which he praised more generously than they deserved; but he was best pleased with his own *Envoi*. Not even in the best parts of his lecture on the English renaissance had he written so well. The long, convoluted sentences wound like a stream in sunlight, reflecting on their way the blossoms of art and literature. They had the limpidity of Pater and the cadences of Ruskin. But Wilde's echoes were not merely imitations. He took the original stuff and exhibited it to advantage, bringing out the best of its design and texture till one forgot the web and woof of which it was woven. More than an introduction to an ephemeral book of verse the *Envoi* was the restatement of his credo; better than a piece of poetry, it was prose raised to rhythmic heights. Wilde knew now what Pater had meant when he said that prose was so much more difficult to write than poetry. He was aware of an added confidence, a joy in his work which he had talked of but never till now experienced. Wilde, the prose artist, came to full growth in America, through the agency of a second-rate book of verse.

With autumn, after a lecture tour in Canada where his hair turned golden in emulation of the magic threads of sunlight which he admonished the Leadville miners to spin, he returned to New York, to an apartment in the lower part of Manhattan. He came in time to meet Lily Langtry at the boat.

It was the 23rd of October. With a group of reporters, theatrical agents and variously interested parties, Oscar Wilde, no longer the admired of all admirers, set out to meet the *Arizona* which only nine months earlier had borne him to America and the mercies of her newspapermen. There were no reporters for him now. As he stood apart from the rest of the men, holding his greeting of lilies for the fair arrival, he roused but a faint stir of curiosity. Press and public had had enough of him. Now that his novelty had waned like the artificial glints in his hair, the people turned to the newest favorite. The king is dead. Long live the queen.

Wilde gazed toward the *Arizona*, a shadow in the foggy dawn. In a few minutes he would be on board. Would Lily remember the poems he had written to her, the hours they had spent together two short summers ago? He had not forgotten. When someone had asked recently whether he had discovered Lily Langtry he answered with little generosity toward Columbus but a great deal toward the fickle fair: "I would rather have discovered Mrs. Langtry than have discovered America."

The meeting was an anti-climax. After the reporters had interviewed Mrs. Langtry and he had a moment alone with her, Wilde offered her the lilies with suitable words of welcome. There was nothing more. Mrs. Labouchère, hovering in the background, took the lovely Helen under her wing, and Wilde, the least important of a long retinue, departed.

The familiar comedy was re-enacted, the press thundering its ballyhoo, the public clamoring for spicier novelties, madder sensations. Lily Langtry rode the crest of the wave, an exultant Aphrodite with no small sense of her worth. Sarony photographed her, paying her, it was said, a staggering sum for the privilege. "You have made me pretty. I am beautiful," she criticized when he showed her the proofs. Even Wilde had not gone so far.

Her debut as Hester Grazebrook in Tom Taylor's *Unequal Match* created a sensation—because of her beauty. Politely the critics skirted the thorny point that the New Helen was no actress and considerately blamed her inadequacy on the crudities of the play. Oscar Wilde, engaged by the *World* to act as its drama critic for the night, wrote a paean on the wonder of her loveliness.

"Pure Greek it is, with the grave low forehead, the exquisitely arched brow," the otherwise sober *World* proclaimed to New York, "the noble chiselling of the mouth, shaped as if it were the mouthpiece of an instrument of music; the supreme and splendid curve of the cheek; the augustly pillared throat which bears it all: it is Greek, because the lines which compose it are so definite and so strong. . . . Greek, because its essence and its quality, as is the quality of music and architecture, is that of beauty based on absolutely mathematical laws."

By converting her, the unattainable, to a mathematical abstraction, Wilde made bearable the intervening time to the 27th of December when he sailed for Liverpool on the *Bothnia*. He had seen little of Lily, and she had remained as aloof, as heartless as ever toward him, though not to others. Scandal sat upon her doorstep and shrieked from the papers of the nation when she accepted too openly the attentions of a young millionaire. But she would not be warned, not even when Mrs. Labouchère rebuked her, and seeing that it was all hopeless, sailed for home leaving her unchaperoned. Lily of love, no longer pure and inviolate.

As the Cunard steamship rolled out toward that disappointing Atlantic, Oscar Wilde despite his melancholy had much to comfort him. He was taking away with him more money than he had ever owned, a commission for a tragedy for Mary Anderson the actress, and the prospect of *Vera*'s production in America through the agency of Marie Prescott. Standing at the rail in clothes as unassuming as his fellow passengers', Wilde cast a backward look upon the fading sky line that had first gazed upon his arrival as Bunthorne. The masquerade had, on the whole, been worth while.

Chapter VIII: In the Gown of Balzac

SPERANZA embarked on a round of entertainments during the first few weeks of January, 1883. Between the hours of five and seven the Irish nationalists, for lack of the hearty brew that had flowed freely in the good old Dublin days of Sir William, took their tea out of china cups and let it grow cold while they listened to their Muse reciting not her own, but her son's poems. She knew them all by heart. With the majesty of an eastern potentate she presided behind the tea table, pouring the tea like the wine of a sacrament, and letting thirst wait upon inspiration as, with the urn in mid-air, she declaimed Oscar's latest. The overcrowded parlor seemed smaller, untidier than ever. Voices rose to a fervent pitch, the shrilling of the women dominating the soberer drone of the males. At Speranza's gatherings the women far outnumbered the men. She had a following among her sex, a sort of rapturous nunnery that offered an antiphonal chant to her eloquence and punctuated with exclamations some particularly happy phrase. High priestess and vestals served two gods—liberty as embodied by the patriot Parnell, and aestheticism as incorporate in Oscar Wilde. At Oakley Street the liberty cap was redder than the accepted shade and the sage green of aestheticism intenser and more prevalent than elsewhere. Speech too became either oratorical or lyrical. Simple prose was left to the outside world.

Everybody now came to Oakley Street. Speranza hoped it was for her sake, but she knew that her "wonderful Oscar" was the drawing card. Willie also knew it. In spite of the delightful way he had of telling an anecdote he could see that his listeners lent him only half an ear, while the other one and a half were pricked up to catch what Oscar was saying in another part of the room, or to the sound of the door knocker whenever he was expected. But he did not mind. The bills in the little lacquer rack over the mantel had been paid fairly regularly since Oscar's trip to

America. There was hope that things would get better rather than worse. Meanwhile he did his duty toward brother Oscar by trumpeting his every move as if he were the Prince of Wales and, to use the mixed figure which was Willie's chief ornament of speech, was content to play second fiddle. Willie was now nearing thirty. Well made and with his brother's Irish beauty, he was always pursued by some gushing damsel inviting him to take advantage of the dimly lighted corners.

For a time the Oakley Street household had half hoped that the gossip in the papers had had some basis in truth when it intimated that Oscar had lingered in America after his lectures to look about for an heiress to marry. He had come back unwed. However, the way to Oakley Street had been pointed out to visitors. As Speranza used to say of the convenient location, "All London comes to me by way of King's Road . . . but the Americans come straight from the Atlantic steamers moored at Chelsea Bridge." Who knows, perhaps eventually fortune herself might step down the gangplank. If not, hadn't Oscar said something about going back to America for the production of *Vera*?

After January, entertainment lapsed at Oakley Street, for with the remainder of the money from his lectures Oscar crossed the Channel to France. With a number of literary irons in the fire, he needed the right atmosphere to beat them into shape. Where better than in Paris, that forge of the intellect, could he find it, and where in Paris except at the *rive gauche*, the left bank of the Seine which counted as many *literati* as cafés and as many cafés as there were leaves on the trees that lined the hospitable boulevards?

At the Hôtel Voltaire he took a suite of rooms, in the quai that also bore the name of that dubious patron saint. From his windows on the second floor he could look out upon the square where, smiling enigmas, Voltaire in stone watched life flow by. Along the Seine wall early in the morning—if he was up—he could see the book vendors opening their stalls, putting out enticingly titled volumes in paper covers for the literate foreigner, and for the illiterate a selection of colored prints that spoke

104

louder than words. Beyond flowed the Seine, changing with the sky. All through the day the river traffic passed under the many bridges, on the right toward Pont Neuf beyond which reared the gray bulk of Notre Dame, insubstantial as a cloud bank on misty mornings, solid as a mountain in the clear light, and on the left to the Pont du Carrousel. Over the river the palisade of the Louvre met the arches that led toward the Avenue de l'Opéra and continued on the river side, framing the lovely formal gardens that concealed all stain of the blood which had flowed when, Louis XVI deposed, Lady Guillotine was raised to the place of authority. Along the quai on the Left Bank, art shops displayed church vestments and oil paintings, scarabs of that inimitable blue which only death can create after centuries of labor in hidden tombs, gross renaissance rings with secret poison chambers, beads once warmed on the breast of a Faustine, anklets that had tinkled to the dance of Salomé, heraldic devices, poniards wrought with an art that lent beauty even to murder—all the strange and wonderful detritus of dead civilizations that gives the spark to creative imagination. It was some such shop that brought to Balzac his idea for *Peau de Chagrin*. Wilde, however, too recently arrived from his American posturing, pretended indifference to the charm that lay beyond his window.

"It's altogether immaterial," he would say airily, "except to the innkeeper who of course charges it in the bill. A gentleman," the lightning smile flashed, "a gentleman never looks out of the window."

Within he arranged for himself the den of a sybarite, a literary sybarite, for he had come to Paris as the littérateur, exemplified by Balzac, whom he was now assiduously reading. The great Frenchman's Lucien de Rubempré more than Balzac himself, however, set the height for Wilde's ambition. He saw himself as another Lucien dreaming of glory and of fortune. Like him he longed for a Vautrin who with unquestioning devotion would serve him in his every wish. But as yet no one came his way, and he encouraged his luxury-loving muse with emulation of the indefatigable Balzac. Robert Sherard, a young journalist whom he had recently met, visited him in his rooms and was astonished at the number of books Wilde had by or on Balzac. "Textbooks with which to study a part," he thought, and he was right.

Wilde was studying the role of the literary man, and the better to identify himself with his model, he adopted his habits as far as possible. Because Balzac, who worked best at night, used to write in a white-cowled monkish dressing-gown, Wilde procured himself one of that fashion. And because Balzac, the dandy, astonished the French bourgeois by carrying an ivory-headed cane set with turquoises, Wilde sported the identical walking stick. But where the French writer in his days of struggle had contented himself with imagining the luxuries which his pen could not afford, and by chalking on the floor of his bare room the place for the Oriental carpet, the cushioned divan, the bookcase and the mirror, lightened his poverty, Wilde had to have the material object to be happy. He knew that his American dollars would not last forever, but while he had them he saw to it that like Aladdin's lamp, they gratified his desires.

Accordingly he lived on a grand scale. The most expensive restaurants on the Avenue de l'Opéra often saw him and his guests; his wines came from the choicest cellars; his button-holes from the most tasteful florists who also provided the bunch of fresh-cut flowers which, together with the box of Turkish cigarettes on his writing table, sweetened his labors. He was never without his cigarettes. In America he had been exasperated by the many *No Smoking* signs placed in public waiting rooms. "Great heaven, they speak of smoking as if it were a crime!" he broke out, shocking the virtuous bluenose.

He had no amourette that anyone knew of. The only feminine thing that Sherard found in the Hôtel Voltaire suite was a print of a Puvis de Chavannes painting showing the meager form of a young girl sitting on her unraveled shroud. Woman and death—an odd choice for a gay man-about-town, yet not so odd considering that the favorite picture of his adolescence, and one that he still loved, was Guido's St. Sebastian pierced with arrows. Was the Puvis de Chavannes adumbrative of change?

106

Stimulated by the literary ferment about him as well as by the example of his model, Wilde buckled down to work. Mary Anderson had given him an advance of a thousand dollars for a "first-class five-act tragedy" as specified by the contract he had signed before sailing. Four thousand dollars were to be his on the approval of the finished tragedy. With the attraction of more American cash before him, and with the white gown of inspiration enfolding him, Wilde finished his tragedy by the middle of March. He was pleased with it. Surely Miss Anderson would find that it answered fully the requirement of first-classness.

Alas, the exacting Miss Anderson was far from satisfied. The play, blanker than its blank verse, was as removed from reality as if the action were taking place in some planet where amorality was the rule and lust the breath of life, with lightning and thunder obligingly furnishing the accompaniment to tragedy and death. To the American public the pseudo-Shakespearean grandeur of the lines would have sounded hollow, the quips flat, the Wildean transvalued values decidedly immoral. As for the three chief characters, never had there been such a complex of villainies as those set forth in the privately printed *Duchess of Padua* whose title page grandly announced that it had been "Written in Paris in the XIX Century."

For the present Wilde who was counting his American chicks, thought well of the Paduan egg. Something else which promised more dollars was hatching in the same nest. Two months earlier Marie Prescott, an astute business woman as well as a clever actress, had held out a pleasant prospect in a letter to him. "I have given up some brilliant offers to go out with *Vera*," she wrote, "and I am confident I have done the best thing for myself." In fact she had shown her confidence when like Mary Anderson she too had given the promising playwright an equally substantial advance. William Perzel, Miss Prescott's husband and co-manager, had at first demurred, but since Marie's "hunches" were usually good, he let her have her way. No doubt he probably had a hand later that year in the advertisement which, inserted by Marie Prescott in the

American press, made public that she had the exclusive right to *Vera,* proclaimed in large print THE GREATEST PLAY OF THE DAY.

As the immediate consequence of that announcement Miss Prescott found herself with a lawsuit on her hands. A Mr. Frank P. Hulette of Dunkirk, New York, had also written a play entitled *Vera* which he described as a "Russo-Parisian society drama." Moreover he had copyrighted his opus and was ready to call upon Washington to substantiate his claim. Naturally Mr. Hulette resented having Wilde's play called the greatest of the day when his own *Vera* was indubitably more deserving of the title. After feverish correspondence the difficulty was solved to the satisfaction of all concerned when Wilde rechristened his drama *Vera; or the Nihilists,* duly recording the change in the copyright office.

Letters flew across the Atlantic as plans for production began to materialize. Wilde dreamed prodigiously. His *Vera* must be the most beautiful play ever to appear in America, just as Rodd's *Rose Leaf and Apple Leaf* had been the most exquisite book.

"I am very much pleased," he wrote to Miss Prescott, "to know that my directions as regards scenery and costume have been carried out. The yellow satin council-chamber is sure to be a most artistic scene." Then there was the dove-gray setting for the last act. In it Miss Prescott must appear sheathed in vermilion silk of a rich depth. If she could not match in America the sample he sent her she must allow him to bring her a piece large enough for her dress. Did she like the sketch he enclosed?

"Your design of the dress . . . is just perfect," Miss Prescott assured him. "No dress is so becoming to me!" One thing she resented, however—his advice that she dispense with her petticoats. "I *never* wear them!" she retorted.

Wilde must be made to realize the quality of the actress who had undertaken to perform his play. Petticoats indeed! Did he think she was Clara Morris who had once appeared like an Egyptian mummy swathed round and round in yards of white muslin? "You cannot imagine my *enormous* victory in the theatrical world as well as with the American public lately," she wrote him in announcing the fact that Salvini's manager had broken his contract with her to engage Clara Morris in her stead for the part of Emilia in *The Outlaw*. "He thought he would make a fortune in his enterprise and it turns out that he has lost in three weeks' engagement so far nearly five thousand dollars." Satisfaction fairly crackled as she added, "Besides Clara Morris is the most frightful *failure* imaginable and has proved utterly incapable of taking *my* place . . . And yet some one said, 'Oscar Wilde wanted Clara Morris to play *Vera* but she declined.' It is absolutely funny, isn't it?"

Wilde may have found it funny for quite another reason which he was wise enough to keep from her.

After finishing *The Duchess of Padua* he was free to take up a poem upon which since Magdalen he had been working intermittently with the cunning of an artificer. Couplet by couplet he wrought the fantastic images, each as carefully limned as the figures of some scroll torn from the bowels of a pyramid—exotic, bizarre, no more of the living world of men than of the realm of the dead, but somehow an end in themselves, like long-dreamed visions eternized to nightmare. What had given Wilde the idea of *The Sphinx*? Had he like Rossetti before the winged figures of Nineveh at the British Museum, caught the burden of the past and with the power of his imagination reconstructed something as intangible as a dream yet perdurable as the universe? Where had he seen the Sphinx that fired his creativeness? Was it at some hearth where "couching on the Chinese mat her eyes of satin rimmed with gold" the domestic pet was invested with the mystery attributed to her by the Egyptians? Did he too well remember the lines of Baudelaire on cats ——

Ils prennent en songeant les nobles attitudes
Des grands sphinx allongés au fond des solitudes . . . ?

109

Whatever the source of his inspiration Wilde made it his own, as if to the original draught he had added the green-gold absinthe of his perverse imaginings till the cloudy glass intoxicated and poisoned. The visions followed, nightmare on nightmare, accompanied by the sinuous music of the verse with its sapient cadences and sudden startling hidden rhymes that bewrayed the senses, like sulphurous flares in the darkness of a cave. He had entered upon the unknown and the nameless. He had produced that new thrill which to the poets of France, deadened by the vision of hell of 1871, meant the rekindling of art. Baudelaire had recaptured that *frisson* for French poetry after renewing inspiration at the fount of Poe. Rimbaud had given it a perverser delight with the hell-born splendor of his genius. Wilde's *Sphinx* belonged with French literature. It was as foreign to English soil as the brittle, gemlike plants that glow in the caverns of the underworld. It was chimerical, sensuous, perverted, evil—a *fleur du mal* transplanted to that innocent vale where the English poet saw only a host of golden daffodils.

Why are you tarrying? Go hence! I weary of your sullen ways,
I weary of your steadfast gaze, your somnolent magnificence . . .

Your eyes are like fantastic moons that shiver in some stagnant lake,
Your tongue is like a scarlet snake that dances to fantastic tunes,

Your pulse makes poisonous melodies, and your black throat is like the hole
Left by some torch or burning coal on saracenic tapestries . . .

False Sphinx! False Sphinx! By reedy Styx old Charon, leaning on his oar,
Waits for my coin. Go thou before, and leave me to my crucifix,

Whose pallid burden, sick with pain, watches the world with wearied eyes,
And weeps for every soul that dies, and weeps for every soul in vain.

It was the true Wilde who in his remotest wanderings had never been far from the foot of the cross.

The French writers whose acquaintance he sued with gift copies of his volume of poems took him into their circle without question. He might be queer, but hadn't they had queerness enough among their own? If they raised their brows at the fur-lined coat in which he arrived and to which he was devoted, it was not because it was eccentric but because fur-lined coats were the proper garb of coachmen in Paris. They had nothing to say of the breeches that had scandalized America, for the masquerading over, Wilde never wore them again. His long hair astonished only those who met him soon after his arrival. Later acquaintances saw him in a moderately short haircut, curled in a coif of ringlets all over the head, as on the bust of Nero in the Louvre which had tempted Wilde to emulation. His affectation of Balzac's cane made them smile complacently. Hadn't Barbey d'Aurevilly, now an old man, worn a crimson silk mantle in the streets of Paris? Poets were allowed their harmless foibles. Some still remembered how Gérard de Nerval used to walk a live lobster instead of a dog on a leash of blue ribbon. To those who met him at the Palais Royal and questioned his peculiar selection of a pet he answered very rationally: "How is a lobster more ridiculous than a dog? I like lobsters. They're placid, serious, they know the secrets of the sea—and they don't bark." The Paris of 1883 had its luminaries. It did not matter if they sometimes left their orbits.

There was one who remained, however, a fixed, if a somewhat spent, star. Like all visiting notables Wilde was escorted to the quaint Place des Vosges to bask in the last sleepy rays of Victor Hugo. The author of *Les Misérables,* the poet of *La Légende des Siècles* had passed his fourscore years. He had become at once a prophet and a shade. Though he was almost completely deaf and the sight of his eyes had dimmed, he held court in the long reception room hung round with his drawings and furnished with odd pieces of furniture which he had made still odder with carvings by his own hand and thick applications of paint. He presided from a throne a foot higher than the chairs of his guests. After dinner when the beneficent calm of wine closed his eyes, reverently his disciples waited, those nearest to him letting slumber descend upon them also till the signal announced that *le cher maître* was again among the conscious and the universe might take its ordered course. Rash indeed the man who interrupted by a word the master's blissful repose! Wilde, accustomed to the amenities of less exalted boards, rushed in where the devotees would never have ventured to tread.

With a start the dozing poet opened his eyes. Solicitous, the faithful clustered round him. They listened, however—listened to a flow of lyrical speech which even in its imperfect French proclaimed the master of language.

"What is it? Who is it?" asked Hugo.

And they told him it was Oscar Wilde, a young fop and a snob who had published a slight volume of verse—nothing much. Had they not had their Parnassians? And now had they not their Symbolists? They liked to think that on the road to Parnassus, as in everything else, it was France that led the way.

From Hugo's shrine Wilde betook himself to that of Edmond de Goncourt, a luminary of equal magnitude. Indeed, in the 'sixties he and his brother Jules had been the twin gods of the literary heavens, the neorealists whose domain included heart and mind, sensibility and an almost scientific research into human conduct. Nothing escaped their dispassionate scrutiny. From the salon they went to the brothel and the sewer until, because life in the raw exhibits itself in all its shameful grandeur, they sought it only among the dregs of humanity. Zola followed them and fell into cynicism. Flaubert, using the same methods independently, diagnosed the malady of the century. But none brought a cure.

With Edmond de Goncourt Wilde carried on in his most extravagant vein. The imp of the perverse possessed him. Seeing before him the humorless old man, a sponge thirsting for facts and yet more facts to add to his compendious *Journals,* Wilde gave him what he wanted and more, especially about the barbarians whose shores he had recently left. In a town in Texas, he told with a twinkle that M. de Goncourt was too nearsighted to see, real criminals were made to act on the stage, and when a hanging was to take place—well, the victim was hanged from the scenery uprights. Once when *Macbeth* was presented, a woman, a notorious poisoner who had been convicted, was selected to play the part of Lady Macbeth—and released from her sentence! Hardly had Wilde left the house when the illustrious *littérateur* set down his conversation, word for word, as a record of human conduct in the United States of America.

In his interview with the actor Coquelin it was Wilde, pleased with his share in it, who made notes in his commonplace book. In fact the result was so good that it might be used somewhere, later. He recorded it, in far from faultless French.

"What is civilization, M. Wilde?" asked Coquelin who evidently meant business.

"Love of the beautiful."

"And what is beauty?"

"What the bourgeois call ugly."

"And what do the bourgeois call beautiful?"

"There is no such thing."

From this aesthetic leapfrog they went to more serious matters—Wilde's play, though which he does not specify.

"My play?" Wilde replied to Coquelin's inquiry. "Nothing but style. Hugo and Shakespeare have divided all subjects between them. It is impossible to be original, even in sin. Hence there are no real emotions—only unusual adjectives."[1]

Had he been serious, or had he spoken for effect? Impossible to be original, even in sin . . . Yet the poet, to be a seer, must reinvent life. He must make the soul *monstrous*, as the sixteen-year-old Arthur Rimbaud had written in a moment of demonic insight. The poet can become a seer only by an immense, willful disordering of his senses. He must seek after all forms of love and pain and exaltation. He must become criminal, accursed, for only then does he arrive at supreme wisdom.

Literary conclaves buzzed with the Symbolist credo in the Paris that Wilde found. In an obscure underground café in the Quai St. Michel sensational theories of art sprang up and grew

[1] Tr. by the author.

with the rapidity of mushrooms. Transplanted to the François
1, on the Boulevard St. Michel, they assumed hothouse colors
that dazzled, shapes and forms that Rimbaud himself had failed
to imagine in the *cauchemar* flora of *"Ce qu'on dit au poète à
propos de fleurs."* Life had become too narrow to hold the
poet's vast desire. Like the creative impulse in some star his
passion, self-derived and self-engendering, must sunder the ex-
istent "I" to other, manifold, unsuspected selves. In divine
madness he must seek truths beyond reason, sensation hitherto
unknown to man, limited by the boundaries of an effete civilization. So current was the new orthodoxy that Wilde jotted down
a definition of art given to him by his garçon: *"L'art, c'est le
désordre."*

And such indeed it was in literature, painting and life. Although Rimbaud, unnoticed except as a sullen, vicious amoral
young beast when Verlaine introduced him to the dinners of
the "Vilains Bonhommes," had outlined the program of the
seer as early as 1871, it was not until long after he had slain
the seer in himself that his ideas began to spread. Now Verlaine
who had been his Baptist was writing about him as one of the
poètes maudits, the Lucifer poets who at the cost of damnation
had discovered a new freedom; Robert de Montesquiou was
modeling his life on the plan of "monstrous" research; while
Huysmans, in *À Rebours* which he was then about to finish,
was producing the Bible of decadence.

Chameleon-like, Wilde colored to his environment. Someone's friend, he jotted in his notebook, kept a gilded tortoise whose shell was set with emeralds. *"Il me faut aussi des
émeraudes: des bibelots vivants,"* he noted. It was Montesquiou who kept that gilded tortoise which was to appear as
des Esseintes' living toy in *À Rebours*. In the meantime the
man who had urged his generation to the discovery of unknown horizons had died on the ledge of his own. It was
another Rimbaud who was living posthumously as trader,
explorer and gun-runner in Africa, a seeker after reality
whose hard earned reward he carried in his belt.

The story of the friendship between Verlaine and Rimbaud was well known in the Latin Quarter. Verlaine had

made no secret of it in his poems. Moreover its sensational climax had been attended by scandalous publicity. In 1871 Verlaine who had published a number of volumes of verse received a letter and an enclosure of poems from a stranger. He was so struck by the power and originality of the verses as well as by the spirit of rebellion that burned the very paper of the letter, that he urged his correspondent to come to Paris. Rimbaud arrived, a gangling sullen youth of seventeen, with eyes blazing defiance and a mouth curled to a sneer. His clothes fit him badly; his hair seemed never to have known a comb. Curtly he greeted Verlaine, the words coming with an effort from that hard yet infantile mouth. Verlaine the patron fell at once under the youth's domination. He had not expected anyone so young. He himself was only ten years older than Rimbaud, but in will power a child in comparison. Fascinated, Verlaine took the boy home with him, to his girl wife, eight months gone with child.

But everything, home, wife, child, family responsibility, became subordinated to the friendship that sprang up between the two poets. The man to whom the youth had gone as to a master bowed before the prodigious stripling whose mouth had been seared with the embers of prophecy, whose words crackled with the fire of his genius. The pale blue eyes in moments of revelation caught the glint of Lucifer's that had pierced unseen hells. Verlaine trembled before them.

"A seer—you must become a seer!" the hard voice commanded, impatient with reality, scornful of the limited language of idea. The poet must create a new and wonderful language that would reveal soul to soul and open the senses anew to perfumes, colors, sounds—a language that would crumble the parapets of the known and reach out to the unknown where alone wonder dwelt. Verlaine read Rimbaud's *Bateau Ivre* and knew that such visions were only for those who had the strength to bear them—and that strength was unholy. To him the lad became a sorcerer working witchcraft on that life which he, a mere man, found so unmanageable even in its simplicities.

"Destroy all known landmarks! Explore the soul!" Drunk

115

with the limitlessness that Rimbaud opened out to him Verlaine followed, blinding himself to the danger. With the wings of Lucifer to bear him he could chance the flight.

It ended in disaster. Never close to reality, Verlaine severed the thread that held him to it, abandoned wife, child and mother, and pursued the vision he saw through Rimbaud's eyes. What matter if it led to the squalor of London's Houndsditch, the slums of Belgium? What if the glories of their perilous experiment came to them only in the smoke of hashish and the cloudy magic of absinthe? They were throwing down barriers. They were revolting against life and discovering the depths of the soul.

Life had its revenge on a stage prepared for comedy with the chief actors wearing the motley of weak, unheroic human nature. In a mean hotel in Brussels Verlaine, in a fit of drunken jealousy, shot the fallen archangel who had threatened to abandon him. But here life revealed its wry humor. The bullet, missing its target, wounded Rimbaud in the wrist. Verlaine was arrested and Rimbaud returned to Charleville, his arm in a sling.

A number of sordid details came out in the judicial investigation, one charging the two poets with immoral relations. Verlaine's wife gave them as the reason for her estrangement from her husband. While he was serving a two-year sentence in the prison of Mons, she was granted a decree of separation. The shock to the repentant Verlaine who had been dreaming of a reconciliation with the girl for whom he had written *La Bonne Chanson* brought him to the Church. From Lucifer to Christ. The cycle was complete even though poor Lélian, as Verlaine called himself, was to alternate in his too human frailty between the rosary on the one hand, and the chalice of absinthe on the other.

And Rimbaud? In 1872 Fantin-Latour had painted one of his characteristic canvases, *Coin de Table,* in which he portrayed a number of his literary friends. Verlaine is shown seated at the head of the table. On his left Rimbaud, with visionary eyes and disdainful mouth, turns his back on the assembled company. The intuition of the artist had foreseen the gesture that was to make Rimbaud soon abandon not only poetry and poets but civilization as well.

He had struggled to tear down the ramparts of life only to find futility. Verlaine he had promised to make a Child of the Sun; instead he had brought him to a prison cell. All nothingness and futility. In splendid revulsion, in an agony of body and mind, he dashed off *Une Saison en Enfer*. There, in his spiritual autobiography written with the coals of the hell he had seen, and in a language that spoke from soul to soul, he took his farewell of poetry and of the corrupt world. What were men but flies "drunk in a urinal"? He would become a Child of the Sun—literally, among the people of Africa. He would slay all his chimeras and grapple with life that was stronger than any dream.

In three tempestuous years he had concentrated a lifetime of literature; and he died. The Rimbaud who now wandered among the ports of Europe seeking among the hulks of tramp ships the phantom of his Bateau Ivre was another man. That vision he could never lose. But the rebellion that had made him seek to tear down the barriers of convention now urged him to raise them up in a protective belt of gold between him and the world.

Wilde knew Rimbaud's strange story, and in the cafés of the Left Bank he often met poor Lélian with his repulsive Socratic mask, his filth and the simple ways of a child. It needed no urging for Verlaine to recite his friend Rimbaud's poems, or better, his own. Suddenly, in the middle of a verse, his throat would go dry, and with unconscious fingers he would push forward his empty glass. Shuddering, Wilde would turn away sick at heart, as the voice behind him chanted of blue skies above the roof, a bell tolling faintly, a singing bird and the rue of a wisdom learned too late:

> *Qu'as-tu fait, ô toi que voilà*
> *Pleurant sans cesse,*
> *Dis, qu'as-tu fait, toi que voilà,*
> *De ta jeunesse?*

117

Chapter IX: Constance

THAT summer the wits who had been languishing in a dull season welcomed Oscar Wilde on his return from France. They scarcely knew him in his Neronian coiffure.

> Our Oscar is with us again; but O,
>   He is changed who was once so fair!
> Has the iron gone into his soul? O no!
>   It has only gone over his hair.

Punch, which had been hard put to it to find matter for laughter with Bunthorne wandering so far from home, welcomed him joyfully. But who was this whose newly found conservative grace proclaimed him, if not of godlike race, at least not of the breed of the buffoon? The professional merrymakers were disappointed. Bunthorne was taking himself seriously. Was he—perish the thought!—was he going to reform? Concerned at the possibility, *Punch* printed a caricature in the grand manner of Frith's canvases, showing General Oscar Wilde leading members of the Salvation Army in a hymn.

But *Punch* need not have been alarmed. Though the sartorial innovations were gone and Wilde appeared regularly in tubular lower garments with the rest of Her Majesty's male subjects, he was still the dandy. Like M. le Comte Robert de Montesquiou, he spent a long time each day preparing his person for the public and like him he could have said to those who charged him with literary indolence that first he must create the man and then the *littérateur*. Wilde was in the process of putting his genius into his personality. In a few months he would be twenty-nine years old. He had only a volume of poems and two as yet unproduced plays to show for his labors. But what a legend of himself he had created on two continents! What other man of his age had done as much? Sometimes, however, the voice of conscience spoke unpleasant truths. He quieted it by pretending he was younger than his years—not a convincing deception, but it gave him the illusion of having youth still before him, youth, the most wonderful of all possessions.

He did not stay long in London—only the time to deliver two lectures, one to the students of the Royal Academy at their club in Golden Square, and the other at Prince's Hall on "Personal Impressions of America." Later, he arranged with Colonel Morse, he would tour the north of England and Scotland. But first he must see about his *Vera* in New York.

On the 2nd of August he went to Liverpool to embark just as Lily Langtry was descending the gangplank, as ravishing as ever but much richer than when she had left for her conquest of the West. Her money bags weighed more than Wilde's. What if the scandal between her and the young millionaire Freddy Gebhardt had turned the public against her? For that reason if for none other people had swarmed to see her on the stage— and to forgive her at the sight of her beauty. Helen is beyond good and evil, as she is beyond mortality. An ancient poet had been to the trouble of telling how he had seen the moldering skull of Helen amid the shades of underground, but for all his witnessing to her mortal decay, mankind still beheld her, flaming on the towers of Ilium. Once again Wilde and Lily met and parted, not too sadly. In his luggage he was carrying a marvelous bit of vermilion satin with which to deck his own creation, Vera.

He arrived in New York in the middle of a hot August to supervise the final rehearsals before Marie Prescott raised the curtain on his Nihilist drama at the Union Square Theatre. He knew the neighborhood well—the small brick house near Seventeenth Street where he had lived; the rows of brownstone edifices in one of which he had been fleeced of a huge sum by card sharpers; the little squares with their pretense at trees pining in the growing city's dust; the commercial hubbub of Fourteenth Street, the quiet dignity of Gramercy with its solid mansions and gracious doorways. Most of their owners were away to escape the heat of the season but he was confident they would all come driving in for the first night of his drama. Marie Prescott was as hopeful as he, though Mr. Perzel grumbled at the lavishness of the mounting. Marie had a clever head on her shoulders, however; and Mr. Perzel was not averse to making a fortune if the gods proved propitious.

On the night of the 20th of August, 1883 in spite of the excessive heat, hundreds of people were waiting under the electric lights to obtain their ticket at the box office. By curtain time parquet and gallery were jammed. Mr. Perzel rubbed his hands. It was something to bring society into town from the seaside resorts. If the critics were kind there was no telling how long the play might not run, as indeed why shouldn't it with such headliners as his wife, supported by George Boniface and Edward Lamb?

Behind the scenes Wilde listened for the reactions of the audience as nervously as Mr. Perzel. He had much more at stake than the manager. If the play failed Mr. Perzel could retrieve his fortunes with another; he had enough of that wonderful American cash at his disposal to challenge fate, while he— But nonsense! *Vera* could not possibly fail, and he would again be returning to London with enough to keep him in funds for a long time. Why, they were actually calling him from the audience after the first act! Should he go out and make his bow? Not yet. An artist must not seem too eager for the applause of the public. The play proceeded. At the end of the second act the cries were repeated, this time so insistently that he stepped out before the curtain and bowed his thanks. The audience was with him. *Vera* was a success.

He reckoned without the fickleness of humankind. By the end of the play the very ones who had been loudest in their applause were filling the house with jeers and catcalls. The Nihilist had failed to charm.

"A foolish, highly peppered story of love, intrigue and politics," said the *Tribune*.

"The play is unreal, long-winded and wearisome," pronounced the *Times*.

120

"It is long-drawn dramatic rot," epitomized the *Herald*.

Against such unanimity of damnation the defense of the gallant *Mirror* sounded like a masked insult: "Just as it stands . . . *Vera* is the noblest contribution to its literature the stage has received in many years." Inwardly Wilde knew it was not so. He was too good a critic not to admit that the truth lay with the opposite camp.

Marie Prescott was in despair. In spite of the yellow satin council-chamber, the splendor of her vermilion gown and the passionateness of her acting, the play lingered one torrid week at Union Square and then the box office closed. The *Pilot*, a New York paper, blamed *Vera's* failure on her acting. It called her an inferior artist who could only scold on the stage and off it. Probably Clara Morris was at the bottom of *that*. Still, all was not lost. She could take the play on the road where the audiences were less exacting. And—she congratulated herself on the idea—she could persuade Oscar Wilde to appear as one of the characters.

Her scheme failed. In September Oscar Wilde returned to London more out of pocket than on his departure, to be greeted by *Punch's* variations on his American fiasco. "Mr. Oscar Wilde's play *Vera*, which the *Herald* dismissed as 'long-drawn dramatic rot'—(they have a neat style of criticism in New York) —was, from all accounts, except the Poet's own, Vera Bad."

He was where he had started a year and a half ago, perhaps rather worse off, for the hounds of the press followed him wherever he went, rousing the public to hue and cry. He had adopted the pose of flippancy as the wisest approach to life; he had raised the paradox to the level of art. Whether he wished it or not, he now had to continue in his pose. Only he knew the anguish of being brought face to face with his true self—the self which none suspected or wished to see when in unguarded moments he revealed it in some flash of irony.

Fortunately he had the lecture engagements which Colonel Morse had obtained for him in the provinces. They offered nothing like the profits of the American tours, but with a little literary hack work they helped him maintain his two small rooms in a house at No. 9 Charles Street not far from Grosvenor Square. He had to walk up several flights of stairs to get to them, but they were pleasant enough with their oak paneling and their old engravings in heavy black frames. The house was run by a retired butler and his wife who kept an excellent table—when their guest had the wherewithal to sit at it.

He was more often to be seen at the Café Royal where over a bottle of *Chateau de Mille Secousses*—discovered by the Butterfly—he made useful mental notes on the master's theories of art. Indeed, if it had not been for Whistler's coaching in June, he could not have addressed the Royal Academy students with such authority. Now that both *Vera* and the *Duchess of Padua* (rejected by Miss Anderson) could no longer be counted upon to make him a fortune, he had to perfect himself in the art which the public wished him to practice.

The Butterfly fixed his monocle and for the nonce sheathed his sting. He had struck none too good-naturedly while Wilde had been away lecturing in America. But he could not long be suspicious of so charming and inspiring a disciple who, somehow, had the gift of bringing out the best in one. Whistler who always spoke brilliantly, excelled himself before those challenging eyes. His wit became wittier in the echo of that laughter that paid him the most flattering of compliments.

Wilde, however, must never forget to keep his place—at the feet of the master, and to use quotation marks in repeating acquired wisdom. He had been careless on the latter point before the Academy students, but because he had declared after his exposition of art, "There is a man living amongst us . . . whose work is a joy for all time, who is himself a master of all time—that man is Mr. Whistler!" the Butterfly had forgiven him. Many, too, thought that Wilde had included him among the martryrs when he said, "The sign of a Philistine age is the cry of immorality against art, and this cry was raised by the Athenian people against every great poet and thinker of their day . . . It was the same with Florence . . ." It had been the same with England when Whistler was awarded his farthing damages.

Wilde started out on his railway circuit. He had prepared a standard lecture for the unsophisticated provinces, one designed to reach and amuse the average intelligence. Experience had taught him that the row of knitters could not be interrupted in counting their stitches by being made to concentrate. The lecture-goer must have his thinking done for him—else why hire a hall?—and woe to the man who presents problems when he is expected to dispense pleasant pellets of a size for all to swallow. Wilde had learned not to overtax his listeners. His lecture on his impressions of America accordingly became a potpourri of the absurdities with which he had regaled the gullible de Goncourt. There may have been in him a latent desire to pay off the humiliations he had been made to suffer, but his malice was of so genial a cast that not even the touchy Americans would have been hurt.

In the outlying towns, therefore, the simple audiences listened gape-mouthed to the tales of this new Munchausen. Americans, he told them, were always in a hurry. They were awakened in the morning by the steam whistle and accompanied through the day by an infernal din. Since art depended on exquisite sensibility, was it any wonder that America had failed in producing beauty? They were good inventors, he avowed, and their machinery had the beauty which their art had failed to attain.

"I was disappointed in Niagara—" He played wittily with the ludicrous situation of Wilde against the torrent. The Mormons in Salt Lake City, the he-men of the West, all were presented to their marveling English cousins. "They were miners —men working in metals," Wilde told them, "so I lectured to them on the Ethics of Art. I read them passages from the autobiography of Benvenuto Cellini and they seemed much delighted. I was reproved by my hearers for not having brought him with me. I explained that he had been dead for some little time which elicited the enquiry: 'Who shot him?' " He was inventing as he went along, but the laughter of the pro-

vincials was worth the fib. "They afterwards took me to a dancing saloon where I saw the only rational method of art criticism
I have ever come across. Over the piano was printed a notice:
Please do not shoot the pianist. He is doing his best. The mortality among pianists in that place is marvelous."

On and on he went, subordinating his message of beauty to
the laugh in the anecdote. He had become the professional
lecturer—everything for the approval of the lowest common
denominator. "So infinitesimal did I find the knowledge of
art," he exaggerated gleefully on those delightful Americans,
"that an art patron . . . actually sued the railroad company
for damages because the plaster cast of Venus de Milo, which
he had imported from Paris, had been delivered minus the
arms." He paused to let the audience have its laugh out. "What
is more surprising still," came the smiling fillip, "he gained his
case and the damages."

Notwithstanding he was not always successful with his audiences. Many a time, especially when he delivered his lecture
on the value of art in modern life, his talk was interrupted by
the creaking of chairs and the shuffle of feet as people got up
and walked out. What interest indeed could the hard-working
farmer have had in the sins of the upholsterer, or the thickness
of the cup out of which he drank his tea? In his part of the
country the upholsterer was as yet unknown, and tea was tea,
whatever the cup. The lecture hall, ordinarily, was only half
full. Yawns and blank boredom too often accompanied the lecturer's finest efforts. Altogether the provinces of England made
harder conquest than the American West.

There was one bright spot in the weary weeks of the lecture
platform when he went to see Miss Constance Lloyd at Ely
Place in Dublin. No one knows how the two first met. It may
have been at one of his lectures; or perhaps Wilde had resumed
an acquaintance of his earlier Dublin days. By the end of the
year, however, acquaintance had deepened to love not only on
the part of Constance but also on that of Wilde who felt it
genuinely for the first time. He did not struggle now to transform the lovely girl with her level gaze and the calm brow of

124

a statue into a cold Hellenic abstraction. He made no comparison between the chiseling of her profile and the faces on the coins of Syracuse. The brown hair with its ringlets that clustered on her temples drew from him no specious similes. He was satisfied with her as she was, a shy, gentle young woman of twenty-six, whose pure soul gazed out of the largest and most glorious eyes he had ever seen, deep thoughtful eyes with that ineffable sadness that shadows all beauty. Simplicity breathed from her. To Wilde perhaps that was her chief charm after his worship at bedizened public shrines. Moreover Constance was well born.

At the time Wilde was courting her she was living with her grandfather as her father, Horace Lloyd, Q.C., was dead. She had a brother, Otho, with whom Wilde was acquainted. Constance had no money of her own, but she had the prospect of a comfortable income from her grandfather who had named her his heir. He would also provide her with a substantial portion when she married.

Like all young people in love Constance and Oscar saw each other as often as possible and exchanged letters when lecturing engagements prevented his visiting her. They were proper Victorian lovers. Gone were the posturings of the callow university youth who spent his nights on the doorstep of his goddess. He would ring the Ely Place doorbell at the established hour like any young man going a-courting, and then he and Constance conversed from opposite ends of the parlor sofa or he listened while her fingers drew music from the keys of the piano. She called him "Mr. Wilde." Until their engagement she remained "Miss Lloyd." Wilde told her of America, of his success as a lecturer, and of his failure as a playwright. He would not pretend to her—he could not before those limpidly earnest eyes.

One day he brought her *Vera* to read. Constance had good judgment. Would she tell him what she thought of the play? Pleased yet unsure of herself Constance read it and on the 11th of November wrote to "Dear Mr. Wilde." She had no pretension to being a critic, she confessed, and she did not even know what constituted a good play. "I was much interested in *Vera* . . . I cannot understand why you should have been so unfortunate in its reception unless either the acting was very inferior or the audience was unsympathetic." Too truthful to say she had liked the play she tried in vain to prevaricate. There was one thing she had been on the verge of telling Mr. Wilde again and again. Now was the time for her to say it, rather, to write it, which made it much easier: "I am afraid you and I disagree in our opinion on art, for I hold that there is no perfect art without perfect morality, whilst you say they are distinct and separable things."

They differed in the one belief that was fundamental to Wilde both as artist and as man, yet by the close of the month the two had announced their engagement. Constance's grandfather, ailing and full of years, gave them his blessing. Otho, her brother, sent Wilde a dutiful note. "I am pleased indeed. I am sure that for my own part I welcome you as a new brother . . . Constance is greatly to be congratulated also to have got your love."

If there was anything of which Constance was aware it was of the fact that she had captured the most coveted bachelor in the realm. She had seen how the women pursued him at his lectures and made themselves captivating for his sake. She had also noticed, however, that while paying them pretty compliments and behaving toward them more familiarly than other men would have dared, there was something impersonal in his very familiarity. They might have been pretty kittens, delightful to play with but soon forgotten.

As for Constance, the moment Oscar declared himself she dropped the veil of reserve that propriety had placed between them and revealed herself glowing with the love she had had to repress. It was no longer "Mr. Wilde" in the letters that passed between them but "My darling love," "My own darling Oscar." She made no secret of the passion she felt for him. Innocent as a child, she was overpowered by the surge of emotions felt for the first time, and disclosed her whole heart to him. Moved by her devotion he confided in her unreservedly.

126

He told her of his peccadillos—so few for his great temptations —and perhaps magnified them for the delightful pain of her forgiveness.

"My darling love," she answered. "You take all my strength away. I have no power to do anything but just love you when you are with me . . . Do believe that I love you most passionately with all the strength of my heart and mind . . . I am content to let the past be buried; it does not belong to me."

For a man as self-indulgent as Wilde there was danger in her generous willingness to forgive. A soft and yielding woman like Constance provided no bulwark against the amorality fostered in the Wilde household and encouraged by the classical exemplars at Magdalen. Constance, nevertheless, felt that she possessed a strength superior to any moral curb. "For the future trust and faith will come," she assured him, "and when I have you for my husband, I will hold you fast with chains of love and devotion so that you shall never leave me, or love anyone as long as I can love and comfort . . ."

Little did she realize that chains cannot bind love, especially the love of one who held that "when a man has once loved a woman he will do anything for her—except continue to love her."

But cynical wisdom found no place in the happiness of their courtship. Wilde lived for the time when he could be with her, and often on a Saturday gave up his lecture—and his supper— that he might see her. Half seriously she scolded: "If you won't promise to have a proper supper you are not to come to see me on Saturday evening. I am still very angry with you for not telling me you were starving last Saturday. . . ."

He made up to her by sending her flowers. "Such a lovely lily has just come from you and I am so happy over it," she wrote on receiving one of his gifts. It was the flower he used to send to Mrs. Langtry. "It is like a flower from Paradise," she added, "bringing memories of Heaven and all lovely things." Not for long. In spite of the care she took to keep the plant alive, the flower withered and died.

The old year passed with the winter and the new had opened

into spring. Constance and Wilde made plans for their marriage, which he announced to Lily Langtry, the "Venus Victrix of the age" as he now called her. "I am going to be married to a beautiful girl called Constance Lloyd—a grave, slight, violet-eyed little Artemis, with great coils of heavy brown hair which makes her flower-like head droop like a blossom, and wonderful ivory hands . . ." Artemis the chaste goddess. The olden aloofness, however, was now belied by Wilde's enumeration of Constance's concrete charms.

It had been difficult waiting, but as later in the season Oscar's lecture tours kept him away for weeks, it was considered best for them to defer the marriage until May. Constance missed him in his long absences. She tried to summon him in his gifts, in the books he sent, in the pet, Jimmy, which he had left with her. At night she could not sleep. Love had come tardily to her as to Wilde; her more delicate organism suffered.

"I don't miss you the least bit in the world, darling," she fibbed to him, "and am quite happy: I know this will please you. Only I wish you would not take all my sleep away with you." She could not get over the wonder that of all women in the world he, Oscar Wilde, should have chosen her to be his wife. Who was Constance Lloyd? A girl less beautiful than some, with a smaller fortune than many. And yet Oscar Wilde had made her the most envied of women. She would try to deserve him by her devotion. In the meantime, unwisely, she told her love, in a need to find expression for it when he was away. "Your letters always make me mad for joy and yet more mad to see you and feel once again that you are mine, and that it is not a dream but a living reality that you love me."

Poignantly a little note flew to him on one of his absences. "Darling—My sweet little Jimmy is dead . . . Is it my fault that everything you give me has an untimely end?"

"There is no such thing as an omen," the superstitious Wilde affirmed in defiance of his belief. "Destiny does not send us heralds. She is too wise and too cruel for that."

They were married on May 29, 1884. St. James's Church, Paddington, where the Rev. Walter Abbott officiated, had never in the years of its existence been the scene of such a wedding as took place there that day—aesthetic to the utmost degree. As the procession filed down the aisle, led by two tiny flower girls dressed in the style of Reynolds' canvases, the reporters who had been invited hurriedly took notes to miss none of the details, for Wilde, even at the altar, had to be attended by publicity. Whistler had begun it at the door with his waggish telegram: "Fear I may not reach you in time for the ceremony; don't wait."

Only a select few were present to enjoy the spectacle. Speranza and her son Willie, a trifle disappointed that Oscar had not fallen in love with a larger fortune, represented the groom. The bride had invited only her intimate family.

Besides the two diminutive flower girls, four bridesmaids, cousins of Constance's, enlivened the wedding pageant in skirts of red surah silk, draped over with pale blue *mousseline de laine*. Long pointed bodices encased their young bosoms. Amber necklaces struck the yellow tone of aestheticism, further nuanced by cream-colored plumes in their high-crowned hats. Yellow roses nestled at their throats, and they carried lilies of the appropriate color. A moon among her paler stars, Constance—a shade embarrassed by the part she was playing for Oscar's sake—floated resplendent in the gown he had designed for her. The delicate cowslip tint of the satin enhanced the color of her cheeks; the low-cut square bodice, with its inset of lace in the high Medici collar, gave her the chaste look of a nun. A veil of the palest saffron India silk gauze embroidered with pearls fell in folds from her hair wreathed in myrtle leaves and white blossoms. The satin of her gown bore clusters of the same funereal leaves which, together with a few white flowers, formed her wedding bouquet. Her slim waist was encircled by a silver girdle of extraordinary workmanship—Oscar's gift.

One of the ladies present drew all eyes by the unusualness of her attire, described by a nonplussed reporter as "an underdress of rich red silk with a sleeveless smock of red plush, and a hat of white lace trimmed with clusters of red roses under

129

the brim and round the crown." None but Speranza could have carried off so daring and original a costume.

And Wilde? It was enough for him to be the impresario of such pageantry. He appeared conventionally dressed and comported himself with a calm dignity few had expected from the notorious Bunthorne. Even *Punch* for once was struck dumb.

They spent their honeymoon in Paris, not, significantly, on the Bohemian Left Bank, but on the other side of the river, at the Hôtel Wagram, Rue de Rivoli. Wilde was a gentleman taking his young bride to the traditional dream city of the romantic. They were as happy as newlyweds can be when their marriage is one of love. Oscar revealed himself the most attentive of husbands. He was proud of Constance who could wear her clothes so gracefully, who could draw so many admiring looks in a city where nearly all women had learned the art of being beautiful.

Paris was at its best that early June. The flower beds of the Tuileries blossomed in their freshest colors. Against the walls of shrubbery the gods and goddesses of stone gleamed in the sunlight as if ready to spring to life. In the Luxembourg Gardens the trees about the fountain of Galatea thrust out toward the lily pool their arms of green shade while ivy wreathed in living bronze the pillars of its border. Along the walks, tubs of pomegranate and orange trees captured in their fragrance an echo of Greece and Sicily. The very streets shone golden in the light that somehow of all cities only Paris knows.

Wilde lived in the happiness of his love. He could scarcely bear to leave Constance alone, and when he did, he would send her flowers at the hotel with beautifully worded messages. Those who had known him wondered at the joy his marriage had brought. His friends were gladdened for his sake and hoped that with his new life would come an end to those ugly rumors which had pursued his flamboyant defiance of middle-class virtues. Others, skeptical, looked on and shrugged.

The honeymoon over, the pair returned to Wilde's bachelor rooms in Charles Street while planning for their permanent home. Nothing was suffered to mar their happiness, though

Wilde's paid engagements dwindled and Grandfather Lloyd developed a remarkable attachment to life. Wilde jested about it. A few months earlier the old man had been lying on what threatened to be his deathbed. "But no sooner had he joined the hands of the young couple and given them his blessing, than, for very joy of the occasion, he suddenly blossomed out into new health and vigor."

In London, as during the honeymoon, Oscar hardly left his wife's side. He would go with her everywhere, and even accompanied her on shopping trips, taking delight in the very things that are the boredom of most husbands. On a bright summer morning he went with her on one of her purchases and waited for her outside the Swan and Edgar's. He was full of the glorious day and his joy and an overwhelming tenderness for the girl who had made him feel. He could have cried out his happiness when suddenly, apparently out of nowhere, a strange young creature appeared, hard-eyed and sinister, stared at him and with a mocking laugh went on. "I felt as if an icy hand had clutched my heart," he said of the experience. Before his mind flashed a vision of folly and disaster, dispelled only when Constance rejoined him, smiling and trustful.

He became an authority on women's clothes, setting himself up as the *arbiter elegantiarum* of Mayfair as he had been of his aesthetic following. In October the *Pall Mall Gazette* published his views on women's dress; the *Pall Mall Budget* immediately reprinted them, much to the discomfiture of the matrons who read that corsets like farthingales, vertugadins, hoops and crinolines were a modern monstrosity, and that dress to be beautiful must be hung from the shoulders of the free and noble body. Wilde knew he could not be wrong. He had the statues of the Greeks to corroborate him in the flow of their sculptured draperies, and he had Constance as the living model for his theories. In her almost hypnotic subjection to him she played a part that was essentially foreign to her ingenuous nature. But if she had any misgivings of her ability to act as was expected of her, she concealed them in a mute willingness to do whatever gave Oscar pleasure.

He responded with poetic ardor. "Dear and Beloved," he wrote to her from Edinburgh in December of that year. "Here am I, and you at the Antipodes—O execrable facts, that keep our lips from kissing, though our souls are one. What can I tell you by letter—? alas! nothing that I would tell you. The messages of the gods to each other travel not by pen and ink and indeed your bodily presence here would not make you more real: for I feel your fingers in my hair, and your cheek brushing mine. The air is full of the music of your voice, my soul and body seem no longer mine, but mingled in some exquisite ecstasy with yours— Ever and ever yours, Oscar."[1]

It was a beautiful letter, almost a poem, that lightened the loneliness of Charles Street for the young bride till Oscar returned home, and made more bearable with its passionate assurances the discomforts of her pregnancy. It was a very beautiful letter such as only Oscar knew how to write.

[1] From the manuscript original at the Morgan Library.

Chapter X: Wilde and the Butterfly

WHEN the Wildes went househunting they naturally turned to London's artistic quarter. In the four-story red brick building at number 16 Tite Street, Chelsea, they found what they wanted. The section had long been a favorite one with Wilde. On that same street in his student days he had been initiated into the mysteries of an artist's life in Whistler's White House, now, alas! fallen to other hands. However, though crushed, the sprightly painter like truth rose again, and in another house, presided over by Maud—"Mrs. Whistler" according to the engraved invitation cards that needed not the benefit of clergy—was even now resuming his American luncheons amid the decorative devices dear to the Butterfly's heart.

Near by in Cheyne Row Carlyle had lived, his bitter mouth clamant for good in a society that would not hear. His shade still haunted the Chelsea Embankment where, immaterial in the flapping folds of his Inverness, he used to take his lonely nocturnal walks, silent as a ghost, the lightning of his eyes alone showing the fire that still burned in him. Now his few possessions were being scattered and sold—the piano on which Jane Welsh Carlyle had accompanied the Scottish songs she sang in her high, eerie voice; the deal board where, while Carlyle sat late into the night working in his study, she mixed and kneaded the bread that alone could still the dyspepsia gnawing at his vitals; the books explored by his knotted hands, the hands of a mason's son; the table on which his elbows had rested when wearily the palms supported the head bursting with the prophecy that few would hear and fewer understand. Wilde bought that table for his own study.

A little distance away in Cheyne Walk, Rossetti's house was again coming alive after the prolonged death-in-life of its tenant. For years before his death in 1882 the rusty iron gate had shut out the living as effectively as the door of the tomb. Wild ivy, lover of graves, had spread unhindered, eating into the moldering brick, enshrouding the windows in its ropes of leaves. Useless precaution! Never washed by the winds of heaven those rooms, laden with memories, remained stagnant with ghosts. Rarely toward the end did the solitary man visit the world of the living, and then only to wander round and round, a prisoner in his weed-choked garden, where one by one his peacocks and his wombats and all the rare caged creatures he kept there showed him the way to death. One night in the heavily curtained bedchamber high up in the house a strange scene had been enacted when amid the stirrings of memory, Rossetti seemed to have heard the flutter of wings. He sent for a priest. "But you're no papist," protested one of the few who ever entered into this nether world. "I don't care about that," said the dying agnostic. "I can make nothing of Christianity . . . I only want a confessor to give me absolution for my sins."

Recently the vine of the dead had been ripped from the old house whose face once more received the sunlight. The neglected garden flowered in tidy beds. The beasts that remained were dispersed. The stones of the walk reappeared through the moss, and the iron gate was shiny under a coat of paint. The living had dispossessed the dead.

The whole neighborhood breathed a rebirth. One by one the gods of the older generation were making way for the younger gods.

In the recently tenanted house on Tite Street everything was fresh like the spirit of the pair who took it on a long-term lease. E. S. Godwin the decorator and Whistler the friend, frequently came for consultation with the newlyweds. The house must be the outward expression of its tenants, a sort of shell, harmonious in form and iridescent with the color of their lives. In spite of Whistler, no fan flights were suffered to soar along the walls. Peacock feathers, because Wilde believed they brought ill luck, were now taboo. He had definite opinions on everything. Having served his apprenticeship, he had been graduated to the position of master, and though he sought advice he reserved the prerogative of not following it.

134

After all, the Tite Street house was to be no mere dwelling but the habitation of poetry and beauty, the showplace of aestheticism. It had to be at once original and impeccable, chaste yet subtly luxurious. None of the shoddy pretense of Oakley Street must be allowed to enter here. Neither must it be invaded by the pseudo-Gothic affectation of carven pieces and tenantless cuirasses, moth-eaten Gobelins and crusaders' banners, that had been Philistia's application of William Morris's medieval revival. Again, in the striving toward originality, there would be none of the hideousness of Carabin whose monstrosities were arriving from France to fill the salons of the prosperous. There might be something of the spirit of the French Revolution in the rows of heads that made up the pilasters of a Carabin bookcase, or in the contorted citoyens who upheld the four corners of a table: they were foreign to the soil of England. Wilde would show the world what he meant by the house beautiful.

The finished home was even more charming than the White House had been, for Wilde, with the Midas touch of the eclectic, turned what he found to gold. He had no concern for period or style. Beauty was sufficient unto itself. Each room like every chamber of the nautilus, must be perfect in unity, an arrangement, a sufficient harmony. The guests who were first admitted into the drawing-room stood in admiration before the effect. No violent colors anywhere—only the low-keyed tones of dull gold and cream on wall and furniture, mingling with the mellowness of antique brocades. A frieze of framed etchings ran along two walls, in the manner of Ruskin's Turners at Oxford. Above the white carved mantelpiece Donoghue's bas-relief gathered in its gilt-copper highlights the glow of the shaded lamps. A few Whistlers, his fine Venetian studies, occupied a place of honor. "Chaste," the connoisseur pronounced the result.

The dining room where the tea was served maintained the same restraint. Here white was the keynote, in the enameled chairs and dado and the shelf that served as a table round the walls, leaving the center of the room free for the standing guests. The seats, copied from Greek frieze and funeral urn, were upholstered in white plush accented with pastel tints of blue and yellow. Blue and yellow were repeated in the choice bibelots that decorated the room in a motif that was almost musical in its harmoniousness. The world came and gaped. It was then, surely, as Max Beerbohm declared, that men and women hurled their mahogany into the streets and ransacked the curio shops.

So far the atmosphere remained objective, almost impersonal, as it should have been, affording the background where contrasting personalities could assert themselves. It was quite otherwise with Wilde's study. Here he brought together everything that he had made his own, the rare, wide-margined first editions which he had begun collecting at Trinity, the cigarette box and the rose jar, the curios he had picked up in the shops of the *rive gauche*, paper knives, knickknacks which under their banal exterior concealed some meaning for his imagination. On the walls, painted a buttercup yellow, there hung a Monticelli and a Japanese picture of romping children.

A drawing by Simeon Solomon beautiful enough to have been placed in the drawing-room he also kept in his sanctum. That slim Eros with his circle of listening youths was too intimate for profane eyes. Poor Solomon! He had glimpsed the ineffable during those early dawns when he had walked forbidden ways in search of experiences that life withheld. He had seen the gods naked and they had taken their revenge. One by one his friends were falling away from him, choosing the narrow but safe path and sparing scarcely a backward glance for the madman teetering on his frail rope over the chasm. Now and then he was seen in some gin shop, his head sunken on his breast, as he drew vague, lost angels which he would sell for the price of a drink. One of his former art patrons had come across him in the Brompton Road, drawing with chalk on the pavement. He was no longer mentioned by those who had once hailed him. Society forgot him more completely than if he had died. Even in the records of the Pre-Raphaelites who had long ago welcomed him, all mention of the pariah was erased by the pious William Michael Rossetti.

Wilde often pondered Solomon's fate. The same love of

beauty linked him to the artist, the same hunger, though as yet restrained, for those terrible pleasures that only the gods may know. In the gaze of Solomon's mystical figures neither male nor female, he read the yearning for visions as yet unseen that burned in his own; in those full curved lips he saw the bloom of the forbidden fruit for which his mouth was parched. Nature was too limited in her offerings for his hunger. Life's pleasures after the first intoxicating moment were flatter than the dregs of champagne in the glass of the night before. Had man never had more than he himself had thus far experienced? Socrates, Plato whose words had opened the pagan world before him, Phidias, Praxiteles and those nameless sculptors who had left their visions in stone—had they been content with the paltriness of everyday living? They had had the joy of their work, but what else, beyond that joy? The cast of the Hermes by Praxiteles that stood on its red stand near Carlyle's writing table vouchsafed no answer to his questioning. Solomon's Eros gave but subtle intimations. Clearest of all had spoken that nude reclining statue in the Louvre, the Hermaphrodite whose ambiguous beauty wounded like a physical pain.

Constance knew little of her husband's obscure yearnings. To her he was a wonderful man, a poet who had chosen her, unworthy, to share the life of the elect. She submitted to every one of his whims. Since he wished her beautiful she made the best of her natural endowments, and since he desired her picturesque she carried on an unconvincing fancy dress in costumes of his designing. At the receptions at Tite Street now she would appear in a Venetian gown heavy with gold lace, and then, hieratic, in medieval draperies loaded down with jangling ornaments, "All of which," said an eye-witness, "she wore with a shy air of deprecation." Perhaps Wilde liked her best in her pale green and cowslip yellow Grecian gown with her hair set off by bands of yellow ribbon.

But soon the lovely dresses had to be put away as Constance's girlish body grew with the burden she carried. A normal man under the circumstances will behave toward his wife with grateful tenderness. Wilde on the contrary hardly concealed his unreasonable resentment against the brutality of a biological necessity which to fulfill itself will transform a beautiful creature to a grotesque. He had a physical horror of ugliness. The sight of Constance ailing, ponderous, a caricature of the girl he had married, was a sin against the holy ghost of the beauty he worshiped. Romance fled. Little by little he began accepting invitations without his wife.

Uncomplaining, Constance let him go. He had work to do in which she had no part, a mission to accomplish which she understood but vaguely and only because of the world's loud responses to everything he did. Since their marriage he had written but little, a mere handful of unimportant articles for the magazines, and yet he was being sought after more than ever before. Everything he said—and he seemed to do nothing but talk these days—was taken up by a thousand echoes. Hostesses fought for the privilege of having him at their tables so that his talk might shed glamour upon their own dull wits. "Have you heard Oscar's latest?" one would ask another, deeming it compensation enough to bask in reflected glory. "And have you read 'The Harlot's House'?"

The poem had taken London by storm. Although it had been written in France, it was not published till April, 1885 in the *Dramatic Review*. Not even "Charmides" which had scandalized by its frank sensuality, had created such a sensation. There had been tradition for that poem in Marlowe's "Hero and Leander" and in Shakespeare's "Venus and Adonis." The two Elizabethans had handled their subject with the candor of their times, shocking no one and delighting generations yet unborn. Wilde's "Charmides" though drawn from the same source, mingled his own intoxicant to the Pierian spring, producing a headiness that had something of the after effect of too much champagne.

"The Harlot's House," however, owed nothing to any influence. It was born of the same bizarre imagination that had created *The Sphinx* except that reality and not an archaic past furnished the shapes of the new arabesques that wove, precise

138

yet monstrous, through their twelve chiseled stanzas. The scene was familiar to any city dweller whether in England or any part of the world—a street, a disreputable house, a man and woman walking past thinking the thoughts that may occur to any man or woman. It is reality perceived through senses sharpened by some potent drug that puts emotion through imaginative revalescence till facts are no longer fact but symbols in a realm out of the reach of known good and evil. The spectator and his companion become Everyman and his Love. The harlot's house with its shadows on the blinds is the stage setting of a Dance of Death.

> . . . We watched the ghostly dancers spin
> To sound of horn and violin,
> Like black leaves wheeling in the wind.
>
> Like wire-pulled automatons,
> Slim silhouetted skeletons
> Went sliding through the slow quadrille.
>
> They took each other by the hand,
> And danced a stately saraband;
> Their laughter echoed thin and shrill.
>
> Sometimes a clockwork puppet pressed
> A phantom lover to her breast,
> Sometimes they seemed to try to sing.
>
> Sometimes a horrible marionette
> Came out, and smoked its cigarette
> Upon the steps like a live thing.
>
> Then turning to my love, I said,
> "The dead are dancing with the dead,
> The dust is whirling with the dust."
>
> But she—she heard the violin,
> And left my side, and entered in:
> Love passed into the house of lust.

Then suddenly the tune went false,
The dancers wearied of the waltz,
The shadows ceased to wheel and whirl.

And down the long and silent street,
The dawn, with silver-sandalled feet,
Crept like a frightened girl.

No far-fetched words marred the poem, like those he had diligently sought as for curious ornaments with which to deck his Sphinx. He, the fastidious, seemed to go out of his way to make poetry out of the commonest parlance; yet with the words of the man in the street he achieved the effect of a Holbein with a rainbow to choose from. Nevertheless "The Harlot's House" marked a beginning and an end. Self-conceived, it carried no seeds but only sterility, for not even Wilde was to reproduce its like. But then, was he not the advocate of "beautiful sterile emotions" for the artist? At Oakley Street Speranza recited it to all comers who were shocked and amazed, then enchanted. Sedulously Willie hailed it in his columns.

For some time a polemical correspondence had been carried on in the pages of *The World* as well as in other papers that gladly furnished space to private quarrels provided they afforded public amusement. The first rumblings of the storm had sounded when Whistler made sarcastic comments on Wilde's accession to the platform. They gained in ominousness after Oscar, poaching on what Whistler deemed his special preserve, lectured on the subject of art—that art which, said Wilde, "Mr. Whistler always spelt . . . and we believe still spells . . . with a capital 'I.'"

"Plagiarism!" accused the Butterfly, thrusting up like a banner of conflict the white lock of hair that gave him such a sinister look. At first he was placated by the offering Wilde had laid at his feet, but the more he thought of his own ideas pluming the headpiece of another, the more pugnacious he became. Wilde's provincial lectures roused his fiendish laughter. Genially Wilde made his rebuttals. He liked "Jimmy." Besides, deep

140

within him he knew that the reproaches were not entirely un-justified.

The darts flew thick and fast until Whistler, to show what he could do when he set his mind to it, delivered his famous "Ten O'Clock" lecture at Prince's Hall on February 20, 1885. He spoke superbly. Swift as Acesta's arrows his aphorisms took fire as they flew. Then, as if to reveal his virtuosity, he painted in words calm landscapes that rivaled in feeling the black and white magic of his Venetian etchings.

"And when the evening mist clothes the riverside with poetry as with a veil," he evoked, "and the poor buildings lose them-selves in the dim sky, and the tall chimneys become campanili, and the whole city hangs in the heavens, and fairy-land is before us—the wayfarer hastens home . . . and Nature, who, for once, has sung in tune, sings her exquisite song to the artist alone, her son and her master—her son in that he loves her, her mas-ter in that he knows her."

Everyone before that evocation, felt himself an artist. Frank Harris, at the adroit persiflage of the lecturer, at the hard, in-tellectual core of his criticisms and the pure beauty of his ex-pression, was prostrate in worship. The lecture, he roared in his loud voice, ranked with the best ever heard in London, and was every bit as wonderful as Coleridge's on Shakespeare and Carlyle's on Heroes. He spoke of them as if he had been pres-ent when the vital words had thrilled upon the air.

Wilde was not of his opinion and made a point of not agree-ing with Whistler in his review of the lecture the following day. He would show "our James" that Wilde could think for him-self. Indeed, his tone was that of omniscience rapping the knuckles of a too clever cockscomb. "The scene was in every way delightful," he wrote. "He stood there, a miniature Mephistoph-eles, mocking the majority!"

Now Whistler had no objection to being called a Mephistoph-eles. He gloried in his satanic reputation. But a *miniature* Mephistopheles was another matter, most of all when the appel-lation came from one with an overplus of inches. "Ha! Ha!"

"That an artist will find beauty in ugliness, *le beau dans l'horrible,* is now a commonplace of the schools, the argot of the atelier," Wilde went on in an endeavor to show that Whistler was not so original after all, "but I strongly deny that charming people should be condemned to live with magenta ottomans and Albert-blue curtains in their rooms in order that some painter (the sting did not miss its mark) may observe the sidelights of the one, and the values of the other. . . . The poet is the supreme artist," he challenged, "for he is the master of colour and of form, and the real musician besides, and is lord over all life and all arts. . . ."

As if warned by some instinct that he had gone too far, he flung at the Butterfly a patronizing valedictory: "That he is indeed one of the greatest masters of painting, is my opinion. And I may add that in this opinion Mr. Whistler himself entirely concurs."

The artist boiled with rage. For months, in fact for nearly two years, in season and out of season, the two men flung the inkpot at each other. Sometimes one hit the mark, sometimes the other; both in the end came out blackened and minus a friend.

The public, however, found in the quarrel much matter for amusement and followed it enthusiastically. "Stick to your painting," was Wilde's admonition to the Butterfly. "Be warned in time, James, and remain as I do, incomprehensible. To be great is to be misunderstood."

Ha! Ha! So Wilde would occupy the field alone! "What has Oscar in common with art," Whistler posed rhetorically, "except that he dines at our table and picks from our platters the plums for the puddings he peddles in the provinces? Oscar, the amiable, irresponsible, esurient Oscar, with no more sense of a picture than the fit of a coat, has the courage of the opinions— of others!"

"This is very sad," countered Wilde, losing his geniality. "With our James vulgarity begins at home, and should be allowed to stay there."

Whistler in the end captured the victor's wreath, a thorny

one, with but few roses. What matter? The Butterfly could still extract from it the honey of triumph.

Through it all Constance fulfilled as best she could her mission as the wife of Wilde. A son had been born to her in June of 1885 and another in November of the following year. Cyril and Vyvyan Wilde called them, choosing names that befitted a poet's sons. Constance from now on rarely accompanied her husband on his rounds of pleasure. She had the children to take care of. Moreover, as an exponent of aestheticism by marriage, she had a small following of her own among young girls and spinsters who adopted her costumes and spread the Wildean views on interior decoration. Bustles and crinolines were thrown out the window. The uncorseted form divine, reveling in the new freedom, propitiated decency by draping itself in yards and yards of Liberty fabrics.

A strange emptiness, in spite of outward brilliance, marked the life of the young household. The early rapture had vanished and as the years passed love settled to an unecstatic alliance—at any rate on Wilde's side. Constance was still devoted to him as in the early days, but she could not help seeing that something, dimly perceived yet increasingly manifest, stood between her and her husband. He had grown more avid for pleasure. The things that had once contented him were no longer sufficient. He must have greater luxuries, stronger sensations. After the birth of the second son he was absent more and more often from her bed. He no longer felt desire toward her. What was it that had come between them? Pure-minded, Constance faced the fact without looking for causes. Perhaps that was what happened in all marriages. Not over-passionate by nature, she found satisfaction for her love in her children and let her husband go his way. She could not have prevented him in any case. He was the strong one in that relation, and she the submissive. Simple and unimaginative, Constance bowed down to life as it came. Yet her unconscious dissatisfaction was stronger than her compliance. Life must have more in it than it gave her. She turned to occultism.

At that time there was a mystical order in London whose

membership was drawn chiefly from women who like Constance needed an outlet for their normal emotions. With the
Comtesse de Brémont she would attend its meetings, study it-
doctrines and find comfort in the illusory sense of power tha
it gave her. After a course of induction she was ripe for initiation. With trembling voice she took the oath that threatened
disaster to the faithless one who revealed the secrets of the or-
ganization. At home, she promptly disclosed to Oscar the mi-
nutiae of the proceedings. Unlike him, she could not keep her
secret.

As for his, she would not have understood. Years earlier, in
America, when that secret was but half-known to Wilde himself, John Burroughs with uncanny observation had guessed it
on first setting eyes upon him. He found Wilde a splendid
talker, handsome "—but a voluptuary. As he walked from you,"
he particularized, "there was something in the motion of his
hips and back that was disagreeable."

Other observers just as keen had had their own suspicions
intimated in their mistrust of the man as well as in the reputation they had foisted upon him long before he merited it
Wilde had had inklings that he was different from others in
the demands he made upon the normal. His marriage crystallized them to certainty. Till then his aberrant desires might
have been attributable to the irregularity of a bachelor life. His
disappointment in marriage, however, proved that those desires had deeper roots than he suspected, far deeper than the
fascination of the Greek cult of beauty, than the influence of
Pater's hedonism which its author came to mistrust. "Yes,"
Wilde would say with mock affliction, "poor dear Pater has lived
to disprove everything that he has written." He, Wilde, would
prove his own convictions to the hilt, however outrageous to
accepted morality.

His life from now on assumed an air of arrogance. He would
do nothing in moderation—except work. But then, his real work
was accomplished when he talked. Before a group of listeners
especially if they were young and handsome and titled, he out-

lid himself. In the spark of their admiration his mind quick-
ned. Epigram followed epigram, one more dazzling, more pre-
osterous than the other, yet always, like the incandescent core
f the firework, with a burning truth at the heart. The articles
e wrote for the reviews, the infrequent poems, were engendered
rom the give and take of such intercourse. The difficulty came
vhen he had to force himself into the chair before Carlyle's
vriting table. How often Sherard caught the look of conscience
n his eyes as Wilde murmured: "I ought to be putting black
ipon white, black upon white."

Sometimes finances at Tite Street presented a serious prob-
em. Suddenly in June, 1887 unexpected help came when Mr.
Cassell of Cassell and Company offered him the editorship of
The Woman's World, a monthly magazine of fashion and so-
iety. The salary was not large—only six pounds six a week, but
t was more than he was getting by his free lance articles. He
ccepted, jesting wryly on himself as the *fittest* for the post.
Many among his enemies agreed with him.

Day after day he went to his offices—Oscar Wilde forcing him-
elf into the mold of Grub Street. Even his worst critics, how-
ver, had to admit that he did his job well. Under his editorship
he magazine with its pink decorated wrappers printed in red
nk, found its way into thousands of well-to-do homes that
dopted the suggestions it contained on the house beautiful,
r simply on Beauty. Through his many connections he ob-
ained an impressive list of contributors. Queen Elizabeth of
.oumania wrote for it, as well as Lady Sandhurst and Marie
Corelli who was beginning to wrest the palm of popularity from
Ouida. Speranza, who had brought out a volume of ancient leg-
nds of Ireland in 1888 was represented in the magazine with
 collection of Irish peasant tales, while Constance wrote with
uthority on muffs and children's dress. Altogether *The
Woman's World* was an exciting venture during the two years
f Wilde's mentorship.

"A beautiful Sappho has broken in Dublin, Miss Romola
'ynte," Father Hopkins wrote to Robert Bridges in 1887.

"Oscar Wylde (*sic*) designed her very becoming costume and she herself, I suppose, her equally becoming name." For the second time the obscure Jesuit poet mentioned the most talked- of man in England. Who could have guessed that he who wrote so lightly was daily crucifying his spirit in a deepening sense of doubt?

Anyone who chanced upon the Jesuit father who was then in his forty-third year would have thought him a boy of eighteen. The straight long palish hair brushed back from the brow and temples concealed the gray. The greenish-brown eyes had youth in them, belied only by the finely etched lines at the corners and under the lids. His body, slim and light, was that of an adolescent despite the conflicts that made it their battleground.

In his passion to serve God in man he had struggled to sever himself from the poetry which, too sorrowfully, he knew was his very life. The manuscripts were scattered, some with Bridges who was gaining recognition with his own poetry, some with Coventry Patmore, the dean of the Catholic literary group. He himself, the avid for life, put on the hair shirt of asceticism; he the singer, vowed himself to silence, seeking fulfillment in serv- ice, and happiness in a hope for the future. Every day some happening took toll of his frail body. Things that others scarcely noticed were for him a personal affliction. Once at Roehampton an ash tree was felled. "I heard the sound and looking out and seeing it maimed there came at that moment a great pang and I wished to die." In his impersonal service there was nothing, no one, he could love. When a golden-crested wren flew in at the window one night he took it in his hands, caressing the orange and yellow feathers that gave him the warmth he could ask of no human being.

For a time he did parish work among the Irish in Liverpool. The filth, the vice and the horror in which man, made in God's image, was compelled to live, nearly killed him. He wrestled with himself, wrestled with God Who allowed such things to be. His anguish overthrowing his vow of silence, made him seek relief in poems that cried his loneliness and frustration.

146

> . . . So what I plead is just,
> Why do sinners' ways prosper? and why must
> Disappointment all I endeavour end?
> Wert thou my enemy, O thou my Friend,
> How could'st thou worse . . . ?

Heart's blood and the sweat of his moral agony made the fluid for his pen; he wrote on his own martyred flesh. But still he believed in the final justice of God, even though he won to that belief through the carrion comfort of despair. The words came salt and single, drop by drop, in the rhythms that he had wrung from his changing heartbeat; and he washed his soul, knowing that

> O the mind, mind has mountain; cliffs of fall
> Frightful, sheer, no-man-fathomed. Hold them cheap
> May who ne'er hung there. . . .
> Here! creep,
> Wretch, under a comfort serves in a whirlwind: all
> Life death does end and each day dies with sleep.

He died in 1889, of typhoid fever contracted in Ireland. He knew that some day his work would come to light. "If you do not like it," he wrote to Bridges of one of his compositions, "it is because there is something you have not seen and I see. . . . If the whole world agreed to condemn it or see nothing in it I should only tell them to take a generation and come to me again."

Just then another generation had come of age.

Part Two

AND THE YELLOW
'NINETIES

Chapter I: On the Threshold of the 'Nineties

THE old century was dying, but in the man-made concept of time, that death betokened a beginning. Heavy with life the chrysalis was about to burst with the century born of the old, yet, for the hopes of mankind, a brighter and more wonderful harbinger of futurity.

The ancients had hailed each birth of time with horoscope and prophecy. Chronos had borne a son. In the span of a hundred years bridging past and future, generations would cross from unknown to unknown, armies march and pestilence break out, while from as yet uncreated wombs new lives would spring forth, walk their allotted way and leave the road clear for those that followed after. It was the time spent on the bridge that counted, before the final step that led to the farther shore. And that time counted more than ever to the generation that was young when the nineteenth century was drawing to a close.

Many things had happened since the beginning of the century. Impoverished Europe, bloodless from the disastrous war that had killed the best of her youth, rose to a recovery which her historians were beginning to call a rebirth. In England after the decade of hardship that followed the victory of Waterloo, industrial prosperity swelled private moneybags which burst from their own plethora, giving birth to other independent fortunes. During the first fifty years the rich grew richer as enterprise flourished. Human flesh and blood could be bought for the machines more cheaply than the provender for my lord's stud horses. The machines throve, and from the digested blood and sweat of the millions gave forth energy in shining gold.

Carlyle, Ruskin and a few other Jeremiahs whose nostrils were offended by the smell of blood raised their voices, pleading with man to have mercy on his fellows. But the machines were

151

loud, and in the windowless countinghouses the rising cries of protest were drowned by the music of the gold pieces. In mill and factory, however, above the uproar of the gins, those cries were heard; the words of hope, mingled with the humming of wheels and the snap of the crank, lifted the heads sunken in brute labor, and the beast remembered he was man.

Reformers took up the cause of the worker. Night schools were founded for his education. Even Parliament awoke to the realization of his existence and passed restrictive labor laws. But the laboring man had been slowly awakened to the knowledge that his strength lay in his numbers and in unity. By the beginning of 1890, therefore, England had had a sample of what that unity could do, both in the free speech demonstration that had covered every inch of Trafalgar Square with people clamoring for their rights, and in the recent Dockers' strike which brought to the fore a new power, the power of the labor leader as seen in Tom Mann and John Burns. A Socialist party had been formed in 1881 by Henry Hyndman. William Morris, once the singer of Guinevere, put his talents to the writing of revolutionary songs for its members, and amid the red flags hailed liberty louder than any. Shabby as any worker, his hands stained from the dye vats, his gray shock of hair unkempt with revolutionary fervor as it had been for poetry, he would be seen at the meetings distributing leaflets among the crowd. Capitalist-Socialist, the sneerers called him, and he let them mock. Over the bier of Alfred Linnell who had been killed by police violence in the demonstration at Trafalgar Square, he knew that from such martyrs would spring the seeds of a society of men not ashamed to look one another in the face. He was not alone among the intellectuals who took to heart the struggle of the masses. In 1883 the Fabian Society called to its ranks such disparate supporters as Bernard Shaw, Annie Besant, the Webbs, Stewart Headlam, Sydney Olivier and many others whose work was still to do.

In literature schools had come and gone. Coleridge and Wordsworth, fanned to poetry by the French Revolution, had turned, the one to the dream dome of Kubla Khan in his escape from a reality that had become intolerable, the other to the sheltered haven of Toryism. Byron and Shelley had had their brief revolt, Byron destroying himself and those linked with him in a satanic descent from godhood toward man whom he sought to remake into the inheritor of the world, Shelley lifting himself upward for the torch to rekindle man's soul dulled to a clod. Each had been successful in his way, though in the following generation the impulse to poetry came from Keats in the banding together of the Pre-Raphaelites. Keats had felt none of the revolt of Byron nor any of Shelley's yearning for that perfect land where love and liberty made men brothers. Prescient of his brief stay on earth Keats had drunk with all his senses the loveliness of the visual world and striven in his poetry to "load every rift with ore." Beauty in its multifarious forms, beauty past and present, sufficed him for his happiness. It should suffice for humanity's also. He mourned only at the thought that beauty had already attained its zenith and that the coming ages would see it dimmed in the smoke of the factory, its colors broken in the spectrum of science.

The Pre-Raphaelites inherited both his worship and his nostalgia, adding to Keats's domain of the visual world the unseen realm of the soul. It remained for Dante Gabriel Rossetti in his "House of Life" to fuse body and soul in a new mysticism.

For the generation that came of age in the last decade of the century the heritage was a heavy one. The pomp of empire that awed the older Briton who had helped attain it made youth sick at heart. Mammon was god, and the young needed something less material to worship. It was a conflict between the world and the spirit out of which at some time it had sprung. How find that spirit, and in finding it find themselves? The Oxford movement under the guidance of its leading exponent had exerted its influence for more than half a century; but when Newman died in 1890 it was no longer the movement he had helped to bring about. How could one aspire to return to the faith of the Middle Ages and re-enact in the complex society of the late nineteenth century the story of Newman's novel *Callista*, wherein the Greek carver of idols is converted to

153

Christianity and dies a martyr? The century's liberalism which Newman rejected had yet found wide acceptance; it too had its martyrs. Nevertheless a group of poets headed by Coventry Patmore and Alice Meynell decided now more than ever to stand on the side of the angels. They had their following from the younger generation.

It was a darker side of Catholic mysticism, however, that seized upon the imagination of those who had been acquiring artistic consciousness in the last quarter of a century, a mysticism that had already had its exponents in France whither they turned for their guiding light. "One can fancy an intense personality being created out of sin," said Oscar Wilde who by 1890 had become one of its devotees.

Indeed, the previous year, as if to ease his soul by confession, he had published "Pen, Pencil and Poison," a brilliant championing of the notorious Thomas Griffiths Wainewright, dandy, poet and murderer with whom he felt a tacit kinship. He might have been describing himself when he wrote of Wainewright: "He loves Greek gems, and Persian carpets, and Elizabethan translations . . . and book-bindings, and early editions, and wide-margined proofs. He is keenly sensitive to the value of beautiful surroundings . . . He has that curious love of green[1] which in individuals is always the sign of a subtle artistic temperament, and in nations is said to denote a laxity, if not a decadence of morals. Like Baudelaire he was extremely fond of cats, and with Gautier, he was fascinated by that 'sweet marble monster' of both sexes that we can still see at Florence and in the Louvre."

Coming so soon after his *Happy Prince*, a collection of exquisitely chiseled tales of the purity of marble, the essay would have been shocking by contrast alone, did not Wilde make his

---

[1] We quote the following for what they are worth from the case histories of inverts. (Havelock Ellis, *Psychology of Sex*, vol. II. *Sexual Inversion*.) "He has a special predilection for green; it is the predominant color in the decoration of his room." . . . "He finds that the love of green . . . is very widespread among his inverted friends." Also from Havelock Ellis's own summation: "It has also been remarked that inverts exhibit a preference for green garments. In Rome *cinoedi* were for this reason called *galbanati*."

position worse by declaring: "Had he lived in imperial Rome, or at the time of the Italian Renaissance, or in Spain in the seventeenth century, or in any land or any century but this century and this land, we would be quite able to arrive at a perfectly unprejudiced estimate of his position and value."

He was simply defending his contention that moral judgments should not be applied to history or to art. He succeeded only in making himself more than ever unpopular with the upholders of the moral structure. In some unconscious striving at catharsis he wrote the essay to win a justification for the career of pleasure on which he had embarked. It was a first attempt in the researches of sin which had long possessed his soul: he thus began paving the way to a dimly envisioned calvary. He had two heroes, Christ and Napoleon, both of whom according to him attained the supreme triumph by ultimate failure. The cross or St. Helena: which would be his?

Meanwhile France had been adding her subtle influences to the spiritual upheaval of the closing century. Gautier, Baudelaire, Verlaine and Rimbaud were well known to the literary of England. D'Aurevilly and Huysmans crossed the Channel in tooled leather bindings. Huysmans' *À Rebours* which appeared in 1884 had been foreshadowed ten years earlier, at least in its outward dealings with luxurious sins, by d'Aurevilly's *Les Diaboliques*. The whole decalogue, however, separated d'Aurevilly's studies in the temptations induced by original sin and Huysmans' explorations of unnatural sensations. The one in its perversity pointed a moral lesson. The other not only presented old sins in a new fashion for the pleasure of the *nouveau frisson*, but invented many more. "Nothing else remains for him," cried d'Aurevilly of Huysmans, "but the barrel of a pistol or the foot of the cross." He himself had reached that point some years before his death in 1889.

He had been a familiar figure in Paris. The men who had known him in his youth recalled the many-colored inks that he used for his manuscripts with their illuminated rubrics, ornamental margins and carefully painted miniatures. Though at first his works were ignored, all Paris knew him as the eccentric who dressed like d'Orsay, posed like Alfieri and had unimaginable amours with mysterious duchesses. Among intimates he was known as Jules le Pâcha, a name he favored for its implications of luxury, indolence and those pleasures which he would have people believe he enjoyed. Whenever he left his apartment in Rue Rousselet, clad in his frock coat with gold buttons, carrying a jeweled cane and walking with the gait of a military man, everyone turned to look at him. At the cafés he had a court of his own for his brilliant conversation. For hours at a time he would hold forth, telling some tale with inimitable grace or waging duels of eloquence with the wits.

When *Les Diaboliques* appeared d'Aurevilly had just passed a spiritual crisis. "I have been a monster of dissipation," he confessed, self-accusing. After surrendering to the urges of his temperament and the suggestions of sin, he knelt at last before two bits of wood in the form of a cross. *Les Diaboliques* was his expiation, his arraignment of sin which he revealed in its fascinating horror the better to unmask it. D'Aurevilly, however, preached no sermons in his work. Seldom did he interrupt the thread of his narrative for religion or morality; yet the power that both wielded over him was implicit, even when he seemed most in league with the Prince of Darkness whose name he assumed in his last years. The stories he told with sensual gusto were woven about six women, products of a decadent civilization. They were wise as Lilith in evil, beautiful as Helen, deceitful as the Serpent. Most of them were of high degree so that luxury might be a fit handmaiden to corruption. He left nothing to the imagination. Writing as if at the devil's dictation, he led the reader through the lowest abysses of human depravity till the very soul shuddered and cried: "No more!"

Huysmans' *À Rebours* concerned itself with no spiritual aspirations. Jean des Esseintes, the hero, had enough as it was experiencing the pleasures of the senses which he pursued with the fixation of genius. A youth of the utmost refinement, he was soon jaded with the unimaginative delights that satisfied most men. He must have pleasures common to none, ecstasies of the senses that would exalt like the beatitudes of the medieval saints. There was no depth to which he would not sink for the pearl of pleasure, no hell he would not explore. A monomaniac, he had no thought but to wring life dry, to extract the last drop that might give him the ultimate thrill of sensual exaltation. As he possessed great wealth he had the open sesame for his every desire. Paintings, women, love, lust, natural and forbidden experience, were his for the wishing. Wearied of the possible, he attempted the impossible to which the body might sink, and yet live. No cult had ever staged such rituals as he devised with his perverse imagination. Paris became another Eleusis, with des Esseintes both highpriest and god, transcending the limitations of sex, impervious to moral laws. In his sybaritic seclusion he surrounded himself with all possible excitements. For his imagination he had books of decadent poetry bound in skins suitable to the subjects. His conservatory bloomed with flowers brought from remote corners of the earth—orchids like still, poised butterflies, bizarre, furry blooms that had maws like beasts and had to be fed with insects, monstrous plants exhaling the fetid breath of unimaginable corruptions. He had an organ of which every note was a perfume; and for the ravishment of his eyes, the suggestive and beautiful evil of Moreau's Salomé paintings.

Wilde, well read in decadent literature, accepted *A Rebours* as the gospel of a fascinatingly wicked religion. Like des Esseintes he too was enjoying pleasures beyond the bounds of vulgar approval. He scorned petty morality, and again, like him, believed that his escape from the mediocre to whatever rapture satisfied his needs was no one's concern but his own. In Paris he had also fallen under the spell of Gustave Moreau.

The symbolic paintings with their suggestion of oriental perversity in jeweled nudities struck the vision like tone poems in color. They could not have been painted in sunlight. The glow that brought out the inmost fire of Salomé's circlet of jewels in the water color of the *Apparition* had never shone on mortal land. Only in the twilit dimness of an undersea cave where vague, silent creatures illumine the depths with fitful phosphorescence had such light been; or in some rocky hollow, fit for a witches' sabbath, when the wraith of a moon in her terrified flight through clouds sends down a pallid beam, and disappearing, leaves but the shadow of her light. Here was a subtler artist and a greater than Simeon Solomon, though of the same perverse breed.

The figures who people Moreau's canvases, those static shadows masked and shrouded and laden with jewels like frightful idols, conceal even from themselves the secret of their sexlessness. Ephebic virgins stand in heraldic attitudes. Youths with the faces of maidens droop in the passion of their own beauty. There is about the men and women the resemblance of consanguinity, as if all had sprung from the same parent, and that parent an androgyne. Over the embraces of lovers hangs the suggestion of incest: all are alike—all beautiful, all ambiguous. Just as Huysmans' book was the evangel of decadence, Moreau's painting was its ritual art. Did he not himself say that he celebrated *"la gloire des sacrifices et l'apothéose des rédempteurs"*?[2]

Neither the novelist nor the painter, however, would have been, at least in the expression peculiar to his art, without Théophile Gautier, the holy ghost of the exotic-aesthetic, satanic-mystical school. When his *Mademoiselle de Maupin* descended upon the earth in 1835, she unloosed a Pandora box of mysteries that have not yet ceased to darken the air. Every predilection of the decadents is to be found in the pages of that magically wrought novel. Once the subject matter was fixed, swarms of disciples more or less endowed, improvised upon the stated themes, till they attained the sensationalism of a Rachilde and a Péladan in France, of a Baron Corvo and an Aleister Crowley in England.

Gautier it was who had first expressed his rapture at the Hermaphrodite as the symbol of completeness. At once a chorus rose up in praise not only of the classic marble, but of the monstrosity itself. For that matter Wainewright, as Wilde pointed out in his essay, had also been enthralled by the dis-

[2] "the glory of sacrifices and the apotheosis of redeemers."

158

turbing appeal of the statue. It took Gautier, however, to discover it as a subject for literature.

From the Hermaphrodite it was but a step to Lesbianism; thus *Mademoiselle de Maupin,* besides much else, is a celebration of its practices. Baudelaire in *Lesbos* and *Femmes Damnées,* Balzac in *Séraphita* and *La fille aux Yeux d'Or,* and later Verlaine in some of his verses, found inspiration at the Lesbian source. In England Swinburne, besides other diableries, perpetrated *Anactoria* and the highly colored *Lesbia Brandon.*

Among sumptuous surroundings that borrowed their *décor* from remote Byzantium, orgies of the body and soul found re-enactment in the imagination, and occasionally in actuality, to believe Huysmans, an active participant in such unholy doings. Sadism flourished anew, adding to the lust of cruelty the spice of sacrilege. At the very time when revivals of faith were filling the churches, impious sabbaths found their celebrants. It was but the other side of religion, a religion turned within itself and become perverted. Huysmans called it a bastard Catholicism, and in *À Rebours* explained: "This curious and ill-defined state cannot indeed be born in the soul of an unbeliever . . . The power of sadism, the attraction it offers, rests therefore entirely on the forbidden pleasure of transferring to Satan the homage and prayer that are due to God."[3]

As in religion, so in life there existed this reversal of allegiance. The normal palled. In the desire for escape the Gautiers, the Baudelaires and other greater and lesser spirits attacked life from the forbidden. "The path is traced, *à rebours,*" announced the poet of *Les Fleurs du Mal.*

In large part, however, such dangerous adventuring took place in the mind. Gone were the days when Byronic romanticists, following the example of the leader, threw themselves bodily into the turmoil of life in search of the great moment. The effete of the waning century were, most of them, armchair Byrons. The imagined adventure satisfied them; indeed, it alone stirred the turbid senses which found their deepest

[3] Tr. by author.

gratification in solitary excitement. What lusts, what raptures did reality afford that they could not better in their imaginings?

> There is nothing nor shall be,

they chanted with Swinburne,

> So sweet, so wicked, but my verse
> Can dream of worse. . . .

They knew their vice and they rejoiced in it. "At bottom," declared Huysmans, "the only obscene people are the chaste."[4] His recondite researches had given him evidence enough that the soul can summon up lasciviousness unknown to the body. Intellectual erethism? Whatever the name, the fact was sufficiently manifest in the productions of the decadents. A des Esseintes had his most poignant thrills in solitary musings.

Wilde was going through a wonderful period of fertility. Since 1886 when he surrendered himself to the subliminal urges of his inverted nature, a new energy seemed to have been released in him, throwing down the psychological barrier between conception and accomplishment. His conversation, friends and enemies agreed, reached greater heights. He no longer had to force himself to put black upon white, although he still much preferred to extemporize his works rather than to write them, and unlike most decadents, to live rather than imagine them. Physically, too, he had changed. His face had grown fuller, heavier about the mouth and chin, giving him an expression of satiety. His clothes, a little too elegant, a trifle too meticulous, made him look overdressed rather than well dressed, creating an impression of artifice like an actor who, leaving the stage, will come out on the street with his make-up still clinging. He continued to sport his continental cane. With his infantile attachment to things—the fur coat which he carefully stored after each season, the knickknacks treasured in his study—he could not bear to give up anything he cherished.

4 From *Certains*. Tr. by author.

Therefore, notwithstanding his conventional garb, he persisted in wearing a huge scarab ring in lapis which affected the orthodox Englishman like a mirror flashed in his eyes by some impudent schoolboy. That, and the gold-tipped cigarettes which he incessantly smoked. One might have thought they were brands of the devil.

Wilde's writings had been appearing in, for him, astonishing succession. Besides his editorial duties which he pursued till 1889, and the articles and letters that maintained his name before the public, he had published a number of short stories; a collection of beautifully written fairy tales in 1888; and the following year, the study of Wainewright, the scintillating first dialogue essay, "The Decay of Lying" and his excursion into Shakespeareana, *The Portrait of Mr. W. H.*

The readers of the July issue of *Blackwood's Edinburgh Magazine* had never seen anything like that clever piece of scholarship, introduced pleasantly in the guise of fiction. The story was simple. Cyril Graham, a youth in whom Wilde unwittingly portrays himself, believes he has discovered the identity of the mysterious *W. H.* in the dedication of Shakespeare's *Sonnets*. It is Will Hughes, a boy player, whose beauty inspired Shakespeare in the creation of his loveliest heroines.

The Will Hughes theory was not original with Wilde. Long before him Malone and Tyrwhitt had derived the name from a play upon words in the sonnets themselves; but they had gone no farther except to add another hypothesis to the two in existence: the identification of *W. H.* with either William Herbert, Earl of Pembroke, or Henry Wriothesley, Earl of Southampton. From internal evidence in the sonnets Wilde's Cyril establishes, however, that Will Hughes was a member of Shakespeare's company during the dramatist's most inspired period, that he left him to join another company, and that as a result Shakespeare suffered from a sense of betrayal. "He (Cyril) felt . . . that the sonnets are addressed to an individual —to a particular young man whose personality for some reason seems to have filled the soul of Shakespeare with terrible joy and no less terrible despair."

The theory is ingenious, and the verses quoted are convincing not only to Cyril, but to the reader. But how establish the identity of Will Hughes as a boy actor? The fact that the name did not appear in the published list of Shakespeare's company does not invalidate the theory: had not Will Hughes left Shakespeare for a rival dramatist? Cyril is so certain of the reality of Hughes that to convince his skeptical friend Erskine he had a portrait forged. Erskine discovers the forgery, whereupon Cyril to prove his conviction to the utmost, kills himself. Erskine must give Cyril's theory to the world, the writer pleads with him. "You forget," answers Erskine, "that a thing is not necessarily true because a man dies for it."

Wilde's story roused more controversy than anything he had yet done and gave ammunition to those who, judging him only by their suspicions, now felt they had tangible evidence. No man would treat such subjects unless they fascinated him. Shakespeare, the world's greatest dramatist, consumed with passion for an effeminate youth! The sublime bard writing love sonnets to a boy actor! It was preposterous, indecent, and only demonstrated the current of Wilde's thoughts. Frank Harris, when Wilde had expounded the theory to him, urged him not to make it public and found the story unfit for his *Fortnightly Review* which had, however, published the earlier "Pen, Pencil and Poison," in many ways a more dangerous piece of work. The sonnets addressed to Willie Hughes? Frank Harris knew better.

"My conviction," he argued with Wilde, "is that Shakespeare was not abnormally vicious. The first series of sonnets proves only snobbishness and toadying and not corrupt passion."

He warned Wilde of the injury he was doing himself. But Wilde only laughed as the barbs flew about him and reveled in the horror and hatred he inspired in the powerful Puritan camps.

Harris deplored Wilde's willful challenge of the Englishman's pet prejudices, yet secretly admired him and was frequently in his company. Well-meaning friends warned him not to go about with Wilde so much.

"Why not?" he asked.

"He has a bad name," they reminded him. "Strange things are said about him. You have only got to look at the man."

"Whatever the disease may be," replied Harris who liked to think he had a pretty gift for repartee, "it's not catching, unfortunately."

The year came to a close. On the threshold of the new decade crowded with youths eager for entry, stood its prophet Wilde adding the last refinements to the gospel of decadence according to himself.

Chapter II: Dorian Gray

The Picture of Dorian Gray appeared in the June number of *Lippincott's Monthly Magazine* for 1890. The title was innocuous enough, although to those who had read *The Portrait of Mr. W. H.* it offered a clue on what to expect. Indeed, the novel opens on the same theme: the domination of an older man—in *The Portrait of Mr. W. H.*, Shakespeare, in *The Picture of Dorian Gray*, Basil Hallward, an artist—by a youth of extraordinary beauty who is at once the inspiration and the cause of sorrow to the man who loves him. In *Dorian Gray*, however, the theme is incidental. Wilde had already done ample justice to it, and the true artist never repeats himself.

Still, the obsessive nature of the subject indicated the trend of Wilde's thoughts. Charmides, the ideal of boyish beauty, had always fascinated him. He had used the name in the most ambitious of his early poems. He reverted to it again and again, confessing to his friends how deeply he had been stirred on reading of Socrates' emotion at the sight of the fair youth.

There was nothing omitted in Jowett's translation of that first of the *Dialogues* of Plato. "Almost all young persons appear to be beautiful in my eyes," Jowett has Socrates say in plainest English. "But at that moment when I saw him (Charmides) coming in, I confess that I was quite astonished at his beauty and stature; all the world seemed to be enamored of him; amazement and confusion reigned when he entered . . ." The old philosophers pushed one another off the benches for the privilege of having Charmides sit beside them. The presence of Apollo could not have moved them more. "And at that moment all the people in the palaestra crowded about us, and, O rare! I caught sight of the inwards of his garments, and took the flame. Then I could no longer contain myself. I thought how well Cydias understood the nature of love, when, in speaking of a fair youth, he warns some one 'not to bring the fawn in the sight of the lion to be devoured by him,' for I felt that I had been overcome by a sort of wild-beast appetite." The reading, hallowed by classic tradition, had made its impression upon Wilde. What had affected the youth became a temptation to the man who, disenchanted with marriage, threw himself into an insensate beauty worship. He could no longer keep his secret. Although no word of it ever passed his lips, he betrayed it in the nature of the company he began to frequent, and in the growing daring of his writings.

The theme of *Dorian Gray*, that is, the central motif of the struggle between good and evil in man, had a venerable ancestry. Not so long ago Poe had treated it in *William Wilson*. It was also adumbrated in Balzac's *Peau de Chagrin* which with others of the Frenchman's works Wilde had studied in his Hôtel Voltaire days when, with Balzac's monkish gown, he would have assumed something of his literary manner. Indeed, the germ of the portrait idea is to be found in the description of the antiquarian's shop that opens *Peau de Chagrin*, where a picture of Christ that exerts a sinister influence is dwelt upon and then abandoned for the more novel idea of a magic skin that granted every wish of its owner. Raphael, Balzac's hero, comes into possession of the magic skin at a moment when he had been contemplating suicide. From then on he plunges into a life of extravagance and dissipation, to discover that with every wish the magic skin shrinks until, in the end, his life ceases with it. Raphael is an ancestor of Dorian. Wilde, however, has improved upon the original; for des Esseintes had come, in the meantime, to heighten sensation with the gamut of the perverse and to teach Dorian new tricks. Here too Wilde proved an apt pupil. Still another master stood at his shoulder as he wrote—his ancestor Maturin whose *Melmoth the Wanderer* had shadowed his boyhood. With Raphael, Dorian is a kin to Melmoth whose feet had marked the path which the two were later to tread.

Des Esseintes, however, is the true blood brother of Dorian Gray who might almost be a twin of Huysmans' hero. Christopher Millard, that strange literary phenomenon better known to the world as Stuart Mason, wrote, "Wilde admitted that in writing *Dorian Gray* he had in mind a French novel entitled *À Rebours*." Even without Wilde's admission the influence is obvious on every page of *Dorian Gray*. Like one whose knowledge is too much for him and must whisper it if only to himself, he introduced Huysmans' novel into his own as "the yellow book . . . the strangest book he had ever read. It seemed to him that in exquisite raiment, and to the delicate sound of flutes, the sins of the world were passing in dumb show before him . . . It was a poisonous book. The heavy odour of incense seemed to cling about its pages and to trouble the brain. . . ." Originally, in his manuscript, he had called it *Le Secret de Raoul*, and its author Catulle Sarrazin.[1]

The same sense of *décor* that filled the canvases of Gustave Moreau, Huysmans had carried over to his own writing. Jeweled words, exotic effects, catalogues of oddities that intoxicated with their very sound, cast a spell over his pages, drugging the senses. Wilde imitated. Des Esseintes had experimented with perfumes: Dorian, therefore, must study them, distilling oils, and burning gums from the East. Des Esseintes had been deeply affected by music; Dorian must follow. "In a long latticed room, with a vermilion-and-gold ceiling and walls of olive-green lacquer, he used to give curious concerts, in which mad gypsies tore wild music from little zithers, or grave yellow-shawled Tunisians plucked at the strained strings of monstrous lutes." Dorian, too, was a lover of jewels, of art and of that mysticism which, imitating the Catholic Communion, had in it the terribleness of sacrilege. One chapter was almost a synthesis of *À Rebours*. Everything was there concentrated and intensified, the element of the monstrous—one of the words Wilde most frequently used—keying to the pitch of ecstasy the senses which "no less than the soul, have their spiritual mysteries to reveal."

Dorian Gray is a modern allegory. The youth whose beauty at the opening of the novel Basil Hallward is endeavoring to

[1] Holograph *Dorian Gray* at the Morgan Library.

capture on canvas, falls under the influence of the clever and perverse Lord Henry Wotton, whose words, brilliant in paradox but poisonous with worldly wisdom, succeed in waking Dorian's slumbering senses to life and desire. Like a flower under forced sunlight Dorian responds. His face attains an expression Basil had never seen. Inspired, he paints it, and the portrait is finished. Possessed by his own beauty and reeling under the intoxication of Lord Henry's dangerous teaching, Dorian—like Melmoth—surrenders to terrible temptation. How sad it all was! He would grow old and horrible while the picture, the lifeless image of himself, would never be older than that particular day in June. If it could only be the other way, that he remain young and the picture grow old! "For that— for that—I would give everything!" he cried. "Yes, there is nothing in the world that I would not give! I would give my soul for that!" And thereby hangs a tale with, wonder of wonders, the tag of a moral, ambiguous to none but *Punch*, the irreconcilable.

Satirically the magazine reviewed Oscar Wilde's "Wildest and Oscarest work," accompanying it with a caricature of him as the "Fad Boy" offering new horrors wherewith to scare virtuous spinsterhood. *Punch*'s style, unlike Oscar's, had not improved. It was still lumbering, and its humor, if possible, more heavy-handed. Amused, Wilde read in the issue of July 19: "The portrait represents the soul of the beautiful Ganymede-like Dorian Gray, whose youth and beauty last to the end, while his soul, like *John Brown*'s, 'goes marching on' into the Wilderness of Sin. It becomes at last a devilled soul. And then Dorian sticks a knife into it, as any ordinary mortal might do, and a fork also, and next morning

'Lifeless but hideous he lay'

while the portrait has recovered the perfect beauty which it possessed . . . If Oscar intended an allegory, the finish is dreadfully wrong."

Though *Punch*'s review laid on humor and censure with a

trowel, it was gentleness itself when compared with the animus in the rest of the magazines. The *St. James's Gazette*, roused on the issue of morality, urged its readers to "chuck" *Dorian Gray* into the fire, and confounding the work with the writer made so personal attack upon him that another would have rushed to the courts with a libel suit. Wilde contented himself with sending out letter after letter, coruscating with paradox, impeccably written, in a vain attempt to teach Mrs. Grundy that art may choose any subject for its purposes and still convert it to beauty. "I am quite incapable of understanding" he reiterated, "how any work of art can be criticised from a moral standpoint. The sphere of art and the sphere of ethics are absolutely distinct and separate."

If Don Quixote had been charging against windmills, Wilde was pitching himself against the British lion—a stubborn beast, with more strength to destroy in each one of its terrible paws when directed by that hard head, than any deadly engine. Wilde's protestations only made matters worse. How, after all, did he expect the outraged public to consider as defensible theories that smelled of the fire and brimstone of their origin? "Bad people are, from the point of view of art fascinating studies. They represent colour, variety and strangeness." That admission in itself was enough to brand the writer who, unabashed, went further: "Good people exasperate one's reason; bad people stir one's imagination." When the critic of the *St. James's Gazette*, a highly moral soul, refused to believe that such creatures as Wilde depicted had a counterpart in life, he brazenly replied: "Quite so. If they existed they would not be worth writing about . . . The superior pleasure in literature is to realise the non-existent."

Wilde was damned not as a writer, for *Dorian Gray*, blown by the wind of scandal, reached thousands of readers who would not else have heard of him, but as a man. No one who knew of him had the least doubt that he was a Dorian Gray and a Lord Henry rolled into one. As the people of the Middle Ages drew away from Dante because they believed he had been in hell, Wilde's contemporaries condemned him for the

168

vision of life he presented in his novel and refused to see its moral. He himself was ashamed of this concession to Mrs. Grundy's pet prejudices. "Yes, there is a terrible moral in *Dorian Gray*," he admitted, "—a moral which the prurient will not be able to find in it . . . Is this an artistic error? I fear it is. It is the only error in the book."

Walter Pater who reviewed the novel of his disciple made much of the moral. Previously he had urged strongly upon Wilde to modify a passage which might have been open to perilous construction. Had he been afraid for Wilde's reputation? And did he perhaps feel some responsibility for the unforeseen development of that soul which, like another Lord Henry, he had seen expanding before his very eyes? Wilde wrote of Lord Henry's way of living as a new hedonism. It was this hedonism that Dorian followed in his urge to live life to the full. A hint of self-extenuation crept into Pater's article: "Dorian himself, though certainly a quite unsuccessful experiment in Epicureanism in life as a fine art is . . . a beautiful creation." The good Oxford master saw in the novel merely an artistically rendered obverse of the Greek belief that beautiful thoughts make a beautiful soul, and a beautiful soul makes a beautiful face.

The Scots Observer spoke out. "Why go grubbing in muckheaps? Mr. Wilde has again been writing stuff that were better unwritten . . . The story—which deals with matters only fitted for the Criminal Investigation Department . . . is discreditable alike to author and editor. Mr. Wilde has brains, and art, and style; but as he can write for none but outlawed noblemen and perverted telegraph-boys, the sooner he takes to tailoring (or some other decent trade) the better for his own reputation and the public morals."

How accurately the Thersites of *The Scots Observer* gauged the public view, and how cruelly the outraged morality of the Calibans would put into effect the advice that Wilde take to some decent trade, a few brief years were to show.

Of all those concerned in the literary storm Wilde alone, especially in the letters he addressed to his critics, kept the coolest head. He was aware of having committed no wrong. In life he might be a *poseur*, a snob, anything his enemies might choose to call him—and they spared no names—but none could impugn his artistic sincerity. However startling his paradoxes, they always contained a germ of truth, apparent even to those who had to test their enjoyment of humor by the microscope. Many found Wilde's charm in the slow, musical tone of his speech, in the voice that would have been music even in uttering the merest commonplace; to them his flashes were the clash of cymbals in some marvelous orchestration. Yet on analysis of the printed page, that music gave evidence of intellectual content as masterly as the mathematical precision of the most conscientious of composers. Wilde was a lord of language, and he was the first to recognize his title. Words to him were the materials of his art. If by their means he built with beauty and sincerity, his artistic conscience—the only conscience he would admit—was satisfied.

When, therefore, *Dorian Gray* was published, greatly amplified, as a book, he ushered it in with a preface in the form of a fugue of aphorisms, derived from his battles with the critics. No artistic credo could have been more explicit. Wilde made no apology. He was what he was, and the fault lay with those who introduced extraneous ethics in their judgment of his work.

"The artist is the creator of beautiful things," he began. "To reveal art and conceal the artist is art's aim." So far so good. Even *Punch* might have nodded approval. It was quite another matter when Wilde asserted: "There is no such thing as a moral or an immoral book. Books are well written, or badly written. That is all . . . The moral life of man forms part of the subject-matter of the artist, but the morality of art consists in the perfect use of an imperfect medium. No artist desires to prove anything. Even things that are true can be proved . . . All art is quite useless."

The closing declaration struck right in the face of Victorian materialism. If all art is quite useless, of what value is art, argued an age that measured worth by percentages? The whole system of nineteenth-century economics was overthrown by those five words affirming that certain productions, which had been found marketable on occasion, indeed, that had a certain monetary value in buying and selling, were—or had to be—quite useless. "Art for art's sake." The phrase was coined and used indiscriminately, its defenders interpreting it as an exaltation of art, its opposers nailing it to the counter as dangerous to established values. As for the statement that there is no such thing as a moral or an immoral book, all right-thinking people shouted in denial. It was the effrontery of a man who because he had offended sought arrogantly to justify his offense. Christian ethics was based on a single great and moral Book. By his contention Wilde was striking at the very basis of moral Christian life. Puritanism remembered and bided its time.

Wilde, if anything, grew bolder in flying in the face of society which insists above everything else, on respect for the prejudices of the majority. Like an eagle, he felt the exhilaration of the storm, and where another would have flown to shelter he sought the densest cloud, for the thrill of the brightness in the lightning flash. Yes, he put his genius into his life, and since genius is a form of godhood, there were no heights or depths forbidden to it. He showed himself less and less with his wife, and more frequently in the company of youths. Shortly after the publication of *Dorian Gray*, he had met a talented young man who might have been the physical counterpart of his hero. By one of those caprices of circumstance, his name was John Gray. "Dorian," Wilde called him, laughing at the consternation he created.

But the boys with whom he was sometimes seen were not all so cultivated as John Gray. To the insinuations of scandal he turned his ambiguous laughter. Harris, not easily shocked, confessed to an unpleasant reaction on coming upon his friend at the Café Royal, sitting at a table with two boys who looked so vulgar that Harris was certain they were no more than grooms. Nevertheless, there was Wilde, talking to them as if they were the flower of British intellect. He was entertaining them with accounts of the Olympic games, describing the golden palaestra, the ivory nudity of the youths, the races, the myrtle wreaths. Harris listened, moved by the evocation of the antique world when one of the boys, in horrible cockney, interrupted:

"Did you sy they was niked?"

"Nude," Oscar answered, "clothed only in sunshine and beauty."

"Oh, my," the boy snickered.

Harris left the table, appalled by the vulgarity, the snickers, and Wilde, Olympian, amid the spawn of a London gutter. But that was the way Harris's unpoetic eye saw it all. To Wilde the two grooms with their rosy-cheeked youth were potential runners in the Greek palaestra; their hair, blown by the wind, might have worn the wreath of myrtle. In itself boyhood was beautiful whether in ancient Greece or in nineteenth-century London. Only an accident of time separated the youths of the past in their sun-drenched nudity from the two lads beside him in their coarse drabness. His imagination, stirred by pagan lore, bridged the centuries, translating to the present a concept which in 1885 had become a crime with its definite name and punishment in the penal code of the realm.

Chapter III: The Lost Generation

LATE in the summer of 1891 two young men came to the door of Number 16 Tite Street. One of them, Lionel Johnson, had been there before; his friend, Lord Alfred Douglas, was making his first visit. They were both of striking appearance. Johnson, at twenty-four, had the face and figure of a boy of fifteen. Slight to fragility, he nevertheless impressed one with a reserve of hidden strength, an intellectual energy that shone out from under his brows with the incandescence of the fire within him. He looked a child, but a wise child, like those infant Christs of the Italian Primitives who bear in their hands the sphere of power and in their gaze the knowledge of all time. He walked, rather, he skimmed the earth, as if his feet like his thoughts were not of it. He was a poet. From New College, Oxford, he had come down to London the previous year, with wings already fully tried in poetry. He had two passions: the Latin classics and the English language; and two mysteries: the Irish Revival which was then coming to the fore, and the Catholic Church toward which he had long been aspiring. At first he had looked toward the priesthood, but since he thought himself of a temper more suited to literature, he abandoned Anglicanism for Rome and vowed himself to poetry. Austerity overlay his work like a sunless sky over a landscape of mingled flowers and ruins. Austerity made him a shadowy crown for his childlike head.

Beside him Lord Alfred Douglas who was only twenty-one seemed like an elder brother although he too had not yet outgrown the charm of the adolescent. He was extraordinarily beautiful—no other word could have been applied to him. His hair of a deep honey color seemed dark against the fairness of his brow. His head was that of a marble of the later Greek period, the sort of head which might have belonged to that Eros whose body, caught in the peak of its boyish grace, trails on

173

the shoulder a long ringlet. There was something in that face too beautiful for a man. The eyes, however, flashed imperious when they were not dreamy. The mouth with its delicate coloring could be scornful. Although of more than middle height, Lord Alfred gave the impression of slightness and delicacy. Like Lionel Johnson he also wrote poetry; a poem of his had appeared the previous year in a literary magazine at Oxford.

Oscar Wilde was delighted with his guests. He took them into his little yellow and red study on the ground floor with its books and its antique cast, and gave them tea. He talked with more than his usual charm, exalted as he was by Lord Alfred's name and position and equally by his beauty. The young man, he learned, was in his third year at Magdalen, his own college. He had as one of his professors an old friend of Wilde's, Warren, who often spoke to Lord Alfred of the days when the author of *Dorian Gray* had walked the quadrangles, pondering some rhyme for his prize-winning *Ravenna*.

Youth was rediscovering Wilde at Oxford, a youth drunk with incense but impatient of the restraints that the soul would put on the body. They were looking for a leader, some one who could make them forget that they were living in an unromantic time, and open wide for them the door to wonderful, yes, dangerous experience. The new youth, however, were tired like the dying century. They wanted their adventure, but not of the active kind that had sent the children of the young century on exploits that defied earth and heaven. Effete, burdened with a causeless disillusionment, they bowed themselves down with the weight of their ennui.

I have outlived my life and linger on . . .

wrote Arthur Symons at twenty-four,

What joy is left in all I look upon?
I cannot sin, it wearies me. Alas!
I loathe the laggard moments as they pass;
I tire of all but swift oblivion.

174

The cry—his and his generation's—rang true, in spite of its echo of Verlaine.

Lord Alfred had been more or less prepared by Johnson for the meeting with Wilde. He had, however, a momentary disappointment. Wilde, in the flashy waistcoats he was again affecting, struck him at first as "comic-looking." He did not like the way the older man began to "make up" to him.[1] But he could not long dislike one who charmed from the moment he opened his mouth to speak, and who, now that he used all his arts to woo, became irresistible. The young man was flattered. And who would not have been? Wilde, the fascinating, the fantastic, the Lord Henry Wotton of his novel was as much captivated by him as Basil Hallward had been by Dorian. It must be glorious to be to an artist what Dorian had been— "the visible incarnation of that unseen ideal whose memory haunts . . . like an exquisite dream."

The two youths finally took their leave, but not before Wilde escorted them to the drawing-room and introduced Lord Alfred to Constance. He lingered on the old romantic name, rolling the syllables on the tongue as if to extract from them the full savor of their tradition. It was a weakness of his, this love of aristocracy. "I love even historic names as Shakespeare did," he defended himself to one who chaffed him. "Surely everyone prefers Norfolk, Hamilton and Buckingham to Jones or Smith, or Robinson." Yet the Joneses and the Smiths were beginning to crop up in his acquaintance with alarming frequency.

There is no record of how Constance behaved on this first meeting with the man who was destined for so dark a part in the drama of her life and Oscar's. Did the occult powers she consulted give her warning? If they did, she said nothing about it. She had grown used to the friendships of her husband. A man had a life of his own to live in which his mate had no share. Every woman knew that, and as the wife of a man of genius Constance extended the boundaries of his ranging. She

[1] Lord Alfred Douglas in *My Friendship with Oscar Wilde*: "From the day when I first met Oscar Wilde . . . he 'made up to me' in every possible way . . ."

drew her happiness from her children to whom, in his own way, Wilde was devoted, and she was satisfied of his fidelity. Sin was a thing impossible to her nature, and perversity inconceivable. Judging everyone by her own purity, a purity that had in it something of ignorance, she saw no evil and therefore thought none. Oscar must have his disciples, the tributaries to his fame, and she asked no questions. It never occurred to her to take more than superficially such aphorisms of his as, "It is better to be beautiful than to be good," and, "I choose my friends for their good looks . . . and my enemies for their brains." Most of his friends had good looks; so far he had no formidable enemies.

Following upon the visit, Wilde received a letter from Lord Alfred. He answered it briefly though graciously. He was frightened. Some inner instinct warned him to beware of the attraction that impelled him toward the young man, and he held away. But he could not be stronger than the strength of his will, all too pliable where pleasure was concerned. After Lord Alfred sent him a poem he answered with less restraint. From then on they saw each other often, dining at the best restaurants together and spending several week ends in Lord Alfred's rooms at 34 High Street in Oxford.

Lionel Johnson looked on and a cloud hung over his face. Had he done well in bringing the two men together? Wilde was a mere literary acquaintance to whose *Dorian Gray* he had written a set of Latin verses—a trifling compliment which a poet may exchange with another. But Alfred was a dear friend. They had both gone to Winchester School; they had read the same books and loved the same things. In Alfred he saw a soul toward which as his senior and as a Catholic he felt a spiritual responsibility. What had he done when he exposed that soul to the wiles of the tempter?

However, Lord Alfred was no innocent, walking blindly to the height where Satan whispered. The Winchester which Johnson remembered tenderly as the cradle of his first aspirations had quite other connotations for Lord Alfred. Besides the place where he had begun to awaken to life, Lord Alfred recalled it as the forcing house of his baser instincts. There had been his friendship with Lionel, and other friendships, equally pure. But there were some which had been neither pure nor innocent.[2] By the time he left Winchester for Magdalen he confessed himself "a finished young blackguard, ripe for any kind of wickedness." Opportunities were not wanting. In Christian Oxford he found many who preferred to live according to pagan ethics. It was daring. It was a revolt against the trivial morality of the despised bourgeois whom Wilde had been trying relentlessly to prick in his foolish self-esteem. Young Oxford welcomed it. From the day of its publication *Dorian Gray* became the handbook of the emancipated.

It gave no little glory to the Oxford undergraduate to have as a friend the man who, against many odds, had succeeded in establishing himself as an influence and a power. The laughter of the mockers had died down. People were beginning to discuss his work as well as himself, though of that subject there could never have been an end. The year the book of *Dorian Gray* appeared, he also published *Intentions*, a volume of essays on which his fame will solidly rest; *Lord Arthur Savile's Crime*, a collection of short stories; and the miniature masterpieces of *A House of Pomegranates*. In February "The Soul of Man Under Socialism" had appeared in the *Fortnightly Review*. The clever social treatise, written with a scintillation that dazzled the Fabians, aroused wonder, discussion and a novel sense of respect. The cavilers found fault with the premises and would have dismissed it for lacking the heaviness always deemed the prime essential of social thought. The young took it to their hearts.

Wilde now possessed everything to appeal to them, even to the banner of an idealism that sought to cure from the root of the social structure. Literary aspirants clustered about him, eager to be discovered. Some time earlier, in an article in the *Pall Mall Gazette*, he had hailed three new poets: Caroline

[2] "But if it is to be assumed by this that I was 'abnormal' or 'degenerate' or exceptionally wicked, then it must also be assumed that at least ninety percent of my contemporaries at Winchester and Oxford were the same." Lord Alfred Douglas, *My Friendship with Oscar Wilde*.

Fitzgerald, Richard Le Gallienne and William Butler Yeats—"My Irish Poet," as Speranza called the new recruit to her Saturday receptions.

Literary coteries flourished, whose members, while drinking English porter, yearned after the absinthe and the larger freedom of France where life could be lived to the full and genius expand. The Rhymers' Club was one of these. In an upper room of the Cheshire Cheese a group of young poets gathered, smoking long clay churchwardens while they listened in the somnolent haze to the latest efforts of their members. Lionel Johnson and his friend Lord Alfred belonged to the Rhymers' Club, and so did Ernest Dowson of the delicate Keats-like face, and Arthur Symons, the ballet enthusiast, for whose sake the meetings were sometimes held in the more mundane precincts of Leicester Square, in a tavern from which he could keep an eye on the stage-doors on either side.

Oscar Wilde in time knew them all, and their friends as well. Like a flame he attracted the young creatures drunk with light who, in their rebellion against cold reality had no thought of the destruction latent in fire. He came to know the artist-prodigy, Aubrey Beardsley with his eternal portfolio under his arm, his dandyism, his sardonic wit, and the way he had of twisting his long lank body like a spider on the arms of chairs. And he met his sister Mabel to whom Aubrey was devoted with the singleness of a man aware that he could never know the normal pleasures of marriage. "What a contrast the two are," Wilde said on seeing them together. "Mabel a daisy, Aubrey the most monstrous of orchids"—to which Aubrey probably responded with a leer of his deathlike face.

He never liked Wilde. He might be a "monstrous orchid"—but it was disease that made him so. With an appetite for life greater even than Wilde's, with the same love of sensation keyed to the pitch of pain, he had been given a body cankered by tuberculosis. He was obsessed by sex. Unable to indulge in its natural expression to the fullness of his desire, he exhausted himself with imaginings. A feverish curiosity led him to the reading of erotica while a preoccupation with his disease brought

178

him, in self-tormenting, to a morbid exploration of medical books. But it was not the knowledge of his malady that he sought. His researches turned most anxiously to the mystery of life. Pictures of the human embryo riveted him to his chair in a terrible hypnosis. He drew it in all stages, employing upon it the subtleties of his marvelous line. Strange foetus-faced monsters crept into his drawings, bulge-browed, with undeveloped limbs folded under them in prenatal involutions. He took delight in presenting humanity's beginning in its most revolting stages. Life? What was it but a caricature, the caprice of a bitter god thrown off in a moment of irony? And yet to create that life people made themselves ridiculous; they committed crimes; they could sometimes be noble. He despised it. And in despising, he admitted how much it meant to him.

From the study of the normal it was but a step to abnormality and vice. He reveled in them. Lusts and strange passions made his mind their playground, and he went among them, a Tannhäuser hardly out of his 'teens, who found nothing shocking, nothing sinful. Like Swinburne he could dream of worse than man's feeble inventions; and in his dreams he was omnipotent.

His immediate acquaintances saw a shy, nervous, self-conscious youth who would unpredictably startle them out of composure by some arrogant outburst. He was far from beautiful. His face, emaciated by disease, had not a little of the fantastic in the beaked sharpness of the nose, full-nostriled and sensitive, in the truculence of the out-thrust underlip, the large spreading ears, the small eyes, slanting like a faun's. As if nature would have added a touch of the preposterous, she gave him hair of a color unknown except to the chemist—an incredible reddish-brown or brownish-red, like nothing ever seen on a human head. Tortoise shell, some called it. Beardsley made the most of it by wearing it like a coif, parted in the middle and drawn down flatly over his immense high forehead. Out of that bizarre frame the unexpectedly ingenuous smile he had for friends and strangers alike shocked as if the curious unreal mask suddenly came to life in the ray of a hidden sun. He dressed immaculately and with an eye to effect, a survival of the early days, perhaps, when with his sister Mabel he had given public recitals on the piano. Music for him was a divine sensuality. It was also a science, mastered so that he could analyze the reasons for its intoxication. He snorted, therefore, whenever Wilde spoke of Chopin's "beautiful sorrows" or of "some mad scarlet thing by Dvorák" who composed "passionate, curiously-coloured things." Himself cruelly sincere, he was intolerant of sham.

Wilde was aware of the fundamental antagonism between himself and Beardsley. The young artist had a strange fixation: that Wilde brought bad luck. He extended the superstition even to Wilde's books which he refused to have near him. Before Beardsley's mocking faun's eyes Wilde lost a little of his ease, and his wit missed fire. There was something intensely disturbing in that youth condemned to die, who burned himself out in a life which he could only live, at best, vicariously, and who had no need of the gracious pose in the grimness of his circumstance.

Ernest Dowson was another of the young men whom Wilde met occasionally in the back room of a public house in Charing Cross Road, the scene of many a Bohemian *cénacle*. Here artists as well as poets convened—the youthful Will Rothenstein whose gravity sent Wilde into gales of merriment, Charles Conder, more at home in Paris than in London, and many another. In the carefree gathering Dowson was the ghost, a tragic figure trailing its mourning to the banquet table. He confided in no one, and his friends, respecting his grief, left him alone with it, reading what they could in his poems where alone he revealed himself.

He was only twenty-four in 1891 but his life was done. The poet alone lived in him, the poet his Adelaide had made when, innocently heartless, she had killed the man. He was a being too delicate for life. Emotions that scarcely touched another man made his soul vibrate with pain. In his imagination he lived in eternities—with love, death and the stars. Then all the accidents of life vanished, and in his dreams he could bear to continue the earthly existence in which he glided, a sleepwalker.

At Oxford as a student he had been avid for sensation beyond the natural by smoking hashish. But it had merely been a schoolboy experiment which ended by convincing him that no power was greater than that of self-induced dreams. Soon after leaving the university he was converted to the Church of Rome. Sincere in his conversion, he was nevertheless attracted by the ritual and the vestments, and most of all by the symbolism that transformed common fact to beauty. He did not feel at home in England. Because of his father's ill health the family had lived much abroad. Italy and the south of France had left their warmth in the boy's blood. His imagination had been stimulated by the vivid life about him. In bleak London he yearned for the scenes of his boyhood, and lacking them found compensation in alcohol. He had to have some form of intoxication to make reality bearable.

For two years he had found it in love. Arthur Symons who knew him at that time remembered him abstracted and more than ever a somnambulist, but one possessed with an ecstatic vision reflected in the gleam of his eyes and the smile that, quick and apologetic, pleaded dispensation for lighting the earth. Who was the immortal who inspired it? His friends were curious, but not a word came from his lips in confidence. They found out at last. The girl for whom he wove his coronals of verse, "violets and leaves of vine," was the daughter of a refugee Italian restaurant keeper in Glasshouse Street, the foreign quarter of London. It was too absurd to believe—Dowson the visionary who wrote with a quill from the wing of some sad cherub, in love with a commonplace little waitress.

They said nothing to him of their shock. He was so happy in his love, and he wrote so beautifully about it. It was as if through passion as fervent as that of some early saint, he had been vouchsafed a sight of the Virgin, so much was there of religion in his worship.

Every evening, like a devotee to his shrine, he used to go to his corner table and wait for Adelaide. Later on, when the dining room was deserted, he would take out his poems and read them to her who sat by, under the eyes of her watchful mother, uncomprehending but graciously smiling. She was a pretty girl, accustomed to compliments from the men who came to dine. There was a waiter, too, an honest decent young man who was very attentive. Meanwhile she sat at the corner table with the poet, nodding, smiling, her thoughts wandering on the soft music of words that came to her with no meaning.

> A gift of Silence, sweet!
>   Who may not ever hear:
> To lay down at your unobservant feet,
>   Is all the gift I bear.
>
> I have no songs to sing,
>   That you should heed or know:
> I have no lilies, in full hands, to fling
>   Across the path you go. . . .

Dowson had no illusions about her love for him. He longed for it as for a gift from heaven, but knew he would never obtain it. He had placed her too high above his orbit. Adelaide and the Virgin both were fused in his devotion; he might only reach upward—in vain. Late at night, leaving the restaurant, his blood tingling from the touch of her hand or perhaps a quick, thoughtless kiss, he would wander about the docks, drinking himself out of human yearning. He could not make Adelaide into flesh. She was virginal and cold to human desire, unapproachable as the moon, and as unresponsive. He could only weep his despair in song. For him there was no hope; she could never understand.

> I would not alter thy cold eyes
>   With trouble of the human heart:
> Within their glance my spirit lies,
>   A frozen thing, alone, apart:
> I would not alter thy cold eyes

After two years of Dowson's impossible worship, Adelaide put an end to it by marrying the waiter. The blow destroyed the lover, but not his love. Adelaide, after all, had been but the vessel into which he poured the pure essence of his adoration. What if the vessel proved unworthy? The gift of love in it made it precious, elevating it to the sanctity of its host.

> Love that is love at all,

the poet sang,

> Needs not an earthly coronal;
> Love is himself his own exceeding great reward,
> A mighty lord!

It was long, however, before he arrived at such resignation. He had first to purge his soul in penance for the shock from which the man had died, but the spirit lived. Abandoning what little hope he had ever had of Adelaide, he hurled himself into all forms of excess. The foulest corners in London now knew the unkempt youth whose deprecating smile suddenly glowed with a strange lost innocence. He looked so small, so young and friendless in the noise of carousing that hardly seemed to reach him, a pallid wayfarer from another world. No one molested him; he troubled no one. Without a word he would empty his glasses and then wander out into the streets, a darker shadow in the shadows. The cabmen's shelters knew him, and the arches under the bridges, frequented like himself by others who had as secret reasons for shunning the bright places. Now more than ever he kept his sorrow to himself, except for the lyric cries addressed to Adelaide. Sometimes he, the wraith, spoke to her, another phantom, in the dim fields of the dead. Sometimes in the houses of the lost he sought her lips, too long denied him, her caresses, never given, in the body of another. In music keyed sad and low he sang all his dead hopes and longings and the pangs of memories that nothing could efface. He was the lost youth of his day, the atoning eidolon of their hunger and their frustration.

183

Eagerly they took up his plaint:

> Last night, ah, yesternight, betwixt her lips and mine
> There fell thy shadow, Cynara; thy breath was shed
> Upon my soul between the kisses and the wine;
> And I was desolate and sick of an old passion,
>   Yea, I was desolate and bowed my head:
> I have been faithful to thee, Cynara! in my fashion.

Adelaide-Cynara: the union was effected between reality and the compensating dream. Because his poem voiced so poignantly the disillusionment of those world-weary though they had barely begun to live; because it sang in Cynara their yearning and their hopelessness, they made it their confession of faith except that they sought the simulacrum in preference to the reality, the wine to the intoxication. With Dowson they could sing their sin and its condoning:

> I cried for madder music and for stronger wine,
> But when the feast is finished and the lamps expire,
> Then falls thy shadow, Cynara! the night is thine;
> And I am desolate and sick of an old passion,
>   Yea, hungry for the lips of my desire:
> I have been faithful to thee, Cynara! in my fashion.

And so the first year of the decade came to an end. Just before its close Arthur Rimbaud, rather, what was left of him, died in a little hospital at Saint-Charles near Marseilles, his face turned to the East that he was nevermore to see. He had come home in search of a cure, obtainable surely, by means of the gold pieces in his belt. He returned only to die. The cancer that had set in at Harrar ate into his flesh, rotted his bones. His leg was amputated and still the malignancy grew, a false limb, gross and horrible, rooting in his living body. Knowing the end near and that the money he had so arduously accumulated was but another illusion against the cruelty of life, he had turned once more toward Harrar where he might die as a Child of the Sun. Too late even for that. With no mourner

184

but a hard old woman who had never understood this prodigious son, and another, in black, his sister, murmuring thanksgiving that the sinner had at last been received into the Church, the maimed body, once so proud, was hidden away in the family tomb at Charleville.

Chapter IV: The Higher Philosophy

ONE night while they were dining at a restaurant together Wilde gave Lord Alfred Douglas a sonnet. It was not the first gift he had made him since their meeting six months earlier, but it was the most complimentary.

> The sin was mine; I did not understand,

it began, progressing to an allegory of the coming of spring, described as an alluring youth.

> But who is this who cometh by the shore?
> (Nay, love, look up and wonder!) Who is this
>   Who cometh in dyed garments from the South?
> It is thy new-found Lord, and he shall kiss
>   The yet unravished roses of thy mouth,
> And I shall weep and worship, as before.

It was delightful. It was subtle and seductive. The young man's head was turned. Here was Wilde, the most prominent literary figure of the day, a poet whose first volume was going into a sixth edition, whose essays furnished brilliance to conversation, whose play, *Lady Windermere's Fan* would soon be having its *première*—here was the wonderful man himself, writing sonnets inspired by him! He did not know that just as during his wooing of Lily Langtry Wilde had made an earlier poem speak for him, he was making a sonnet, published in the *Court and Society Review* for December 13, 1887 serve him in his present suit.[1] To Wilde there was nothing wrong in the deception. The sonnet was lovely; it throbbed with genuine feeling. The young man had no suspicion that he was not its

---

[1] Lord Alfred has not yet discovered the deception for in *My Friendship with Oscar Wilde* he says: "He wrote a sonnet to me, and gave it to me at dinner one night." Elsewhere Lord Alfred refers to the sonnet as the one quoted.

"onlie begetter." Scruples of conscience, therefore, were as unnecessary as they were absurd; for Wilde was practiced in the
ways of seduction.

Late in 1891 he had come across a young clerk at his publisher's office and had been struck by a certain sensibility in
the youth. Edward Shelley loved books. He had a vague ambition to write. When, at the end of a brief period, Oscar Wilde
asked him out to dinner, Shelley felt that some dream of the
Arabian Nights had come true. Later Wilde invited him to
Tite Street. He had him meet Constance and the two little
boys. He gave him copies of his books with flattering inscriptions, and recommended others for his reading. The boy hung
eagerly upon his words, giving him the adoration that was
manna to Wilde's ego. People accused him of cultivating the
society of women and boys instead of addressing himself to
intellectual equals. There was some truth in the charge; but
as Wilde himself would have answered, "Beauty is a form of
genius—it is higher indeed than genius, as it needs no explanation . . . Youth is an art . . . Beauty, real beauty, ends where
an intellectual expression begins."

A few weeks after the preliminaries Wilde invited Edward
Shelley to smoke a cigarette with him, not at Tite Street, this
time, but at a hotel. The boy accepted, in spite of the jibes of
his fellow clerks and the overt references to Mr. Wilde's peculiarities. They had dinner in the main dining room where
champagne of the finest brand flowed freely. Then Wilde suggested that they finish their bottle in his room. The boy remained all night, returning again to see him in the course of
the following day. He was a nervous, high-strung lad. At the
time Wilde was offering Douglas his initiatory sonnet he was
getting bored with Shelley who showed distinct signs of mor-
bidity mingled with moral qualms that had no place in the
practice of the higher philosophy.

Lord Alfred, however, was no bookseller's clerk. One had
to be careful and circumspect. Hence the early friendship established itself on an intellectual footing. The two had much
in common. Both were poets; both had an ego that admitted

no superior. Wilde readily granted the excellence of the verses brought to him by Lord Alfred, but— The reservation spoke much of what he felt in making comparisons with his own. As for Douglas, he knew the value of his work. He had only begun to try his poetic power, but he bowed before no one. At Oxford he was the center of a group of aspiring *literati* clustering about *The Spirit Lamp*, a magazine of which he became the owner and editor. "The New Remorse," Wilde's sonnet, was published in it, with Douglas's verses and contributions which he solicited. Not every undergraduate magazine could boast such a name as Wilde's.

From the first there had been a reciprocal attraction between the two men. Douglas, who had won the two-mile race at the Magdalen College athletics, appealed to the most sensitive in Wilde. For him the youth embodied the ideal he was ever envisioning. He saw him in the athletic field, a Charmides wreathed with victory, clothed only in beauty and sunshine— except that this Charmides was of flesh and blood, and of today. As if his reality were not alone sufficient he was also a poet, a nobleman—and a pagan, for of his own spiritual emancipation Lord Alfred left him in no doubt. The mystical ferment of Oxford that had made Lionel Johnson think of taking orders had had the opposite effect on Douglas. He joined the ranks of the rebels—often the choice of the devout who must first put their souls to the trial and, conquering, align themselves on their true side in the end.

The friendship was not to remain on a platonic plane.[2] Before the year was out Wilde and Douglas flaunted their intimacy without a care for consequences. They gloried in their alliance. Wilde, proud of his aristocratic conquest, took Lord Alfred with him everywhere. In the excitement of the new life college routine became too limited for the youth. He left Magdalen without taking his degree and entered avidly into the scenes that, a Greek of the decadence, his mentor opened out to him. But Douglas was no victim, nor had there been se-

[2] "Familiarities," as Lord Alfred calls them, began about nine months after his meeting with Wilde. See *My Friendship with Oscar Wilde*.

duction in the true sense of the word. He was of age and fully aware of the seriousness of his action. He had had, moreover, other passionate friendships at Winchester and at Oxford, though none of the prominence of Wilde's. With precocious canniness he knew that Wilde was under a mad infatuation, and because he was young and spoilt, he took full advantage of it. In the relation it was Wilde, gentle and weak, who was dominated, and Douglas who ruled, as is often the case; for the one whose love is greater is perforce the weakling, yielding so that the other may be spared.

Lord Alfred came often to Tite Street where Constance began to take his presence for granted. Money was coming in from Wilde's books and from his play at St. James's Theatre. People were beginning to seek out Constance, the great man's wife; there were even little paragraphs in the society papers about her and her "at homes." If, as it sometimes happened when Lord Alfred was present, Oscar turned sharply against her in inexplicable ill temper, Constance excused it on the ground of overwork and the round of activity with which he would let nothing interfere. She might have wished that he spent a little more time at home, or that he saw more of his children and less of Lord Alfred; but she did not complain. She knew he loved the two boys and took delight in their childish ways, telling amusing tales out of the nursery to his literary friends. Vyvyan, he would say, was a thinker. One day he had found the child lying on a sofa. "What are you doing?" he asked.

"Leave me—I am thinking," the little one answered, waving him away with just such a gesture as he himself might have used. It pleased him to see himself in that tiny mirror.

Like Edward Shelley, Lord Alfred received copies of Wilde's books. "From Oscar, To the gilt-mailed Boy" read one of the inscriptions; and another, in *Intentions*, "Bosie, from his friend the author . . . In memory of the higher Philosophy." He loved to call Lord Alfred by the pet name his mother had given him—Bosie, little boy. It was sweet, cajoling, tender and infantine. It suited perfectly his spoilt charm—until something

189

happened to displease him, when he would turn about, his face contorted with rage, a true son of the formidable Marquis of Queensberry. A violent blood surged in him, rising passionately from the heart to the head. Wilde was in terror of these sudden changes that transformed Bosie to something he scarcely knew. Most of the time, however, Lord Alfred was "My own dear Boy" of the letters that filled the gap of their enforced separations.

Wilde could write very charming epistles. When he sat down to them he composed them with the art he put into his poetry, till, moved by the words themselves, he had no care for the meaning which prosaic eyes might derive from them. Besides, they were meant for Bosie's eyes alone.

"My own Boy," he wrote to Lord Alfred from Torquay, on receiving some verses. "Your sonnet is quite lovely, and it is a marvel that those red rose-leaf lips of yours should have been made no less for music of song than for madness of kisses. Your slim gilt soul walks between passion and poetry. I know Hyacinthus, whom Apollo loved so madly, was you in Greek days.

"Why are you alone in London, and when do you go to Salisbury? Do go there to cool your hands in the grey twilight of Gothic things, and come here whenever you like. It is a lovely place—it only lacks you; but go to Salisbury first.

Always, with undying love,
Yours, Oscar."

It was a lovely letter, worthy of being sent by a poet to a poet. But others besides Lord Alfred read it. Pierre Louys, a young French writer whom Wilde had met in Paris, turned it into a sonnet[3] which appeared in *The Spirit Lamp*. Then suddenly,

[3] Lord Alfred echoes the last paragraph of the letter in his poem "In Sarum Close:

> Tired of passion and the love that brings
> Satiety's unrest, and failing sands
> Of life, I thought to cool my burning hands
> In the calm twilight of gray Gothic things."

with others of Wilde's letters addressed to Lord Alfred, it disappeared from his rooms at Oxford.

By some peculiar aberration Wilde who had scarcely been prudent in his dealings with society, now began throwing all discretion to the winds. It may be that his association with Lord Alfred encouraged boldness by lending the seal of nobility to a course of life that could not but fill most people with loathing and horror; it may be, too, that inflated with success, he lost his sense of proportion in a world scrupulously defined between the boundaries of right and wrong, the moral and the immoral.

For a long time in England as well as in the metropolitan centers of Europe, homosexuality had had a subterranean though by no means an obscure existence, to judge by the criminal records. In London, in the first half of the eighteenth century, it had taken such hold that detectives connected with the Old Bailey were planted in the neighborhood of notorious resorts to spy upon its practitioners and bring them to justice. Punishment for sodomy was death, which was known in some instances to have been inflicted. On the whole, however, the courts were satisfied with fining the accused, placing them in the pillory, and sometimes sentencing them to prison. Not infrequently they were reprimanded and acquitted. "Mollies," as effeminate men were called, generally served as subjects for laughter rather than for moral wrath. The philosophers of Greece had not yet been brought forward to lend the sanction of classic tradition to the practice which existed simply and baldly as a sexual derangement, little understood and hardly investigated by the medical profession. "Mollie houses" were as well known as houses of prostitution, and Upper Moorfields became as frequented a place of assignation for pederasts as certain parts of London, Berlin or New York are today.

In 1726 Margaret Clap, or Mother Clap, as the records call her, was brought before the Old Bailey for keeping a Mollie house in Field Lane, Holborn. The case was tried in a matter-of-fact way, with no moral indignation on the part of the public, no fulminating oratory from the judge. It was all in the

191

order of the day. Found guilty, Mother Clap was sentenced to stand in the pillory and to imprisonment for two years; scarcely a ripple disturbed the course of contemporary life. Mollie houses continued; Upper Moorfields remained as popular as ever. "In our country," Smollett has Lord Strutwell say in *Roderick Random* nearly a quarter of a century later, "it (homosexuality) gains ground apace, and in all probability will become in a short time a more fashionable vice than simple fornication."

The passing years proved the prediction true. During the nineteenth century the practice was so widespread that it became the subject of art. It was almost *de rigueur* for marquis or marquise to have an ambiguous friend. Wealthy Englishmen, exhausting the possibilities of home, traveled for their pleasure, finding what they sought in Italy and in the Orient, always a field of exploration for the exotic. There humanity exhibited itself with wonderful candor. No labels of right and wrong marked the lawful or forbidden. One purchased what one required and no questions were asked. Women and men lent themselves to every solicitation, but it was the male who was the more sought after. Flaubert who kept a journal of his Oriental journey in the middle of the century left a description of the "dancing men" of Cairo. Two young scoundrels, dressed in trousers and jacket but with the lower torso exposed, advanced and withdrew to the music of flute and tambourine. Their features were rigid, almost immobile. It was their body that spoke, lascivious, insinuating in the quivering of the abdomen, the undulation of the flanks. "It is too beautiful to excite," he commented. Nevertheless the dancing places were always crowded with foreigners. If anything they gained in popularity as they continued to be discovered by greater numbers of the confraternity. English, French and German visitors predominated.

London society had its extensive circle of homosexuals, become more circumspect since the passing of the Criminal Law Amendment Act of 1885 with its attendant police surveillance of shady resorts. The members knew one another. They frequented certain haunts and shared their information on places of interest in Florence, Naples, Cairo, Biskra. In discreetly masked houses in Pimlico they made their assignations; they had orgiastic parties in the private rooms of Soho restaurants. Although homosexuality at that time was no more prevalent than it had been, the public conscience was awaking to its existence. In 1883 John Addington Symonds began a study of pederasty, later privately printed under the title *A Problem in Greek Ethics*; in 1891 he brought it up to date in *A Problem in Modern Ethics*. Obviously it was a subject which had to be carried into the open.

Oscar Wilde's name came uppermost in the association of ideas. Innuendoes had begun as early as 1881. Now, however, emboldened by his disregard of the most elementary prudence, scandal found matter a-plenty—and not only for speculation. Wilde's *outrecuidance* increased with increase of prosperity. He was well fed, and like the horse in the Italian proverb, he kicked from very surfeit of well-being. Lord Alfred's youthful recklessness egged him on. He must reveal himself a daring idol-breaker before his aristocratic friend; he must show that he bestrode the world with both feet, conculcator of convention. Out of regard for the higher philosophy, respectability became something to be despised; he was above and beyond the judgment of his intellectual inferiors.

His intellectual inferiors, however, failed to see their inferiority. They might not have wit—indeed sobriety has no use for wit—but they did possess positive views on the subject of decency. Wilde affronted those views. Whenever he was seen with his youthful companions at the Café Royal or the Berkeley, men made a point of looking the other way to save themselves the embarrassment of greeting him. They understood nothing of his love of youth. He might reiterate that youth is art, that there is nothing more beautiful than youth: they could see only a gentleman of thirty-seven consorting with grooms and valets in their 'teens. They found the relation evil. What if Wilde pleaded his case in *Lady Windermere's Fan*, saying it was absurd to divide people into good and bad since they were only either charming or tedious, and he preferred to associate with the charming? He and his companions were thrust into moral pigeonholes for judgment when the time should come. It was not for nothing that Victoria had ruled for so many decades.

"England has done one thing," Wilde remarked with more truth than levity. "It has invented and established public opinion, which is an attempt to organize the ignorance of the community, and to elevate it to the dignity of physical force." Nevertheless he seemed to center his effort in flouting public opinion like one who, knowing the violent character of the lion, will persist in teasing it.

He did not always take snubs with docility. Robert Ross invited him one evening to be his guest at dinner with a group of friends. Later they went together to the Hogarth Club of which Ross was a member. The moment they entered one of the men at the club stared pointedly at Wilde and then rose to go. His move was noticed by others, some of whom in turn made as if to follow his example. Wilde took in the situation at a glance. Striding up to the first man he said in a loud voice for the benefit of the assembly: "How dare you insult a member of your own club? I am Mr. Ross' guest. An insult to me is an insult to him. I insist on your apologizing to Mr. Ross." Thus boldly bearded, respectability had no choice but to make excuses. But it bore rancor. "A man cannot be too careful in the choice of his enemies," Wilde was fond of saying. As in everything else, he was the last to follow his own advice.

Little by little Wilde began frequenting places of ill repute in his search for adventurous acquaintance. In October, 1892 a friend of his, the son of Colonel Schwabe, introduced him to a certain Alfred Taylor who was living in an attractive little apartment at Number 13, Little College Street, Pimlico. It was by no means an address to be proud of despite its nearness to the Houses of Parliament; but Wilde, the man who took it as an insult if his friends did not receive him in the best of restaurants or entertain him in the highest style, was frequently to be seen in the neighborhood of Little College Street.

194

Alfred Taylor he found a delightful person and a gentleman. He had been educated at Marlborough School; he played the piano and possessed many gracious accomplishments. He seemed also a young man of some fortune, though in temporarily straitened circumstances, having lost much of the money he had inherited from the cocoa business in which his family was engaged. There was no servant in the apartment, more out of caution, perhaps, than of economy. The rooms were tastefully furnished. At the window no fewer than three pairs of curtains, a dark pair, one of lace and one of art muslin, shut out the vulgar daylight; only the mellowest of candle beams were allowed to fall upon the chairs and the luxurious divan a foot above the floor. The caretaker of the house thought well of her tenant. He was a fine, soft-spoken gentleman, proper and moral. No woman was ever seen to enter his doors. He had an amiable eccentricity. He loved to lounge about in dressing gowns, rather feminine in cut, and he would sometimes wear a wig from his wide collection. One in particular had a brace of braids fully a yard in length. Friends came to see him often. Sometimes he would have parties for them—all nice, good-looking young men. Now and then older gentlemen would come to visit him. He was always prompt in paying his rent; he was, indeed, a perfect tenant. It would have amazed the landlady to learn that her house, particularly Taylor's apartment with its variety of curtains, was suspected by the police.

Who can explain what strange processes were working themselves out in Wilde? He loved Lord Alfred and frequently assured him that his love for him was in essence spiritual. Notwithstanding, the ideal, now realized, did not prevent his seeking pleasure elsewhere. In his complex nature, however, fickleness touched that ideal not at all. The friendship was pure and pagan; it existed on its own plane, unaffected by whatever else might take place in the lower levels of satisfaction. Something had been let loose in his physical and spiritual make-up, resulting in an unbalancing which he had no longer the power to control. The moral guide was dead; he was driving willessly to his destruction, bearing with him everything and everyone connected with him.

And Lord Alfred? The young man, both influencing and influenced, was as blind to the danger as Wilde himself in the stimulation of their friendship. Each egged on the other in a mad pursuit of pleasure—not happiness, for happiness Wilde considered a negative state of being. "Nothing ages like happiness," he would say. "Pleasure is the only thing to live for."

The young man took him literally. But there was a difference in their approach. For all his sophistication, even with Winchester and Oxford behind him, Lord Alfred was comparatively a child in experience. Life which he was seeking in its heightened colors was still new whereas with Wilde it was beginning to be a faded thing. "Sin is the only real color element in modern life," he declared. He looked for that color element to relieve his days of drabness, and derived a perverse pleasure in trying the body with the soul.

As the friendship began to be talked about Lord Alfred's family became alarmed. His mother sent him away to Florence hoping thereby to put an end to Wilde's influence, but when the youth returned the ties were closer than ever. Lord Alfred at that time was as essential to Wilde and his creative impulse as the air he breathed. He had never enjoyed such productivity. Ideas were coming to him in great number; despite the pace of his living he found time to put some of them down.

Suddenly, in the air laden with rumors, the particularly ugly one spread that Wilde was being blackmailed for certain of his letters to Lord Alfred. Evil tongues linked with it Lord Alfred's sudden departure for Egypt as Lord Cromer's honorary attaché, a post which had been obtained for him by his relatives.

This time the rumors were founded on fact. A little before leaving Oxford Lord Alfred had missed a number of letters which Wilde had sent him. He had given a suit of his to a man by the name of Alfred Wood, one of the frequenters of Taylor's little Bohemian apartment, and in the pockets of the suit, it seemed, the letters had been discovered by Wood and his unscrupulous associates. One day, while Wilde was rehearsing at the Haymarket, Beerbohm Tree handed him a copy of the note wherein he, Wilde, spoke of Lord Alfred's "slim gilt soul." The actor looked very grave as he remarked to Wilde that those were dangerous sentiments to have written, since they could so easily be misconstrued.

A few days later Alfred Wood came to Wilde with the letters in question. Wilde paid him thirty pounds—that he might go to America and break away from undesirable acquaintances—and Wood, pocketing the profits of his blackmail, left. On looking through the papers, however, Wilde discovered that the letter of which Beerbohm Tree had shown him a copy was missing. He thought no more of it till one night a fellow by the name of Allen called on him at Tite Street.

"I've got a letter of yours which you ought to have," Allen began, feeling his ground.

"I suppose," said Wilde lightly, "I suppose you have come about my beautiful letter to Lord Alfred Douglas? If you had not been so foolish as to send a copy to Mr. Beerbohm Tree I should have been very glad to pay you a large sum for the letter, as I consider that it is a work of art."

"A curious construction could be put on that letter," Allen insisted.

Wilde, too fully aware of the fact, turned it deftly aside. "Art," he smiled, "is seldom intelligible to the criminal classes."

Allen would not be discouraged. "A man has offered me sixty pounds for it," he said.

"If you take my advice," Wilde answered, "you will go to him and sell my letter to him for sixty pounds. I myself have never received so large a sum for any prose work of that length. But I am glad to find that there is someone in England who will pay such a large sum for any letter of mine."

"The man is out of town," hedged Allen, uneasily.

"He will come back," Wilde comforted him, adding, "I assure you, on my word of honor, that I shall pay nothing for the letter."

The scoundrel then changed his tune. He was very poor, he said; he hadn't a penny.

"Well, I can't guarantee your cab expenses," said Wilde;

197

but feeling sorry for the man who had come to blackmail him, he handed him half a sovereign and showed him out.

He sat down, pondering on the interview and on the mischief the letter might do him, when there was a knock at the street door and another fellow, more disreputable looking than Allen, entered. The scoundrels came in droves! Wilde lost his temper. "I cannot be bothered any more about that letter," he said to the man who announced himself as Cliburn. "I don't care tuppence about it."

"But Allen has asked me to give it back to you," said Cliburn.

"Give it back? Why does he give it back to me?"

"Well, he says that you were kind to him, and that there is no use trying to rent[4] you as you only laugh at us."

Wilde took the letter, very much soiled by the hands through which it had passed. He was aggrieved. "I think it quite unpardonable," he said, "that better care was not taken of an original letter of mine." Cliburn shifted uneasily, whereupon Wilde gave him half a sovereign for his errand. "I am afraid you are leading a wonderfully wicked life," he remarked.

"There's good and bad in everyone of us," said the homely philosopher.

Constance knew nothing of the interviews, nor of the specimens of London's underworld who came to knock on the Tite Street door.

Lord Alfred did not continue long in his diplomatic post and was soon back in England. Lionel Johnson who saw his friend changing before his eyes to a soulless automaton for whom nothing existed but the senses, his bright youth tarnished, his very beauty an evil thing because it inspired evil, went through agonies of conscience for having brought Douglas and Wilde together. Like Beardsley he had been fascinated by Wilde as by some magnificent corrupt force, but he had never liked him. The brilliance he deemed worldly; the attraction Wilde exerted, meretricious. To him the man was Satan walking the earth in one of his disguises. Douglas, on the other hand, he remembered as the boy of the shining hair at Winchester, as

[4] English slang for "blackmail."

198

the youth, dedicated like him, to poetry. In the dark room of his conscience the chiaroscuro was intensified, the white becoming whiter, the black of deepest shadow. Good and evil wrestled before him as in some miracle play; it was evil that conquered.

> I hate you with a necessary hate,

he addressed Wilde in a terrible sonnet.

> First, I sought patience: passionate was she:
> My patience turned in very scorn of me,
> That I should dare forgive a sin so great,
> As this, through which I sit disconsolate:
> Mourning for that live soul, I used to see;
> Soul of a saint, whose friend I used to be:
> Till you came by! a cold, corrupting, fate . . .
> Say you my friend sits by me still? Ah, peace!
> Call you this thing my friend? This nameless thing?
> This living body, hiding its dead soul?

Within himself too, however, good and evil struggled under the dominion of that Dark Angel, the shadow of whose great wings had fallen over the whole generation. A Catholic, he saw it as a tangible being, whispering temptation and pointing with its mighty hand the way to perdition. None could escape its dread solicitations. In vain Lionel Johnson exorcised it in verse.

> Because of thee, no thought, no thing,
> Abides for me undesecrate:
> Dark Angel, ever on the wing,
> Who never reachest me too late! . . .
>
> I fight thee, in the Holy Name!
> Yet, what thou dost, is what God saith. . . .

After all, seeking the anti-self was perhaps part of the divine scheme.

Chapter V: Success

WHEN success had come to Oscar Wilde at last it caught him so unawares that from the shock he lost his self-possession. It was *Lady Windermere's Fan* that had propitiated fortune. On the 20th of February, 1892 when she smiled upon him on the boards of St. James's Theatre, he was so taken aback by the splendor of her ingratiation, so overwhelmed by the plaudits of the fashionable world, that when he was called out to make his curtain speech he did an unforgivable thing: he, the impeccable, the mirror of good breeding, came out before an audience which he had miraculously wooed away from Pinero, Jones and Sydney Grundy, with a half-smoked cigarette in his hand. Nevertheless the enthusiasm of the audience was so great that men and women rose up and cheered as he came forward in his black velvet jacket, lavender trousers, and variegated waistcoat. Again and again the cheers filled the house, giving Wilde time to compose himself for the sally which he knew the public expected.

"Ladies and gentlemen, I have enjoyed this evening immensely," he said with sublime arrogance, and praising his play, congratulated his audience on its good taste. "I feel sure," he ended, "that you estimate its merits almost as highly as I do myself."

He was made. Gone were the precarious days when Constance had had to borrow small sums from her neighbors; gone the hack work and the struggle to keep up appearances. George Alexander, the producer, had a box-office success in *Lady Windermere's Fan*. Oscar Wilde was assured of money and more money as long as he could work the vein which, by the way he felt, was inexhaustible. He had found himself. How far away, how much the work of another man now seemed his first attempts at drama! Comedy was his field. It had been so easy for him to create his play. Most of it he had extemporized.

200

As for the paradoxes and witty sayings, he had already tried them on dozens of delighted listeners. He had only had to set them down. As usual the effort of writing what he talked so easily bored him; but he succeeded in keeping to the grindstone. The finished comedy, however, betrayed none of the drudgery. Spontaneous as a gushing spring, the dialogue flowed fresh and exhilarating, breaking into laughing ripples at self-imposed obstacles, glancing and sparkling in the sunlight of Wilde's wit. The situation was trite; little originality distinguished the plot from many another that had preceded it on the stage. Yet Wilde had made of it a novel thing. He had taken a piece of shoddy, and weaving it with the shimmering threads of his fancy, produced a work of art.

Of course not all the critics praised it. Some of them, accustomed to the Oscar Wilde who stood for the symbol of affectation, dismissed *Lady Windermere's Fan* as another of his amusing trifles. "For the present . . ." wrote one Solomon of this play and of *A Woman of No Importance* which followed it, "we may content ourselves with the reflection that there is no serious danger to be apprehended to the state from the vagaries of a butterfly."

The people, however, had learned to laugh again as a new spirit of comedy pointed out the absurdity of their foibles, their ethics, their high respectability. Not that Wilde set out to preach. He had no concern but to amuse. If the theme of *Lady Windermere's Fan* skirted on the moral, and if *A Woman of No Importance* contained a mild indictment against society for its treatment of the unmarried mother, it was not because Wilde saw himself as a social critic: the subjects lent themselves to dramatic treatment, that was all. Once he had the armature he could model his creation upon it, making a Galatea where the prosy dramatists before him had succeeded only in producing moral scarecrows. He had no thought for absolute reality. His Lord Darlington and Lady Windermere, his Mrs. Arbuthnot and Lord Illingworth traveled in a world of their own which was yet recognizable as the fashionable society in which Wilde was most at home. His characters, highly artificial, were nonetheless alive, acting, moving and talking in a manner that life itself might have envied.

Indeed, before long all London society coruscated with conversational sparks borrowed from Wilde's fire. "Nowadays to be intelligible is to be found out," people quoted from *Lady Windermere's Fan.* "London is full of women who trust their husbands . . . They look so thoroughly unhappy . . . Nothing looks so like innocence as an indiscretion . . . What is a cynic? A man who knows the price of everything and the value of nothing." One could be daring with impunity and brilliant without taxing one's brains. "What are American dry goods?" one would ask another after *A Woman of No Importance.* And the answer came back: "American novels." How delightfully turned, and how well calculated to fill the British breast with consciousness of superiority!

It was amazing how much Wilde knew about women. "Twenty years of romance make a woman look like a ruin; but twenty years of marriage make her look like a public building . . . Men always want to be a woman's first love . . . Women have a more subtle instinct about things. What they like is to be a man's last romance . . . Women love us for our defects. If we have enough of them, they will forgive us everything, even our gigantic intellects . . . The history of women is the worst form of tyranny the world has ever known. The tyranny of the weak over the strong." Thrilled, the women acclaimed him. As "sphinxes without secrets" they enjoyed being made much of, even if sometimes with a spice of malice. They were being noticed, and that was what counted. Gradually they were emerging from the Pre-Raphaelite languors imposed upon them. Burne-Jones' bloodless maidens were becoming a trifle outmoded with the advent of the artistic sophisticate. It was Wilde who managed her debut as in the 1880's he had managed Beauty's.

Harris who attended Wilde's triumphant first night did not have to wait for the final curtain to know that a vivifying wind had passed over British drama. Himself a small tornado, he huffed and he puffed in the circle of the critics in the foyer, attempting to sweep them off their feet. But nothing could budge the huge bulk of Joseph Knight, as stolid within as he was solid without.

"I might say in Oscar's own peculiar way," he said, " 'Little promise and less performance.' " And he exploded into a guffaw appreciative of his own wit.

"That's the exact opposite of Oscar's way," Harris retorted. "It is the listeners who laugh at his humor."

"Come, now," Knight insisted, unwilling to grant that Wilde could transcend his popular repute. "You cannot think much of the play."

"I have not seen the whole play," said Harris. "But so far it is surely the best comedy in English, the most brilliant— isn't it?"

That was too much for Knight. "Ha! Ha! Ha!" he laughed. "*Lady Windermere's Fan* better than any comedy of Shakespeare! Ho! Ho!"

Harris rose to his full five feet and some inches, and with the uproarious voice that should have belonged to a Gargantua, defended the work of his friend. "Yes," he insisted, "wittier and more humorous than *As You Like It* and *Much Ado*. Strange to say, too, it is on a higher intellectual level. I can only compare it with the best of Congreve, and I think it's better."

Perhaps in the privacy of his rooms he offered up a prayer for forgiveness to Shakespeare who was one of his divinities, but in public he maintained his championship of Wilde. Independently of Harris, however, others began making literary comparisons. If Wilde was not the peer of Shakespeare, he was certainly comparable to that other witty Irishman, Sheridan. And as he repeated his first success, he received a full measure of intellectual acclaim. William Archer placed him in a niche apart from other living dramatists, not alone for his wit or his paradoxes.

"It is (for) the keenness of his intellect," he wrote, "the individuality of his point of view, the excellence of his verbal style, and above all, the genuine dramatic quality of his inspirations."

One thing more remained to achieve for unquestioned triumph, and wonder of wonders, it was accomplished! Through Mrs. Ada Leverson, one of Wilde's most sympathetic admirers, *Punch* declared a truce on its belaborings and opened up its columns to her clever parodies of Wilde's wit.

Wilde could scarcely believe his good fortune. He took it as a gift of the gods, but he could not help wondering why it came through his plays rather than through others of his writings which he considered of greater literary worth. The workings of chance always left him in awe, though its fruits he took gladly with both hands, reaching out for more in his insatiable desire. Mischance, indeed, frustration of any kind, left him resentful yet powerless. He would have wanted life to be a road pleasantly shaded against inclemency, opening out, as one advanced, more and more glorious prospects. Even though his two heroes, Christ and Bonaparte, had taught him that in the one case the end was Calvary and in the other the rock where the Eagle rotted in chains, he deluded himself with the hope that with him it would be different. He, the Lord of Life, would carve his way to the summit where Beauty lay revealed. He would not know defeat. Nevertheless, in the depths of his being an obscure fear gave warning. He heard it in his rare silences; sometimes it spoke to him through his own mouth in allegories that held meaning through indirection. What crown of life excelled the crown of martyrdom? Christ without His thorns, Bonaparte without his chains— would they have lived on to tenant the souls of men forever?

"Now when the darkness came over the earth," a prophetic Wilde would speak, "Joseph of Arimathea, having lighted a torch of pinewood, passed down from the hill into the valley. For he had business in his own home. And kneeling on the flint stones of the Valley of Desolation he saw a young man who was naked and weeping. His hair was the colour of honey, and his body was as a white flower, but he had wounded his body with thorns and on his hair he had set ashes as a crown.

204

And he who had great possessions said to the young man who was naked and weeping, 'I do not wonder that your sorrow is great, for surely He was a just man.' And the young man answered, 'It is not for Him that I am weeping, but for myself. I too have changed water into wine, and I have healed the leper and given sight to the blind. I have walked upon the waters, and from the dwellers in the tombs I have cast out devils. I have fed the hungry in the desert where there was no food, and I have raised the dead from their narrow houses, and at my bidding, and before a great multitude of people, a barren fig-tree withered away. All things that this man has done I have done also. And yet they have not crucified me.' "

Wilde felt keenly one disappointment in the midst of his triumph—his failure to have his play *Salomé*, produced either in England or in France. He had written it in French in 1891. For some time, especially since his reading of *À Rebours* with its descriptions of Moreau's paintings, the vision of Salomé had come before him, haunting him as it had haunted des Esseintes, except that to her jeweled nakedness was added the perverse innocence of Flaubert's daughter of Herodias. Wilde admired Flaubert's rendering of the story and he had read it carefully. The archaeological magnificence of *Hérodias* seemed to carry over to the nineteenth century the lust and strange cruelties of a Byzantium whose colors Moreau had fixed forever in those great dream canvases instinct with perversity. Flaubert's and Moreau's became one with Wilde's vision of Salomé, Flaubert's infantine princess with her childlike hesitancies borrowing in her rebirth Moreau's suggestion of sin. Flaubert's heroine was tortured with no lust for Jokanaan. She was the guileless instrument of her mother's revenge, dancing her dance at the bidding of Herodias and asking her monstrous reward in words that, from the uncertainty with which she uttered them, betrayed their source:

"I will that you give me in a charger the head . . . (she had forgotten the name, but she continued, smiling)—the head of Jaokanann."[1]

[1] Flaubert, *Hérodias*.

Wilde was obsessed with the innocence of Salomé. In his transforming mind, however, it became an evil chastity, a sin blacker than any lust. For that matter there was nothing novel in the transvaluation. Since the dawn of romanticism it had become a well-established axiom that nothing is so sinful as innocence. Salomé, therefore, was chastity rotting at the core, innocence violating itself with dreams. Wilde needed but the language in which to make his Salomé speak. He found it in Maeterlinck whose *Princesse Maleine* and *Les Sept Princesses* talked a simple unreal idiom, as of beings in a trance. Nothing is ever exact. All is a repetitious allusiveness, a childlike babbling pitched in a low key yet irresistibly moving, a language of nuance, the overtones saying what the words fail to express.

Consummate artist that he was, Wilde adopted the speech and made it his by imparting to it the quality of his poetic prose. The story grew in his mind, Salomé attaining imaginative reality with the Tetrarch, superstitious and fearful, with the evil Herodias, and the prophet Jokanaan, at first a voice uttering imprecation upon the daughter of Babylon, then the terrible apparition, thin as an ivory statue, with eyes like black holes burned by torches in a tapestry of Tyre, black as lakes troubled by fantastic moons. . . . The characters took on life; they lived their drama, Herodias devoured with vengeance against the prophet who cursed her, Salomé consumed by the lust engendered on her virginal body by the chastity of Jokanaan. "He is like an image of silver. I am sure he is chaste as the moon is. . . ." Here was Wilde's central theme: the love of the princess Salomé for the man of God.

As was his way, before he sat down to his writing Wilde had first to be kindled by his immediate audience. In Paris, one day, he was surrounded by a group of young French writers, Adolphe Retté, Stuart Merrill the American Frenchman, and a number of others. He told them his play, his imagination taking fire from the rapt silence of his listeners. Clothed in the living word, his characters started to life; new figures came into being, the young Syrian with his hopeless love for Salomé, the disputatious Jews, the Nazarenes, all playing their part in that drama of lust and death. Over them, chill, white and chaste, floated the moon, ruling their actions like an implacable destiny.

Back in his rooms at the hotel, he began writing his play. It was mid-afternoon. For hours and hours he sat, filling the blank pages with the flood of his inspiration. The *garçon* came to light the gas lamp, and still Wilde wrote, possessed by Salomé who in turn, influenced by the moon, burned in the white heat of unutterable desires.

"I am sure she is a virgin," the princess speaks. "She has never abandoned herself to men." Like herself. But the voice of the prophet has rumbled from the depths of the cistern where he is imprisoned, and the sound of that voice has left her body shaken like the string of a lyre that passion has plucked. She must see the prophet; she must behold the mouth that had such power to move her, even though it uttered nought but curses. Jokanaan is brought out of the cistern. "Oh! How strange the moon looks. Like the hand of a dead woman who is seeking to cover herself with a shroud. . . ." Fascinated, Salomé draws near him. "Ah, but he is terrible, he is terrible! . . . How wasted he is . . . Jokanaan! . . . I am amorous of thy body, Jokanaan! Thy body is white like the lilies of a field that the mower hath never mowed. Thy body is white like the snows that lie on the mountains of Judaea. . . . Suffer me to touch thy body."

Monotonous as a chant Salomé's words hypnotize her senses till she is oblivious of everything but her passion, growing with the spell of her utterance. As the prophet repulses her, ardor and revulsion seize upon her, till love becomes hate and hate love, and the object of her lubricity at once wonderful and horrible. "Thy body is hideous. . . . It is like a plastered wall where vipers have crawled. . . . It is like a whitened sepulchre full of loathsome things. . . . It is thy hair that I am enamoured of, Jokanaan. Thy hair is like clusters of grapes, like the clusters of black grapes that hang from the vine-trees of Edom. . . . The long black nights, when the moon hides her face, when the stars are afraid, are not so black as thy hair. . . . Suffer

207

me to touch thy hair. . . . Thy hair is horrible. . . . It is like a knot of serpents coiled round thy neck. I love not thy hair. . . . It is thy mouth that I desire, Jokanaan."

The kiss becomes a terrible fixation. "Suffer me to kiss thy mouth. . . . I will kiss thy mouth, Jokanaan!" The young Syrian kills himself before her eyes, but not even death can swerve her from her compelling desire. "Suffer me to kiss thy mouth, Jokanaan. . . . Suffer me to kiss thy mouth. . . . I will kiss thy mouth, Jokanaan." Again and again, through the words of the page boy mourning the immolation of his friend, through the warnings and curses of Jokanaan, pierces Salomé's desire, blood-red as the sword of passion that has ravished her chill chastity. From now on she lives for that kiss alone. Parched with lust, the lips of the virgin must slake themselves on the mouth of the saint.

Not Flaubert with his immense lore, not Moreau with his imagination loose amongst heraldic luxury, had been able to read such meaning in the story of Salomé. Flaubert for all his artistry had only amplified with scholarly embellishment the sixteen verses in the gospels of Matthew and Mark; Moreau had lingered only on the details of the dance, preparing for that moment when with one hand outstretched in imperious command and with the other holding to her face the mystic lotus, Salomé, poising on her toes the wonder of her body, gives promise in the first vibration of her resplendent robes that the Tetrarch will look upon it bare.

It was near midnight before Wilde who had not ceased writing since the afternoon, realized that he was feeling faint from hunger. He had reached the dance of Salomé; he must release his tension before he could go on with the rest of the play. The Grand Café was at the corner of the Boulevard des Capucines and the Rue Scribe, not far from his hotel. Leaving his notebook open, he walked to the café. As usual the tables were crowded, for Rigo, the leader of the gipsy orchestra was playing. Wilde gave the *garçon* his order and then called Rigo to him. "I am writing a play," he told him, "about a woman dancing with bare feet on the blood of a man who has slain himself for her sake, while she is craving to kiss the lips of another whom she loves and so must die. Play me something in harmony with my thoughts."

Rigo played. He drew such wild and terrible music from his *tziganes* that all talking ceased and the people looked at one another as if some doom were impending. Then Wilde returned to his hotel and wrote till he had finished his play.

He sustained the mood to the end. Over the indefinite yet sumptuous landscape the moon with animate purpose directs the drama's weird unfolding. Frightened, the Tetrarch cowers at every change that comes over her face. "She is like a madwoman who is seeking everywhere for lovers. She is naked, too. . . . She reels through the clouds like a drunken woman. . . ." Like Salomé, reeling in the dominion of her passion. The Tetrarch must be amused. Will Salomé dance for him? "Whatsoever thou shalt desire I will give it thee, even to the half of my kingdom. . . . Ah! look at the moon! She has become red. She has become red as blood. . . ." And in blood, in the bitter taste of death, Salomé spent from her dance, her dove-white feet ruddy from the spilt life of the prophet, slakes her desire on his dead mouth. "Ah! I have kissed thy mouth, Jokanaan, I have kissed thy mouth." The cry of her triumph resounds through the darkness as a great cloud crosses the moon.

Wilde came very close to writing a masterpiece. As a drama *Salomé* had its limitations, but they were defects inherent in the decadent school—too high an emotional pitch, a rarefied unreality like a moral swamp whose miraculous blooms exhaled poisons that made men mad, and a brooding immobility, the trance of the anchorite whose fixed state beholds what the soul may not see and survive. The characters in the play were not human beings but incarnate passions. Salomé herself might have been an embodied holiness, a sister to Jokanaan. She is likened to a dove, to a narcissus trembling in the wind, a silver flower. The mystery of white things clings to her. She is the shadow of a white rose in a mirror of silver. She is the saint whose desert loneliness, troubled by the demons of imagination, succumbs to the lure of sin, and in saving the soul loses it utterly. Salomé sought to fathom the mystery of love and death. From the severed head of Jokanaan on the shield before her she learns what she had sought. "Well I know that thou wouldst have loved me, and the mystery of love is greater than the mystery of death."

Sarah Bernhardt upon hearing the play read, saw herself at once as the daughter of Herodias. The language was exquisite. As on a pattern of *mille fleurs* in some elaborate tapestry the poetic imagery enhanced the central design. The French was of the simplest, yet by the cunning use of his limited instrument Wilde was able to draw such music as made his poet friends wonder and admire. There were a few crudities here and there, but on the whole the cadences had a Biblical majesty and the *décor* the grandeur of the scenes painted with simple art on the tombs of the Kings. Sarah Bernhardt was responsive to the spirit. "The word," she said, "must fall like a pearl on a crystal disc. There must be no brusqueness of motion, only stylized attitudes." With the eye of the artist she had caught the quality of the drama whose inception lay in the immobile splendors of Moreau.

Salomé went into rehearsal with Sarah Bernhardt in the title role and M. Albert Darmont as Herod. It was to have its opening at the Palace Theatre, London. The settings were planned, the costumes designed, but suddenly, when the play was ready for production, the Lord Chamberlain refused to license it because of the old bugbear that it introduced Biblical characters. Wilde was beside himself. After the success of *Lady Windermere's Fan* a few months earlier, the prohibition of the censor came as a covert attack upon his morals, and it was so that Wilde took it.

"I shall publish *Salomé*," he defied. "No one has the right to interfere with me, and no one shall interfere with me . . . The action of the censorship in England is odious, and ridiculous."

Indeed, what could be said of a board that prohibited the showing of Gounod's *Queen of Sheba* and Rubinstein's *Judas Maccabaeus* and gave its sanction to the dramas of Sardou? Worse, at that very time a burlesque on Wilde, *The Poet and the Puppets,* was running at the Comedy Theatre without any protest from the censor who saw no wrong in having a prominent literary man ridiculed before initiated audiences as "O'Flaherty, a poet."

Wilde had taken the burlesque good-naturedly as grist to the publicity mill. Charles Brookfield, however, had written it with malice. He had a detestation of Wilde amounting to monomania. Once they had been fast friends. Then they quarreled, and when the quarrel was made up, though it left Wilde as genial as ever, it rankled with Brookfield till every success of Wilde's affected him as a personal defeat, every word of praise as a rebuff to his own clever but limited talents. There had never been rivalry between them: the forces were too unequal. Brookfield, nevertheless, considered himself Wilde's superior and grudged him every triumph that came his way. With social address that he thought greater than Wilde's, a facility which could turn out a play in a few days, and a gift for ridicule that gave him a certain popularity on the stage, he considered his comparatively obscure position as an injustice on the part of fortune, and therefore hated fortune's darling. It was an obsessive hate. He could hardly be in anyone's company for a moment without bringing up the subject of Wilde and expatiating upon it with unconcealed rancor. Whatever the quarrel it must have had deep roots.

At first Wilde took the Lord Chamberlain's action so much to heart that he made the mistake of losing his temper. He would leave England and settle in France, he said; he would renounce his British citizenship and become a naturalized Frenchman. How could he continue living in a country that showed such narrowness in its artistic judgment? "I am not at present an Englishman," he announced. "I am an Irishman, which is by no means the same thing . . . I shall transfer myself to another fatherland . . . There is only one Paris . . . and Paris is France. It is the abode of artists . . . To me there are only two languages in the world: French and Greek."

Immediately a giant laugh rang through the tight little island. Wilde a French citizen? Ridiculous! The *Pall Mall Budget* that June relished the joke, showing Wilde as "Monsieur Vilde" a French abbé. *Punch* for July 9 made of him a French conscript carrying in his knapsack the despised *Salomé*. "A Wilde Idea. Or more injustice to Ireland," ran the caption. Even the staid William Watson used his classical stylus to indite for the *Spectator* a heavy-handed mock threnody.

When the laughter died down Wilde remained a British subject, and only *Salomé* left with Sarah Bernhardt for Paris where the diva promised to produce the play in her own theatre at the Porte St. Martin. Easily swayed by the whims of chance, and not immune to public opinion, Mme. Bernhardt thought it best to mark time before putting through an expensive production that might loose as troublesome a hornets' nest in Paris as it had in shopkeeping London. As the weeks and then the months passed, she enjoyed less the prospect of the risk she might run, and answered evasively Wilde's inquiries. Finally *Salomé* was avoided as a topic of correspondence and there was no more question of the word dropping like a pearl on a crystal disc.

Wilde had to content himself with publication. But before the manuscript left for the printers he decided to have the French text edited. Stuart Merrill had the first trial. He found it no easy task to have the author agree to his corrections. For example, almost all the long speeches began with the expletive *enfin*. "*En ai-je assez biffé des enfin!*" exclaimed the harassed editor. Wilde, however, doubtless because Merrill had been born in Long Island and was therefore no true Frenchman, had no great confidence in him, whereupon the young man turned over the manuscript to Retté. If possible, Wilde trusted Retté even less. Before *Salomé* finally passed for the press, it had been doctored by Pierre Louys and last of all by Marcel Schwob. "*A mon ami Pierre Louys*" read the dedication of the tasteful volume in its bright purple wrappers lettered in silver.

While still at Oxford Lord Alfred Douglas had made a translation of *Salomé* at Wilde's request and for friendship's sake he also published an article on the French play in his undergraduate paper. The translation was a labor of love, and with infinite skill Lord Alfred chose a medium in keeping with the somber theme. Strangely enough Wilde was not pleased, calling it a schoolboy exercise, and when Aubrey Beardsley came to him assuring him that he could make an excellent translation of the play since he felt such kinship with the spirit of it, Wilde gave him a free hand. Alas, when Beardsley brought in his drudgery of a month Wilde could hardly conceal his disappointment. "Utterly hopeless," he confessed to Lord Alfred whose translation, after some revision, he brought to Mathews and Lane for publication.[2] Aubrey Beardsley was commissioned to illustrate it.

He had already done one drawing. After the French version had appeared, sending a chill down the spine of those who read the exultant cry of Salomé: *"J'ai baisé ta bouche, Iokanaan, j'ai baisé ta bouche,"* Beardsley made an illustration of it, putting into his masses of black and white such subtleties of evil and sadism that everyone who saw it in *The Studio* accompanying Joseph Pennell's article on him was divided between awe of the subject and horror of the illustrator. Elkin Mathews and John Lane, however, knew that here they had found their man. At the sign of the Bodley Head in Vigo Street they had recently established themselves as publishers of *belles lettres* and of such brave, original books as received little encouragement among the timid ones of the trade. They took pride in the beauty of their work, and already their reputation was being made by people of taste who, frightened away by the too great solemnities of Morris's Kelmscott Press, wanted their literature new, bold and beautiful. What better combination than Wilde and Beardsley?

Wilde, however, was ill at ease. He could not understand the originality of Beardsley's art and mistrusted it. The veiled indecencies that found their way into the drawings, the elaborate sex symbolism running like a recondite text through the decorations, repelled his beauty-loving nature. He experienced a phys-

[2] Robert Ross in the appendix of Frank Harris' *Oscar Wilde* writes: "Douglas' translation omits a great deal of the text and is actually wrong as a rendering of the text in many cases. . . . I believe Douglas is to this day sublimely unconscious that his text, of which there were never more than 500 copies issued in England, has been entirely scrapped; his name at my instance was removed from the current issues for the very good reason that the new translation is not his."

Lord Alfred Douglas has disavowed the translation in *My Friendship with Oscar Wilde*. "I do not regard the present translation, which is usually attributed to me . . . as mine at all . . . I think my own translation, as a matter of fact, was much better."

ical revulsion at the lovingly drawn hideous abortions, at the leering dwarfs lolling their tongue before the gauze-clad body of Salomé, at the blood treated as an ornamental medium, at the grotesque and the decadent where he had intended the strange and the subtle. What if in the purity of his line, in the tender, drooping body of the dead Salomé, Beardsley had gone as far as an artist could go in technical perfection? Wilde, to whom the content in this case meant more than the execution, saw only the two abhorrent monsters thrilled with lust at the beautiful dead nudity in their arms.

"Dear Aubrey's designs," he said, "are like the naughty scribbles a precocious schoolboy makes on the margins of his copy books." He resented having his *Salomé* so used. In Beardsley's presence he was more tactful with his criticism, although it took no keen psychologist to detect the basic dislike.

"Absinthe is to all other drinks what Aubrey's drawings are to other pictures," he said one night when he, Beardsley and a number of friends were drinking together. "It stands alone . . . it has about it the seduction of strange sins. It is just like your drawings, Aubrey. It gets on one's nerves and is cruel. Baudelaire called his poems *Fleurs du Mal*. I shall call your drawings *Fleurs du Péché*—Flowers of Sin."

Beardsley thought his private thoughts. Secretly he was ambitious of literary fame, and Wilde's unceremonious rejection of his translation rankled, especially since he disliked the play. He took a schoolboyish revenge in his drawings by introducing caricatures of Wilde in "The Woman in the Moon," "Enter Herodias," "The Eyes of Herod," wherein he made him particularly repellent, and in the "Platonic Lament."

A number of drawings were canceled as too bold at the request of the publishers. One, "Enter Herodias," in its early form came into the hands of Frank Harris with Beardsley's inscription:

> Because one figure was undressed
> This little drawing was suppressed.
> It was unkind, but never mind,
> Perhaps it all was for the best.

214

Chapter VI: Enter the Marquis of Queensberry

JOHN SHOLTO DOUGLAS, Marquis of Queensberry, at last came upon the stage in the private drama of his son Lord Alfred and Oscar Wilde. He was a violent man. The representative of a family that was a thousand years old or more, he still blustered, "the dark gray man" of fantastic adventure, whose deeds of derring-do had livened many a page of Scott's romances. But there was nothing chivalric about Queensberry. A man of much natural endowment, he made little of his gifts, taking an evil pleasure in encouraging all that was dark and passionate in his nature. His father, it was suspected, had committed suicide. At any rate he was found shot in the family park at Kinmount, Dumfrieshire. Queensberry succeeded to the title.

He was a stocky man of middle height, vigorous and younger-looking than his years, his ruddy cheeks clean shaven but for a streak of fiery red whisker matching his thinning hair. He dressed like a sportsman. In his younger days he had been an amateur lightweight boxing champion and author of the famous Queensberry rules. He was also an adroit horseman, but so reckless that there was hardly a bone in him that had not been broken by some fall during his hunting and steeple-chasing. With his equals he had a bluff courtesy ill concealing, however, an irritable temper that needed but a word to rouse it to combativeness. Toward inferiors he acted with aristocratic insolence. His sullen face, energetic in spite of the drooping underlip, caught a lurid fire from his eyes. He was a man to watch and to beware of. Many stories were current of his captiousness. At the House of Lords he had lost his seat as a Scottish representative peer for refusing to take the oath on the ground that he was an atheist. It was a sore point with him. On another occasion when Tennyson's *Promise of May* was given at the Globe Theatre, he had got up in his box and interrupted the performance, shouting his agnosticism and condemning the play for going counter to his unbelief. He dared everything and was afraid of nothing in a disregard of conventions that had in it something more than the aggressiveness of his rank. He was a fine instrument turned to evil uses, a Scott hero gone to the devil.

In 1887 he had been separated from his long-suffering wife, whose gentle nature found solace in her favorite son Alfred whom she spoiled. The marriage had never been a happy one. A household tyrant, the Marquis of Queensberry believed in exercising authority while offering the worst examples for his children to follow. As it was, they saw little of him, his horses, dogs and women taking up more time than he could spare for them. Weeks, sometimes months, passed before he put in an appearance. Finally he took rooms in London, visiting his family for a night or two whenever he remembered it. He made no mystery of his affairs. Patiently Lady Queensberry bore his infamous treatment, but even her forbearance could stand no more when the Marquis suggested bringing his latest mistress to his wife's house and forming a *ménage à trois*. In 1893 he married a Miss Ethel Weedon, a girl some thirty years younger than himself. The new marriage already showed signs of heading toward the rocks.

Lord Alfred had never loved his father. As a boy he had had a great admiration for the picturesque in his seemingly heroic exploits, but he had not been close to him. Later, when he began to understand the enormity of his behavior toward his mother, he turned against him, loyally clinging to the woman whose favorite he had always been. Queensberry hated his wife. Like all those whose consciousness of guilt will not let them rest, he turned it to resentment against her whom he had wronged, and against those through whom he could hurt her. Lord Alfred, naturally, came first to his mind. Father and son saw each other occasionally. By one of those freaks of comedy which relieve even the grimmest circumstances, John

Sholto Douglas, eighth Marquis of Queensberry, appeared as a poet in that same *Spirit Lamp* which had published Wilde, Lord Alfred and Pierre Louys!

Queensberry had met Wilde at a gathering years earlier when the young Professor of Aesthetics had come down from Oxford. Neither had had anything to say to the other. Once again, in November, 1892, chance brought them together at the Café Royal, when Queensberry happened to come into the dining room while Wilde and Lord Alfred were lunching there. At first on seeing them he had sat at his table, sullen and forbidding, not from any suspicion of illicitness in the friendship of his son and Wilde, but because of the gossip of the clubs that found the author—as who did not?—a richly rewarding topic. Lord Alfred after a few minutes invited his father to Wilde's table, whither Queensberry allowed himself to be led. In no time Wilde had engaged him in lively conversation—of all topics, on atheism! The minutes passed, and still Wilde and the Marquis pursued the fascinating subject, the Marquis warming toward the man whom he had begun by heartily disliking. Lord Alfred became impatient, then bored, as the minutes turned to hours. Finally he was obliged to excuse himself because of an appointment, and left his friend and his father together, still in the heat of argument. Wilde had made another conquest.

It was no surprise to Lord Alfred to receive a letter from Queensberry shortly after the accidental meeting, assuring his son that Wilde was "perfectly all right," and that he had misjudged him. Unfortunately Queensberry was exposed to influences even stronger than Oscar's charm, influences that pleaded in the name of propriety and morals. Who was he to ignore the props on which stood the peerage and Britannia's empire? For the time, however, the Marquis took no action.

It was from Percy, Lord Douglas of Hawick, Alfred's elder brother, that had come the first inklings of uneasiness with regard to the growing intimacy between the two men. Lord Douglas knew Wilde and liked him; he knew, as well, a number of his acquaintances. However, when rumor began having sinister repercussions, he sent his brother a tactful letter pointing out the dangers. Then Lady Queensberry sent her relative, George Wyndham, on a mission to Wilde who acquitted himself so well during the interview that Wyndham left fully convinced of the innocence of the friendship. How could he doubt the word of a gentleman who, looking him straight in the eye, had answered satisfactorily to the embarrassing questions put him? Nevertheless Lady Queensberry was still uneasy. It was then that she contrived to send her son abroad.

Wilde, indeed, had begun to have forewarnings of what his acquaintance with Lord Alfred might entail. Before the young man was expedited on his journey Lady Queensberry herself had discussed the step with Wilde who readily concurred in it, for his own sake as well as for Lord Alfred's. Wilde, it is true, had enjoyed a creative resurgence in consequence of the friendship. At the same time the presence of Bosie, bidden and unbidden, often usurped the solitude required by his writing. The young man, mad for pleasure and exacting of time and money with the thoughtlessness of his years, basked in his friend's success without considering that it came as a result of hours spent in lonely labor. He was forever suggesting that Wilde take him on trips abroad, to pleasure resorts and expensive watering places.

In his infatuation Wilde weakly acquiesced, putting aside his half-finished plays in pursuit of the beauty that enslaved him. Often, however, Lord Alfred showed himself far from beautiful. At the least pretext, if he were crossed or if Wilde did anything to displease him, he would fly into a fury and make scenes before the helpless man, a bewildered pachyderm goaded by a brilliant, maddening, savage creature. After one such altercation he wrote Lord Alfred a pathetic letter, pleading with him not to repeat the scene as he could not bear to see him, so Greek and gracious, distorted with passion. The careless youth left the note trailing in a hotel room from where, like others of his letters, it disappeared.

Lady Queensberry had her moments of anguish concerning this son of hers in whom, she confided to Wilde, she saw too clearly embodied the fatal Douglas temperament that had brought one man to self-murder and another, Lord Alfred's own father, to acts so irrational that madness was feared.

As for Wilde, he had no illusions, as time elapsed, about the terrible attraction in the friendship. Still he could not tear himself away. Try as he might, at the first contrite telegram, at the sight of the familiar handwriting on an envelope, his weakness would get the better of him and once again he would submit to the domination of the young man whose influence he grew to dread yet whose fascination he could not resist. Concentrating all his will power, he tried to make a clear break after the departure for Egypt. Bosie, however, besieged him with letters and telegrams, angry, cajoling, desperate, recriminating. He even threatened to commit suicide. Finding Wilde for once firm, he prevailed upon Lady Queensberry to plead for him, and when her entreaties left Wilde unshaken, he besought Constance to make her husband write to him. Little knowing what she did, and seeing only that Oscar had turned hard and unkind toward the friend he professed to love, the poor woman in her guilelessness did as Lord Alfred asked, though she had never liked him and was dimly conscious of the power—not for the better—that he exerted over her husband. And so Wilde and Douglas were brought together again, for better or for worse, according to the eyes of those who looked upon them. When Lord Alfred quitted his post and went to Paris, Wilde was already waiting for him. On their return to London the old life recommenced, more openly imprudent than ever.

"Have you heard the latest about Lord Alfred and Oscar?" men asked one another. "They are being watched by the police."

Whether or not the police were indeed on the trail of Wilde and Lord Alfred, they were certainly vigilant in the neighborhood of Little College Street. Too many young men with no known employment went in and out of Alfred Taylor's apartment. Taylor himself was suspect, even though there was no tangible evidence against him. Often Wilde came to his afternoon tea parties; and often Taylor came to see him, either in Tite Street or in the chambers which for some time Wilde had been occupying in St. James's Place—to write in quiet, he said. Not infrequently Taylor was accompanied by youths in their 'teens whom he would introduce to Wilde. Sometimes he made arrangements for young men to meet the author in restaurants whence they would adjourn either to St. James's Place or to a suite which Wilde had at the Savoy Hotel. The gift of a silver cigarette case usually betokened Wilde's pleasure in his youthful companions. He ran up a considerable bill on cigarette cases at Thornhill's in Bond Street. Through Taylor he came to know some half-dozen boys and young men—Ernest Scarfe who had been in Australia; Charles and William Parker, gentlemen's servants out of employment whom Wilde entertained at Kettner's Restaurant with a sumptuous feast and the best iced champagne; Sidney Mavor, whose acquaintance he had made in Little College Street; and a number of others. Both Charles Parker and Sidney Mavor had been the recipients of Wilde's silver case as well as of gifts of money. Charles' cigarette case, it seemed, cost one pound, Mavor's four.

One night in 1894 the police took action by raiding a house on Fitzroy Street. Taylor and Charles Parker had been invited, from their own accounts, to entertain at what was euphemistically called a benefit concert. When they arrived, dancing was going on in a private suite of rooms. There were only men at the gathering, youths and gentlemen in their middle years— more or less the same clientele that used to frequent the Little College Street tea parties. Cabs had begun to drive up at eleven. It was near midnight when the police on guard saw a hansom appear with an astonishing group: two women, one of them holding a fan, and a man in ordinary clothes sitting on their laps.

The group entered the house, the police, unseen, following close behind. When they burst in upon the party they discovered that the women were female impersonators, and that among the guests a number had police records and were known as men of the vilest possible character. Eighteen in all were

226

arrested, among them the pair in masquerade. One of them changed into trousers before he was brought to court, but the other, who had not taken the precaution to bring along his proper apparel, stood before the bench in a ridiculous gown of black and gold. Taylor and Charles Parker were taken with the rest before Mr. Hannay the magistrate at Marlborough Street, but as nothing could be proved against them, they were dismissed.

Wilde read an account of the raid in the papers. Although it involved men with whom he had been, and was still, on familiar terms, he lost not a jot of his insouciance and continued his visits to Taylor's rooms.

Some of his companions he found without Taylor's mediation. Edward Shelley he had discovered for himself; but for a long time he had not seen the lad. After a few months Edward, shattered by his experience and further bedeviled by the insinuations of his fellow clerks, left his position and was lost sight of. Religious melancholia gripped him. He could not overcome his sense of guilt and sin, while at the same time lamenting the fickleness of the great man who had been interested in him, awakened his love of books, and then dropped him. In the midst of his conflict he wrote Wilde a letter revealing the part he played in that poor wrecked life, and asked him for the loan of ten pounds that he might go away and try to regain his health. Wilde, oddly enough, laid the blame at Edward's door. "As he betrayed me grossly," he wrote to Bosie, "I, of course, gave him money and was kind to him. I find that forgiving one's enemies is a most curious morbid pleasure—perhaps I should check it." Edward Shelley an enemy? Wilde had indeed gone far in his subversal of values.

In the summer of 1894 Wilde took a furnished house at Worthing for himself and his family. Constance was glad to escape the heat of London. Besides, the children would enjoy being near the water, with their father to take them swimming and boating. They had a lovely time together. With Cyril and Vyvyan Wilde would spend hours at the waterside watching the sail craft coming in, the sailors pulling in the boats. Wilde made friends with them. There was a lad he saw one day towing a boat. His young torso straining with the effort showed the strong interlacing of the muscles under the sun-browned skin. He was eighteen, one of that colony of boys of no definite occupation, to be found in every beach resort. Wilde took a fancy to him. He was good-looking and with that ingenuousness of youth which for Wilde formed one of the chief beauties of adolescence. Soon he and Alphonse Conway were on a firm footing. He talked to the lad as if the gamin had stepped out of the pages of antiquity, and in the transposal so natural to him, he made the shores of an English beach the borderland of the Aegean sea. But Alphonse belonged wholly to the nineteenth century. He understood nothing of Wilde's fine speeches though he had no difficulty in realizing that here was a rich bloke who would give him what he wanted most—a blue serge suit, a silver-handled grape-vine cane and a straw hat with a ribbon of red and blue.

Wilde was charmed with the lad's naïveté. He gave him what he asked for and stayed overnight with him at Brighton. Back in Worthing he introduced him to Constance and the children and they all dined together. Constance saw nothing questionable in the acquaintance. By now she was accustomed to the youths whom Wilde brought home. This one, at least, had the virtue of being a playmate to their boys.

After a while Constance and the children left Worthing and Oscar stayed on. He made more friends. Lord Alfred at the time was staying with him, and his happiness was complete, as it had been at Babbacombe where he wrote *A Woman of No Importance* and at Goring, the summer of the previous year where he had commemorated Lord Alfred's presence by noting on the first draft of his play, *An Ideal Husband:* "Bosie present." The three months' vacation had cost him £1,340. He was now writing another sparkling comedy. He had to be surrounded with youth and life and joy.

"Dear, dear boy—you are to me more than any one of them has any idea," he wrote when Lord Alfred left Worthing. "You are the atmosphere of beauty through which I see life—

222

you are the incarnation of all lovely things— When we are out of tune—all colour goes from things for me—but we are never really out of tune—I think of you day and night . . ."

Lord Alfred knew it. He too found joy and inspiration in the friendship although there was much in it that was base. The very letter that spoke so idealistically of Wilde's love for his friend contained passages which gave terrifying glimpses of the morass in which that love was rooted. "Percy left the day after you did. He spoke much of you— Alphonse is still in favor— He is my only companion along with Stephen— Alphonse always alludes to you as 'The Lord'—which however gives you I think a Biblical Hebraic dignity that gracious Greek boys should not have. He also says from time to time, 'Percy is the Lord's favourite' which makes me think of Percy as the infant Samuel—an inaccurate reminiscence as Percy was Hellenic. . . ."

On Wilde's return to London the Marquis suddenly decided to take matters into his own hands and cut short the relations that were, as he thought, dishonoring his ancient name. He had already warned his son in no indefinite terms. "Alfred—it is extremely painful to me to write you in this strain . . ." he began. "Firstly, am I to understand that having left Oxford as you did, with discredit to yourself . . . you now intend to loaf and loll about and do nothing? . . . I utterly decline, however, to supply you with sufficient funds . . . You are preparing a wretched future for yourself, and it would be most cruel and wrong for me to encourage you in this . . . Secondly, I come to the more painful part of this letter—your intimacy with this man Wilde. It must either cease or I will disown you . . . I am not going to try and analyze this intimacy, and I make no charge . . . With my own eyes I saw you both in the most loathsome and disgusting relationship as expressed by your manner and expression. Never in my experience have I ever seen such a sight as that in your horrible features. No wonder people are talking as they are. Also I now hear on good authority, but this may be false, that his wife is petitioning to divorce him for sodomy and other crimes.

223

Is this true or do you know of it? If I thought the actual thing was true, and it became public property, I should be quite justified in shooting him at sight. These Christian English cowards and men, as they call themselves, want waking up." The letter, sent on the 1st of April, 1894, was signed, "Your disgusted so-called father, Queensberry."

Inchoate though it was, libelous and uncontrolled, it yet might have been interpreted as the inconsidered expression of a wrathful parent on seeing his son in harmful company; and perhaps had Lord Alfred answered with the dutifulness Queensberry expected, he might have placated him, at least for the time. But Lord Alfred had not a little in him of his father. Instead of replying to the letter itself, he sent a telegram, remarkable for its studied insolence: "What a funny little man you are."

If Lord Alfred had expected a storm, he got a hurricane. The Marquis lost all control of himself—little in hand at the best of times—and gave his violence free rein. It did not occur to him that his solicitude for his son's welfare expressed itself rather late in the day. Alfred was twenty-three. All his life he had gone his way, the Marquis scarcely concerning himself with him except in the matter of giving or withholding a meager allowance.

But reasons other than the explicit prompted Queensberry's move. Since his divorce from Lady Queensberry he had overlooked no way of wounding her; Alfred he had always resented out of jealousy for his devotion to her. The young man, therefore, became the logical butt for the Marquis' vengeful spite. On his part Lord Alfred opposed interference with the intransigence of his nature, and hurled defiance at Queensberry's threats. He was fond of Wilde. Not anyone or anything was going to force him to give up his friendship. Queensberry's meddling, therefore, only drew the two men closer, bound now by persecution as well as by their mutual sympathy.

"You impertinent young jackanapes!" the Marquis addressed his son. "I request that you will not send such messages to

224

me by telegraph, and if you come to me with any of your impertinence I will give you the thrashing you deserve . . . All I can say is that if I catch you with that man again I will make a public scandal in a way you little dream of."

Rebellious, Lord Alfred plied him with more insulting telegrams. The Marquis boiled with rage. Hate for the mother merged with hate for the son. The two combined to make a maniac of him, anxious only to destroy. Honor, decency, nothing was spared in the insane letters he sent to Lord Alfred. "You reptile," he exploded in one missive. "You are no son of mine, and I never thought you were." Again, "No wonder you have fallen a prey to this horrible brute."

At the time Lord Alfred was receiving such endearments from Queensberry the "horrible brute" was writing: "My own dear Boy . . . It is really absurd—*I can't* live without you. You are so dear, so wonderful—I think of you all day long, and miss your grace, your boyish beauty, the bright sword play of your wit, the delicate fancy of your genius . . . and above all, you yourself . . . I know that early in January you and I will go away together for a long voyage—and that your lovely life goes always hand in hand with mine . . . Write me a line and take all my love—now and forever."

Unfortunately the world and the men affected saw their relations from entirely opposite aspects—and the world was on Queensberry's side.

On the 16th of June, 1894, the Marquis, accompanied by a gentleman to act as witness, called upon Oscar Wilde at his home. The servant led the visitors to the library and there Wilde received them, standing near the fireplace.

"Sit down!" said Queensberry rudely.

Calmly but firmly Wilde enunciated, looking at him fixedly: "I do not allow anyone to talk like that to me in my own house or anywhere else. I suppose you have come to apologize for the statement you made about my wife and myself in letters you wrote to your son. I should have the right any day to prosecute you for writing such a letter."

225

"It was privileged, as it was written to my son," retorted the Marquis who was well posted on his legal rights.

"But how dare you say such things about your son and me?"

"You *were* kicked out of the Savoy Hotel at a moment's notice for your disgusting conduct," he insisted.

"That is a lie!" cried Wilde.

"And you have taken furnished rooms for him in Piccadilly."

"Somebody has been telling you an absurd set of lies about your son and me. I have not done anything of the kind."

Queensberry would not be convinced by mere denial and stood his ground, whereupon Wilde asked him bluntly: "Lord Queensberry, do you seriously accuse your son and me of improper conduct?"

"I don't say you are it," said the Marquis cautiously, "but you look it and you pose it, which is just as bad." Then he turned to him, menacing: "If I catch you and my son together again in any public restaurant I will thrash you." His small epileptic hands clutched the air in the exigence of his wrath.

Wilde drew himself up with dignity. "I don't know what Queensberry rules are," said he, "but the Oscar Wilde rule is to shoot at sight. Leave my house at once."

"It is a disgusting scandal!" Queensberry sputtered.

"If it be so, you are the author of the scandal, and no one else."

As the Marquis made no move to leave his place in the embrasure of the window, Wilde summoned his servant who escorted the visitors to the hall. "This," said Wilde, indicating the stocky, red-whiskered nobleman, "is the Marquis of Queensberry, the most infamous brute in London. You are never to allow him to enter my house again."

It was in surroundings far different from the pretty red and yellow library, presided over by the calm Grecian Hermes, that the two men were again to confront each other.

226

Chapter VII: *The Green Carnation*

THERE were times when over the brightness of his pleasures Oscar Wilde saw the shadow of the wings of doom. Stubbornly he closed his eyes to it, admitting its presence only in his art where alone he permitted himself no pose. There he spoke of it, reiterating the fears in his heart, and working out symbolic prefigurements of the wages of sin. Pleasure will bring forth misery just as surely as sin will suffer its consequences. In "The Young King" long ago he had made the bishop say to the kneeling boy: "Is not He who made misery wiser than thou art?" Significant words they were, but to Wilde who had written them they had not yet revealed their full meaning. In *Dorian Gray* the note of doom, as he himself admitted, ran like a purple thread through its texture; upon it he had woven the whole of the *Soul of Man*, that brave investigation into the sorrows and injustices of the civilized world which, among much that was only brilliant paradox, contained deep and bitter truths. Doom was the leitmotif of *Salomé*; it was also the symbol in the prose poem of the man who from the bronze of the image of the Pleasure that liveth for a moment, fashioned in the end the image of the Sorrow that abideth for ever.

Wilde was still preoccupied with the Pleasure that liveth for a moment. It was incarnate in the young men on whom he lavished the jewels of his speech for the cheap joy of their marveling uncomprehension, their admiration that was balm to his vanity, the flattery of their upturned faces, their youth that intoxicated him like the headiest wine. It was both body and spirit in Bosie—at least so he thought when their friendship was in complete harmony and nothing of crude reality came to mar the life which he lived as a high art.

Robert Sherard, Frank Harris and Robbie Ross his most faithful and loyal disciple, looked at the friend they had known and found it hard to recognize him. He had grown fat. The fine head with its noble forehead and eyes still wonderful despite the telltale pouches beneath them, had the excessiveness seen in the busts of the Roman decadence. The mouth, once of the purest cut, was now thick and coarse; his cheeks oozed self-indulgence. The very veins of his temples stood out in the exertion of the pace he was leading, while his breath came in quick pants, like a runner's going beyond his speed.

Invariably, except when abroad by himself, Lord Alfred was to be seen with him, a slight, slim shadow, the nervous movements of whose hands had in them some reminiscence of Queensberry's as Wilde had seen them clutching the air in the impotence of exasperation. For all the difference between father and son there was something disturbingly alike in them —something that came to Oscar as a warning which, however, because it was of reality and not of art, he willfully ignored. Lady Queensberry had put that warning into words when she spoke of the dread Douglas temperament. Lord Alfred himself stood as its personification when, pale with passion, he spat out at his friend cruel and bitter words in their frequent quarrels. Nevertheless Wilde persisted in seeing in him the Charmides of his imagination.

"You must really be painted, and also have an ivory statue executed," he told him in his infatuation, and carrying out his suggestion, commissioned young Will Rothenstein to make a drawing of Bosie. Money which he flung about with the carelessness of a pasha was too impure a medium of barter for the portrait of the gilded youth. "Enclosed is an absurdly coloured thing—" he wrote to the artist, "which foolish bankers take in exchange and for which they give, in reckless moments, gold both yellow and red . . . "

It was a charming way of making payment, a way suited to the personages of an urbane tale. It was one with the luxuries of the Savoy Hotel, with the champagne parties at Kettner's or the Solferino, the luncheons at the Café Royal, the vacations at Goring and Worthing, the trips abroad, the drives in hansoms and the choice boutonnières which he ordered at the florist's—one for himself and another, appropriately smaller but no less expensive, for his coachman. It was all pleasure, enchantment and unreality, a beautiful, imaginative way of living that followed the shape of life but which, like the green carnation he took pride in having invented, assumed a hue it had never had. He loved it because he was the chief character in it, round whom as round the sun, all satellites had perforce to shine by the light he shed.

The most exalted dinner tables made room for him as a distinguished guest, and swollen with pride, he grew bolder and less considerate of personal feelings. His talk, now that he felt he could dispense with tact, soared unrestrained. His repartee came as a lightning flash, blinding minds accustomed to commonplace. They enjoyed and resented it at the same time, every spark of his wit showing up by contrast the deficiencies of their own. At a luncheon with Margot Asquith and her husband at Upper Grosvenor Street, round a table that had among its guests Ribblesdale, Reggie Lister and Wilfrid Scawen Blunt, Wilde was easily the most scintillating talker of them all. Where the less prosperous Wilde would have shown a certain deferential tactfulness, saying the things that would have delighted his hosts, he took a malicious pleasure in challenging first one and then the other to verbal duels, desisting only when his opponent had been made ridiculous. Asquith, for some perverse reason, he selected as his special target, making such outrageous fun of him that Blunt commented on it in his journal. It was not the highest wisdom to make so free with the Home Secretary—or, for that matter, with anyone who had human feelings and no less human frailties. As carelessly as he drank his champagne, and with as little thought, Wilde had made himself an army of enemies that needed but the signal to charge against him.

That fateful year of 1894 a book appeared which did Wilde inestimable harm. It was a novel, *The Green Carnation,* offered anonymously to the curious London public. *A roman à clef,* it required no stretch of the imagination to identify the characters which the author, with wit and daring, held up to ridicule. Esmé Amarith with his affectations and visible aura of evil was none other than Wilde, but a Wilde seen through the unsympathetic eye of the critic whose moral standards the protagonist himself would have dismissed as the ultimate in the inane—the middle class. The novel accomplished its destructive work, however, the malice in it, no less than the cleverness, making for instant success. Who had written the book that captured so perfectly Wilde's turns of speech, his manner, the very essence of his affectations? It must have been someone intimately connected with Wilde—Wilde himself, perhaps.

Scornfully Wilde repudiated the suspicion. "I invented that magnificent flower. But with the . . . mediocre book that usurps its strangely beautiful name I have . . . nothing whatsoever to do. The flower is a work of art. The book is not."

For that reason, nevertheless, the novel went into a number of editions and its young author, Robert Hichens, had his first taste of popular fame. The remarkable thing about it was that Hichens had not met Wilde. Like the rest of the world he had heard the stories, true and invented, that were current about him, and they had stimulated his facile pen. As luck would have it, before writing the book he had found himself in Egypt with Lord Alfred Douglas and a number of other men who knew Wilde. Their conversations gave him more than he needed for his satire. Back in England he lost no time in putting his material to good use.

Beyond disavowing authorship of the novel Wilde did nothing more about it. What if the old rumors gained new force? It was all part of fame. Wilde and the world stood at opposite poles in their ethical judgments. Where the despised middle class saw matter for condemnation and would have dragged Wilde down from the pedestal from which he spurned them with the foot of scorn, he saw the aureole that marked him the chosen among men. "I am one of those who are made for exceptions, not for laws," he declared. He was a rebel like Byron, but of more significance than Byron because whereas the older poet's relations had been with the passions of his age and its world-weariness, he stood in symbolic contact with the art and culture of his day. He had realized it at the dawn of his manhood; he knew it now in the affirmation of his acknowledged genius. In the beautiful unreal world of art he was king, and that was the only crown he sought. For did he not make the boast that he treated art as the supreme reality and life as a mere mode of fiction? He had genius, position, intellectual daring. He had succeeded in making art a philosophy and philosophy an art. Whatever he touched he had made beautiful in a new mode of beauty. He had so awakened the imagination of his age that it created legend about him. *The Green Carnation,* the whispered stories—what were they but the myths that follow in the wake of the heroes of life?

Life itself he had sought to know in its heights and in its depths. He had experimented with it as the alchemists of old had done with creation and with death in their search to transmute dross into gold. He too had striven to draw experience of beauty out of the baser passions, even out of sin, maintaining with unwonted earnestness that Christ had regarded sin and suffering as in themselves beautiful holy things and modes of perfection. "It seems a very dangerous idea," he argued. "It is—all great ideas are dangerous. That it was Christ's creed admits of no doubt. That it is the true creed I don't doubt myself. Of course," he elucidated, "the sinner must repent . . . The moment of repentance is the moment of initiation."

Importunately his obsession thrust itself forward in his mind as if, against the brightly lighted window of his enjoyments a dark form passed and vanished, only to return blacker and more menacing. Sometimes the shadow had the shape of his sin. Sometimes it bore the form of his love. Always it was the shadow of his fears. Neopagan though he was, he could escape no more than the mystical Francis Thompson the pursuit of the Hound of Heaven.

> Nigh and nigh draws the chase,
>   With unperturbèd pace,
> Deliberate speed, majestic instancy;
>   And past those noisèd feet
>   A voice comes yet more fleet—
> "Lo! naught contents thee, who content'st not Me."

Inwardly he had to admit that his life remained unfulfilled. Its triumph, wrought so elaborately in every detail, lacked the one thing that gave it significance. Years ago he remembered standing with tears of ecstasy before that wonderful Rubens painting—the pageant of horse and rider at the Crucifixion, through the evocation of which he had sought to awaken wonder in his American audiences. His life, it seemed to him, was like that pageant. The joy of art and the triumph both were there; there the flying banner and the plumes tossed by the wind; but not the Christ whose bleeding feet made the whole scene meaningful.

He knew he had been designed for some strange and terrible fate. His career from the very beginning had had in it much of the spectacular. Now that he was at the peak and could rise no more he must prepare for the descent. Consciously he did not wish it. He had always yearned after the high places, the topmost fruit of the branches on the sunny side of the garden of the world. He had avoided the shadow, indeed, he had lived life as if all had been sunshine. It had always been springtime in his heart, and the joyousness that was in him communicated itself to everyone about him, calling forth like the light and warmth of the sun the brightest blossoms of geniality and laughter. All who entered his radiant presence became better than their best. The tongue-tied found words that made them marvel at themselves; the dull shone with unaccustomed light. Failure, disgrace, poverty, sorrow, despair, the tears of anguish and the broken words of pain were to him merely the dark values in the chiaroscuro of literature. He avoided them in life.

When he was still a youth his mother, apprehensive at such capacity for joy, used often to quote him Goethe's lines inscribed in a book which years ago Carlyle had given her:

> Who never ate his bread in sorrow,
>> Who never spent the midnight hours
> Weeping and waiting for the morrow,—
>> He knows you not, ye heavenly powers.

Vehemently Oscar denied the truth hidden in those words. Weeping and suffering could have nothing in them of holiness. "I will not eat my bread in sorrow," he would defy her. "I will not pass any night weeping and watching for the dawn!" Sorrow did not enter into his scheme of life. It held no place in his philosophy. But now that he had crushed against his palate every fruit of the joyous garden, he knew that he must enter the places of shadow where grew the thorns and bitter things and where the dew had the salt taste of tears.

By some inner warning (though outward circumstances were not lacking) he linked Bosie with his premonitory fears. He had found through him immeasurable joy. Would he, the "Hyacinthus whom Apollo loved so madly" now make him know disaster and despair? "It is what we fear that happens to us," a ruined man who had learned deep wisdom said years later.

Once more Wilde, during a stay at Brighton with Lord Alfred, sought to make an end of the friendship that struck him, as he saw himself subjugated against his will, akin to that relation between the Greek of whom Aeschylus tells, and the beautiful lion cub which he cherished till, manifesting its true nature, the full-grown creature destroyed him, his home, and all that he held dear. Douglas was as beautiful as that lion cub—and, with his heredity, as dangerous. Wilde had had frequent occasion to draw parallels between father and son since the Marquis' visit to him at his home three and a half months earlier. He knew that Lord Alfred loved him better than he loved anyone else, and with a love which, though inspired by the fascination of his personality, his position in the world of art, his lavishness with money and his wonderful, improbable way of living, had in it something beyond all these that turned to him for himself alone. But stronger than his love, Wilde discovered, was Bosie's inveterate hatred for his father. It was a mania, a passion of such dimensions that it dwarfed and overshadowed even his love for Wilde. The letters exchanged by father and son seemed incredible in their unnatural loathing. Wilde experienced a creeping chill whenever he was shown them, and that horror grew as he found himself bandied between the two men, the helpless pretext of their expressed enmity.

In the inconsiderateness of his youthful vanity Lord Alfred relished the part he was playing. Oscar Wilde, the most famous author of London and the Marquis of Queensberry engaging in a terrible quarrel over him! It was flattering and delightful. So far the duel had been a paper one with the Marquis sputtering his disordered invective in his letters while Wilde kept his disdainful distance. Since the Tite Street interview, however, Queensberry had been threatening a public scandal, and followed Wilde about for the excuse to wreak upon him the storm of his long pent-up fury. Oddly enough, in some freak of latent paternity, he had no wish really to injure his son. In his distorted imagination Wilde became the arch villain of the piece, the corrupter, and it was upon him, therefore that after the preliminary skirmishes with Lord Alfred, Queensberry focused the force of his irresponsible hate.

Everyone knew he was a man to be avoided, a violent, combative creature who was known in every club for the scenes that at some time or other he had precipitated. To the arrogance of his class he added the recklessness of his insane temper which made him enemies even among those of his own blood. At the Pelican one night he insulted a man who proved to be more than his match. After putting up with Queensberry's taunts, he turned upon him and caught him full in the face, making him sprawl amid a circle of onlookers. Slowly Queensberry rose. His nose was bleeding and an eye was almost shut. He did not resume the fight as another man might have done; neither did he leave the club. Instead, he took a seat at a table and there remained, sullen and terrible, his shirt stained with blood and his face disfigured—a beast at bay, suppressing with a mighty effort an outburst that might have been murderous. Such was the enemy whom Wilde had made for himself.

Lord Alfred comported himself with adolescent bravado. He stood by Wilde against his father, but in his defiance he

234

did his friend great harm. In a chivalrous moment he went so far as to buy a pistol which created quite a sensation at the Berkeley when it suddenly went off while he was testing it to see whether it was charged.

Meanwhile Wilde was trying to fulfill his obligations toward his producers. His plays had taken the public by storm and the managers were clamoring for more. Stimulated by his fame, ideas came pouring in upon him, but alas, he could hardly find the time to collect his thoughts. At his suite in St. James's Street he was interrupted by visitors. The Savoy was linked with too many associations; the Albermarle had its drawbacks. Even the Café Royal was no longer safe from the incursions of his boon companions.

"There's a dreadful youth waiting for me in Regent Street," he said to Vincent O'Sullivan one day at the Café Royal. "He is pacing up and down before the door like a wonderful black panther. I think he must be there yet. Do go and see," he begged, much distressed. "If he is, I shall go out by the side door."

O'Sullivan obliged him and went out on the Regent Street side. Surely enough there was an unpleasant-looking youth stalking back and forth as if waiting for someone. More and more the panthers, wonderful only to Wilde, were closing in upon him.

For the sake of his work he went into retirement at Worthing, hoping for the solitude in which to finish his new comedy. Hardly had he settled down to his writing when Bosie appeared with a companion. Work was of course abandoned. It was nothing unusual. Bosie had the marvelous faculty of stimulating him to his best endeavor while at the same time he deprived him of the calm necessary to creation. A few days later Bosie's friend left and Wilde and he remained alone. It was October. The season was over and there was little for Lord Alfred to do. He was bored—bored with the place and with Wilde who, with his mind on his play, did not give him the attention he desired. He wanted life, excitement, pleasure. Why should they not go to the Grand Hotel at Brighton?

Wilde could refuse Bosie nothing and so to Brighton they
went, the play put aside for the sake of the immediate pleasure.
At Brighton, however, Lord Alfred fell ill with influenza,
and for five days Wilde nursed him, not leaving his side for
a moment. He entertained him with his most delightful inventions; he read to him. And because Bosie did not like the
grapes the hotel provided, he sent for some from London. As
it happened, no sooner had Bosie recovered than Wilde had
to take to his bed. But Bosie had had enough of illness. Instead
of tending Wilde, sitting by him, reading, or bringing him
flowers and fruit, he left him alone and went about his pleasures with the eagerness of one too long deprived. When he
came back there were reproaches, sharp words, scenes. Wilde
was deeply grieved, Lord Alfred annoyed and disenchanted
at the sight of Wilde ludicrously red-nosed and watery-eyed
like any common sufferer from a cold. Plaintively Wilde contrasted his behavior with his friend's. His remorse converted
into rage, Bosie turned upon him with Queensberry fury,
coming forward toward him at one moment so menacingly
that Wilde, filled with horror, rose from his bed ill as he was
and made his way barefooted down two flights of stairs to the
sitting room. Lord Alfred returned to London, and Wilde determined never to see him again.

The 16th of October was Wilde's birthday. Letters and
telegrams of well-wishing were brought to him, among them
an envelope from Bosie. He had expected a contrite note or
perhaps some word of repentance and affection. He read a letter of peculiar rancor, one sentence of which cut him like a
knife. "When you are not on your pedestal you are not interesting."

More than anything else in the letter, and there was much
in it to wound, the brutality of that cold, sinisterly revealing
declaration brought Wilde to with the pain of the shock. In
a vision of intense lucidity he saw the part he had played in
that relation. "When you are not on your pedestal you are
not interesting." It was not Oscar Wilde the man, with his
human weaknesses, to whom Lord Alfred had been drawn,

but the eminent author, the dispenser of largesse. The "my darling Oscar" of Bosie's affectionate address had been the triumphant figure before the footlights, bowing to an audience wild with applause, the monarch of the dinner table, the lordly friend who thought nothing of spending fifty pounds on a mere Christmas gift simply because Bosie had set his heart upon it. Next time Wilde was ill, the letter continued, he, Douglas, would disappear at once.

What would happen to that friendship if instead of illness, disgrace and poverty hurled him from his pedestal? Life, as Wilde had learned from his study of the Greek tragedies, gave no one assurance of continued success. At any moment the crown might be wrested from the king, the laurel from the warrior. The sword of Damocles held by its single hair hung over him as over all who had made the climb to the heights of glory. Where would be Bosie when the pedestal crumbled— Bosie who, he comforted himself in moments of doubt, loved him for himself as much as for his fame?

He determined on a final break. The following week on his return to London he would go privately to Sir George Lewis, Queensberry's attorney, and request him to write a letter in his name urging the Marquis under no circumstances to allow his son to visit Wilde, or to be seen in his company. He set the appointment for Friday. He was about to start out on his way when, on opening the newspaper, he read the appalling notice that Drumlanrig, Queensberry's firstborn son and heir to the title, had been found dead in a ditch, his empty gun beside him. Wilde could not go on with his errand. Pity for Lady Queensberry who had doted on her son, for Bosie and Lord Douglas of Hawick, altered his determination, none too firm in the first place. Instead of seeking out Sir George he sent a telegram of condolence to Bosie, and in the letter with which he followed it, invited him again to come to see him.

And Bosie came. Before the youth in his suit of mourning, his face pale and his eyes dim with sorrow, Wilde forgot his resentment and opened to him once more his heart as well

237

as his home. Not a word of reproach for the revolting scenes or for the letter that had given him so much pain.

Within a few weeks, before the flowers on Drumlanrig's grave had withered, everything in the drama of Wilde and the Queensberry family resumed its course. Queensberry, unbalanced by the strokes of fate in the death of his son and his recent scandalous divorce from his second wife, took up his persecution of Wilde with insane zeal. Every club heard his defamations; he scarcely met anyone without pouring out to him the venom of his hate. Wilde and Bosie continued defying him.

"My dearest Boy," Wilde addressed the youth from whom a few days earlier he had determined to break, "I have been very lonely without you . . . How strange to live in a land where the worship of beauty, and the passion of love are considered infamous—I hate England: it is only bearable to me because you are here."

Fate was weaving her intricate threads, the chief character of her concern seeing the snare yet beating his wings in the sun, ever nearer to it. Now and again people he had known in the past met with him in his dizzy flight and went on. Not long since, on a wet February day, as he was crossing the Strand in a fine carriage, the white flower in his buttonhole and the smaller one in his cabby's bringing a touch of spring to winter, he was startled by the coach's sudden stopping. Through the rain he saw to one side a man, splashed with mud, whom the horses had barely missed.

"Hullo, Ned Carson! How are you?" he cried, jumping out of the carriage as he recognized his old rival of Trinity College days. Quietly Carson greeted him and they exchanged a few words, the playwright and the rising advocate feeling slightly uncomfortable in each other's company.

"Fancy your being a Tory," Wilde said airily, "and Arthur Balfour's righthand man! You're coming along, Ned. Come and dine with me one day in Tite Street."

The polite invitation was never meant, and Carson never for a moment believed it was. He did not go to Tite Street. Fate had designed a different meeting for them.

Chapter VIII: *The Yellow Book* and *The Savoy*

THE decade was running its course but it was only in 1894 that it acquired the designation of "yellow." The color had been a favorite one with Rossetti, Morris and Burne-Jones who had first discovered it in the richness of medieval panels, then nearer at hand in the sunflower of rural gardens. Whistler had made subtle use of it in his Japanese paintings; and Wilde both in England and America had never wearied of extolling the hue of gold and of sunlight, making it so popular that yellow satin evening gowns became the fashion and a helianthus at the whip hand of an equipage the proper decoration for young ladies driving in the park. The color had been further popularized by an increasing interest in the work of the French novelists whose books, because of the tone of their paper covers, were commonly known as "yellow backs."

There was something vivid and daring about the color, something of the times, like the golden bloom of the age on a century that was nearing its close—not to death but to greater achievement. Yellow and *fin de siècle* began to have connotations open to many meanings but all leading to a definable sense of modernity, challenge, emancipation. People were no longer afraid to live. They responded sympathetically to the color that tinted their daily living, from the buttercup yellow of their breakfast crockery to the hue of the billposters on the hoardings under the city lights at night. Toulouse-Lautrec in Paris had been lavish of yellow in the poster paintings which he lifted to an art. London decorators were not slow to see its effectiveness. The public became yellow-conscious. Aubrey Beardsley who did not believe in half measures, went the whole way by having his new studio in Warwick Square decorated by Vallance with deep yellow walls and black woodwork.

The final fillip was given by the appearance on the market of *The Yellow Book* in April, 1894, issued by Mathews and Lane at the Bodley Head which, though young as a publishing house, was to be more closely identified with the *fin de siècle* in literature than any other firm in England. Books by Oscar Wilde had already been issued under its imprint, and before the century was over it had mustered to its sign some of the most significant writers of the day, ranging from the Catholic sibyl Alice Meynell, her protégé Francis Thompson, William Watson, the guardian of morality, and John Davidson, to the roguishly precious Max Beerbohm, Richard Le Gallienne, Lionel Johnson, "Michael Field," the two women who wrote as one man, Kenneth Grahame, Laurence Binyon, George Egerton and many another belonging either to the Catholic revival or to the decadence, yet all finding eager welcome with the intrepid publishers.

"Have you seen *The Yellow Book?*" Oscar Wilde asked Mrs. Leverson in a petulant little note soon after the magazine burst upon the scene. "It is horrid and not yellow at all." He was still more candid with Bosie. "*The Yellow Book* has appeared. It is dull and loathsome: A great failure—I am so glad."

His feelings were hurt. In the flaming quarterly issued—*mirabile dictu!*—solely for the benefit of literature and art, a magazine which contained no vulgar advertising and preached no moralities, which stood for the beauty and joy of creation, there was nothing by him, Oscar Wilde. Between its yellow covers with their striking black design by Beardsley—one of those Aubreyish women which Wilde could not abide—amid the writings of youths whom he looked upon as his disciples—Arthur Symons, Le Gallienne and Beerbohm—amid the decorations by his friends, Will Rothenstein and Walter Sickert, there was not the least reference to him, the prophet of art for art's sake. The format of the book, the very color owed something to his influence. At the time the magazine was preparing, was he not bringing out through Mathews and Lane themselves, his poem, *The Sphinx,* in a small quarto, with exquisite designs in the new manner by the talented Charles Ricketts, and with text printed in red, black and green?

Why had he been excluded? Beardsley's dislike of him was one of the reasons, and as it happened Beardsley, a founder of the magazine with Henry Harland and John Lane, was its art editor. He was very proud of the enterprise and with his superstitious dread that Wilde brought ill luck, he refused to have anything to do with him. John Lane had no more desire than Beardsley to include Wilde among the contributors. It was one thing to publish a man's books and another to have him figure in a publication designed to reach a wide and diverse public. Wilde's dealings with the boy Shelley who was now drifting, a hopeless human wreck, as a result of the great man's interest, had made its impression upon Lane. Moreover, in itself *The Yellow Book* was startling enough, and carried with it a discernible aura of decadence without the addition of Wilde whose notoriety was not exactly of the kind sought by the magazine's sponsors. For the beginning it was better to have safe names like those of Richard Garnett, Edmund Gosse, Henry James who contributed "Death of a Liar" and Sir Frederick Leighton, P.R.A. who very generously sent in the frontispiece for the first number.

In spite of Wilde's jubilation that *The Yellow Book* was a failure it created a furore. The public was intrigued by a quarterly bound, as with hope of permanence, like a book, and selling for five shillings. The title and the color of the binding struck the right note. The Beardsley drawings, hitherto accessible only to those who could afford the luxury of a limited edition, revealed to the world at large an art that captured the time spirit within the confines of his black-and-white pictures. Women who saw Beardsley's portrait of Mrs. Patrick Campbell aspired to look like his conception of her with that slim long body and enigmatic head weighed down by the dense black of the hair as with oppressive dreams. They yearned for those overdecorated boudoirs in which he loved to place his voluminously draped figures whose heavy lids and sullen lips imparted to the face the suggestion of forbidden adventure. He played with powder boxes, rouge pots, phials and puffs with aggressive sensuality. And always there were the candlesticks, so constant that even without his adoption of them as his symbol they might have served as a signature.

Beardsley became famous. Now whenever he went to the Café Royal there was no need for people to ask who he was. The loose-limbed, gaunt apparition in a black cutaway, silk hat and lemon-colored gloves held in the long spidery hands, the youth with the startling hair and cold, agate-like eyes, moving feverishly among the tables as if every instant had to be lived, was as well known as the type he had invented. He might almost have stepped out of one of his drawings. Everyone was soon talking of the "marvelous boy" and society came forth to meet him. Vain, Beardsley let himself be courted. He missed nothing. First night audiences and concert crowds became familiar with the angular, fleshless face drinking in life from avid eyes. One cold night a friend was shocked to see him on the steps of the Opera House, wearing no overcoat.

"Aubrey, you will kill yourself!" he remonstrated.

"Oh, no . . . I am always burning."

And he was, always burning with the fever of an urge that knew it had little time in which to fulfill itself. He was already walking among graves, as real as those through which, that July, Haldane Macfall had seen him stumbling, panting for breath, from the unveiling at Hampstead Church of the bust of Keats who like him had fought a losing fight with consumption.

For the present, however, he took the pleasures that success gave him and enjoyed the scandal which, through *The Yellow Book*, he was creating. John Bull threw up both hands at the idea of a magazine devoted to art and literature, of all things, and could not tell what shocked him most—those wicked drawings, the preciously written, tongue in cheek essays of Beerbohm who had also a mean stylus for caricature, or the high quality of the work of a group of obscure young writers. His press hastened to express consternation, the *Westminster Gazette* going so far as to demand among other repressive measures, "a short Act of Parliament to make this kind of thing illegal."

"What kind of thing?" asked the thousands who found the magazine delightful. And Mostyn Piggott told them in Jabberwocky language:

> Beware the Yaller Bock, my son!
> The aims that rile, the art that racks,
> Beware the Aub-Aub Bird, and shun
> The stumious Beerbomax!

It only added to the general fun, as merrily "the minim potes did mime and mimble in the cafe," whilst "footly were the Philerotes and the Daycadongs outstrafe."

Now less than ever in childish pique would Wilde hear a good word for the magazine that was occupying the place he usually held in the spotlight. "My dear boy, do not say nice false things about *The Yellow Book*," he said to Ricketts assuming a mock-injured look preparatory to spinning out a ridiculous yarn. "I bought it at the station, but before I had cut all the pages, I threw it out of my carriage window. Suddenly the train stopped and the guard, opening the door, said, 'Mr. Wilde, you have dropped *The Yellow Book*.' What was to be done? In the hansom, with the subtlety of a poet, I cunningly hid it under the cushions and paid my fare . . . when came a loud knocking at the front door, and the cabby, appearing, said, 'Mr. Wilde, you have forgotten *The Yellow Book* . . .'" And so on, Wilde putting on the absurdest expressions in a mimicry that was irresistible in its ludicrousness. He could not bear the thought that a luscious pudding of publicity was cut before his eyes and he was not given a crumb, especially since Beardsley and Lane were, so to speak, the hosts. He took it out in little feline jabs at Beardsley's French affectations.

"Yes, dear Aubrey is always too Parisian. He cannot forget he has been to Dieppe—once!"

Despite the stir he made, however, Beardsley did not re-

243

main long with *The Yellow Book,* for with the fourth number he ceased to be its art editor. Not through any wish of his own. William Watson, who found deeper meanings of perversity in the drawings than were implicit in them, could not tolerate having his unimpeachable morality bound in the same sheets with them and sent the publishers an ultimatum saying that if Beardsley's work was not withdrawn he would take back his poem. Lane had the choice to make and decided in favor of Watson. Since his break with Mathews he had veered steadily toward the conservative side. *The Yellow Book* showed the effect through the rest of its thirteen numbers.

Long before it ceased, the qualities of daring that had distinguished it at its inception had submitted to such modification that by the end it differed little from the literary magazines which sprang up to imitate it in the course of the 'nineties—the *Pageant,* the *Hobby Horse,* the *Dome,* the *Quarto,* the *Parade,* the *Evergreen,* the *Butterfly,* the *Venture*—some as ephemeral as their title, others very quickly denying the duration of their greenness.

The Savoy, following shortly upon Beardsley's rupture with John Lane, was alone of them all comparable to *The Yellow Book.* In some ways it surpassed it as an exponent of the *fin de siècle,* for Arthur Symons, its founder and editor, had been deeply imbued in the currents of French decadence. He knew French poetry which he rendered into excellent English verse; he knew some of the poets themselves and the influences that made for their modernity. A critic of genius, he could discriminate between the mediocre work of a well-known name and the excellence of an unknown writer. Without prejudice or predilection, but with the conviction that beauty justified its existence, he culled for *The Savoy* the finest flowers in the fields of literature and art. "We are not Realists, or Romanticists, or Decadents," he announced in the preface of the first issue in January, 1896. "For us all art is good which is good art."

The birth of the magazine came to Beardsley as a new lease of life. After his dismissal from *The Yellow Book,* not through any fault of his own but because a mistaken prejudice had

244

linked him with the sins of Wilde who was then at the height of his scandal with the Queensberry family, he had taken to his bed where, powerless to work, he brooded on his brief year of glory. Then unexpectedly one day Arthur Symons came to see him as the emissary of a mysterious Leonard Smithers who was willing to put up the money to finance such a magazine as *The Yellow Book* had started out to be. Symons found Beardsley lying upon a pile of cushions, so horribly white that he thought him to be dying. Fearful that he had come too late, he made haste to tell the sick man his errand. The thought of editing a rival of the offending *Yellow Book* brought color to Beardsley's cheek. Eagerly he discussed its prospects. How large a page would it have? Why not make it a quarto so that his drawings would not have to be too much reduced? What should they call it? "Why not *The Savoy*?" he suggested. Symons seized upon the title and *The Savoy* was born.

Beardsley left his bed and worked as never before. He usually made his designs at night. Placing the sheet between the flames of his two candlesticks, he ran his pencil over it, covering it with what seemed meaningless scrawls which he rubbed and scraped and blocked till there was hardly an inch of the surface that was not marred. Then with a fine gold pen and Chinese ink he picked out his design, working in the shadows, elaborating the ornamental traceries, insinuating with a mischievous boyish smile the rococo details that marked the work his and his only.

For *The Savoy* he worked out a title page in marvelous line, showing two veiled mysterious figures, a man and a woman, standing against curtains spangled with grotesque roses, and inviting the reader toward the mirrored recess where between lighted candles lay a mask and a fan. It was the cover design for the first number, however, that showed him at his best, making his imitators throw down their pens in despair. The Beardsley woman occupies the left foreground; but she is beautiful and stately, without the smirk that had turned the Watsons against him. Dressed in a riding habit, and with her heavy black hair flowing behind her, she carries a whip in her gloved hand while before her a plump child, naked but for a plumed hat and a coat covering its shoulders, looks down contemptuously. The background is a fairyland of clear sky and shadowy boscage, furnished with the terminal god, temple and sun dial dear to the heart of the decadent Pierrot that Beardsley fancied himself. From the trembling delicacy of the flowers in the fore to the tufted tree in the center, a palette of colors and textures fills the surface in a technical virtuosity that Beardsley now completely achieved. In a mood of spite against *The Yellow Book* he had at first made the child depict too realistically its contempt for the magazine; but on second thought he decided to serve art alone. With the appearance of *The Savoy*, its predecessor found itself thrown into the shade.

But alas! Symons and Beardsley and their financing angel had taken too glowing a view of the English intellectual temper in thinking that by adding wings to the shoulders and feet of the paunchy John Bull, and by endowing him with the instruments of art as Beardsley had done in the design for the prospectus, they could make him other than he was. At the end of twelve months *The Savoy* had to admit defeat, Symons unburdening himself in the final number of his newly acquired wisdom: "Comparatively few people care for art at all, and most of these care for it because they mistake it for something else." Even at half-a-crown, the price charged by *The Savoy*, the public found it too expensive a luxury.

So far as they were concerned the editors had nothing to regret in their conduct of the magazine. In no instance had they truckled to the scruples of Mrs. Grundy, and not once had they been guilty of compromise against their artistic judgment. A number of the contributors to *The Yellow Book*, the younger and bolder vanguard, joined the venture, sending in poems and illustrations which their reformed quarterly would have frowned upon. Throughout, *The Savoy* maintained its *fin de siècle* tone, though true to its promise, it rejected nothing that bore the stamp of art. Thus Bernard Shaw who would have reared at the charge of decadence, was represented with an essay, "On Going to Church." Havelock Ellis, a pioneer in the new psychology, contributed a study of Nietzsche, while Joseph Conrad, Mathilde

246

Blind and Selwyn Image saw nothing amiss in their appearing with George Moore, W. B. Yeats, Lionel Johnson, Ernest Rhys, William Sharp-Fiona Macleod, Arthur Symons himself, and others identified with the time spirit.

The Savoy was moreover remarkable for introducing Aubrey Beardsley as a man of letters. Beardsley had always been anxious to write, to emerge as a sort of decadent Rossetti. Association with Wilde and his literary circle sharpened his ambitions. He felt he had the talent to shine with the best of them, and they, knowing the bright frail ghost doomed, encouraged him. Everyone marveled at how he was able to accomplish so much. He was only twenty-three years old; nevertheless, besides the five hundred or more designs for the *Morte d'Arthur*, the drawings for *Salomé* and the many illustrations which he was producing for Smithers who had made up his mind to supplant John Lane in the production of books that were as beautiful as they were suspect, he still found time to break into a new career. He was never seen idle. Wherever he went his leather portfolio went with him. Sitting apart at a concert he would be seen to jot down some thought suggested by the music for his phallic version of the legend of Venus and Tannhäuser, *Under the Hill*. He always carried the manuscript with him, changing a word here, adding some bit of ribaldry there, underscoring a licentious suggestion or amplifying the examples of sexual aberration that marked the progress of the errant knight in the court of Venus.

The erotic concentration of his adolescence was aggravated as he grew older. His friends who read the unexpurgated *Under the Hill* which appeared, much chastened, in *The Savoy*, spurred him on in his dangerous cleverness. It was an amazingly successful experiment in the rococo style of literature, they argued —something so modern and shocking that hypocrisy would be stricken dumb. Like John Lane who glossed the embarrassment which Beardsley's drawings caused him by explaining them away to the interviewers as "pitiless satire" and Beardsley himself, the flower of the decadence, as "the modern Hogarth," they read everything in the story but what was patent for them to see. Beardsley was no satirist. He created his drawings and wrote his fancies from the profoundest impulse of his nature. He gloried in the unconventional. His interest in sexual perversions was as much inherent in himself as the magic of his line, and he could no more have satirized the era in whose vices he rejoiced than Wilde could have mounted the pulpit to preach that nothing is beautiful but what is moral. Each in his way was representative of the age's struggle for the emancipation of the individual, and each was to pay his price.

With the fragment of *Under the Hill, The Savoy* also published two rococo poems, "The Three Musicians" and "The Ballad of a Barber." Beardsley meant to shock and he did it thoroughly, not so much by the form which showed some metrical adroitness, as by the suggestiveness of the subjects that suddenly hit the unwary reader with such force that like the tourist in "The Three Musicians" he

> . . . gives a furious glance,
> Red as his guide-book grows, moves on, and offers up a prayer . . .

Beardsley was as happy as a child with his new éclat. He beamed whenever anyone praised him, his face where already the skeleton showed, startling with the unexpectedness of his smile. One night while visiting the Pennells, he was made ill at ease by Whistler's dropping in. He knew Whistler had never liked him and that he had been furious with him for his most decadent of decadent drawings, "The Fat Woman" in whom the Butterfly had detected with reason a reminiscence of Mrs. Whistler. He trembled, therefore, when Joseph Pennell brought him his portfolio, expecting him to show the master his latest series, *The Rape of the Lock,* illustrating Pope's mock epic.

Nervously Aubrey opened it while the Pennells stood by, no less nervous for their knowledge of the Butterfly's unaccountable humors. One by one Beardsley took out the drawings—"The Dream" with its singing line and its subtle textures, "The Baron's Prayer," "The Rape of the Lock," that captured as music might, the spirit of the eighteenth century, and finally the prodigality of "The Toilet" and "The Battle of the Beaux and Belles." Nursing his grudge, Whistler looked on, indifferent. Little by little he cocked his head and his beady birdlike eye lighted with interest, the artist winning over the man. In the end he turned to Beardsley and said slowly:

"Aubrey, I have made a very great mistake—you are a very great artist."

Beardsley burst out crying.

"I mean it— I mean it— I mean it," stammered Whistler, who for once was at a loss for words. It was to his credit that he whose struggle had been so long and embittered could admit the genius of the successful boy.

Still, had it not been for Smithers who bought everything that Beardsley drew and kept him busy with commissions to illustrate reputable and not so reputable masterpieces, the young artist might have starved for all the material recognition the public gave him. He was a prodigy, a subject for parlor conversation— but one could live without his art. Smithers and his list of private subscribers, fortunately, came to the rescue.

Nothing but gossip was known of the sandy-haired, thick-set man with his single eyeglass and conspicuous wedding ring who came down from Sheffield to open a one-room bookshop in a hole and corner section of London. Behind its glass door, curtained by a dirty muslin peep blind, a surreptitious commerce was carried on, sufficient however to keep him dapper in silk hat and morning clothes. Smithers did not remain long in Wardour Street. By mysterious transactions which had to do with books sold under the counter, he came into funds, and ever ready to build him more stately mansions, he blossomed out into a shop in the Royal Arcade where besides selling books he began publishing them.

Strange tales were current about Smithers. Some said he had been an attorney at Leeds where for reasons unknown he was thrown out of the profession. Others credited him with a still shadier past. Whatever his interest in law might have been, he was certainly a passionate bibliophile. A fine edition affected him more than a beautiful woman. Indeed, in the matter of women he was so little discriminating that Oscar Wilde spread the legend that he collected about him the ugliest in the world. At any rate he was always to be seen at home and abroad with a varied assortment of Mrs. Smitherses for whose sake in turn he sported his wedding band.

It was said he founded his fortune on Burton's manuscript of the *Arabian Nights* which he acquired by a trick that only he could have conceived. One Friday afternoon, with a check book but little cash with which to cover his signature, he started off to Lady Burton's in the country to inveigle her into selling him Burton's unexpurgated translation. Lady Burton at first would not hear of it, but such was his power of persuasion that she let him have the manuscript for a few thousand pounds, convinced that through Smithers' offices her husband's work would be preserved for posterity. Craftily Smithers dated the check for the following Monday. The rest of that night and all of Saturday he spent in a frenzied endeavor to find a buyer for the manuscript. No one wanted to touch it. In despair he rose early Sunday morning and followed up all possible leads. Finally he tracked down a purchaser—for five thousand pounds. There was still Lady Burton with his check which might already be on its way to the bank. Not bothering to go home, Smithers installed himself, silk hat, monocle and cane, on the doorstep of his bank, and there, bright and early, the porter found him, tenderly nursing the slip of paper that just in the nick of time had saved him from a session in the law courts—on this side of the bench. Subsequently he edited the Bombay edition of Burton's *Arabian Nights*.

While at the Royal Arcade in his most flourishing period, he opened a bookshop of rare and *recherché* editions in Old Bond Street. His stock was of such sort that he lived in daily dread of the police. But unlike many another who allowed himself to be caught and serve a sentence in gaol, Smithers was ever ready with his ruses. At the threat of unwelcome attentions he bundled the most incriminating of his stock into Gladstone bags kept in readiness for such emergencies, and checked them at the various railroad stations until the danger was past.

Whatever his weaknesses—and he had them all for women, wine, song and later drugs—he possessed a genuine love of books and a flair for art and letters surprising in one with so strong a Yorkshire accent and not always impeccable h's. He knew the most recondite of books, swore that he had done the prose version of Burton's verse translation of Catullus—which he was ready to prove by quoting the Latin at the least challenge— rivaled Swinburne in his cult of the Marquis de Sade, and in every way was as incredible a figure as the most bizarre of that improbable decade. He was acquainted with every artist and writer of the 'nineties—indeed, many of the younger men found it to their advantage to know one who boasted that he would publish anything that others were afraid of. He had made the boast good in the case of Beardsley, left adrift by John Lane, and he had bettered it by taking Dowson under his wing for the translation of *La Fille aux Yeux d'Or* with illustrations by Conder.

Beardsley, however, remained his special protégé. Some hidden tenderness in the rough Yorkshireman was touched by the youth contending for his genius against death itself, and he saw to it that Beardsley should want for nothing. Smithers might be unscrupulous in his dealings with others. He might cheat and defraud for the thrill of the thing. But to Beardsley he was always a generous friend.

Many a time with Dowson, Symons, Beardsley and Conder, Smithers would take a fleeting trip to Dieppe with its beautiful old churches and its bathing beach. He was not the best chaperon for them, knowing as he did all about bad wine and bad women and abetting them in their various remedies for the malady of the century. Wilde found him "wonderful and depraved" a man who "went with monsters to the sound of music." To Beardsley and the pathetic Dowson, and to Conder already tainted by excess, he was an angel—but an angel of destruction.

Chapter IX: The Marquis Leaves a Card

WHILE *The Yellow Book* was reaching heights without benefit of Wilde, an obscure little Oxford magazine containing a contribution by him received unfavorable attention from the pen of Jerome K. Jerome in his journal *To-day* for December 29, 1894. Jerome was shocked. Considering the fact that the offending magazine, *The Chameleon,* circulated only to the extent of a hundred copies and that it was edited by an unknown John Francis Bloxam of Exeter College, the space taken by Jerome seemed unwarranted were it not that, as a protector of public decency, he called attention to what he considered highly objectionable matter.

The Chameleon looked inoffensive enough. A small quarto, the sixty-page magazine had so far scorned the rage for yellow as to appear in green wrappers, with pages printed in a darker shade of the same color. Outwardly there was little to distinguish it from the dozens of arty ephemera that were issuing from the commercial and university presses. Its contents, however, had a striking consonance of tone which, whether intentionally or by accident, strove to comply with the descriptive subtitle, taken from Stevenson: "A Bazaar of Dangerous and Smiling Chances."

Oscar Wilde's contribution, a set of aphorisms entitled "Phrases and Philosophies for the Use of the Young" had the place of honor on the first three pages. There was no other name to compare with his in the index of titles. To men like Jerome K. Jerome who laid great stock by literary dignity, and indeed, to the majority of people, it seemed odd, to say the least, that a man of Wilde's standing should allow writings of his to appear with the outpourings of undergraduates. Originally he had intended publishing them in *The Saturday Review*, but when Lord Alfred came to him one day asking as a personal favor that he contribute something to a magazine about to be started by a friend of his, Wilde, to please him—what did he not always do to please him?—gave him the aphorisms re-titled to suit the college publication. He knew nothing of the young man who was editing it, and even less of the material it would contain. Bosie wished something of him—that was enough.

Judging everyone's level of intellect by his own, Wilde saw no harm in presenting his worldly wisdom to youths in their formative years. Intelligence would know how to interpret, and discrimination how to separate the merely clever from the profound. He therefore sent uncensored—though for that matter he would sooner have cut off his right hand than propitiate morality—such dangerous sparks as: "Wickedness is a myth invented by good people to account for the curious attractiveness of others . . . Those who see any difference between soul and body have neither . . . Religions die when they are proved to be true . . . Science is the record of dead religions . . . Pleasure is the only thing one should live for . . . No crime is vulgar, but all vulgarity is crime . . . Vulgarity is the conduct of others . . . Nothing should reveal the body but the body . . . To love oneself is the beginning of a life-long romance."

Had "Phrases and Philosophies" appeared in any other magazine they would have attracted only the notice allotted to any writer's fugitive pieces. Before contributing to *The Chameleon* Wilde had published "The Disciple" and "The House of Judgment" in Lord Alfred Douglas' *The Spirit Lamp*, where, but for the limited circle of the subscribers, they would have remained had he not given them wider publication through his incomparable gift as a raconteur. *The Chameleon,* however, because of the matter it contained, lent his aphorisms special significance by throwing a lurid light on what would otherwise have passed, as indeed it had, for the usual Wildean parlor cleverness.

It was the story, "The Priest and the Acolyte" that made Jerome K. Jerome sound the alarm. Even for a contribution in a daring college magazine it went beyond the limits of boldness. Briefly, it told of the attachment of a priest for the young boy who was his acolyte, and of the fulfillment his nature found in a relation that he sublimated into spiritual perfection. One

253

night he was discovered with the boy; the only possible interpretation was put upon it. Rather than undergo the loss of the sole being he had been able to love, the priest had the acolyte drink a poisoned chalice and then killed himself. For added spice the anonymous author employed in the poison scene the words of the sacrament of the Church of England. The whole was written with a grim sincerity which made parts of it, such as the priest's confession to his rector, read like some analogous case history in Havelock Ellis' studies in sex inversion. It was the old concept of pagan boy worship, here tricked out with the mystical paraphernalia that made it a product of the *fin de siècle*. In France the genre had long been outmoded with Barbey d'Aurevilly and bolder disciples who had carried it to extremes; in England it was the newest of the new. However, the young author, whoever he was, wrote not so much to shock, except perhaps by his daring in treating such a theme, as to give artistic presentation to something none could help seeing who kept his eyes open in the byways of contemporary life.

Yet even the story might have roused only a passing snarl from the censor had it not been for the presence in the same issue of two poems by Lord Alfred Douglas—a sonnet that called itself "In Praise of Shame" and a longer poem, "Two Loves," which began with a reminiscence of Keats and ended with such conclusions as the earlier poet would never have imagined. In both, as in the rest of the magazine, the content was open to singular interpretation, notwithstanding the artistic subterfuge of the dream vision. Few however could miss the allusion in the sonnet's lines:

> "I am Shame
> That walks with Love; I am most wise to turn
> Cold lips and limbs to fire; therefore discern
> And see my loveliness, and praise my name."

"Two Loves" spoke more plainly still. After describing a flowery landscape the poet has a dream wherein, escorted by a youth in a strange garden, he is shown shadows of the world.

And lo! within the garden of my dream
I saw two walking in a shining plain
Of golden light. The one did joyous seem
And fair, and blooming, and a sweet refrain
Came from his lips; he sang of pretty maids
And joyous love of comely girl and boy . . .
But he that was his comrade walked aside;
He was full sad and sweet, and his large eyes
Were strange with wondrous brightness, staring wide
With gazing; and he sighed with many sighs . . .
A purple robe he wore, o'erwrought with gold
With the device of a great snake whose breath
Was fiery flame; which when I did behold
I fell a-weeping and I cried, "Sweet youth,
Tell me why, sad and sighing, thou dost rove
These pleasant realms? I pray thee speak me sooth
What is thy name?" He said, "My name is Love."
Then straight the first did turn himself to me
'And cried, "He lieth, for his name is Shame,
But I am Love, and I was wont to be
Alone in this fair garden, till he came
Unasked by night; I am true Love, I fill
The hearts of boy and girl with mutual flame."
Then sighing said the other, "Have thy will,
I am the Love that dare not speak its name."

It was a skillful poem which, like the sonnet, showed poetic
feeling and a sense of form that placed it above the apprentice
verse usually found in undergraduate magazines. Imitative it
was, like all early poetic efforts; but the models could not have
been better—the poet of "I stood tip-toe upon a little hill" and
that Dante who interrogated the spirits of Paolo and Francesca
in Hell. Its place, however, within the same wrapper as the story
of "The Priest and the Acolyte," allied "the Love that dare not
speak its name" with the passion that formed the theme of the
prose tale.

Wilde was as horrified on seeing the printed *Chameleon* as
Jerome had been, though for different reasons. He had no idea
when Bosie had come to him for a contribution that such un-

conventional matter, to put it mildly, was to be ushered in by his comparatively innocuous "Phrases and Philosophies." Standing as he did on the very ledge of a moral precipice, he saw the danger of every little pebble in his way—and *The Chameleon* was by no means the least negligible. Acting contrary to his character, he wrote to the authorities protesting the publication of the story. The magazine which had already received more notice than its editors had dared hope for was withdrawn. But greater mischief than Wilde knew had already been done. One of the hundred copies of the first and only number of *The Chameleon* had fallen into the enemy's hands. Furthermore, such was the association in people's minds that the authorship of the story was attributed to him.

Discounting his personal problems which were hourly becoming more complex, Wilde found himself in 1895 at the zenith of his career. Since the performance of *Lady Windermere's Fan* no play of his had been off the boards. On the 3rd of January *An Ideal Husband* opened with éclat at the Royal Theatre in London while his newest and most scintillating comedy was in rehearsal with George Alexander. The gold coins without which Wilde could never be happy were dropping down from heaven in grateful showers. Zestfully he flung them about him as quickly as they came in, enjoying the glitter and music they afforded. Bosie, as ever, was at his side, though behind them, and engulfing them, loomed the ever-present shadow of Queensberry.

On St. Valentine's Day, Little King Street teemed with the bustle and stir that always preceded a gala opening at the St. James's Theatre. *The Importance of Being Earnest,* announced the poster, would be having its first performance that night. The day had dawned stormy and chill, and as the evening drew on the wind hurled the drifting snow in banks along the street. The coachmen in the hansoms breathed upon their numbed fingers for warmth; the horses snorted into the frozen air. Nevertheless broughams, cabs, equipages of all kinds lined both sides of the street, and still they continued to arrive. In the lobby the women threw off their snow-flecked furs and held against their shoulders sprays of white lilies. Single blossoms adorned the lapels of the dandies who held tall Whistlerian ebony canes with ivory tops in their white-gloved hands, and minced about in the shining pointed shoes that were the fashion.

Queensberry would not miss the occasion. Several hours before the opening he blustered in carrying a grotesque bouquet of vegetables which he intended hurling at the author when he was called upon to make his curtain speech. A prize fighter accompanied him. The box office which had been warned of some such visit stopped the Marquis and his bodyguard at the door. But they would not be deterred. For three hours they prowled about, closely watched by the Scotland Yard men who had been posted there to prevent disturbance, and finally, after the doors were closed, they left, Queensberry shaking his head in wrath and muttering to himself.

Within, almost from the instant the curtain rose, the house resounded with laughter from the completely sympathetic audience. With a stroke of his peculiar magic Wilde had captivated it from the very first exchange between Algernon Moncrief who had been playing the piano offstage, and Lane, his manservant.

Algernon: Did you hear what I was playing, Lane?

Lane: I didn't think it polite to listen, sir.

Algernon: I'm sorry for that, for your sake. I don't play accurately—anyone can play accurately—but I play with wonderful expression. As far as the piano is concerned, sentiment is my forte. I keep science for Life.

Lane: Yes, sir.

The mood of absurdity and extravagance was set. From that moment the audience entered Wilde's imaginary world and became part of it in an intimate communion which only the highest art can achieve. The dainty youths with their black-stitched white gloves all felt themselves potential Algernons in their cleverness; the women found it difficult to choose between Gwendolen and Cecily. Throughout, a fountain of the most preposterously delightful dialogue jetted and played. A man who could write like that must be of another order of humanity, a being like those vivid summer creatures that cannot live except in the light. Unreality became real from the instant he touched

257

it. The fantastic was the order of the day. Once the threshold of probability was crossed, no one found anything strange in Worthing's sententious: "It is a very ungentlemanly thing to read a private cigarette case," or in Cecily's confidences to her diary long before the events she recorded. The light loves, the lighter pains, the fleeting emotions and the still more transitory circumstances that called them forth belonged to a supra-lunary world where anything so deep as a sorrow was unknown. In that realm life and death were equally a jest and morality as absurd as the thing that prompted it.

Chasuble: Your brother Ernest dead?

Jack: Quite dead.

Miss Prism: What a lesson for him! I trust he will profit by it.

Through the three all too brief acts the audience shared with Wilde the pleasures of his kingdom and forgot the annoyance of life in the catharsis of laughter. The critics whose function it is to find analogies that they may go home and sleep soundly agreed that not since the days of So-and-So had English comedy come to such flowering. They would have been aghast indeed to learn that *The Importance of Being Earnest* was dashed off in about a fortnight; and probably their reviews would have been colored by the knowledge. With Wilde his special gift did not express itself in the capacity for taking infinite pains. The methods of a Flaubert who struggled for a week over a passage and held himself chained to his writing table for hours every day, would have atrophied any quality of imagination in the Wilde who nonetheless admired him. But to every man his method. It is not the time required, nor the sweat of the brow, that constitutes the excellence of a *Madame Bovary.* Many have slaved and sweated with nothing greater to show than the *mus ridiculus.* Still, Wilde had a certain naïve reverence for the sacrifices of the artist and was inclined to favor *Dorian Gray* and others of his works that mingled a faint smell of the midnight oil with their exotic perfumes, to the airy nonsense of his comedies.

During the intermission Wilde went into Mrs. Leverson's box where among other guests sat Aubrey Beardsley and his sister. Wilde was glowing from his triumph. As soon as he appeared the air became electric with his presence. Life and gaiety entered with him; he seemed transformed in the almost supernatural joy that emanated from him, softening the sensuality of his face, the grossness of his features marred by overindulgence. As with Dorian Gray the spirit concealed the ravages of sin— except that in Wilde the soul expressed itself in a contagious euphoria that, like wine in water, colored the blankness of life.

Once the success of the new comedy was assured Wilde and Bosie took one of their vacations together, this time to Algiers. Wilde had long been looking forward to it, and as early as the previous spring had written to Douglas about it. When they started out, however, it was under the cloud of Queensberry's threats, exacerbated by his unsuccess in drawing Wilde into a public scandal. Vengeance alone existed for him now. He would have it, no matter what he had to destroy on the way.

The pair, like hungry men who feel their food may soon be taken from them, made the most of their time. They knew the country. Traveling from one place to the other they visited well-known haunts, taking their enjoyments where they found them. Wilde was a notorious figure. Wherever he went he was escorted by a mob of young scamps shrieking, laughing, dancing like fauns in the train of a Bacchus. He enjoyed it and threw them money. Everything could be bought for money.

One day André Gide who happened to be traveling in Algiers at the same time, found as he glanced down the slate of his hotel, the names of Oscar Wilde and Lord Alfred Douglas at the end of the list. He started. Then almost instinctively he erased his own and left for the station with his luggage. On the way he pondered his action. Why had he rubbed out his name? He had known Wilde in Paris; they had had delightful luncheons together; they had friends in common in Pierre Louys and many another from among French writers. He liked Wilde. But the man had acquired a bad name. People in Paris as well as in London were talking about his scandalous life. Ashamed of himself for his action Gide tried to rationalize it into a desire for solitude. Then thinking that perhaps Wilde had seen his name on the blackboard, and feeling ashamed of his flight, he turned back to the hotel.

They met, as was inevitable, Gide with difficulty concealing his dismay at the change in Wilde. It was not physical so much as spiritual. Something in him, a reserve that he had once scrupulously observed, was gone; in fact he took pains to flaunt his complete amorality. No longer did he speak in the beautiful fables that had charmed his listeners. He had become hard, undisciplined.

Almost the first words he spoke to Gide were about Bosie whom he compared to a "charming god." Gide who was soon introduced to Lord Alfred failed to perceive his divinity, but noticed on the other hand, that his mere presence incited Wilde to recklessness. But it was a recklessness which came, as Gide could not help remarking, as a reflex of Lord Alfred's who possessed something so violent, so impelling in his nature that it carried everyone, including himself, with it. It was more than his pouting manner of a small boy, his imperious insistence on his own way in trifles, that made Wilde yield to him at every turn.

"Oh, isn't he terrible . . . terrible?" he would ask Gide, half-proud, half-pathetic. And Gide, before the flaming eyes of the possessed youth admitted the terribleness of the domination.

They went out, all three together, in search of pleasure, under the tutelage of a professional procurer.

"My special duty," declared Wilde, "is to plunge madly into amusement. Not happiness! Pleasure. One must always set one's heart upon the most tragic."

He said he hoped they would come across some young Arabs. *"Beaux comme des statues de bronze,"* he added with a laugh and a deprecating wave of the hand. He spoke French well with scarcely any accent, attenuating with a touch of mockery, as in this instance, the pretentiousness of the phrase. He had gone far since he shocked the perfectionist Stuart Merrill with the unpardonable, *"Et puis, le roi il est mouru."*

"These guides are so stupid," said Lord Alfred, putting his

arm through Gide's. "No matter what you tell them they're always taking you to cafés full of women."

They found the amusements they sought. Wilde, Gide observed, laughed loud and often with a hysterical immoderateness in his outbursts. It rang like laughter that was near to sobs. After Lord Alfred left for Blidah for a few days Gide had occasion to study Wilde more closely. Together they set out in quest of adventure, Wilde knowing the tortuous streets and alleys better than any guide. Then it was that Gide learned how terrible indeed was the change that had come over the man. Beardsley with his uncanny sensitivity had felt it and told it to the world when he caricatured him as a drunken Bacchus with vine leaves in his hair, gross lips and eyes leering their solicitations. Wilde was no longer satisfied merely to enjoy his pleasures. He must have the added thrill of corrupting others to his ways.

During their intimacy Gide prevailed upon Wilde to talk about himself. "Would you like to know the great drama of my life?" Wilde asked. "It is that I have put my genius into my life— I have put only my talent into my works."

That genius, unhappily, was in its decadence.

Finally, unburdening himself, Wilde told the young Frenchman of his persecution by the Marquis of Queensberry and of the dangers that menaced in London.

"Do you know the risk you are running?" Gide asked him.

"It is best never to know," said Wilde strangely. "My friends are extraordinary," he continued. "They beg me to be careful. Careful? But how can I be careful? That would be a step backward. I must go on . . . I cannot go much further—something is bound to happen—something else."

What that something was he learned the moment he set foot in England.

According to his custom he went in the late afternoon of February 28 to the Albermarle Club of which he was a member. On arriving there the hall porter, Sidney Wright, came over to him with an envelope. "Lord Queensberry desired me, sir, to hand you this when you came back," he said

261

Wilde took the envelope and looked at it. On the back he read his name and a notation, evidently in Wright's hand: "4:30; 18-2-95." Inside he found a printed visiting card of Queensberry's with some words scrawled upon it in the all too familiar hand. For a moment he could not believe his eyes, but there, at last, in writing, was the terrible accusation in the Marquis's own peculiar spelling: "To Oscar Wilde posing as a somdomite."

Had the porter read what was written on the card? Had anyone else seen it? He questioned Wright. Yes, he had looked at the card, but he did not understand it. Since the Marquis had given him the uncovered square, he put it into an envelope, wrote Mr. Wilde's name and the date upon it, and put it away against his coming. He had let no one else see it.

Had the brilliant author shown the same discretion as the porter no one else need have known about it and the story of Oscar Wilde might have been different. But that something else which was bound to happen, the fatality which had followed him like his own shadow, could no longer be ignored.

From the club he drove to the Avondale Hotel, Piccadilly, where he sometimes stayed. He could not possibly go to Tite Street and reveal to Constance a thing of which she had not the remotest suspicion. How would she understand the implications of Queensberry's card?

He could think of only one friend whose advice he wanted under the circumstances. Robert Ross was young, but what balance and sanity he had in everything that concerned him! In great agitation he dashed off a note to Ross asking him to come to see him at the hotel and indicating the trend of his thoughts: "I don't see anything now but a criminal prosecution—my whole life is ruined by this man. The tower of ivory is assailed by the foul thing. . . . On the sand is my life spilt—I don't know what to do." Even now, behind the real fear betrayed by the note, was discernible Wilde's enjoyment of his role of martyr, assailed by the foul thing, his life spilt on the sand.

Lord Alfred was all for prosecution.[1] He said, in fact, that

262

his relations would be happy to bear the expenses of a trial if they could be sure to place under lock and key, and beyond the possibility of further mischief-making, the man whose sole purpose seemed to be the wrecking of their lives. Percy, his brother, echoed him. After a conference with him Oscar wrote to Bosie: "Percy is on our side. I feel now that, without your name being mentioned, all will go well."

The only thing Ross could do, once Wilde made up his mind, was to advise him to consult Messrs. Humphreys and May, a reputable firm of solicitors. On the last of March, accordingly, Wilde presented his case to Mr. Charles Octavius Humphreys, the senior partner, who listened with amazement as he unfolded his story. It was unheard of for a man of Wilde's class to be subjected to such inhuman persecution on the part of Queensberry. But Mr. Humphreys wished to make certain of one thing before he undertook the case. Point-blank he asked Wilde on his solemn oath whether there was any truth in the libel.

"I am absolutely innocent," Wilde swore.

"If you are innocent," said Mr. Humphreys, "you should succeed."

Elated at this assurance of success, and oblivious that it had been based on his own lie, Wilde went down personally to the Police Court to apply for a warrant for Queensberry's arrest on the charge that the Marquis had made and published a libel against him. The following day Queensberry was arrested at Carter's Hotel, charged with the libel at the Marlborough Police Court, and released on bail until the hearing.

[1] Here as elsewhere information derives from the so-called unpublished *De Profundis* checked and collated with Lord Alfred's various versions of the circumstances.

Chapter X: The Booby Trap

Pending the deposition and the trial Wilde and Bosie went
to Monte Carlo. It had not been Wilde's idea. Several times
between the afternoon he received Queensberry's card and the
day he applied for a warrant some instinct told him to give up
the suit. But a will stronger than his own imposed itself upon
his wavering resolve. A will, and circumstance. Soon after he
had engaged rooms at the Avondale Hotel Bosie came to stay
with him. He remained for ten days, and in the interval Wilde's
bill mounted to one hundred and forty pounds. As the time
approached for his taking active steps against Queensberry,
Wilde, with the hunted animal's impulse for flight, packed his
luggage and prepared to cross the Channel. But alas! that life
which he had scornfully treated as a mode of fiction took one
of the many little revenges it had in store for him. With crude
realism the proprietor would not let him go until the bill was
settled, and Wilde, after the Algiers excursion, was temporarily
out of pocket. Since he could not get the sum together at a moment's notice he had to abandon his plan of flight and went, instead, for the warrant for Queensberry's arrest.

Once the Marquis was committed Bosie suggested spending
the weeks before the trial with Wilde abroad. As usual Oscar,
again in funds, let himself be persuaded and went off with
Bosie instead of staying in London near his lawyers to prepare
himself for a case which his better judgment told him held many
a slip betwixt prosecution and triumph. The publicity had been
stupendous. On the continent and in America the wires hummed
with the details of a case that promised more than ordinary
sensation. The brilliant Wilde suing for libel a noble lord with
whose son he had long had an ambiguous friendship: it was
enough to send the circulation of the press soaring, a desider-
atum which the newly established yellow journalism did its
best to further.

Meanwhile at Monte Carlo Wilde who had no love for *roulette* found leisure to ponder his position while Bosie stood riveted to the gaming tables of the casino. What was awaiting him in England? True, in the beginning he had been elated at the prospect of a case in which he would be the central figure, with the newspapers reporting his clever sallies, the artists sketching him and the whole world resounding with his name. He would be the hero crushing the Philistine brute under his heel to rescue beauty from the mire of prejudice. He would force the lie into Queensberry's throat and himself explain the meaning of a friendship which ignorance persisted in misunderstanding. But was Queensberry's charge really a lie? "To Oscar Wilde posing as a sodomite." The insertion of the word *posing* had the cunning of the very devil in it. How could he, who affected so many poses, deny that one? He would be called into the witness box. He would be forced to answer many questions on his mode of living—he who had never troubled to conceal certain aspects of his life, but on the contrary had made a boast of them.

Sometimes when he succeeded in tearing Bosie away from *roulette* he tried to discuss with him the many angles of the case. Impatiently, Bosie turned away. Was Wilde showing the white feather? Could he possibly be afraid to face Queensberry? And with scathing words he taunted the weakling who allowed himself to be intimidated by a mad old man.

Nevertheless, all was not as Wilde had at first believed. At Monte Carlo the manager of the hotel at which they had first applied refused to receive them, so rapidly had the news spread. Like that prudent man the rest of the world might have a different concept of a hero from the one which he, with the egging on of Bosie and his brother, had been led to create for himself.

In London on his return his friends besought him to give up the suit. Bosie stormed against them for meddling in the affair, and renewed his taunts. Wilde must go on with the case. It was the only way to render harmless a brute who was a menace to society. Once more Wilde allowed himself to be overruled, even though convinced that he might have to brazen it out in the box with "absurd and silly perjuries."[1]

On the 29th of March he set out to make his deposition at the Marlborough Police Court, already packed with a crowd conspicuous for the absence of women. There was a stir when the carriage and pair, with liveried servants, drew up and out stepped Wilde accompanied by Lord Alfred Douglas and Lord Douglas of Hawick. No sooner had the trio entered than the presiding magistrate turned to Lord Alfred and ordered him to leave the court. The interrogation was brief. Wilde answered his counsel's questions, rehearsed his acquiring of the libelous card and then, before signing his deposition, asked to have it read again.

"If you would just attend, this would not have happened," the magistrate reproved him.

The die was cast. On Wednesday, the 3rd of April, at the Old Bailey, life caught up with the artist Wilde.

The mean little courtroom was filled to the last square foot of space. For centuries the judges had complained of the sordidness of the court of law where even they, upon entering, were oppressed by a weight of doom. The prisoners' bench which could hold thirty criminals, was the roomiest place in it, whereas the counsel and the public had to make the best of what little accommodation the miserable old building afforded. On the present occasion the room was so packed that the dock itself had to be turned over to the fashionable crowd that kept on gathering, milling at the entrances and lining the walls.

Of the parties concerned Queensberry was the first to arrive. He came alone, looked at no one, spoke to no one, hardly aware of the whispers that arose as the people identified him by his red whiskers and the Cambridge-blue hunting stock that as a sportsman he affected instead of the common collar and tie. Someone made a jest on "the importance of being early" and there was a laugh quickly subdued by the imposing figure of Oscar Wilde, squeezing his way through the crowd, followed by Lord Alfred. Wilde had taken special pains with his toilette

[1] Wilde's own phrase. From the so-called unpublished *De Profundis*.

266

that morning. His rich brown hair, carefully parted, was banked in waves on top of his head. His dark, tight-fitting frock coat that seemed hardly to contain his immeasurable girth was topped by a collar with wide points. He wore a black tie, carried a very tall, conical-shaped silk hat, and light gloves. He had removed his long Melton overcoat which hung carelessly over his arm.

A contagious well-being emanated from him. One might have thought he came to the court as he went to his own plays for the exaltation he derived from the delight he inspired. Confidence was written all over his face, in the ease with which he joined Sir Edward Clarke, Q.C., his counsel, in the carelessness of his gestures. After all, wasn't it old Ned Carson who was acting for Queensberry? How could he have any qualms about an old Trinity schoolfellow whom he had surpassed so effortlessly in their classical rivalry? Hence he chatted genially with Sir Edward and his other counsel, Charles Mathews and Travers Humphreys.

Edward Carson, Q.C., long and lean, more than ever looking the nickname of Rawbones that his classmates had given him, sat forbiddingly grave near Queensberry and the two other defending counsels, Mr. C. F. Gill and Mr. A. Gill. When, in the beginning of March, young Charles Russell whom Queensberry had approached to answer the charge of criminal libel was looking about for the best man to handle a case of such difficulty, he had gone to Dr. Johnson's Buildings in search of Carson. At first Carson had rejected the case. There was no definite evidence against Wilde, and the documents on which Queensberry wished to build his defense were not enough to substantiate the charge of "posing as a sodomite," although on the literary side evidence for the pose could easily have been adduced. Moreover Carson hated cases of that nature, and not so long since had thrown a shady brief out on the landing, shouting at the men who had brought it: "If there is anything I loathe and detest above all else, it is the raking up of a public man's private affairs against him. We're all sinners."

That undeviating sense of right, however, which prompted him against taking Queensberry's defense when he thought the accusation unwarranted, made him turn to it fanatically when the Marquis's partisans and detectives, working overtime, uncovered a mine of far from literary incriminations. On that evidence which, with detective Littlechild, Wilde's former friend Brookfield had helped to unearth, Carson based his attack. Queensberry who had been frantic with joy when Wilde had fallen into "the booby trap" that he boasted to have laid for him, rubbed his hands at having obtained Carson to make the kill. On his side Wilde felt secure in his intellectual superiority over Carson and in his having to plead for him Sir Edward who was the leader of the Bar.

The crowd was beginning to grow restive while waiting for the judge. At last the usher's three knocks sounded at the door (Did Wilde think of the three knocks that announced the rising of the curtain at the Comédie Française?) and everybody stood up as the exalted presences crossed the threshold. First, august in scarlet and ermine, came Mr. Justice Henn Collins; behind him, in court dress and sword, followed the High Sheriff of London.

The gentlemen of the Bar bow to the Judge. Graciously he acknowledges their greeting and sits down. Before him a bouquet of flowers—a survival of the days when they were carried against the plague—obstructs his view. He takes it up and lays it to one side. The Marquis of Queensberry is motioned to the dock. Looking neither to the right nor to the left he takes his stand and the charge is read to him. Suddenly turning toward Wilde with a truculent look he answers in a voice that echoes through the court: "Not guilty." The words, he continues, were true, and published in the public interest. The trial has begun.

With a dignity that added cubits to his small stature Sir Edward rose and opened the case for the prosecution. He had no doubt of Wilde's innocence—had not Wilde sworn to it on oath? —and he spoke with conviction. For more than an hour he sketched in Wilde's background, told of his distinguished university career and dwelt on his literary achievements. Patiently he traced Wilde's friendship with Lord Alfred and rehearsed his few meetings with Queensberry. The audience listened with

268

polite interest. It was all necessary, if rather boring. What was the respected leader of the Bar leading to, people asked one another? His colleagues nodded approval of his form—but what line was he choosing in conducting the case?

Gradually Sir Edward came to pertinent facts. He narrated the attempts at blackmail made upon Wilde by men who had come in possession of certain letters that he had written to Lord Alfred—perfectly innocent letters, such letters as an artist might write to some cultured young poet whom he admired. Indeed, Sir Edward would read one of those letters, a sort of prose sonnet which had, as a matter of fact, been rendered into French verse by a friend of Mr. Wilde's. And with admirable equanimity, as if he were dealing with the figures of a census, Sir Edward read the letter that Wilde had reclaimed from Allen and Cliburn.

The audience sat up as one man. At the phrases "red rose-leaf lips," "madness of kisses," "your slim gilt soul walks between passion and poetry," "Hyacinthus whom Apollo loved so madly" men exchanged glances and then looked from Wilde to Lord Alfred and at the Marquis, mumbling under his breath in the dock. The jury sat stonily.

"What is the date of it?" the foreman asked darkly.

It was not dated, Sir Edward told him, and quickly changed his tactics.

Sidney Wright, the hall porter of the Albermarle, was then sworn in, and after he told of how he had received the card from the Marquis of Queensberry—to establish the point of the publication of the libel—Wilde was called to the witness box to be examined by Sir Edward. Every eye was fixed upon him as he kissed the Book and then turned toward his counsel a face that would have inspired confidence in a misanthrope. As he answered the preliminary questions he leaned over the narrow rail, his hands, with their long, beautifully shaped nails toying with a pair of gloves. Shifting his position in the dock the better to see him, Queensberry gave him a look wherein contempt mingled with hate.

On being asked his age Wilde replied, "Thirty-nine."

Carson, who until that moment had been sitting in apparent abstraction stared at him fixedly and then made a note. Blithely Wilde answered his counsel's questions as if he were participating at a dinner conversation, traced the story of his friendship with Lord Alfred who, he stressed, was also acquainted with his wife, and related with amusing detail the visit of Allen and Cliburn to his home. The court was with him. Even the jury relaxed the tenseness into which the reading of the letter had put them; a few of the men were seen to control their smiles as with confident good humor Wilde told how he had outwitted the blackmailers, as if such encounters were the most natural in the world. In the dock the Marquis gave vent to subdued and angry muttering, increasingly violent as Wilde told of the interview at his home between Queensberry and himself.

The high spot of the day was yet to come, and the court keyed itself up to it like an audience at the theatre when Carson rose to cross-examine the witness. Many of them knew that the two men had been schoolmates together. Intently they watched for some sign of recognition, as the man who was known to have made hardened criminals weep, came forward to face his victim. Wilde greeted him with a wide, frank smile. Embarrassed, Carson pretended not to notice and plunged immediately into his questioning. His Dublin brogue—so much admired by Lady Londonderry's circle that the women went about gushing that he simply must not lose it, it was so adorable—contrasted unfavorably with Wilde's perfect enunciation which gave to each syllable the value of a note of music. Carson, moreover, suffered an added disadvantage in that he had a cold. He made up for everything, however, by the cunning of his opening attack.

"You stated that your age was thirty-nine," he challenged. "I think that you are over forty. You were born on the 16th of October, 1854."

"I had no wish to pose as being young," Wilde retorted. "I am thirty-nine or forty."

"But, Mr. Wilde, doesn't 1854 from 1895 leave forty-one?" With a mock courteous bow and a wave of the hand, Wilde dismissed the subject. "You have my certificate and that settles the matter."

Years ago, on his visit to America, Speranza's son, inheriting her dread of growing old, had given his age as twenty-six instead of twenty-eight. No one had run to verify it by his birth date, and it would have made no difference in any case. But Wilde's foolish lie in answer to almost the first question put to him after he kissed the Book had its effect upon the jury and the court when Carson exposed it. There was yet another motive, one that neither Wilde nor his counsel anticipated, in this stress on Wilde's true age.

Deftly Carson changed his lead, now that he was accomplishing his purpose, and went on to the subject of literature. Both Sir Edward and Wilde had expected that the defense would build up its justification on the prosecutor's writings. Wilde regained his assurance, therefore, though a cloud seemed to pass over him when Carson introduced "Phrases and Philosophies" and other publications in *The Chameleon*. How quickly one's most insignificant actions caught up with one, and what proportions they took!

"You read 'The Priest and the Acolyte'?" asked Carson.

"Yes."

"You have no doubt whatever that that was an improper story?"

"From the literary point of view it was highly improper . . ."

"You are of the opinion, I believe, that there is no such thing as an immoral book?"

"Yes."

"May I take it that you think 'The Priest and the Acolyte' was not immoral?"

"It was worse—it was badly written."

Everybody laughed. Carson rattled his papers and went on with his interrogatory. Let them be amused by the frivolous mountebank. In his rigid code Carson knew the worth of such easy triumphs.

"Do you think the story blasphemous?" he hammered away in an attempt to show Wilde as irreligious as well as immoral.

"I think it violated every artistic canon of beauty," Wilde countered.

"That is not an answer."

"It is the only one I can give."

"I want to see the position you pose in."

"I do not think you should say that."

"I have said nothing out of the way," Carson caught himself. "I wish to know whether you thought the story blasphemous."

"I think it is horrible. 'Blasphemous' is not a word of mine." Wilde's voice throbbed with feeling. Such sincerity about mere artistic matters came as a revelation to all who had thought Wilde genuine only in his pose. Carson clung stubbornly to his attack.

"So far as your works are concerned, you pose as not being concerned about morality or immorality?"

"I do not know whether you use the word 'pose' in any particular sense," said Wilde.

"It is a favorite one of your own." Carson made his thrust.

"Is it?" said Wilde with quick fire. "I have no pose in this matter. In writing a play or a book, I am concerned entirely with literature—that is, with art. I aim not at doing good or evil, but at trying to make a thing that will have some quality of beauty."

There was a stir of applause, immediately suppressed. By imperceptible degrees the court was being divided into ranks, those standing with Wilde in upholding art, and the others, the Philistines, as Wilde would have dubbed them, who shook their heads at what appeared to be the victory of evil over right. Carson, as he made his innuendoes more pointed, began to betray signs of ill temper. He was not accustomed to so deft an opponent. He questioned Wilde on *Dorian Gray*.

"This is in your introduction," he said, reading. " 'There is no such thing as a moral or an immoral book. Books are well written or badly written.' That expresses your view?"

"My view on art, yes."

"Then I take it that no matter how immoral a book may be, if it is well written it is, in your opinion, a good book?"

"Yes, if it is well written so as to produce a sense of beauty, which is the highest sense of which a human being can be capable. . . ."

"Then a well-written book putting forth perverted moral views may be a good book?"

"No work of art ever puts forth views. Views belong to people who are not artists."

Carson went on doggedly. "A perverted novel may be a good book?"

Wilde winced at the word. "I don't know what you mean by a perverted novel."

"Then I suggest *Dorian Gray* as open to the interpretation of being such a novel."

"That could only be to brutes and illiterates," said Wilde with spirit. He no longer toyed with his gloves. He stood tense and aware, ready to better every blow.

"Have you ever adored a young man madly?" asked Carson after reading a passage from the novel.

"No, not madly. I prefer love—that is a higher form."

"Never mind about that," said Carson grimly. "Let us keep down to the level we are at now."

"I have never given adoration to anybody except myself," Wilde lightly skirted the pitfall. But he underestimated Carson.

" 'I have adored you extravagantly,' " the counsel went on quoting.

"Do you mean financially?" Wilde asked innocently.

"Oh, yes, financially! Do you think we are talking about finance?"

"I don't know what you are talking about."

"Don't you?" Carson echoed. Then with menace in his tone he said, "Well, I hope I shall make myself very plain before I have done."

He was as good as his word, although as yet he had not drawn upon his secret store of evidence. "Why should a man of your age," he continued, after reading the letter which Sir Edward Clarke had presented earlier in the day, "address a boy nearly twenty years younger as 'My own Boy'?"

273

"I was fond of him. I have always been fond of him . . . I think it is a beautiful letter. It is a poem . . . You might as well cross-examine me as to whether *King Lear* or a sonnet of Shakespeare's was improper."

"Apart from art, Mr. Wilde?"

"I cannot answer apart from art. . . ."

"I can suggest for the sake of your reputation that there is nothing very wonderful in this 'red rose-leaf lips of yours'?" Carson put into the words a hint of ridicule.

"A great deal depends on the way it is read."

There was laughter, for indeed, even Lady Londonderry's circle could have found little to admire in Carson's rendering of the letter.

" 'Your slim gilt soul walks between passion and poetry.' Is that a beautiful phrase?"

"Not as you read it, Mr. Carson."

"I do not profess to be an artist," Carson broke out, "and when I hear you give evidence I am glad I am not! . . . Have you often written letters in the same style as this?" he resumed more equably.

"I do not repeat myself in style," said Wilde warily.

Carson looked for something among his papers and began reading: " 'Dearest of all Boys—Your letter was delightful red and yellow wine to me; but I am sad and out of sorts. Bosie, you must not make scenes with me. They kill me, they wreck the loveliness of life. I cannot see you, so Greek and gracious, distorted with passion. I cannot listen to your curved lips saying hideous things to me . . . I must see you soon. You are the divine thing I want, the thing of grace and beauty; but I don't know how to do it . . . Why are you not here, my dear, my wonderful boy? . . . Your own Oscar.'—Is *that* an ordinary letter?"

Wilde, to whom the reading had summoned up the turbulent scenes with Bosie and presented in a flash the fatal complexity of a relation that had given him great depths of joy and of pain, had yet enough presence of mind to conceal his feelings in a flippant retort. "Everything I write is extraordinary. I do not pose as being ordinary, great heavens!"

But how had Carson obtained that letter written by him in one of those moments of despair when, while struggling to free himself from a tyrannous domination he made himself the more its slave? How had Bosie ever let that pathetic plea out of his hands? Unthinking, careless Bosie who left his most intimate papers in the pockets of the suits he gave away, or lying among the heaps of unwanted rubbish in vacated hotel rooms!

In the afternoon the cross-examination fell from the literary plane to an inquisition on matters of a very mundane nature. Wilde was taken unawares. Sir Edward Clarke who had prepared his case from Wilde's information and was therefore pursuing the line that he was suffering an unjust persecution, appeared visibly disturbed by the specific evidence with which Carson was confronting the witness. Neither he nor Wilde had the least suspicion that Queensberry's detectives had not only done their work, but that they had done it thoroughly. As the afternoon wore off and the waning daylight filled the courtroom with shadows, the names of Wood, Mavor, Alfred Taylor, Fred Atkins, Shelley, Conway, William and Charles Parker took on substance like evil spirits summoned by enchantment. They followed Wilde out of the court when at last he had a respite from Carson's badgering; they were with him all night, to resume their places before him in the courtroom when again he took the witness box the following morning.

As at the opening session he was meticulously dressed. Not a wave of his hair was out of place; his lapel held its usual morning flower. But Wilde himself, though waiting smilingly for his opponent to begin, had neither the gaiety nor the buoyancy of the first encounter. He was less flippant in his answers, as if before pronouncing the words he were weighing their power to injure him.

Carson had now abandoned the literary attack altogether and confined himself solely to the task of getting Wilde to betray the nature of his relations with Alfred Taylor and the young men whom he met at the tea parties in Little College Street. Was there not something peculiar, Carson insinuated, in the perfumed, curtained apartment of a man all of whose guests were boys? Had he not met Sidney Mavor in Taylor's rooms— and others whose names he mentioned? And did he not get Taylor to arrange dinners for him to meet young men? Did he not know that Taylor was being watched by the police and that he and Charles Parker had been arrested in a raid? Was it not true that he had given money and presents to at least five of the youths whom he had met at Taylor's?

To all the questions Wilde answered with apparent directness. (The time had come to brazen it out with "absurd and silly perjuries.") No, Taylor's rooms did not strike him as peculiar except that they were furnished in better taste than ordinary. As for Taylor, he was a young man of taste and intelligence, a public school boy, and a friend of his. Yes, it was true that he had given money and presents to the young men mentioned: they had given him nothing.

Carson then interrogated him on a dinner party to which Taylor had brought Charles and William Parker. "Taylor accepted your invitation by bringing a valet and groom to dine with you?"

"That is your account, not mine."

"Were they persons of that class?"

"I am surprised at your description of them," Wilde retorted. "They did not seem to have the manners of 'that class.' . . . Charlie Parker told me he was desirous to go on the stage."

"Did you call him Charlie?" Carson quickly picked up the slip.

"Yes . . ."

"Was it a good dinner?"

"Kettner's is not so gorgeous as some restaurants, but it was Kettner at his best."

"With the best of Kettner's wines?"

"Yes, certainly."

"All for the valet and the groom?"

"No—for my friends . . ."

276

"Now, after dinner, did you say referring to Charles Parker, in the presence of Taylor and William Parker, the brother, 'This is the boy for me'?"

"Certainly not!"

"Do you drink champagne yourself?"

"Yes, iced champagne is a favorite drink of mine—strongly against my doctor's orders." Wilde smiled, seeking to break the tension.

"Never mind your doctor's orders, sir."

"I never do . . ." He laughed his irresistible, infectious laugh. The court had to be called to order.

"What was there in common between this young man and yourself?" persisted Carson, referring to Charles Parker. "What attraction had he for you?"

"I delight in the society of people much younger than my-self," Wilde answered truthfully. "I like those who may be called idle and careless. I recognize no social distinctions of any kind, and to me youth, the mere fact of youth, is so wonderful that I would sooner talk to a young man for half-an-hour than be even—well, cross-examined in court."

Carson ignored the taunt and continued pressing him on his friendship with valets, grooms and bookmakers, playing on the prejudice of the class-conscious Briton that no gentleman would have associated with inferiors from any honorable motive. Name after name was brought up in the scandalous category and Wilde was forced to admit his knowledge of each one. Yes, he had known a young man, Fred Atkins, employed by a firm of bookmakers. Fred had been introduced to him by— (Here, be-cause Schwabe, the intermediary, was a nephew of Sir Frank Lockwood, Q.C., M.P., the hush-hush policy was adopted of suppressing his name.) He had taken Atkins to Paris with him. He had called him "Fred" and Atkins had called him "Oscar." He had given him three pounds to buy his first song for the music hall stage for which he was ambitious. That was in March, 1894. There had never been any improprieties between them . . . Yes, he knew Ernest Scarfe. He had met him through Taylor who told him he knew a young man who had become acquainted with Lord Douglas of Hawick on board ship going out to Australia. . . . Sidney Mavor he had first met in September, 1892. He gave the young man a cigarette case. Mavor stayed with him one night at a hotel in Albermarle Street because he had just returned to London from Scotland, and his house being empty, he preferred passing the time with a pleasant companion.

His answers came mechanically. Now and then he would pass his hand through his hair in a gesture of weariness. He had been in the witness box for hours. He was no longer smiling. Carson watched him, ready to swoop. His man was where he wanted him.

"Do you know Walter Grainger?" he asked without altering his tone.

"Yes," replied Wilde to whom the name brought up a plain boy in the house in High Street, Oxford, where Bosie had rooms.

"How old is he?"

"He was about sixteen when I knew him . . . Grainger waited at table. I never dined with him," he forestalled the inevitable question. "If it is one's duty to serve, it is one's duty to serve; if it is one's pleasure to dine, it is one's pleasure to dine." Decidedly, Wilde must have been bored and tired to utter such platitudinous nonsense.

Carson looked at him narrowly and leaning forward asked him suddenly: "Did you ever kiss him?"

"Oh, dear, no," said Wilde, expressing disgust at the thought. "He was a peculiarly plain boy. He was, unfortunately, extremely ugly." He seemed unable to leave the subject. "I pitied him for it."

The jurymen sat up tense. The very benches stiffened. Carson's had been a deadly snare; this time Wilde by his flippancy had caught himself in it.

Almost with exultation Carson shouted his next question:

"Was that the reason why you did not kiss him?"

"Oh, Mr. Carson! You are pertinently insolent!" He drew back in the witness box.

Now that he had him at his mercy Carson came closer, hissing his words almost into his face: "Did you say that in support of your statement that you never kissed him?"

"No. It is a childish question." Wilde was obviously at a loss, which made Carson ruthlessly press a point that the most innocent person present understood too plainly.

"Did you ever put that forward as a reason why you never kissed the boy?"

"Not at all." Wilde's words came with difficulty; several times he tried to say something in justification and at each attempt the syllables caught in his throat in incoherent cries.

"Why, sir," Carson badgered him, "why did you mention that this boy was extremely ugly?"

"For this reason. If I were asked why I did not kiss a door-mat, I should say because I do not like to kiss doormats. I do not know why I mentioned that he was ugly, except that I was stung by the insolent question you put to me . . ."

"Why did you mention his ugliness, I ask you?"

"Perhaps you insulted me by an insulting question."

"Was that a reason why you should say the boy was ugly? Why, why did you add that? Why?"

In the narrow box Wilde reeled as if he were about to fall. His usually colorless face was flushed, his eyes glistening with tears. Instinctively he recoiled and his hands went up to shield him against the sting of that cruel "Why? Why? Why?"

After an interval of unbearable suspense the court heard him say in a voice that he tried valiantly to control: "You sting me and insult me and try to unnerve me, and at times one says things flippantly when one ought to speak more seriously. I admit it."

"Then you said it flippantly?"

"Oh, yes. It was a flippant answer," he said contritely.

Too late. The harm had been done. As far as the jury was concerned the case was lost to him.

At the end of the cross-examination, during which Carson took the opportunity of questioning him on specific instances of an incriminating nature, Sir Edward Clarke re-examined. He knew now that he was prosecuting for a guilty man.

Chapter XI: Morality Versus Art

S IR EDWARD stood faithfully by Wilde nevertheless. The defense, as none could doubt, had somehow or other secured evidence of the most damaging nature against his client; but Sir Edward was too old a practitioner of the law not to know certain shady ins and outs in the obtaining of testimony, So far Carson had only mentioned names, easily procured in hotel registers or from informers who had no scruples on how they earned a sovereign or two. On his side he too had testimony— the unnatural, hate-filled letters of a father to his son, letters that questioned that son's legitimacy and threatened him with violence.

While Wilde was still in the witness box, shaken after his cross-examination, Sir Edward read to the jury Lord Queensberry's letters. The whole court was aghast. It was not so much by Sir Edward's reading, done in the imperturbable manner of some eighteenth-century parson whom he most of all resembled, as by the scene that ensued. As the first letter was introduced Queensberry, flushed and trembling, rose in his seat staring fixedly at Wilde and then toward the opposite end of the courtroom where, since the trial began, Lord Alfred had been sitting. The court watched in painful tension. A sinister drama quite different from the sparkling comedy offered at the first session, was unfolding itself before them, their conflicting emotions wandering from one character to the other as with every scene some new aspect was uncovered. Hardly breathing, they listened as Sir Edward's equable voice read from the paper he was holding: "Secondly, I come to the most painful part of this letter—your infamous intimacy with this man Wilde. I must either cease, or I will disown you ——"

The men sitting near Queensberry were conscious of a strange sound. The Marquis, his head shaking violently, was grinding his teeth in the renewed stress of the fury that seized him on hearing his own words. He looked as if at any moment he might hurl himself upon Wilde, slumped helplessly in his box.

Sir Edward read on: "Never in my experience have I ever seen such a sight as that in your horrible features. No wonder people are talking as they are . . ." From one letter he went to another, his emotionless voice lending an eerie quality to the burning words: "If you are my son, it is only confirming proof to me, if I needed any, how right I was to face every horror and misery I have done rather than run the risk of bringing more creatures into the world like yourself, and that was the entire and only reason for my breaking with your mother as a wife, so intensely was I dissatisfied with her as the mother of you children and particularly yourself, whom when quite a baby, I cried over you the bitterest tears a man ever shed, that I had brought such a creature into the world, and unwittingly had committed such a crime. . . ."

At this point Queensberry, still alternating his gaze from Wilde to his son, had the greatest difficulty to restrain his emotion. The tears welled to his eyes, making him bite his lips to keep them back. Many at the reading pitied the father who must have suffered inhuman provocation to write such words of his own flesh and blood. Carson who missed nothing of their effect, which the prosecution had expected to be quite other, made his notes.

Sir Edward then took the witness and examined him about certain letters which Edward Shelley had written to him when they had first become acquainted. In this case, at least, Sir Edward meant to show that there had been nothing in the relationship but the admiration of a young man of literary inclination for a prominent and successful author. Carson smiled sardonically at what he must have considered a mere child's dart against his array of deadly ammunition.

The examination over, everyone confidently expected Sir Edward to call Lord Alfred to the witness box which Wilde had finally vacated. After all, Lord Alfred's friendship with Wilde was the pivot of the case. Moreover, he had been in the courtroom from the very first session, and was more than anxious to give evidence against his father. What was the court's astonishment when Sir Edward gathered his papers together and closed the case, reserving to himself the power "to call evidence to rebut anything that may be sprung upon him." So Lord Alfred would not be called! Was Sir Edward afraid that the son's testimony against his father would only prejudice the case for his friend? Or was it that he feared Lord Alfred would be no more of a match than Wilde had been for the deadly cunning of Carson's questions?

Late in the afternoon Carson finally opened the case for the defense. It could not have been more perfectly timed. As on the day before, the gloom of dusk descended upon words of such foreboding that everyone felt as if his own fate were hanging on their meaning.

Lord Queensberry, Carson told the jury, took nothing back in the charge he made. What he did he had done to save his son. Lord Queensberry undertook to prove that Mr. Wilde was *posing* as guilty of certain vices. Indeed, as far as he, Carson, was concerned, he thought that if the case had rested solely on Mr. Wilde's literature, Lord Queensberry would have been absolutely justified. "A more thinly veiled attempt," he continued, "to cover the real nature of the letter to Lord Alfred called a sonnet, has never been made in a court of justice. My learned friend has said that Wood had stolen the letter from Lord Alfred Douglas. But who was Wood? He too was Alfred, the friend of Wilde, the friend of Taylor. One of the lot . . . Taylor, the old public school boy, might have given a little useful information. He was Wilde's bosom friend . . . Why has he not been called? . . . Why did Wilde give Wood sixteen pounds? The one thing that he was anxious for was that Wood should leave the country. So he paid his passage, and after a farewell luncheon, he shipped him away to New York and, I suppose, hoped that he would never see him again."

He paused dramatically. "But," he thundered, "he is here, and will be examined."

At this point the Judge who had laughed with the rest at Wilde's quips of the previous day was seen to bury his head in

282

his hands. Wilde's friends realized by this action that all his hopes lay in the dust.

Still Carson pursued his powerful advantage, charging against Wilde not only his aphorisms in *The Chameleon* but also the things he had not written. He spoke of Lord Alfred's poems, laying particular stress on "Two Loves." Wilde had seen it before publication. Was it not a terrible thing that a young man on the threshold of life, who had for several years been dominated by Oscar Wilde, and had been "adored and loved" by Oscar Wilde as the two letters proved, should thus show the tendency of his mind on this frightful subject? What should be the horror of any man whose son wrote such a poem? "Before the jury condemns Lord Queensberry let them read Wilde's letters and say whether the gorge of any father ought not to rise . . . In view of these disgusting letters . . . I wish to know, are you going to send Lord Queensberry to gaol? I ask you to bear in mind that Lord Queensberry's son is so dominated by Wilde that he threatened to shoot his own father. Lord Queensberry did what he has done most deliberately and he is not afraid to abide by the issue of the court."

In the falling night the session adjourned before the conclusion of the address. Wilde, stunned at all that had been brought against him who had foolishly thought to outwit justice as he had conquered life, left the Old Bailey like one in a nightmare. He was powerless to think except of the humiliation of the scenes in the witness box, powerless to make any decision. Yes, he had been caught in Queensberry's booby trap, and struggle as he might, there was no escape. The trap itself might change, like the shifting locale of a dream. It became a courtroom, a witness box, a pillory—and all the time he was caught there, alone. The loyal friends who stood by him urged him to escape abroad. Dolefully he shook his head, hardly listening to their words.

Besides, Bosie and Lord Douglas were with him, ready to stand by him to the end. He could not like a craven abandon the field and throw down the lance he had taken up for them— certainly, for Bosie. His pride would not allow it, nor a certain

283

exaggerated sense of honor that increased with every humiliation put upon him. Moreover, he did not wish Bosie to go on the witness stand. On that point, at any rate, he and Sir Edward and the Marquis of Queensberry were in agreement. Some of his friends who recalled Carson's closing words on Wilde's domination of Lord Alfred left the lost man with a bitter smile.

The following morning, the 5th of April, the stage at the Old Bailey was again set with its posy for the Justice, the glass of water for the witness. There was not a seat in the courtroom that was not occupied, the crowd overflowing to the door and gathered densely outside. Now and then when a carriage approached, the name of Wilde was heard. Then there was a lunge forward, accompanied by ominous boos, and quiet was restored only when the information spread that Wilde was already in the building. Roused by the accounts in the newspapers, public feeling had been mounting against him, for with the oversimplification of journalism the issues had boiled down to one: that of a father protecting his son against the influence of an immoral companion.

After the Judge and the gentlemen of the Bar had again indulged in their formalities, Mr. Carson rose at once to resume his address. His lean face was set to decisive lines, his eyes before which the most hardened criminals had flinched, burning with moral indignation. Beside him Sir Edward, white and drawn, fumbled with his papers. The people looked for Wilde. He was nowhere to be seen. Lord Queensberry, on the other hand, sat conspicuously, surrounded by his friends. He looked composed, in fact, almost cheerful, as he exchanged glances and nods with his cronies.

Carson after a few preliminaries struck at once into the heart of his address. "I now unfortunately approach the more powerful part of my case. It will be my painful duty to bring before you the young men . . . who have been in the hands of Mr. Wilde, to tell their unhappy tales . . . But let those who are inclined to condemn these young men for being dominated,

284

misled and corrupted by Mr. Wilde, remember the relative positions of the two parties."

It was here discovered that Sir Edward Clarke had risen the moment Carson indicated that he would present his witnesses and quietly left the courtroom.

"Let me say," Carson went on, unconscious of the interruption, "whether these young men are not more sinned against than sinning . . . All of the young men introduced to Mr. Wilde were of something like eighteen or twenty years of age. The manner of their introduction, and the way in which they were subsequently treated with money and presents, all lead me to the conclusion that there was something unnatural between the relations of Mr. Wilde and these young men."

Stimulated by the sensation he made, he used his words boldly and with effect. In the close interest of the audience it was hardly noticed that Sir Edward had re-entered and was now resuming his seat next to Carson.

"There could be no explanation of the facts but this," he was saying, "that Taylor was a procurer for Wilde, as he undoubtedly was . . ." He then enumerated the young men whom he had summoned to testify. "After you hear the evidence," he said, "you will wonder, not that gossip reached Lord Queensberry's ears, but that the man Wilde has been tolerated for years in society, as he has."

Just then Sir Edward was seen to lean forward and pluck Carson by the gown. The court's indulgence was asked while the two men consulted. They spoke in a low voice, inaudible even to the gentlemen of the Bar sitting near them. For a few minutes the whispered conversation continued and then, to the astonishment of everyone, Carson who had reached the very climax of his address, sat down. What had been said? Why was Mr. Wilde not in the courtroom? Why had Sir Edward absented himself soon after Carson had begun speaking? When his counsel sat down Queensberry had a start of surprise. What was the meaning of this mystification at the very point when "the man Wilde" was going to be exposed for the corrupter he was?

There was no time for conjecture for Sir Edward rose and addressing the Judge said in a voice faltering with embarrassment: "May I claim Your Lordship's indulgence while I interpose to make a statement which, of course, is made under a feeling of very great responsibility?" The Judge nodded whereupon Sir Edward, his drawn cheeks flushed with humiliation at the thing which after many years of an honorable career he was compelled to do, addressed the court. It was no easy matter, and many a colleague sympathized with him; but he acquitted himself with dignity. It had become clear to Mr. Wilde's advisers during the case, he said, that the jury might well justify Lord Queensberry *as a father*, for using the word *posing* in the expression he had employed.

"Under the circumstances," he continued, "I hope you will not think I am going beyond the bounds of my duty . . . if I interpose and say on behalf of Mr. Oscar Wilde that I would ask to withdraw from the prosecution . . . I trust this may end the case."

In brief, Sir Edward was admitting Wilde as *guilty* of the lesser charge of *posing* in order to avoid his having to face charges of a graver nature. Again the element of irony was not lacking: Wilde, sincere only in his art, was accused of a meretricious pose in regard to it.

At Sir Edward's suggestion Carson interposed to point out that a verdict of *not guilty* for the defendant would mean a verdict of justification on the whole plea—a point in which the Judge concurred.

"Then," said Carson quickly, "the verdict will be that complete justification is proved, and that the publication was for the public benefit."

For some minutes, indeed, from the moment Sir Edward made his suggestion to withdraw, the dock where Queensberry had been sitting was surrounded by rejoicing friends who extended their hands in congratulation. At the verdict of *not guilty* loud applause came from his partisans, and the clapping was taken up by the great crowd that had been milling about outside all morning.

286

Wilde, with whom Sir Edward had consulted in an upper room where he had been waiting during the proceedings, had inconspicuously left the Old Bailey in a brougham drawn by two brown cobs—he thought white were unlucky—and had got off at the Holborn Viaduct Hotel where he had earlier reserved a sitting room. A few minutes later Robert Ross, Lord Alfred Douglas and Lord Douglas of Hawick, followed shortly by George Wyndham, M. P., their cousin, joined him there. Mr. Wyndham had come to warn Wilde to flee abroad at once as a warrant would surely be issued for his arrest. Wilde would not listen to him. The same will-lessness that had numbed him since the turn of his case rendered him incapable of decision. He was like some victim of witchcraft, like the prince in the *Arabian Nights* who was conscious of everything about him, but whose limbs were stone. Wilde too saw the horror of his position, but he could no more make a move to save himself than if his frame were cased in iron.

Nevertheless he did send out a letter to the editor of the *Evening News* to explain his withdrawal from the spectacular trial. "It would have been impossible," he wrote, "for me to have proved my case without putting Lord Alfred Douglas in the witness box against his father. Lord Alfred Douglas was extremely anxious to go into the box, but I would not let him do so. Rather than put him into so painful a position, I determined to retire from the case, and to bear upon my own shoulders whatever ignominy and shame might result from my prosecuting Lord Queensberry." Thus simply the discrowned lord of life put on the martyr's thorns.

After the final session, as Sir Edward and Carson were leaving the Old Bailey together, they had to make their way through a mob of loose women tossing their skirts in a wild dance.

"What a filthy business!" cried Sir Edward at the sight. "I shall not feel clean for weeks."

He did not know, as Carson did, that they had a private reason for rejoicing as members of the oldest profession, and that it had been one of their sisterhood who had given the clue to the discovery of the strongest evidence against his client.

287

Soon after Wilde had charged Lord Queensberry, detectives had ransacked the underworld of London and Paris to collect material in substantiation of the Marquis' accusation. For weeks they had carried on their search, but all they had for their pains was proof that Wilde had stayed at various hotels with Lord Alfred—a fact which was already known and which was certainly not one on which a father, anxious for the protection of his son, would have wished to build his case. At last, when the search was about to be abandoned, one of the detectives who happened to be in a "shop" that was under constant police supervision, asked a young woman employed there whether her business was thriving. "Not at all," she answered, adding that it was all on account of that man Oscar Wilde.

"Why do you say that?" he asked.

And she told him, saying that if he went to a certain flat near the Houses of Parliament, he would find proof enough that she knew whereof she spoke. The man wasted no more words. He went to the flat which Taylor had recently vacated, and there among useless refuse, discovered a sort of post-box full of papers, letters and notebooks containing the names and addresses of many young men who, through other documents found in the same box, were subsequently linked to Oscar Wilde. Upon those papers Carson had built his damning defense.

But not only the prostitutes of London cheered Queensberry's victory. The most respectable British press rejoiced as at a personal triumph, leaving to the defeated man no shred of achievement, no page from the plays that were even then entertaining vast throngs, with which to cover his shame. It is man's nature to despise the beaten. With one accord enemies and erstwhile friends, except for a faithful few, showed themselves all too human.

After luncheon Wilde with Robbie Ross, Bosie and Lord Douglas took a carriage and drove to Lord Alfred's rooms at the Cadogan Hotel, Sloane Square. Wilde sank back, silent and apathetic, his face impenetrable through the masklike rigidity that used to fall upon his features whenever speech did not quicken them. The carriage drove past the milestones of

288

his life—Fleet Street where he had struggled, an obscure journalist on his coming to London, and worked during the early years of his marriage; the Chelsea Embankment, associated with Rossetti, Carlyle, Whistler, the house beautiful, his dreams and ambitions; the Savoy Hotel, scene of his hours of triumph—and now connected with his fall. What were his thoughts as he passed by? His companions knew only that they were driving as in a funeral cortege with a man who to all intents and purposes might as well have been dead.

At the London and Westminster Bank Lord Alfred and his brother stopped to cash a check. Wilde and Ross drove on to the hotel where some minutes later Bosie and Lord Douglas again joined them. What was to be done now? As George Wyndham had warned, Wilde's arrest might be expected at any moment, for no court of law could think of leaving at large a man under such suspicions as had been brought up against him. As it was, Queensberry's solicitor, Charles Russell, had already sent a memorandum to the Hon. Hamilton Cuffe, Director of Prosecutions, together with a copy of the shorthand notes of the trial and the witness' statements—"in order that there may be no miscarriage of justice."

The Hon. Hamilton Cuffe took the hint, and on examination of the documents a warrant was immediately issued for the arrest of Oscar Wilde, under Section XI of the Criminal Law Amendment Act devised by Labouchère.

Meanwhile at the Cadogan Hotel the doomed man was turning listlessly the pages of *The Yellow Book*—how had it known so early that he was one to be avoided?—as he drank mechanically glass after glass of hock and seltzer. The room was littered with newspapers, scanned and thrown aside. Only bitterness there—for what voice would have dared to raise itself against the general hue and cry to say a word in defense not of the man, but of the man's work? Indeed, the moralists found many a text for their sermon, the *Westminster Gazette* putting it most concisely: "It is untrue to say that art has nothing to do with morality. Wilde's art rests on a basis of rottenness and corruption." The only plea for it came from the producers of *An Ideal*

Husband who, prompted by their concern for the welfare of the box office, informed the people through *The Times* that it was "an entirely innocent play, which has been accepted by the public and the press as an agreeable evening's entertainment, and has already been performed over 100 times."

Again Wilde's friends renewed their entreaties that he escape abroad. He was still in time to make the train to Dover. Mutely he shook his head. He had no strength even to speak, so completely had he been crushed by his defeat. One thing he did ask of Robbie Ross: that he go to Constance and tell her the dreadful news. He could not go home. How could he face her—and the children? He seemed to have but one desire—to drink himself into a merciful stupor.

Ross went to Constance and as gently and delicately as only he could, tried to make her understand the import of the court decision. She could only weep in bewildered despair. She knew a shameful thing had happened to Oscar, something that brought him lower than the lowest criminal, that would make people hesitate to admit they ever knew him, that somehow cast the shadow of his dishonor over her and the children. But he was the man to whom she had given the fullness of her first and only love, even though from the beginning they had disagreed on the very thing that now brought him so low. Had she not told him, even then, "I hold that there is no perfect art without perfect morality, whilst you say they are distinct and separable things . . ."? How had she found the boldness to warn him?

"Poor Oscar! Poor Oscar!" she kept repeating between her sobs. "I hope he is going away abroad."

Some such decision must have been made for him, for later that afternoon, toward 6:45, Lady Wilde was seen at Tite Street superintending the loading of a cab, already piled high with luggage. Majestically she gave orders to the men, concealing her heartbreak by the proud lift of her head. As the last box was being carried out of the house, a newsboy was coming up the street, like many others all over London, shouting till the buildings rang again: "Arrest of Oscar Wilde!"

About half an hour earlier Detective Inspector Richards and Sergeant Allen, armed wtih a warrant, had arrived at the Cadogan Hotel and had been shown to Room 53. Bosie and his brother were still with Wilde, slumped low in an armchair, smoking one cigarette after another.

"Mr. Wilde, I believe?" Inspector Richards asked courteously, identifying him.

"Yes?" said Wilde as if roused from his thoughts. "Yes?"

"We are police officers and hold a warrant for your arrest."

"Oh, really?" There was a note of relief in his voice.

"I must ask you to accompany me to the police station."

Wilde inquired where he was to be taken, and Inspector Richards told him.

Unsteadily he rose, put on his overcoat, and taking his hat and gloves followed the officers down to the street. He was drunk. The three then entered a cab and went first to Scotland Yard and then to Bow Street where Wilde was placed in the station dock with other alleged criminals waiting to be charged. As the warrant was being read over to him, accusing him of committing acts of gross indecency on March 20, 1893 and other dates, he leaned over the side of the dock, smiling wanly. He offered no comment on the charges, but asked to have the dates repeated. He was so poor about dates!

After being searched he was taken to a cell and the door locked behind him. The court kept as exhibits several writs against Wilde for money owing on cigarette cases and jewelry, and a note addressed to Sidney Mavor from Taylor which read, "Dear Sid—Could not wait any longer. Come at once and see Oscar. He is at Tite Street. I am there."

The dulling effect of the alcohol long since dissipated, Wilde became acutely aware of his degradation, brought back to him by the reporters whom the jailers allowed to come and peer at him through the wicket in the door. All night long he paced the cell, unable to sleep, powerless to throw off the loneliness and despair. He did not know that Bosie had come to bail him out, only to be told that under no circumstances could his application be entertained. Wilde was a criminal with other criminals, and the law admitted no distinctions.

Chapter XII: The Love That Dare Not Speak Its Name

THE following day Wilde was transferred to a cell in Hollo-way Prison to await his trial—merely a legal formality for in the eyes of the world, and indeed, in his own estimation, society had already judged him when it gave its verdict in the Queensberry case. "All trials are trials for one's life—" He was beginning to learn that truth; and as he had lived more lives than one, he was to suffer more deaths than one on the pedestal that had become a place of execution.

He had plenty of leisure to think of his situation during the nineteen days of his confinement in the apartment which justice provided for the alleged criminal. As he paced the cell, diminishing his long stride across the length and breadth of the narrow room, stumbling now against the deal table with its water jug and its Bible under the high, barred window, now against the pallet, laughably covered with a quilt in harle-quin patches, he had moments of resentment for the weakness that had prompted him, against the proud individualism of his life, to his one unpardonable and contemptible action, when he appealed to society for help and protection. And how was society answering? "Have you been living all this time in defiance of my laws, and do you now appeal to those laws for protection? You shall have those laws exercised to the full. You shall abide by what you have appealed to." So far he had been beaten. What could he expect from such a be-ginning?

He thought of Constance and the boys. How much longer would she be allowed to live in their house in Tite Street? His money was gone. Already he was learning that his books were being withdrawn from sale, that his plays, running so successfully, were suspended to placate public feeling. Meanwhile Constance was hounded by the creditors; everyone to whom he owed anything was taking out judgments against him. And there were the seven hundred pounds which had to be paid to Queensberry for court expenses. An execution, he knew, would be put upon his house. Where would Constance go? Fortunately she had her income from her grandfather's estate to provide for her and the children. Poor Constance who still remained loyal to a man who had brought upon her worse shame than woman had ever known!

Pity and remorse mingled in his thoughts of her. How different their life might have been if—! But in the word lay a deeper sundering than their best intentions could have healed. He reflected upon the early years of his friendship with Bosie when Lady Queensberry, afraid to speak to her son lest he unloose his violent temper, would write to him, the friend, begging him to do things for which she had not the courage. With unfailing regularity those letters would come to Tite Street, and always their envelopes were marked *Private*, till Constance laughingly twitted Oscar on the high society romance he must be carrying on. Always, too, came the admonition in the postscript: "Please do not let Alfred know that I have written to you . . ."

Bosie now was sweet and kind. Every day during visiting hours he would come to see him. They were not allowed to be alone. There were no such facilities in the prison and even if there had been, Wilde's charge was of too grave a nature. At the appointed hour each day Bosie would take his place with other visitors in one of a row of stalls separated by a corridor from the side where the prisoners were brought. A guard during the interview paced up and down the narrow space, between the stalls and the prisoners. With tears running down his cheeks at the indignity and pathos of the surroundings, Wilde would gaze at Bosie and he at him, the words they shouted across to each other becoming lost in the confusion of voices talking, sobbing, pleading at once.

Back in his cell Wilde would write to Lord Alfred, grateful for those moments they had together, for the knowledge that he had not been wholly forsaken. During those times he would think of the careless, beautiful youth as of someone like himself under the curse of some force beyond human power to explain. He wrote ceaselessly to Ross, to More Adey, to Robert Sherard who, leaving no stone unturned, was trying to raise money for Wilde's counsel even from the tight-fisted divine Sarah, lavish of tears and promises for her poor *Vilde*—but of nought else. Wilde also wrote to Mrs. Leverson who with her husband was ready with all kindnesses. It comforted him to write to her for, as to none other of those who knew him, he could speak freely of Bosie.

In their loyalty to him Ross and Sherard blamed Lord Alfred for Wilde's fall. Wilde, however, realized that they thought as they did because they were not acquainted with the whole truth—that his life long before Lionel Johnson brought the young man to meet him, had been full of perverse pleasures. True, he had been spurred on to greater rashness in his emulation of daring youth. He had been led to extravagance and had thrown prudence to the winds in his desire to live to its utmost his "wonderful life."

He had experimented with human beings, and played with dangerous criminals as a snake charmer plays with the poisonous cobra. "They were to me the brightest of gilded snakes," he said of them. "Their poison was part of their perfection." Whenever he dined with them, it was like feasting with panthers. How could such hazardous play have been understood by the average Englishman who must know the antecedents of a man's grandfather before he invites him to his cold mutton?

Lord Alfred Douglas of the beautiful name that to Wilde rang like the name of a flower—Bosie had proved more dangerous to know than the Allens, the Parkers and the Cliburns together. But when Wilde wrote of him to Ada Leverson after each comforting visit, he remembered only an angel of mercy in a place of shame. "I write to you from prison where your kind words have reached me and given me comfort though they have made me cry—in my loneliness—not that I am really alone— A slim thing, gold-haired like an angel, stands always at my side. His presence overshadows me— He moves in the gloom like a white flower. With what a crash this fell! . . ." Sometimes he wrote of him as Dorian, or gave him other lovely names. He had to concentrate on the beauty he had found in the friendship to gather the strength to defend it from the prisoner's dock.

Besides his grief for Constance whose innocence had been so brutally violated by the disclosures of his arrest, he knew the keenest heartache for Lady Wilde. In his filial affection he placed her as the peer of Elizabeth Barrett Browning in spirit and with Madame Roland in historical importance. How she had gloried in his success, and how great her pride in talking of her brilliant son, the high-soaring eagle of her eyrie!

Nowadays she hardly left her house. In her indifference to material concerns as age crept upon her, she gave little thought to her surroundings except to keep the red-shaded lamps dimmer than ever, and the doors and windows shrouded. Down below the bell pull was broken in the hall. The vestibule, piled high with cloaks, waterproofs, walking sticks and old umbrellas, and funereally lighted like the rest of the house, menaced the safety of those who came to pick their way through the confusion. She still gave her receptions, when majestically draped and veiled, she would descend from her rooms on the upper floor which ordinarily she seldom left, and take her place behind the tea table. No one, not even William, heard her utter a word about Oscar, and her face, more thickly painted than ever, allowed nothing of her sorrow to break through the mask. Only those who like the young Irish poet Yeats professed to understand what lay too deep for words could guess the depths of pain as with averted eyes she said, "I must go and live up Primrose Hill. I was an eagle in my youth."

In the meantime preliminary hearings had been going on at Bow Street before Sir John Bridge in preparation for Wilde's trial and that of Alfred Taylor who had been committed with him. Staunchly Sir Edward Clarke stood by Wilde where no other counsel, with less at stake than the leader of the Bar, would have defended him. Refusing all payment, he did it all out of admiration for the artist and from a desire for fair play in a case wherein, judging by the prejudice shown even by the law, the prisoner was treated as guilty long before he met his trial. In spite of the fact that the charge against Wilde was technically a *misdemeanor* and not a *felony*, and that under the circumstances he was entitled to bail, it was refused him at every application.

On the Saturday following his arrest a police van called at the Holloway Prison and Wilde was driven under escort to the Bow Street Station yard. Quickly the gates were shut upon a crowd of roughs who jeered and hooted as the van came past. Once again he was put into a detention cell from where he was summoned at half past ten and led to the prison dock. The people who had seen him not so long since, noted the dark rings under his eyes and the lines of strain which broke through the rigidity of his seeming unconcern. He sat wearily, one arm extended over the back of the rail and his head supported on the other, the elbow resting on the end rail.

A few minutes after Mr. C. F. Gill, the Public Prosecutor, had begun to review the case a dark, black-haired man of about thirty, well dressed and of gentlemanly bearing, was brought into the courtroom and escorted to the dock. Wilde recognized Alfred Taylor. The two bowed to each other as if they were meeting in a salon; Taylor smiled, and Wilde courteously rose to let the prisoner pass to the farther end of the dock.

Just then Charles Parker was called to testify for the prosecution. Wilde, who had been shielding his face with his arm, looked up quickly as a slim, brown lad, wearing a well-cut light gray overcoat with velvet cuffs, entered the witness box. The boy smiled. Taylor, leaning forward, responded with a sneer. Both had expected to see Parker in uniform, as he had joined the army. Considering the kind of testimony he had to give, however, the prosecution had furnished him with a complete wardrobe out of regard for the Queen's colors.

His face burning with shame Wilde had to listen to a series of truths, half-truths and downright lies from "the brightest of gilded snakes" with whom it had been his whim to play.

Charles Parker contributed little that Carson had not already reviewed in the Queensberry trial. But now, brought face to face with the thing itself, Wilde saw how slight were his chances of getting—not justice, which was out of the question—but clemency from society. The scene, the words he heard, became after the first shock like the hallucinations of a drug. He listened in a kind of somnolence till time and place were confounded, one day merging with the other, one session with the next, except for some moment, more vivid than the rest, some arresting bit of dialogue that captured his interest as if he were another, watching his own trial.

"For what purpose did Taylor wish to introduce you to Mr. Wilde?" asked Gill.

"He said he was a good man," said Charlie Parker.

"But," interposed Sir John Bridge, "did he say why he wanted to introduce Wilde?"

"Because he liked boys."

The court desired the details to fill in the lurid picture. What happened after the dinner at the restaurant? Where did Charlie Parker go? What did he do? Charlie obliged, talking with admirable objectivity.

"Mr. Wilde said, 'This is the boy for me' . . . It was about ten o'clock. He took me to the second or third floor of the Savoy . . . No one else was there. Whisky and soda for two was brought."

"After the waiter had gone, what did Wilde say to you?"

"'Come into my room.' There was a door leading to it from the sitting room. Both of us went in." Parker talked on till Mr. Gill, with eloquently timed reserve, turned to the magistrate. "I don't propose to take this farther, Sir John," he said.

"Misconduct took place?" Sir John asked the witness.

"Yes. I was there about two hours. He gave me two pounds and told me to come again . . . I went . . . He gave me three pounds that time."

"Did you see him again?"

"I saw him again from time to time . . . I had a room at Park Walk, Chelsea, and he visited me there. He kept his cab waiting. After that there was some unpleasantness with my landlady, and I left . . . I visited him once at the Albermarle Hotel. I was taken there by——"

"Never mind," said Mr. Gill. "I don't want to introduce any other name into this case."

"I last saw Mr. Wilde about nine months ago. He drove up past me in Trafalgar Square and stopped his cab. He shook hands and said, 'You are looking as pretty as ever.'" Parker laughed at this. No one else showed amusement.

Mrs. Ellen Grant, the caretaker of the Little College Street house testified. She described Taylor's apartment, said that many young men came to see him, and that she had seen women's clothes there, and wigs for fancy dress. No, she could not identify Wilde, but she had heard Taylor address someone as *Oscar* and another as *Charlie dear*.

Alfred Wood, tall, fair, about nineteen, joined the procession. He had met Wilde at the Café Royal and had had supper with him.

"A good supper?" Mr. Gill drew him out.

"Yes, a very nice supper with champagne and liqueurs. After that I went with him to Tite Street, to his house."

"Where was the family?"

"He told me they were at Torquay . . . He let us in with a key. We went to his room and had drinks there."

When Gill asked whether improprieties took place, Wood replied, "Yes." He spoke plainly of what had occurred though he excused himself for having been the worse for drink. Wilde gave him money to leave for America in March, 1893.

Sidney Mavor, a soft-spoken youth, said he had been one of a dinner party at Kettner's with Taylor and Lord Alfred Douglas. Wilde sent him a cigarette case a week later. They stayed overnight at a hotel together. When asked the inevitable question on what had taken place, he said, "Nothing." They

298

had stayed at the hotel simply because it was so late. Hurriedly the court dropped him.

For once Wilde's face wore the suggestion of a smile when Antonio Migge, who styled himself a Professor of Massage, was wounded in his *amour propre* when counsel dared to suggest that he had been employed by the Savoy Hotel. He only *attended* there to massage his clients, he insisted. Wilde's smile immediately faded when Professor Migge gave his evidence. Some time in March, 1893, he said, he entered Mr. Wilde's room without knocking one morning, and there saw a young man in bed. At first he thought it was a young lady as he could see only the head; it was someone about sixteen or eighteen years of age. Mr. Wilde was in the same room, dressing. The Professor never attended Mr. Wilde again.

Jane Cotter, chambermaid at the Savoy, corroborated Mr. Migge's testimony. Other employees, housekeepers and caretakers added their stone to the mound under which Wilde's reputation was forever buried. Day in, day out, during the examination, London's lowest specimens, protected by law, incriminated themselves while accusing Wilde of the vilest practices. The name of the man which at first had been written down privately for the court out of concern for the feelings of his kinsman the Solicitor-General, was inadvertently pronounced in the full hearing of the jury. Lord Alfred Douglas too was mentioned more than once as participating in the parties. Fred Atkins, a pale-eyed representative of London's underworld seemed to take special delight in letting slip the very things which the prosecution wished to conceal. After speaking broadly of his Paris excursion with Wilde, his visits to the Moulin Rouge and his return to the hotel early the following morning, he said he had found Wilde in the company of another person.

"That was Schwabe," he added for good measure.

"Leave that for a moment," Mr. Gill broke in.

The court sat up, as it had occasion to do a few minutes later when on describing a certain dinner at the Florence, Atkins said that he had thought it funny that Mr. Wilde kissed the waiter and put his arms round his, Atkins', neck. "And he had his arms round Douglas's neck, too."

"Ah, leave that!" Mr. Gill repeated sharply.

A most inconvenient witness, and likely to do much damage for the prosecution. As it turned out Atkins was exposed at the cross-examination as one of a group of blackmailers under the notorious "Uncle Burton" whose game it was to have young scoundrels like Atkins and Charles Parker lure men to their rooms, when he would surprise the victims and extort hush money. Parker, on examination by Wilde's counsel, admitted having shared in such money, together with Allen and Wood. At one point Atkins was thrown out of court after Sir Edward Clarke proved him guilty of perjury.

The criminal trial itself which took place at the Old Bailey before Mr. Justice Charles, had begun on the 26th of April, 1895. There were twenty-five counts in the indictment referring to acts of gross indecency alleged to have been committed by Oscar Wilde, and the procuring of the said acts by Alfred Taylor. Sir Edward Clarke fought ably on certain technicalities that might have helped Wilde, but to no avail. On the subject of special consideration for the prisoner as an artist and a literary man the court remained unmoved.

Wilde appeared sunk in the profoundest dejection. His haggard face had lost its hearty handsomeness. His hair, once so shining and carefully arranged, fell in damp strands over his forehead. He looked all of his forty and a half years. From the moment he entered the dock where Taylor preceded him, sleek, smiling and neatly dressed, he would slump into his place, and leaning his arm on the rail, rest his head upon his closed hand. Through the long hours he would hardly move. The impenetrable face told less than ever. It might have belonged to a corpse. Now and again, at some especially inculpating evidence, the knuckles of his hand would whiten and he sighed deeply.

300

For three interminable days, interrupted only by the Sunday holiday, the trial continued, the same witnesses outdoing one another in the boldness of their testimony as they retailed without embarrassment the indecencies they alleged to have committed with Wilde and with Taylor. No horror was omitted, nor was tragedy lacking in the witness Edward Shelley who, deranged by moral conflict, kept talking incoherently of his *sin*. Wilde groaned. If all the others who appeared there against him betrayed themselves by their very words as blackguards, criminals and blackmailers, Edward Shelley stood like the embodiment of his own guilt.

On Tuesday, the 30th of April, Sir Edward succeeded in having the charges of conspiracy between Wilde and Taylor withdrawn, but he was not successful in preventing Mr. Gill from putting Wilde once more under cross-examination on the poems of Lord Alfred Douglas. As it turned out, the questioning had unexpected results both for the prosecution that had insisted upon it, and for the defense which had tried to avoid it.

"It is not for me," said Wilde, in a voice grown hollow with suffering, "to explain the work of anybody else. It does not belong to me. But the word *shame* used in the poem 'In Praise of Shame' is used in the sense of *modesty*. I mean that I was anxious to point out that 'Shame that turns cold lips'—I forget the line exactly—'to fire' is a quickened sense of modesty."

"Your view, Mr. Wilde," said Mr. Gill, "is that the *shame* mentioned there is that shame which is a sense of modesty." He spoke with a hint of sarcasm.

"That was the explanation given to me by the person who wrote it." Loyally he did not mention the name of Lord Alfred who at Sir Edward's insistence had left England for the Continent the day before the commencement of the trial.

Mr. Gill, however, would not be turned aside. "During 1893 and 1894 were you a good deal in the company of Lord Alfred Douglas?" he asked.

"Oh, yes."

"Did he read that poem to you?"

"Yes."

"The next poem is one described 'Two Loves' . . . Was that poem explained to you?"

"I think that is clear."

"There is no question as to what it means?"

"Most certainly not."

"Is it not clear," Mr. Gill asked innocently, "that the love described relates to natural and unnatural love?"

"No," Wilde answered firmly.

"Then what is the 'Love that dare not speak its name'?"

"The 'Love that dare not speak its name,' " said Wilde, "in this century is such a great affection of an elder for a younger man as there was between David and Jonathan, such as Plato made the very basis of his philosophy, and such as you find in the sonnets of Michelangelo and Shakespeare. It is that deep, spiritual affection that is as pure as it is perfect. It dictates and pervades great works of art like those of Shakespeare and Michelangelo, and those two letters of mine, such as they are." His hand waved a deprecating gesture. His voice which had risen to a throbbing crescendo from the slow, reflective tone with which he had begun, paused for the briefest second. "It is in this century misunderstood, so much misunderstood that it may be described as the 'Love that dare not speak its name,' and on account of it I am placed where I am now. It is beautiful, it is fine, it is the noblest form of affection. There is nothing unnatural about it. It is intellectual, and it repeatedly exists between an elder and a younger man, when the elder man has intellect, and the younger man has all the joy, hope and glamour of life before him. That it should be so the world does not understand. The world mocks at it and sometimes puts one in the pillory for it."

He ceased. In that whole courtroom, the air of which had shuddered to the foulest abominations, few remained unmoved by the beauty and sincerity of Wilde's defense. For he was sincere, with the sincerity of one who saw before him the wreck of his life caused by the world's failure to understand that love. It may have been all too often in the mire, as he admitted, that he and Lord Alfred met. It was nonetheless true that at its best

302

heir love had given them moments of spiritual exaltation which ould ennoble Wilde and make him reach heights such as in he grimness of the Old Bailey he had attained even now while eeking to convey what it meant to him.

When he finished speaking, after a few breathless moments here was loud applause, sternly quelled by Mr. Justice Charles. Mr. Gill, taken aback by the unforeseen sensation, endeavored o bring Wilde down to a commoner level.

"With regard to your friendship toward the persons I have mentioned," he suggested, "may I take it, Mr. Wilde, that it vas, as you describe, the deep affection of an elder man for a ounger?"

"Certainly not," Wilde retorted earnestly. "One feels that once in one's life, and once only, towards anybody."

It was seven o'clock and already dark when court adjourned after Sir Edward had made a moving appeal in which he stressed he proved untruthfulness and immorality of the witnesses for he prosecution. With his few words Wilde had turned the senti- ment against him to sympathy. Sir Edward hoped for the best.

The morning of May 1 passed in addresses, a review of the evidence and the summing up. Questions were put to the jury. At about half past one Wilde was removed from the dock and a few minutes later the jury retired to deliberate. There had been no interval for luncheon. Nevertheless the Judge waited on the bench as if he expected a speedy decision. But the hours passed and still there was no word from the jurymen. Luncheon vas sent in to them. Finally, at a quarter past five, the jury returned, Wilde was brought back to the dock and the foreman spoke. The jury could not agree on certain counts. Mr. Justice Charles asked whether the jury wished to put any question to him, and whether there was any prospect of their coming to a conclusion after further deliberation.

"My Lord," replied the foreman, "I fear there is no chance of agreement."

And so the trial ended—in the disagreement of the jury. It vas a more propitious conclusion than Sir Edward had dared hope for, and he seized the occasion for presenting a verdict of *not guilty* for Wilde on the conspiracy counts. That attained, Sir Edward put in another application for bail, which was granted. A re-trial was then set for the next session so that the Treasury might have the opportunity of considering how the case should then be introduced.

It was not till the 7th of May that Wilde left prison, a comparatively free man, with a price of five thousand pounds on his limited freedom. He himself had given personal surety for half the sum. Lord Douglas of Hawick and a total stranger, the Rev. Mr. Stewart Headlam, made themselves sureties for the rest. That Lord Douglas should have come forward to help surprised no one. But a storm of protest arose when it was learned that an English clergyman had furnished bail for one whose name the vulgar were bandying about the streets. In spite of letters to the press and other less gentle pressure put upon him, the Rev. Mr. Headlam stood firm. Wilde, he said, through his work, "had shown him beauty on a high hill."

On leaving Holloway Wilde drove with Lord Douglas to the Midland Hotel at Saint Pancras where two rooms had been engaged for him. He no longer had a home. While he was still awaiting trial all that he owned in Tite Street had been put up for sale to satisfy his creditors.

Some of his friends, who had gone there the afternoon of the 24th of April to buy back for him what little they could afford, described the painful scene. From the moment the doors opened, the house had been mobbed by idlers, dealers and thieves who went through the rooms helping themselves to whatever they could lay hands on before the sale began. Letters and manuscripts, among them the originals of *The Woman covered with Jewels* and *The Portrait of Mr. W. H.* vanished without a trace. Later, bundles of Wilde's most prized books, autographed authors' copies, etchings, prints, went for almost nothing, while the mob tramped about, pillaging, forcing doors and drawers for valuables till the police had to be called to restore some semblance of decency to the proceeding. Carlyle's writing table, the Simeon Solomons that had colored Wilde's adolescence, his old blue and white china, his casts from the

Greek and his Oriental curios, the Chippendale chairs and the Persian carpets of the drawing-room—everything fell under the hammer, no one seeming to know or to care about the value of anything. A Whistler painting of a young girl went for six pounds, and the portrait of "Willie Hughes" that Charles Ricketts had painted to illustrate *Mr. W. H.*, fetched only a guinea. Will Rothenstein bought the Monticelli that hung in Wilde's little study for eight pounds. There was nothing which the ruthlessness of the law spared the fallen man. The last pathetic object to be knocked down was a rabbit hutch which someone bought for a few shillings. Constance had not a bed to sleep on. With her two boys she had gone after the sale to stay with friends who, with her relatives, aggravated her misery by urging her to divorce her husband.

Wilde and Lord Douglas had hardly sat down to the dinner they had ordered when they heard a commotion below, soon explained by the appearance of the manager who, telling Wilde that he knew who he was, rudely bade him get out. A crowd of prize fighters, it seemed, engaged by Queensberry, had followed the brougham to the hotel and exposed the unhappy man. He had no choice but to go. All night long the same story repeated itself. Where Wilde was not refused admittance, he was sure to be expelled with the coming of Queensberry's roughs who threatened to sack the hotel if the manager did not do their bidding. Soon after the Midland Hotel experience Lord Douglas had had to leave him. Alone, the hounded man knocked vainly at all doors. Society had no room for him.

At last, faint from hunger and staggering with fatigue, he went to the only door that he knew would be opened. It was long past midnight. He had not gone there earlier for dread of the grief and reproach in his mother's eyes. But he could not remain in the streets. Willie came down to open at his knock.

"Give me shelter or I shall die," Wilde pleaded.

Willie dragged the fainting man into the house. Some time later when in his typical style he told of his brother's plight to Robert Sherard, even the element of burlesque entered into the tragedy, as Willie said dramatically: "He came, tapping with his beak against the windowpane, and fell down on my threshold like a wounded stag."

But nothing lightened the remorse of Lionel Johnson who, after the collapse of the Queensberry case, had had to be carried to his rooms in Gray's Inn stupefied with drink. The companion who brought him home saw the portraits of Oscar Wilde and Lord Alfred on the poet's table, and caught the significance of the anguish that made the poor youth, suddenly terribly conscious, break into sobs, crying, "My God! My God!"

Chapter XIII: The Trap Shuts Down

W HAT would be the outcome of Wilde's third trial by society? In the house of lost hopes at Oakley Street Oscar's fate was a foregone conclusion. Speranza virtually put on mourning. The large, pale face, so much that of the son whom she had wished a girl, had set to stony grief. She hardly left her room even for the haphazard meals of that undisciplined household. When she did, she stalked the cluttered corridors, a monumental phantom bent under her wordless despair. Oscar, a descendant of the poet kings of Ireland, a crowned lord of the intellect before whom the hated English had had to bow, was worse than dead in his dishonor. She could not believe the charges against him. In the moral apartness to which her life with Sir William had forced her to withdraw, there was no room for such base concerns. Oscar could never have been guilty. As her son he was above right and wrong. Society hounded him as it had hounded all great spirits, Socrates, Dante. It might even succeed in bringing about his death. To her he remained one of the royal line whose name, once the present cloud had passed, would shine as bright as the face of the sun.

When she descended to realities, however, and read the foul outpourings of the newspapers that outdid one another in their condemnation, or when she looked at her son, lying like a dead weight on the spare camp bed much too small for him, she knew that no power on earth could save him from his destiny. He was like Melmoth whose last words must have rung their echo through her mind: "I have been on earth a terror, but not an evil to its inhabitants. None can participate in my destiny but with his own consent . . . I alone must sustain the penalty." The penalty, yes. But how many victims Oscar carried with him in his ruin—Constance and her broken life; his fatherless children; Lord Alfred who even if he lived to be a hundred, must always be associated with him in his guilt and dishonor; herself whose old age he had burdened with shame!

Willie who could feel nothing deeply extracted a kind of self-importance from the notoriety attaching to his brother. It was a terrible thing, of course, having everybody saying such awful things about Oscar, and the newsboys shouting his name through the streets. And it had been dreadful, the way he had come home that night, nearly struck to death by his persecutors. But Oscar, after all, was famous. If he had not risen so high he could not have fallen so low. It was a genuine Aristotelian tragedy—the fall of the eagle as against the fall of the sparrow. Had Oscar been merely a sparrow no one would have heard anything of the case. It would probably never have reached court. At the worst he might have been warned by the police, like some men he knew in English society, and like them he would have taken the first boat to Calais. But Oscar, like a true Irishman, had remained to take his punishment. He would keep on taking it honorably to the end, no matter what his friends tried to make him do. Whenever, therefore, people came to Oakley Street, they had to scheme their way past a benevolent Cerberus who dinned into their ears the fact that as an Irish gentleman, "Oscar must stay to face the music."

Sherard and Harris, Ross and even Lord Douglas who could ill afford to forfeit his portion of the bail, were again urging him to escape while he still had time. In unutterable depression Wilde stood firm. The gloom of the house had aggravated his despondency. He could only lie on the cot, where Sherard had found him, a limp arum lily mourning over his head from a glass on the mantelpiece.

Knowing he could do nothing with Oscar in those surroundings, Harris came one day to take him out to lunch. Willie intercepted him. "It's most kind of you, but he can't go."

"Why not?" asked Harris, walking past him.

"There would be a scandal. Someone'll insult him and it would do harm—set people's backs up."

"Oh, Frank, I dare not," Wilde echoed weakly.

Harris won over all objections and took Wilde with him to

a restaurant in Great Portland Street where they dined in a private room. With relentless logic Harris reviewed the two trials, pointing out how everything had gone from bad to worse for Wilde and how, with his spirit so broken, he could scarcely expect to win in the third ordeal against the sordid evidence of chambermaids and blackmailers.

"Oh, Frank," Wilde interrupted pitifully. "You talk with passion and conviction, as if I were innocent."

"But you are innocent, aren't you?"

"No, Frank," said Wilde. "I thought you knew that."

It is to Harris' credit that Wilde's avowal made no difference in his friendship, except, perhaps, to impress upon him that at all costs the unhappy man must be prevented from once more facing the law. One night after he and Wilde had dined together at Ada Leverson's, he took him unsuspecting to Queen's Gate where he had a brougham and a fast pair of horses waiting to carry them to a steam yacht anchored at an obscure landing place up the Thames. With all the persuasiveness in his power Harris endeavored to make Wilde realize that there would be nothing heroic in his remaining to be condemned a third time —for no other issue was possible, what with public feeling rising, and the law, because of the nature of the case, forced to exercise justice untempered with mercy. A rapid drive to Erith, Harris coaxed, the yacht—and the promise of another life ahead, with England and her sudden crisis of morality forgotten.

With the tears streaming down his cheeks, Wilde could only repeat: "It is impossible, Frank, impossible. It would be too wonderful—but it's impossible!" Harris renewed his entreaties, threatened, prophesied. Wilde could not be moved. "I am caught in a trap, Frank," he said. "I can only wait for the end."

When he was prevailed upon to enter the carriage he remained only after Harris, pitying him yet exasperated with what he interpreted as unforgivable weakness, flung at the driver, "Oakley Street—Oakley Street, Chelsea." He would sooner have taken him to prison. In silence they drove through Queen's Gate and the dim London streets, till they reached the house with its broken bell and black, blind windows. Filled with foreboding Harris waited outside till the door closed behind the man compelled by his irresoluteness to suicidal heroism.

Fortunately for Wilde the Leversons succeeded in making arrangements for him to stay with them until the day fixed for the trial. In the cheerful surroundings, and with his hosts as gracious and friendly as if nothing had happened, Wilde shook off some of his torpor. After the Leverson children had been put to bed and he came down, a most welcome guest, he could even talk lightly at table as in the past and make his hosts laugh at some refulgence of his wit. Occasionally he went out and in deceptive optimism pretended that he had perhaps taken too dark a view of the case. He became actually hopeful, in a confiding, childlike way, after a palmist predicted to him that he would ultimately triumph.

He was now once more receiving letters from Bosie, one of them, sent to him on the 15th of May from the Hotel des Deux Mondes in Paris, full of trust and affection. "My darling Oscar— It seems too dreadful to be here without you, but I hope you will join me next week . . ." Who knows, perhaps he might if all went well during the trial, set for the 20th. "They are very nice here, and I can stay as long as I like without paying my bill which is a good thing as I am quite penniless . . ." When wasn't he, the thoughtless boy? But who could refuse anything to one who wrote with such artless affection? "Do keep up your spirits, my dearest darling. I continue to think of you day and night, and send you all my love. I am always your loving and devoted boy, Bosie."[1]

Then Constance came to see him one day. For two hours they were alone together and when she left Mrs. Leverson was grieved to see her in tears. She had come at her lawyer's behest to persuade Oscar to leave the country. Indeed, what man or woman who wished him well, from his own counsel, good old Sir Edward, to his sureties, had failed to urge flight upon him? Only Speranza and Willie Wilde, tender of the mythical honor of the kings of Ireland, encouraged his resolve which perhaps Frank Harris interpreted aright when in mingled loyalty and impa-

[1] Manuscript from the collection of Dr. A. S. W. Rosenbach.

tience he branded resignation as the courage of the irresolute. Wilde, except for his few moments of hopefulness, was ruled by inertia, waiting and doing nothing, placing more stock in the prophecy of a fortuneteller than in the terribly corroborative certainties awaiting him in the court of law.

Some time between the Queensberry trial and Wilde's appearance at the Old Bailey as the accused, he had come across the painter, Toulouse-Lautrec whom he had met in Paris three or four years earlier. He had a horror of the misshapen homunculus with his stunted body and too searching eyes, though he had never betrayed it out of an even greater horror of inflicting pain. Moreover, something about the artist, apart from the very important fact that Lautrec could boast of as noble a lineage as his own, attracted Wilde. Many a time he had gone with him and others of their circle to certain notorious haunts in Paris. But each had found there what he himself had brought.

Wilde, as he said of another, exemplified the pathological tragedy of the hybrid—the Pagan-Catholic. Lautrec, on the contrary, had almost the scientist's objectivity. Where Wilde heightened lust with sin-consciousness, Lautrec, ruthlessly realistic, saw it as another manifestation of human nature—nothing to shock, if nothing to admire. He was known to have lived for weeks in a brothel, setting up his easel in parlor and inspection cabinet as if they were the most natural places for an artist. From the Moulin Rouge and its dancers, La Gouloue, Nini Pattes-en-l'air, Rayon d'Or and many others in their foamy lace and black silk stockings, he went with equal ease to Le Hanneton and La Souris where short-haired women dressed and behaved like men. He knew them all by name, put them in his canvases, and left to others ridicule or condemnation. It is doubtful that he would have smiled at a bon mot of Wilde's on a certain inverted actress in his company: "Poor dear —, she is one of nature's gentlemen." Everything in that lurid, abnormal life furnished material for his art, an art which was certainly, among much else, *fin de siècle*.

That night in London Lautrec spent a few hours listening to Wilde's story and carried away with him a picture of the man in his torment, bitterness and disintegration. When he set down his impression he softened nothing of what he remembered. He had never had any particular liking for Wilde; neither had he disliked him: there was no room for emotion in his make-up. For the time the man became a subject for the art of Lautrec who saw him with inhuman dispassionateness as a voluptuary, no longer young, whose indulgences had caught up with him. With the utmost economy of stroke and color Lautrec painted the portrait, in a simplification that had in it the hard clarity of an anatomist's drawing and not a little of the symbol. Against the veil of a London mist, with a background of the Thames and one of the towers of the Houses of Parliament—was it to suggest the proximity of Little College Street?—a heavy yet feminine face peers out in tragic brooding. The eyes are pouched from sleeplessness and worry, with, in their gaze, the fixity of one who would not be distracted from some compelling vision. The jowls hang ponderously. The classical mouth, here tightened to the rosebud of the courtesan, seems outlined with rouge. Despite the hardness of the lines and the vibrancy of the brush strokes the softness of decay has loosened the flesh from the skull. The very greenish blue of the coat and cravat, and the sickly yellow highlights convey a feeling of putrescence. It is a cruel portrait, not so much of Wilde, as of his moral disintegration.

As the day for the final trial approached Wilde struggled to conceal his feelings but anxiety showed clearly on his face. He spoke often of the palmist's prophecy—might there not be something in it?—and those who listened to him had not the heart to contradict him. On the night of the 19th of May, Wilde asked Mrs. Leverson to put a sleeping draught on his mantelpiece. But he did not take it. The following morning he dressed with his usual care. He looked better than on his previous trial, and an exalted look strove with the lines of worry on his face. Since he had to face his ordeal anew he would do it like a hero who had chosen to suffer rather than to flee. "A dishonored name, a haunted life," he had written to Bosie, "are not for me to whom you have been revealed on that high hill where beautiful things are transfigured." In that frame of mind he would face Sir Frank Lockwood the Solicitor-General, and the pitiless Mr. Gill.

Just before stepping into the little pillbox brougham with More Adey he turned suddenly to Mrs. Leverson and said in a voice he controlled with difficulty: "If the worst comes to the worst, you'll write me?"

Once more, in the now familiar setting of the Old Bailey, Wilde took his place in the dock with Alfred Taylor, and the case opened before Mr. Justice Wills—the Solicitor-General, Mr. Gill and Mr. Horace Avory conducting for the prosecution. Immediately before the jury was sworn, Sir Edward Clarke proposed a separate trial for the two prisoners which the Solicitor-General opposed, pointing out that in such a case Taylor would have to be first.

"I should object to that," Sir Edward said sharply.

The Solicitor-General insisted, and repeating what he had said, added, "I hope Mr. Justice Wills will not allow my learned friend to dictate to the prosecution."

The note of antagonism boded no good for Wilde. It was apparent from the first that the Law had had enough of the case and was anxious to make an end. At length, after much wrangling, it was decided that Wilde and Taylor be tried separately. But although, as Sir Edward pointed out, the name of Wilde stood first on the indictment and the first count was directed against him, his case was placed after Taylor's.

"I and the jury," said Mr. Justice Wills, "will do our very best to take care that one trial has no effect on the other."

"I am sure you will do that," Sir Edward agreed, "but there never was a case in which that duty was more difficult to discharge."

The only concession Sir Edward could obtain was that Wilde be let out on the bail he was carrying during Taylor's trial, which occupied the whole of the following day. The jury found Taylor *guilty* on the counts of indecency with Charles and William Parker, and *not guilty* on the charge of procuring Wood for Wilde.

Though only the faintest hope glimmered for Wilde in the

decision, the Marquis of Queensberry found it enough to infuriate him. With him to feel a thing was to act upon it. No sooner had the court adjourned than he went to the post office in Piccadilly and sent an offensive telegram to Lady Douglas, his son Percy's wife, commenting on Percy's looking "like a dug up corpse" perhaps because of "too much madness in kissing." He was just about to cross the street when he came upon Lord Douglas himself, who seeing his father leaving the post office, came toward him angrily, asking him if he intended continuing to pester Lady Douglas with his obnoxious communications. There was a set to at once, the author of the Queensberry rules applying his technique so thoroughly that by the time the police intervened Lord Douglas of Hawick had a scientifically discolored eye. They were both charged with disorderly conduct, and at the Marborough Police Court they were bound over in the sum of five-hundred pounds to keep the peace for six months. While the charge was being read over to him the Marquis, pointing to Percy, said out of a clear sky: "That is my son who bailed Oscar Wilde." It was enough for him to look upon Lord Douglas as an enemy.

On the 22nd of May, after Taylor's jury had been dismissed and a fresh one procured, Wilde's trial was re-opened, the indictment comprising charges dating from February 20, 1892 to October 2, 1893. The session was taken up with the recalling of the witnesses Shelley, Wood and Charles Parker, the last of whom was made to admit publicly by Sir Edward that since the previous trial he had been living at the expense of the prosecution. Parker, this time, made an unfavorable impression, and Wood, if possible, a worse one. Edward Shelley, more than ever overwrought, unwillingly repeated the story he had already told. The jurors listened, visibly puzzled. How could they accept the testimony of a young man who admitted having been mentally ill, and whose allegations were completely uncorroborated?

To their surprise, on the case's resumption the following morning, Ascension Day, Mr. Justice Wills proposed to withdraw the counts dealing with Shelley, a portion of the charge which had until then been regarded as the strongest against

Wilde. For the first time the accused sat upright, while the counsel for the Crown, unprepared for this turn of events, rummaged through dusty law books for precedent. The Solicitor-General immediately put in an objection, ably countered by Sir Edward who quoted authorities and took the opportunity to plead movingly for Wilde. His speech came as a relief that day, during which the bells of St. Paul's, heard from the Old Bailey, had rung their chimes through some of the most loathsome evidence ever heard in a court of law.

On Friday the 24th, Wilde again testified in his own defense. For the third time he swore to his innocence upon oath, admitting the testimony of the witnesses against him to the point where they charged gross indecencies when, he said, all of them lied. The Solicitor-General showed him no mercy. One by one the steps of the trial were retraced, all the youths involved mentioned again, every cigarette case with its inscription brought forward as proof of guilt against the accused.

Before calling Wilde to the witness box Sir Edward sought to rouse sympathy for him by pointing out how different a man he was from the self-assured prosecutor of the Queensberry trial. Good Sir Edward might have spared his words. Few who had seen Wilde then would have known him. He leaned over the witness box, not as before, to play with his gloves, but heavily, as if glad of its support. Even his voice had changed. He made no attempt at cleverness now, and answered the questions of the cross-examination briefly and to the point. Once only, when the Solicitor-General, remembering Carson's success with the "slim gilt soul" letter interrogated him about it, did Wilde show a trace of his former self-assurance.

"Were you speaking of a love between men?" the Solicitor-General asked, quoting, "Always with undying love."

"It was not a sensual love," said Wilde.

"Is that again poetic imagery or an expression of your feelings?"

For the first time a smile broke on Wilde's immobile countenance. With a bow he answered, looking straight at his oppo-

315

nent: "That is an expression of my feelings." He would not disclaim the love that had brought him where he now was.

That day the court adjourned in the middle of the Solicitor-General's address, which was resumed early the following morning, May 25. The case had dragged out longer than the prosecution desired. Justice must no longer be balked. Here and there from the packed courtroom a familiar face penetrated Wilde's consciousness through the weary somnolence into which he had again fallen. There was Robert Sherard, sitting behind the Solicitor-General, and there near him Ernest Dowson who had come to lend moral support to the doomed man. Somewhere in the background, like the head of a hideous ape, Queensberry's bobbed and nodded as the Solicitor-General made his appalling denunciations.

From his place in the dock Wilde listened and was sickened with shame as crime after crime was laid at his door. It was horrifying—like a thing out of Tacitus, it seemed to him, like a passage in Dante, like one of Savonarola's indictments of the Popes of Rome. But it was of him, Oscar Wilde, that the Solicitor-General was speaking. Suddenly with a queer stirring of conscience it occurred to him, "How splendid it would be, if I were saying all this about myself!" A man's highest moment, he reflected, is when he kneels in the dust, and beats his breast, and tells all the sins of his life.

He was only dimly aware of what followed: the Judge's summing up, the review of the evidence, a brief dialogue between His Lordship and the foreman of the jury.

"In view of the intimacy between Lord Alfred Douglas and Wilde," the foreman asked, "was a warrant ever issued for the apprehension of Lord Alfred Douglas?"

"I should think not," said Mr. Justice Wills taken by surprise. "We have not heard of it."

The foreman insisted. "Was it ever contemplated?"

"Not to my knowledge," confessed His Lordship. "A warrant in any case would not be issued without evidence of some fact of something more than intimacy . . . I think you should deal with the matter upon the evidence before you."

316

"But it seems to us," the foreman pressed, "that if we are to consider these letters as evidence of guilt, and if we adduce any guilt from these letters, it applies as much to Lord Alfred Douglas as to the defendant."

"Quite so," said His Lordship urbanely. "But how does that relieve the defendant? Our present inquiry is whether guilt is brought home to the man in the dock. We have got the testimony of his guilt to deal with now. . . ."

The luncheon interval fortunately released Mr. Justice Wills from his embarrassing predicament. Sir Frank Lockwood, the Solicitor-General, too, welcomed the intermission. His nephew Schwabe's name had leaked out in more than one incriminating situation. If justice were to take its full course— Murmurs rose among the people who saw the relevancy of the foreman's questions. Guilty or innocent, Wilde had had to face the most shameful ordeal. Why, as Sir Edward Clarke had pointed out, was Wilde being tried, whereas Wood, Parker and all the blackmailers of London, by giving evidence, had managed to establish for themselves a sort of statute of limitations? Why, they asked with the foreman, had no warrant been issued for Lord Alfred Douglas?

Evidently Mr. Justice Wills felt that he owed the public further explanation, for when the court reconvened he began of his own accord: "There is a natural disposition to ask, 'Why should this man stand in the dock, and not Lord Alfred Douglas?' But the supposition that Lord Alfred Douglas will be spared because he is Lord Alfred is one of the wildest injustice—the thing is utterly and hopelessly impossible . . . You must remember that no prosecution would be possible on the mere production of Wilde's letters to Lord Alfred Douglas. Lord Alfred Douglas, as you all know, went to Paris at the request of the defendant, and there he has stayed, and I know absolutely nothing more about him."

Imperceptibly, from the moment of Wilde's entrance to the witness box, the sympathies of the public had turned toward him. It was evidenced in the applause that broke out at Sir Edward's pleadings, and at the silence that fell after the Solicitor-

317

General had thundered forth his denunciation. There were some who saw a heroic loyalty in Wilde's requesting Lord Alfred to go abroad.

Perhaps because he sensed this change, His Lordship was unduly virulent in his summing up, although when the jury retired the Solicitor-General whispered to Sir Edward: "You'll dine your man in Paris tomorrow."

The old man shook his head. "No, no, no," he said disconsolately.

For two hours the jury deliberated, disagreed, retired again, and toward dusk returned to their seats. Hardly a breath stirred when the verdict rang in the tense room. *Guilty*. *Guilty* on all counts except that involving Edward Shelley.

A buzz of approval rose up from the gentlemen of the Bar. Among the public there were signs of displeasure impatiently quelled. The Marquis of Queensberry was seen to beam with exultation; the booby trap had shut down on the victim at last.

A few more formalities and the case would be over. Mr. Justice Wills cleared his throat to pass sentence as Taylor was conducted into the dock beside Wilde whose pallor, when the verdict was pronounced, had given place to a purplish flush. He seemed to be gathering all his strength to remain on his feet while the fatal words were uttered.

"That the jury have arrived at a correct verdict in the case," said His Lordship, fixing the two defendants with his hard gaze, though the men near him saw that his hands shook as in a palsy. "I cannot persuade myself to entertain the shadow of a doubt . . . It is no use for me to address you. People who can do these things must be dead to all sense of shame, and one cannot hope to produce any effect upon them. It is the worst case I have ever tried. That you, Taylor, kept a kind of male brothel it is impossible to doubt. And that you, Wilde, have been the center of a circle of extensive corruption of the most hideous kind among young men it is equally impossible to doubt.

"I shall, under such circumstances, be expected to pass the severest sentence that the law allows. In my judgment it is totally inadequate for such a case as this. The sentence of the Court is

318

that each of you be imprisoned and kept to hard labour for two years."

The Judge had hardly finished when the room resounded with cries of "Oh! Oh!" and "Shame!" His Lordship looked sternly about him. Calmly indifferent, Taylor accepted the sentence. Wilde made a move as if to address the Judge; his lips formed words, drowned by the sensation the sentence had created. Scornfully, His Lordship waved him away to the warders who touched him on the shoulder and led him toward the stair well whence, after a lost wild look round that sea of faces, he sank below.

That night the curious who passed by the St. James's Theatre, the scene of Wilde's most brilliant successes, looked in vain for the poster advertising *The Importance of Being Earnest*. The building, with its classic white portico, seemed deserted. There was a placard, however, the color of the sunflower, attached to the railing at the entrance to the theatre, the huge black letters coming alive in the street lights: WILDE VERDICT! OSCAR GUILTY! SENTENCE TWO YEARS HARD LABOUR!

In how brief a time had he fallen "from an eternity of fame to an eternity of infamy!"

Chapter XIV: *De Profundis*

CLAPHAM JUNCTION presented an unusual scene in the early afternoon of November 13, 1895. Toward two o'clock a gang of convicts, manacled and chained together, were herded on the central platform to wait for the train that was to take them from Wandsworth prison, whence they had come, to Reading Gaol. They were a wretched looking lot. Their prison uniforms, grayer than the gray November day, showed dark spots as the rain fell upon them. Shivering in the wet, and insufficiently protected, they huddled together, their handcuffs clinking, their feet shuffling uneasily as each train that stopped unloaded its passengers to stare at them. The crowd grew. It was not every day that the public was treated to such a spectacle of social justice. Who were these men? What had they done? Laughing, the people stood by and exchanged remarks on the ridiculous garb, the foolish attempts the convicts made to keep from being drenched to the skin. Already their uniforms showed an uneven darkness with the wet; rivulets of rain fell from them, and still they waited for the train that never came.

Suddenly one of the crowd, more percipient than the rest, shouted "Oscar Wilde!" and going toward a prisoner shrunken to make himself as small as possible, expressed his contempt in the only way he knew. His brave fellows immediately followed his example, mocking and jeering the miserable man. Wilde had already served six months of his sentence at Wandsworth. His moral agony, the insufficient bad food, the confinement, the labor, and finally his weeks in the hospital ward from where he had been taken that day without warning, all told upon him. He had grown thinner. His face, burned a brick red by the enforced exercise in the prison yard, still retained an unhealthy look. From the sleeves of his coat his hands hung lined and scarred, the long nails worn down to the quick, the fingers calloused and misshapen. Among other humiliations, his hair was shorn.

No bitterer caricature of him could have been drawn by his worst enemy—yet there he was, a caricature in the flesh, a living example to the self-righteous who invoke the wages of sin. They had no way of confronting one man's punishment with the lot of other Englishmen, guilty but untried, who had thought it best, after Wilde's downfall, to carry their sins to pleasanter and more tolerant climates. Dieppe for more than a year was overrun with them; Paris had never seen so many of them before. In their opinion Wilde had been a fool to face English law in one of its periodic fits of morality. The result of the tremendous scandal appeared more than anything, in an awakening of the vulgar to peculiarities of which they had not known. Now no man could show himself in London wearing a cloak, or with hair longer than John Bull's, without eliciting from the street arabs the greeting, "Hello, Oscar!"

The half hour spent by Wilde on the platform of Clapham Junction became for him a period of mourning. Every day at the same hour he wept for the same space of time—as much for man's inhumanity as for the tragedy that had brought him so low. Long ago, while in the sunshine of his wonderful life, he used to say that he could bear a real tragedy if it came to him in purple pall and a mask of noble sorrow, but that the dreadful thing about modernity was that it put tragedy in the raiment of comedy. "It is said that all martyrdoms look mean to the looker on,"—as mean and ludicrous and repellant as that of the rain-soaked convict in his garb of shame. The world in moral justification thought Wilde's punishment more lenient than he deserved—had not the Judge declared as much? It took a poor thief in Wandsworth to read into Wilde's bitter humiliation, and in the husky prison voice that comes of compulsory silence, to speak to him words of sympathy. "I am sorry for you. It is harder for the likes of you than it is for the likes of us."

When Wilde went to prison to serve his sentence he entered in an elevated state of mind, vowing eternal devotion to Lord Alfred and imploring him in heartbreaking letters never to forsake him but to wait for him until he came out. He comforted himself that he had acted heroically. Not once during the badgering of the opposing counsel in court had he denied "the Love that dare not speak its name." Often, however, when the spiritual ecstasy waned before the hard glare of reality and he saw himself without name, despised, dishonored, his home destroyed, his own children about to be taken legally from him as unfit for them, when he faced the bankruptcy court, the drying up of his income, of his very genius, he turned against Lord Alfred as the instrument of his destruction. Then his heroic self-sacrifice became the most foolish of the thousand foolish acts of his life, and he told himself: "The sins of another were being placed to my account. Had I so chosen, I could on either trial have saved myself at his expense, not from shame indeed, but from imprisonment." But would it have been so? Proving another guilty would not have made him innocent. Moreover, English justice would never have been satisfied with a less notable example than himself in its moral housecleaning.

The first shock Wilde suffered in his dream of Bosie, the Jonathan of his stirring court speech, occurred when in the darkest moment of his tragedy a messenger associated with his counsel came, and while the warder was standing by, whispered something that he was obviously reading from a slip of paper in his pocket: Prince Fleur de Lys sent greetings. At first Wilde stared at him blankly. The man repeated his message. When he saw that even then Wilde failed to understand he explained in an undertone that the gentleman of the greeting was at the moment abroad. Then the meaning dawned upon Wilde, and for the first time in his entire prison life he laughed. Prince Fleur de Lys! Then it had all been in vain—his own trial, the terrible punishment that he was yet to undergo! Nothing that had happened to him, Wilde, had made Douglas realize a single thing. Bosie, he saw, remained in his own eyes still the graceful prince of a trivial comedy. . . .

At Reading Gaol his disillusionment fed upon his sorrow. Month after month he waited for Bosie to write, but no word came. Robert Sherard had come to see him at Wandsworth, cheering his despair with hope; through his loyal efforts Constance on the next visiting day was prevailed upon to see her husband again in the sordid prison reception room. She who had every reason to despise him did not come in bitterness but with words of forgiveness which held the promise that on his release she would perhaps set up house with him again together with Vyvyan and his little Cyril whose golden head and sweet child ways companioned him in the ghost-filled nights till his conscience knew no rest.

Then there was Robert Ross, most devoted of the faithful. The tears came to Wilde's eyes whenever he thought of his selfless love. In prison a man lives only on memories, and among them one came to renew his faith in the nobility of human nature whenever he found himself sinking too deep in hopelessness. The scene was the bankruptcy court whither two policemen had brought him for the final indignity. While he was passing through the long corridor between a lane of the curious ready to mock at his handcuffs and convict's garb, he saw Robbie who was standing there among them gravely raise his hat to him as he drew near and so shame them to silence. Too moved to acknowledge so sweet and simple an action, Wilde passed him by with bowed head, but he thought to himself that men go to heaven for smaller things than that. In this spirit saints knelt down to wash the feet of the poor, and stooped to kiss the leper on the cheek. But from Bosie, not a syllable. An utter stranger, a Professor Frederick York Powell of Oxford, drew up a petition to Her Majesty for the mitigation of the prisoner's sentence; sympathetic articles on the harshness of his punishment were appearing in the papers on the Continent. Still, from Bosie, nothing. Prince Fleur de Lys had lost interest in one who, far from being on a pedestal, occupied the most shameful place into which society can put a man: a cell three paces wide and three paces long—in the third, Block C, of Reading Gaol, the third cell in the third landing. Prince Fleur de Lys had known Oscar Wilde. He had no acquaintance with the convict designated a "C.3.3." outside whose door the card which

323

usually gave the name of the occupant bore, out of some strange sense of decency, only his initials.

The prison ruling was of the harshest, and under the governing of Lieutenant Colonel H. Isaacson, a man who believed in the strict letter of discipline, life was a hell to the inmates under him. They could not talk; smoking was forbidden. A thousand trivial tasks were prescribed, each with its penalty for infraction. A thousand rules and regulations had to be observed—all under threat of punishment, merciless and brutalizing. After divine service every morning the prisoners went out into the paved yard for exercise about the stone-paved circle. Round and round in an inner and an outer ring, the prisoners kept three paces apart, so that they could not talk to each other when they were out of earshot of the warders. Wilde always walked in the outer circle among those who were strong and healthy. With his rapid stride—the stride which as the Philadelphia reporter had noticed long ago kept him far in advance of even the eager rush of an American crowd—Wilde was soon on the heels of the convict in front of him, which immediately brought the warder to him, that the three-pace interval might be maintained.

For two hours the convicts took their joyless walk, repeated for two hours more in the afternoon. The rest of the day they spent at hard labor after they had washed out the floors of their cells and cleansed their prison utensils. Broken in spirit as he was, Wilde had no heart for rebellion. In the morning if the keeper forgot to bring him water for the scrubbing, C.3.3. quickly reminded him. His water pail, the tin prison plates and cups were conscientiously scoured and arranged over and over again in their fixed places: too severe were the penalties for him to wish to incur them more than once. He was so cowed by the regulations that he would sometimes start up from his plank bed in the middle of the night and grope about the cell to make sure that everything was in order for the morning inspection. He had had his encounters with Lieutenant Colonel Isaacson and he was not anxious to repeat them. "I will see to it that your whims be plucked out of your system," he threatened the prisoner. He was a man of his word.

For the first year or more C.3.3. was put to oakum picking. He could not get on with it. The tough tarred ropes which he had to shred cut his fingers till the tips grew insensitive with pain. "What an ending! What an appalling ending!" he would murmur through closed lips that the warder might not see and add to his punishment by a week of solitary confinement in the dark cell—the penalty for speaking.

And then the terrible hunger, never appeased by the scant rations of loathsome prison food, the nauseous black bread, the revolting gruel. There was no suffering, no expiation that society spared him in his chastisement. He who had lived like a king had to do the tasks that a menial despised; the lord of language was compelled to be mute, the singer silenced. All that he had joyed in doing became the rod of his humiliation, his virtues as his perversities. Because he had written plays that had brought back the golden age of comedy to England, he was deprived of pen and ink; because he had delighted in the good things of life, he was made to starve.

How often he tormented himself with thinking of the dinners he used to order for himself and Bosie at the Savoy—the clear turtle soup, the delicate ortolans on their beds of Sicilian vine leaves, the 1880 Dagonet champagne, Bosie's favorite wine that had the color and the taste of amber! Now he was paying for them with hard crusts and water. And the suppers at Willis's after the theatre—those delightful suppers with the choicest *paté de foie* from Strasburg, and the *cuvées* of Perrier-Jouet, always reserved for them. When would they ever be paid for in full? Needless for him to expect Bosie to pay. It was not Bosie's way of life to pay. "What you did someone else must pay for," he accused in his lonely recriminations. And not only in a financial sense. What was he doing every moment of his imprisonment but paying for that friendship because of which the name of Wilde had become a byword among low people, a synonym for folly; because of which he would sit forever in the judgment of posterity between Gilles de Retz and the Marquis de Sade? And Bosie? He would be considered as the child Samuel, while the Marquis of Queensberry became a hero.

Brookfield, the actor, had arranged a banquet on his conviction for the Marquis to celebrate his annihilating shame. Would not the future too deem Queensberry a hero, and the man who walked into his booby trap the incarnation of the lowest evil?

With such thoughts Wilde nurtured his resentment at what appeared Bosie's neglect of him, turning his love to hate and his friend to an enemy. How could he ever have loved one so worldly, so shallow, so lacking in imagination? "The supreme vice is shallowness," he repeated again and again, not altogether in justification of Bosie. Always the shadow of that friendship walked with him. At night it wakened him, flashing before him with the lightning of memory and keeping him sleepless till dawn when unlike other visions, it remained to haunt him. In the prison yard it made him talk to himself as he tramped round. Nothing that had happened in those ill-starred years but reenacted itself in his imagination, to the least strained note of Bosie's voice, every word, every twitch and gesture of those nervous hands, to the very position of the shadow of time on the dial. And always he thought: had he wished it he could have saved himself at Bosie's expense. But he had refused. Such a course of action would have been beneath him. "Sins of the flesh are nothing," he rationalized. "They are maladies for physicians to cure. . . . Sins of the soul alone are shameful."

But did Bosie think for a single moment that he was worthy of the love Wilde was showing him then, or that for a single moment Wilde thought he was? "The aim of love is to love; no more and no less," he discovered as the pitiful Dowson had discovered long since to his own destruction. "You were my enemy, such an enemy as no man ever had. I had given you my life; and to gratify the lowest and most contemptible of all human passions, hatred and vanity and greed, you had thrown it away." But he could not really hate Bosie. Every morning he would say to himself, "I must keep love in my heart today, else how shall I live through the day?"

Though the prison walls kept him from the temptations of the world they did not shut out sorrow. He had been in Reading Gaol three months when Constance came again to see him. She had traveled all the way from Genoa where she was living as Mrs. Holland with her children, to tell him of his mother's death. She knew his grief would have been too great to bear had he heard of his loss from another. For what seemed interminable hours she sat in the gray and brown waiting room, listening to the ticking of the clock before the dreaded interview. How would Oscar look? Would she have the strength to face him? At last the guard came who led her through a yellow corridor and up a staircase; she gripped the iron rail. A glass-paneled door, the visitors' parlor—and there stood Oscar. The sight was too much for her; she broke down. It was the last time they were ever to meet.

Constance had softened the blow with all the gentleness of her nature; but Wilde could never be free of remorse at his mother's death. He had seen the change that had come over her after his disgrace, like a kind of spiritual extinction; he had known even then that the bodily would soon follow.

A still more bitter grief came to him when he learned that his children had been taken away from him by law. Now he had absolutely nothing left in the world that he could call his own. At first when he was told of this last revenge on the part of society, the shock was so appalling that he could not grasp its import. It was only when he found himself alone in his cell that the full meaning dawned upon him, throwing him on his knees in a paroxysm of tears. How long he lay there he did not know till he roused himself from his despair, murmuring, "The body of a child is as the body of the Lord: I am not worthy of either." That moment seemed to save him; he saw then that the only thing for him to do was to accept everything.

From then on he bore up against adversity, facing each sorrow with a fortitude he had never known, as he strove to convert every blow that fell to spiritual experience. Prison life dulled itself to routine. In July of 1896 a note of humaneness entered into it with the coming of Major J. O. Nelson as governor of the gaol to replace Isaacson who had been transferred to Lewes prison. C.3.3. was relieved of his tasks of shredding rope and turning the crank that supplied the prison water, and put instead to bookbinding. Soon he was also allowed to receive books which his friends eagerly supplied after the governor passed upon the selection. But Wilde was still forbidden to have paper and pencils. No matter what seethed in his brain which was never at rest, he could not give it expression.

Occasionally with Warder T. Martin, an intelligent, kind-hearted man who in his liking for his prisoner infracted the rules to smuggle in to him some little luxury, he would permit himself to talk in an undertone and behind the locked cell door. Warder Martin drank in the amazing monologues. Nothing seemed to stump the wonderful prisoner. Sometimes Martin, who used to pass the long hours off duty reading, plied Wilde with questions for the improvement of his mind. Too often the names Wilde mentioned—Voltaire, Renan, Dante, Dostoievsky—were Greek to the good man, but he did not hesitate to lead the wanderer nearer home. Amused, Wilde talked with his tongue in his cheek.

"Charles Dickens, sir," the warder would say, "would he be considered a great writer now?"

"Oh, yes—a great writer. You see, he is no longer alive."

"I understand, sir," Martin nodded. "Being dead he would be a great writer."

Once the name of John Strange Winter came up. "What do you think of him, sir?" he asked.

"A charming person," said Wilde very gravely, "but a lady, you know, not a man."

"Thank you, sir. I did not know he was a lady, sir."

"Excuse me, sir," Martin began on another occasion. "But Marie Corelli, would she be considered a great writer?"

"Now don't think I have anything against her moral character," Wilde smiled, "but from the way she writes she ought to be here."

"You don't say so, sir! You don't say so!"

There was some ruffling of feelings in England when it was learned that *Salomé* was given its first showing at the Théâtre de l'Oeuvre in Paris on the 11th of February, 1896. The work of a convict performed? Outrageous! In London after Wilde's disgrace, the sensitive managers had blacked out his name from the theatre posters while continuing to collect box-office profits from his plays; his books when sold were extracted from under the counter. And yet in Paris he was boldly announced as the author of *Salomé*, the handsomely printed program bearing upon it a lithograph of the portrait by Toulouse-Lautrec! Lugné-Poë, the director himself, a man of considerable repute, appeared in the part of Herod. The play was at once hailed as an artistic triumph.

"It is something that at a time of disgrace and shame I should be still regarded as an artist," Wilde wrote to Ross who kept him in touch with everything that was going on. But he felt no real pleasure, seeming dead to all emotions except those of anguish and despair.

Both emotions were painfully aroused when some time later he heard from Sherard that Bosie was about to publish an article about him in one of the French reviews. When it appeared finally in *La Revue Blanche* it did Wilde great harm. Henry Bauër, championing the unfortunate man, left no doubt of his feelings about the writer. "One might have hoped," he said, "that Wilde, forgiven, might find on his release from prison the hospitality of French letters. The recent success of *Salomé* augured well for it. But now here comes Douglas who with a scandalous, self-advertising article ruins everything . . . In England he made a convict of him; he is now depriving him of the possibility of living in France: he brought him to hard labor; now he makes Paris impossible for him on the morrow of his release. And all, so that he may make a noise about his pretty person and get some advance publicity for his forth-coming verses."[1]

At this time another application for the commuting of Wilde's sentence was drawn up by his sympathizers, but like Professor Powell's it never reached the point of being submitted to the proper authorities. It would have been useful; the law would

[1] Tr. by the author. Lord Alfred Douglas' poems were eventually published by the *Mercure de France*.

not be deprived of its full meed. Moreover, the Home Secretary to whom the case was brought, remembered certain quips at his expense at a dinner where Wilde was his guest, and he may have thought that mortification was good for his soul. At any rate the Home Secretary discouraged the presentation of the petition, saying in a letter, that upon investigation no grounds, medical or other, had been found to justify special privilege. Wilde who had deluded himself with hope, had still another disappointment to bear. "For myself, dear Robbie," he wrote to Ross, "I have little to say that can please you. The refusal to commute my sentence has been like a blow from a leaden sword . . . I had fed on hope, and now anguish, grown hungry, feeds her fill of me as though she had been starved of her proper appetite."

However, the fact that sympathy had been shown him helped to draw him from the spiritual isolation which had been to him a source of terror and trouble. Besides, through the kindness of Major Nelson, he was now permitted to write. At first except for the long letters he sent to Ross, Sherard and More Adey, he could do little else. But he put himself to the study of German, read Dante, and made excerpts and notes for the pleasure of using pen and ink. After he had had to spend several weeks in the sick ward he was put on light labor and medical diet, and was later absolved from all work except that of keeping his cell clean. He now wrote most of the day, using the planks of his bed for a table on which he placed the sheets of blue stamped prison foolscap paper. Every morning the chief warder would take them for inspection to the governor's office, and after Major Nelson had glanced at them, brought them back to the prisoner who was soon bending over them again with passionate intensity.

It was a letter, the only form in which he found it easy to express himself since his imprisonment; yet it was more in the nature of a confession addressed to Bosie, for only to him could he speak from the depths of his anguished spirit. When he began writing he was still suffering from Bosie's unimaginative callous-

330

ess in publishing an article which could not but be injurious
o him.

> I think they love not art
> Who break the crystal of a poet's heart
> That small and sickly eyes may glare and gloat.

He had written those lines after a sale by auction of Keats'
ove letters. Strangers had put those letters on the market, and
trangers had bought them. In his case it was the very man to
vhom his thoughts had oftenest turned who was offering his
nmost secrets to the basest curiosity. Hurt and resentful, he
poured out his grievances, and as he wrote the pent-up misery of
eighteen months in gaol, the gnawing thoughts of what had
prought him there, Bosie, Queensberry, his trials and his disgrace took such possession of him that he who had never been
ble to write a bitter word became all bitterness. Accusations
proke from him, violent convulsions of the spirit, uncon-
rollable now that he could express them; old wounds opened
ind bled anew; and pitying himself for his martyrdom, he made
Bosie his executioner. The fates had been more than kind to
Bosie. "The head of Medusa that turns living men to stone, you
have been allowed to look at in a mirror merely. You yourself
have walked free among the flowers. From me the beautiful
world of color and motion has been taken away." Each and
every one he traced the stations of his downfall till at last he
ound himself in the lowest mire of Malebolge. The visions of
his past that had possessed the nights in his cell he set down in
heir spectral hues, and through them Bosie walked, not the
Greek and gracious lad of his idolatrous letters, but a twisted
igure of evil, a Dorian who in himself bore the marks of his
corruption.

Gradually as he saw his own sins face to face, he who had
never had the courage of his paganism beheld it for what it was:
he weariness of the decadent who must glut on new sensations
even to the destruction of his soul; and having recognized it he
realized of how little worth it had been. As if by a miracle his

331

bitterness left him, and the still small voice that had spoken to him even at the height of his depravity rose loud and clear, till at its bidding he could forgive Bosie and the no longer splendid sinner that was himself. In the example of Christ he found the noblest beauty and the fount of all creation, "the note of pity in Russian novels, Verlaine and Verlaine's poems . . . the troubled romantic marbles of Michelangelo . . . and the love of children and flowers—for both of which, indeed, in classical art there was but little place, hardly enough for them to grow or play in, but which, from the twelfth century down to our own day, have been continually making their appearance in art under various modes and at various times, coming fitfully and wilfully, as children, as flowers are apt to do; spring always seeming to one as if the flowers had been in hiding, and only came out into the sun because they were afraid that grown-up people would grow tired of looking for them and give up the search; and the life of a child being no more than an April day on which there is both rain and sun for the narcissus."

Gropingly he was seeking his soul, though how far as he wrote he was still from its true temper he could not but realize in the changing moods of his letter. "But do not forget," he warned "at what a terrible school I am sitting at my task, and incomplete, imperfect as I am, my friends have still much to gain. They came to me to learn the pleasures of life and the pleasure of art. Perhaps I am chosen to teach them some thing more wonderful, the meaning of sorrow and its beauty."

In his search he learned the meaning of pity that like an invisible guide brought him close to others who suffered and were dumb. Sometimes he would slip a note on a scrap of paper or the inside of an envelope to Warder Martin, asking him to do a kindness for his sake to some fellow prisoner. "Please find out for me the name of A.2.11.," he wrote toward the end of his confinement, "also the names of the children who are in for the rabbits and the amount of the fine. Can I pay this and get them out? . . . Please, dear friend, do this for me. I must get them out. Think what a thing for me it would be to be able to help three little children . . ."

Among the prisoners there was one, Charles Thomas Wooldridge, formerly a trooper in the Blue Royal Horse Guards whose fate had made a deep impression not only upon Wilde but upon the rest of the "trial men" who had tramped with him the weary hours in the exercise yard. He was young, not quite thirty. His step, as he walked, seemed light and gay, but never had Wilde seen anyone look so wistfully upon the bit of blue overhead with its clouds drifting by. What hunted thought quickened his step? What crime had brought him there? Suddenly one day the man behind him whispered to Wilde: "That fellow's got to swing." The prison walls reeled round him; the sky became like a casque of steel. Wooldridge must pay for having murdered his wife in a fit of jealousy. "The man had killed the thing he loved, and so he had to die."

For six weeks Wooldridge took his place in the circle of gray-clad marchers, and then he came no more. He was standing in the black dock, Wilde knew, and none of them would ever see him alive again. Like two doomed ships he and Wooldridge had crossed each other in a storm, without a sign. Then one evening in July, as the prisoners were tramping in from work, their hearts stilled with terror of the fate awaiting the man who was not there, they came upon a yawning yellow grave dug in the prison asphalt. They saw the hangman with his little bag go shuffling through the gloom, and each man trembled as he crept into his cell.

Shortly after seven o'clock the following morning, the bell of St. Lawrence's Church began tolling. The prisoners who had been awakened as usual at six o'clock to clean their cells stood still. Half an hour passed, three-quarters. Then there was a sound of steps in the yard, and they knew that the man who was about to die was being led to the mean little shed where the prisoners used to be photographed but which now was the scaffold.

At eight o'clock Wooldridge stood under the gallows beam. His arms were pinioned behind him. Without a word or a gesture of protest, he allowed the hangman to fasten his feet. The cap was drawn over his head, the noose fastened, and quickly the executioner drew the bolt. A strangled scream and in a few moments all was over, Wooldridge dying without a struggle. Hardly had the body ceased to swing when the black flag was hoisted over the prison to show that justice had been done.

That morning the chaplain held no service for the prisoners —his heart was far too sick for the office—and until noon the men were kept in their cells. When they were let out at length into the yard their faces were as pale as death and none dared to look at the other for fear of what he might read. Up and down, as usual, the keepers paced among their human herd. They were wearing their Sunday uniforms, though it was Tuesday, and the prisoners noticed that their boots were spotted with lime. As they passed by the prison wall where, the night before, the grave had yawned as for a living thing, they saw only a stretch of mud and sand, and a little heap of burning quicklime. Underneath the man who had walked with them lay wrapt in a sheet of flame.

As the time approached for Wilde's release his friends made preparations to receive him. They had to be extremely careful, for the hurt his imprisonment had inflicted was deeper than they knew and everything made it bleed. At first he dreaded the thought of facing a world that did not want him. "Horrible as are the dead when they rise from their tombs," he wrote to Ross, "the living who come out from tombs are more horrible still." How was he to take up the threads of his life when the most essential had been irretrievably snapped? He could never live with his wife and his children again. Constance had a full right to her freedom, even though in her pity for him at Wandsworth she had generously promised to take him back after a period of probation. He knew now how wrong it would be to have her tie herself to him out of a sense of duty. Life had been cruel for her as it was, forced to conceal by an assumed name that she had ever been bound to him. It was kinder for him to sign a deed of formal separation, granting her full custody of their two sons. This he did, in return for which she pledged herself to give him an allowance of £150 a year. It was very little, a mere pittance to one who had paid that amount for a pair of cuff buttons for a friend. But, Constance's lawyers may have argued, Oscar would soon be writing again.

Deep within himself Wilde had no such confidence, though he could hope. The very fact that people would recognize him wherever he went would force upon him the necessity of reasserting himself as an artist. "If I can produce only one beautiful work of art, I shall be able to rob malice of its venom. . . ."

It was to Ross that he turned in the large as in the small matters of his readjustment, revealing a serious outlook entirely new to him. "I want you to be my literary executor, in case of my death," he wrote, "and to have complete control of my plays, books and papers. As soon as I find I have a legal right to make a will, I will do so." In the meantime he was most concerned about giving into his keeping the letter he had written in prison. As he was not permitted to send out the manuscript, he made sure that Ross would receive it as soon as he himself left prison.

"When you have read the letter," he told him, "you will see the psychological explanation of a course of conduct that from the outside seems a combination of absolute idiocy with vulgar bravado. Some day the truth will have to be known: not necessarily in my lifetime . . . but I'm not prepared to sit in the grotesque pillory they put me into, for all time . . ." The letter must be copied, he directed—typewritten, preferably. "I assure you that the typewriting machine, when played with expression, is not more annoying than the piano when played by a sister or near relation . . . The lady typewriter might be fed through a lattice in the door, like the Cardinals when they elect a Pope; till she comes out on the balcony and can say to the world: '*Habet Mundus Epistolam*'; for indeed it is an Encyclical letter, and as the Bulls of the Holy Father are named from their opening words, it may be spoken of as the '*Epistola: in Carcere et Vinculis.*' "[2]

Two things he wanted when he went back to the world—a few books that he might call his own, and his old fur coat which

[2] When Ross published it, very much expurgated, in 1905, he called it *De Profundis*. The original manuscript is now in the British Museum.

he had vainly tried to save with others of his few belongings after the debacle. Perhaps More Adey could get in touch with the people who had sold or pawned it. He had had it for twelve years before he was sent to prison. "It was all over America with me; it was at all my first nights; it knows me perfectly, and I really want it."

Chapter XV: *The Ballad of Reading Gaol*

THE mob of the curious who had been drawn to Reading Gaol the morning of May 19, 1897, at the announcement that Wilde that day would be released from prison, waited long in vain. For once the law deprived them of the edifying spectacle of seeing how an artist would look after two years at hard labor. In justice to that moral body, however, it must be said that the contretemps had been entirely unintentional, caused by the strict observance of rules and regulations without which the very fortress of order would have been assailed. It was the rule that a prisoner must be released from the gaol where he had first been confined. The night of May 18, therefore, Wilde, for the first time in ordinary clothes which Harris and others of his friends had provided for him, left Reading in a closed carriage with the chief warder, also in plain clothes, took a train at the local station a few miles distant, and rode on to Paddington. From there he was escorted to Wandsworth Gaol and discharged the following day.

Robert Ross, Mrs. Leverson and two or three others who were there to meet him looked at him with mingled feelings of pity and gratification. He had grown much thinner, and his face, freshly shaved, had a healthy outdoor tan. But he had lost a great deal of hair. A bald patch was discernible on the crown; the hair itself showed streaks of gray amid the brown. Ross saw with relief that his eyes no longer had that horrible vacancy that had chilled him on his first visits to Reading when, without listening to what was said, Wilde would interpose with the question: "Do you think my brain seems all right?" The old smile beamed on his face, lighting his glance with that sunniness of heart which prison had clouded but not extinguished. By the transmutation of suffering and enforced regular living, the bloated, arrogant voluptuary of 1895 had again become the Oscar Wilde of the past, sweet, gentle, and with a new humility.

He was anxious, he said, to withdraw from the world for a little while, a few months, perhaps, till he could find himself and gather the strength to meet life. "I must not be afraid of the past," he told himself. "If people tell me that it is irrevocable I shall not believe them. The past, the present and the future are one moment in the sight of God, in whose sight we should try to live." He must go to a Roman Catholic retreat.

His friends looked at one another at the announcement, and their hearts sank. But Oscar would not be dissuaded. In spite of them he wrote a letter and sent it by cab to one of the Fathers of a near-by Oratory, begging that he be allowed to retire there for six months. During the hour of suspense they tried to distract him by talking of other things. Finally the man returned with an answer; Mrs. Leverson, Robbie and the rest turned away as he read it. They knew it was none other than they had expected when in the midst of his reading Wilde broke down and sobbed. The Fathers could not admit him to the retreat on a mere impulse, the refusal read; such a step must be considered for at least a year—a year for the man who had had twenty-four months of spiritual agony in which to know his mind.

England was out of the question, at least for the present. There was no time to lose. That same day Wilde left from Newhaven accompanied by Ross and Reginald Turner, and went on to Dieppe. How often before had he lightheartedly made the crossing! But now it was like a flight heedlessly delayed for two years. Although he had served his sentence, society had not forgiven. It had no place for him and offered none. Long before leaving Reading Gaol he had known it. Nevertheless, being human, he hoped that just as he had learned pity and forgiveness while serving the sentence imposed upon him, society too had softened toward him.

He hated Dieppe and went there with a heavy heart. He was too well known. Moreover the many residents and visiting Englishmen in the little resort saw to it that he should not lack the moral chastening which according to the unimaginative served both to exalt the chastiser and improve the culprit. Hence wherever he was recognized, whether at the hotel where he stayed, or in some public café, he was reminded that his presence infected the rarefied atmosphere in which all Englishmen travel. He had been the victim of one such insult when Fritz Thaulaw, the painter, walked up to him and in a booming voice invited him to dine with his wife and his children at his home.

Gratefully Wilde went, finding there Charles Conder, a little chastened, perhaps, and already marked for death, but still materializing his Laodicean dreams of changeless beauty amid ever-blooming nature to which he escaped from his chronic poverty. "Dear Conder," Wilde used to sigh as he watched him trying to sell some lovely bit of decorated silk. "With what exquisite subtlety he goes about persuading someone to give him a hundred francs for a fan, for which he was fully prepared to pay three hundred!"

While at Dieppe he was pained to learn that Warder Martin had been discharged from Reading Gaol for the great crime of having given some sweet biscuits to one of the imprisoned children for whom Wilde had pleaded. He had seen the three children, on the morning before his release, standing in their prison dress and carrying their sheets under their arms. They were no older than his own sons. One of them, indeed, was so tiny, that the prison could not provide clothes small enough to fit him. Wilde had seen many children in prison, especially at Wandsworth, but never one so young as that poor, terrified mite who must spend twenty-three hours of the twenty-four until discharged in a solitary cell, a punishment harder than that inflicted on a murderer—and all for having attempted to steal some rabbits. Warder Martin had been no less affected. When he noticed the following morning, that the little fellow had not touched the crust of black bread that comprised the prison breakfast, he returned after the other prisoners of the block had been served, and rather than see the child starve, coaxed him with a few sweet biscuits which he managed to smuggle in to him. The boy, astounded by this beautiful action, spoke of it in his innocence to one of the senior warders who promptly reported Martin and had him dismissed.

Remembering the keeper's many kindnesses to him Wilde

wrote a letter describing the inhumanity of prison conditions, especially toward children, justified Martin for his deed, and sent the communication to *The Daily Chronicle* where it took up two columns of the edition for May 28. His sympathizers read it with tears in their eyes, while the British public at large sighed piously at the uplifting example of the sinful man who, through his punishment, had been made to know the pity they could not feel. The letter, however, succeeded in bringing about prison reform.

Since every day Dieppe became more impossible for him, Wilde found himself a place of refuge in the little town of Berneval-sur-Mer, not very far away yet beautifully secluded amid its deep meadows, forest land and the bordering sea coast. At the Hôtel de la Plage where he took two rooms he registered as Sebastian Melmoth. He had given himself the name after his own marked him out for infamy even in the remotest corners that his former fame had failed to reach. Sebastian for the martyr—had not he, the artist, suffered the arrows of the Philistine?—and Melmoth for the lonely wanderer rejected of society, for whom nature alone had a place where he might hide. "She will hang the night with stars so that I may walk abroad in the darkness without stumbling, and send the wind over my footprints so that none may track me to my hurt."

There, amid simple folk who asked no questions and learned to like him for himself, he tried to obliterate the marks of the convict and recreate the artist. His brain teemed with ideas once more. He would finish his *Florentine Tragedy* and then begin work on two Biblical plays that he had outlined in his mind—*Pharaoh* and *Ahab and Jezebel*, which he pronounced Isabel. Ross and More Adey who received regular accounts on his activities rejoiced at his intentions. Perhaps after all Oscar could adjust himself to the life of simple living and high thinking forced upon him by the small allowance from Constance and the fund that had been raised for him while he was in prison. His first letters from Berneval certainly brought back the old Oscar with springtime always in his heart.

"I am going tomorrow on a pilgrimage," he wrote happily.

"I always wanted to be a pilgrim, and I have decided to start early tomorrow to the shrine of Notre Dame de Liesse. Do you know what Liesse is? It is an old word for joy . . . It will take at least six or seven minutes to get there, and as many more to come back . . . Need I say that this is a miracle? I wanted to go on a pilgrimage, and I find the little gray stone chapel of Our Lady of Joy is brought to me. It has probably been waiting for me all these purple years of pleasure, and now it comes to me with Liesse as its message."

To others of his correspondents to whom, because he loved them less, he could reveal his true state he wrote more candidly. "I have no storage of nervous force," he confided to Frank Harris. "When I expend what I have, in an afternoon, nothing remains." The least drain on his intellect or emotion exhausted him and deprived him of his sleep at night. He found himself incapable of any protracted creative activity. Somehow it took more than the quiet life he was leading, with its healthful sea-baths, simple food and regular hours to charge his cells for him. To André Gide he gave a clue to his increasing unrest. "Alfred Douglas writes me terrible letters. He says he does not understand me, that he does not understand that I do not wish everyone ill, and that everyone has been horrid to me. No, he does not understand me . . . But I keep on telling him that in every letter: we cannot follow the same road. He has his, and it is beautiful—I have mine. His is that of Alcibiades; mine is now that of St. Francis of Assisi."

Doubtless he wrote in all sincerity. The nearness of the chapel of Our Lady of Joy made him feel a kinship with that Brother Francis who after a youth wasted in search of pleasure, found perfect happiness in a mystic marriage with Lady Poverty. Nevertheless the remembered ways of Alcibiades could not but waken the old torment. "I had hardly any sleep last night," he wrote to Robbie on again hearing from Bosie. "Douglas's letter was in the room, and foolishly I had read it again and left it by my bedside." That night he had one of his recurrent dreams. His mother appeared to him, as she had appeared once before in

341

prison, and spoke to him with some sternness. "I can see that whenever I am in danger she will in some way warn me. . . ."

But that tone of piety was adopted rather to reassure Robbie who dreaded more than anything else a reunion between Wilde and Lord Alfred, than out of any real conviction that he could indeed succeed in keeping away from the man at whom, nevertheless, he had addressed his merciless prison letter. The note to Ross bore the date of May 28. On the 6th of June, Sunday night, he was writing to "My dearest Boy": "I must give up this *absurd* habit of writing to you every day. It comes of course from the strange new joy of talking to you daily . . . Dear boy, I hope you are still sweetly asleep—you are so absurdly sweet when you are asleep . . . Remember, after a few days, *only one letter a week*—I must school myself to it." He signed himself *"Oscar— Poète-forçat."*[1]

No, neither Speranza, returned to warn him from the grave, nor the prayers of his friends could alter what two years in prison had been powerless to change. It served no purpose to confess the truth to Robbie; it would merely mean unpleasantness and the cessation of his allowance, granted to him under a very explicit proviso. He resorted to duplicity, writing his affectionate letters to Bosie while to Ross he turned a face of repentance, feebly seconded by protests that he tried to make convincing. Constance also wrote to him again, and sent him photographs of Cyril and Vyvyan in suits with little Eton collars. She would visit him twice a year, she said, but made no promise to allow him to see the boys. "It is a terrible punishment, dear Robbie," he complained, "and oh, how well I deserve it! But it makes me feel disgraced and evil, and I don't want to feel that."

Shortly after he settled at Berneval Wilde left his hotel for the Chalet Bourgeat, a pretty little house not far from the good innkeeper and his wife who had befriended him. He furnished it himself, removing from the hotel his small shelf of books, a graceful little Gothic madonna on a high pedestal—was it Notre

[1] "Oscar—convict poet."

Dame de Liesse?—and Nicholson's portrait of Queen Victoria which he hung on the wall in his study. He had an inexplicable admiration for Her Majesty with whom he had been incongruously juxtaposed in the case of *Regina versus Wilde,* a sardonic fulfillment of his schoolboy wish. To Berneval, Will Rothenstein came to see him, and others of his former associates who were not intimidated by public opinion; and there for a time he took in Ernest Dowson whom he rescued from his landlord at Arques-la-Bataille, after Smithers, too much preoccupied with the dying Aubrey Beardsley, had left him stranded.

Monsieur Melmoth became a well-loved figure in the community. Many an evening he might be seen taking a walk by the sea with the old curé of Notre Dame de Liesse, mingling his voice with the plash of the waves, while the holy man listened, sweetly smiling. The customs officers borrowed his Dumas *père*; the children flocked to him, especially after he invited the whole school and the schoolmaster to celebrate Queen Victoria's Diamond Jubilee at an outdoor *fête* where they were all served strawberries and cream, cakes, sweets and tea. What wonder the delighted youngsters raised the cry, *"Vivent Monsieur Melmoth et la Reine d'Angleterre"* whenever they caught sight of him passing through Berneval-le-Grand!

In England the nation was in a frenzy of aggressive jubilation celebrating the sixtieth anniversary of Queen Victoria as ruler of Great Britain. The empire had extended its dominion over the world. Guns and battleships protected its supremacy. It was an era of prosperity and power, expressed symbolically in the pageants and ceremonies of that glorious July. The exaggerations of the earlier 'nineties had subsided after the scandal of 1895 which, while putting their most prominent exponent on trial, came as an indictment of the daring, indulgent life. Art and letters fell into disrepute. Spiritual aspirations and schemes of social reform became suspect. England put its faith in the material things of life, and of blatant patriotism, fattened on the spoils of conquest, created itself a god.

On the morning of July 17, the day after the pageant, a poem

343

appeared in the London *Times*, accompanied by editorial comment; for indeed Rudyard Kipling's "Recessional" called for a word of explanation when into the orgy of imperialism triumphant it brought its spiritual warning. "In this moment of exaltation," said the *Times*, "Mr. Kipling does well to remind his countrymen that we have something more to do than to build battleships and multiply guns." Kipling did more than that. He pricked the pride-glutted conscience of the nation to the values it had neglected.

> The tumult and the shouting dies;
>   The Captains and the Kings depart:
> Still stands thine ancient sacrifice,
>   An humble and a contrite heart.
> Lord God of Hosts, be with us yet,
> Lest we forget—lest we forget!

From the singer of imperialism, it was an admonition to be heeded.

A year earlier Alfred Edward Housman had introduced into his first volume of verse, *A Shropshire Lad,* a poem celebrating the Queen's fiftieth year of rule in which he recalled to the reader what the building of the empire had meant even to the remotest corners of Britain whose lads had been taken from the fields to fight the wars abroad.

> The skies that knit their heartstrings right,
>   The fields that bred them brave,
> The saviours come not home tonight:
>   Themselves they could not save.

> It dawns in Asia, tombstones show
>   And Shropshire names are read;
> And the Nile spills his overflow
>   Beside the Severn's dead.

Everyone had read the poignant little volume, even though it came while the exponents of *The Yellow Book* and *The Savoy* were still enjoying their popularity. The ballads and short lyrics had little in common with the elaborations of the aesthetic poets in their terse simplicity, akin, rather, to the verses of the Greek *Anthology*. There was, however, an affinity in the philosophical pessimism of the poems and the pervading sense of defeat and decay in the writings of the aesthetes that gave Housman's book undeniable modernity, though he could never be classed with the predominant school.

Reginald Turner had given Wilde a copy of *A Shropshire Lad* not long after it was published. It affected him deeply, coming as it did after suffering had brought the hedonist close to the simplest and most universal emotions. The unaffected cadences of Housman's book telling the simple annals of common folk in their acceptance of life, cruel, brutal and noble in turn, harmonized with the ideal of spiritual perfection which he had put before himself.

He had come out of Reading Gaol anxious for vindication as man and artist. For the first few weeks he had been unable to do anything. With the summer, however, he set seriously to work on what was to prove his sincerest creation and his noblest poem. Because it was the genius of Wilde that invested it, *The Ballad of Reading Gaol* disputes with none its place as the most moving of English ballads for the universality of its appeal and the blood drops of pity that sear the page with a terrible burning life. Scholars have been anxiously tracing influences and derivations. Whatever the outward garb, *The Ballad of Reading Gaol* shows Wilde humanized and therefore exalted. Unlike Dante who had seen Hell and came back to flay his fellows, Wilde who had lived through the worse hell of an English prison returned to speak the pitiful message he had learned.

He took the hanging of his fellow convict Wooldridge as the central theme; it was as simple as that, and as great: the expiation of a soul in pain for the sin which society judged without understanding.

As one who sees most fearful things,
    In the crystal of a dream,
We saw the greasy hempen rope
    Hooked to the blackened beam,
And heard the prayer the hangman's snare
    Strangled into a scream.

And all the woe that moved him so
    That gave that bitter cry,
And the wild regrets and bloody sweats,
    None knew so well as I:
For he who lives more lives than one
    More deaths than one must die . . .

The man in red who reads the Law
    Gave him three weeks of life,
Three little weeks in which to heal
    His soul of his soul's strife,
And cleanse from every drop of blood
    The hand that held the knife.

And with tears of blood he cleansed the hand,
    The hand that held the steel:
For only blood can wipe out blood,
    And only tears can heal:
And the crimson stain that was of Cain
    Became Christ's snow-white seal.

In the heart-wrung stanzas of the ballad he attained the peak
of his poetic achievement. Higher he could not go: there was no
greater elevation. It had remained for the convict poet to sur-
pass the best of the lord of language by the lowliest device of
speaking to the heart of humanity that knows all tongues as all
silences.

But alas, even while he was writing his Christian poem he had
to wrestle with the temptation of seeing Bosie once again. Fran-
tically Ross sent him letters appealing to his will for strength to
resist, and reminding him of how much he risked if he succumbed at this stage. Constance would forever be alienated from

346

him: she herself wrote to him more forcibly than she had ever done. It would mean never seeing his children, never again returning to the society that will sometimes take back the regenerate sinner. Oscar was doing so well; he was writing the work he had dreamed of in prison. Once he could prove that prison had recreated the artist Paris would take him back, perhaps even London. But he must not sacrifice his salvation to his weakness.

With seeming docility Wilde would appease him. "I have had no time to write lately, but I have written a long letter of twelve pages to Douglas to point out that I owe everything to you and your friends . . . I also wrote to him about him calling himself a *grand seigneur* in comparison to a dear sweet wonderful friend like you—his superior in all fine things."

All this he may have written to Bosie. Nevertheless his weakness won. In the beginning of September Will Rothenstein sent him a check of fifteen pounds, the proceeds of the Monticelli which he had bought at the Tite Street auction and sold to an art dealer. A few days later Wilde sped to Rouen to meet Bosie who was waiting for him at the station. In his emotionally unbalanced state Wilde burst into tears. Arm in arm the two spent the day walking through the town. No bitterness marred their meeting. Next day Wilde returned to Berneval after they had arranged to meet again in Naples a few weeks later.

Wilde's castle of strength which he had been so painfully building collapsed forever. Bosie had won against the devotion of those who had sought to guard Wilde from himself. To Wilde duty had never been a pleasant taskmistress: against "the Love that dare not speak its name" it became a despised middle-class convention.

"My own Darling Boy," he wrote to Bosie from Berneval soon after their parting. "I got your telegram half an hour ago—and just send you a line to say that I feel that my only hope of again doing beautiful work in art is being with you. It was not so in old days—but now it is different, and you can really recreate in me that energy and sense of joyous power on which Art depends. Everyone is furious with me for going back to you—but they don't understand us. I feel that it is only with you that I can do anything at all— Do remake my ruined life for me—and then our friendship and love will have a different meaning to the world. . . ."

Forgotten were the recriminations he had poured out in the prison letter that Bosie had never seen. In the sunlight of the presence that for him transfigured all things to beauty the disgrace of his fall, poverty, humiliation, suffering, his broken home and his pariah state vanished like the bad dreams of a night. With Bosie under the same roof he would finish the ballad. He must have his quickening nearness for the power of creation. Berneval became insufferable as Notre Dame de Liesse abdicated to Apollo.

Lord Alfred too responded to the stimulus of their association, for soon after the Rouen meeting he wrote "The Ballad of St. Vitus." As in the past in London, it was impossible for them to remain apart. By the third week in September they were occupying the Villa Giudice in Posilipo, near Naples. The house was small, but the servants were plentiful, what with Carmine the cook to take care of the kitchen, the maid Maria for the housework, two boys Peppino and Michele to wait on the milords, and an old witch, complete to the beard, to tell their fortunes and exorcise the rats which by common consent had left Norway to settle the pleasanter Mediterranean shores. Money alone was scarce, Wilde's three pound weekly allowance adding little to Lord Alfred's eight. However, since masters and servants could be fed on twelve lire a day even the shortage was not hard to bear.

Ross in vain endeavored to bring Wilde to reason by writing him as harshly as he dared. Wilde retorted with silence. The letters angered and distressed him, and in those moods he could not write to Robbie, of all people. When he did, finally, he tried to propitiate him by promising to work on *The Florentine Tragedy*, and later on the Pharaoh play. Douglas, he added, had written three sonnets. "They are quite wonderful!"

Pressed for money and with the anticipation of a thunderbolt from the solicitor, stopping the allowance from Constance, he hopefully banked on the publication of *The Ballad of Reading*

Gaol. "Unless Pinker gets me three hundred pounds," he wrote on October 3, "I shall not be able to get food. Up to the present I have paid for almost everything . . ." On three pounds a week?—Ross might have asked.

In a little while it became clear that all was not well at Villa Giudice. The disparate temperaments of the two men again wrought upon each other in their original force which nothing of what they had experienced had been able to modify in any essential. As Wilde was to learn, there was no such thing as reforming in life. "One merely wanders round and round within the circle of one's personality." In the friction of daily living the renewed friendship, wearing down the first enthusiasms, showed in all its hopelessness.

Wilde's letters formed one long complaint, the theme of poverty varying with that of Lord Alfred's lack of imagination in his regard. To make matters worse, Pinker the agent could not place the *Ballad.* No reputable publisher had the courage to bring it out even without the name of Oscar Wilde; and as for the three hundred pounds that the author had optimistically anticipated, it dwindled to a mere twenty when his friend Leonard Smithers, true to his boast that he would publish anything the others were afraid of, resolved to try his luck with the poem of an ex-convict.

While Oscar was busy with the revisions, an unforeseen blow came when Lady Queensberry threatened to cut off Bosie's allowance if he still continued living under the same roof with Wilde. The situation became indeed desperate. Without a penny, his wife and his friends bitterly disappointed in him, Wilde saw himself thrown into the streets. In his panic he no longer knew where to turn. "I need not tell you that Douglas could not give me three shillings a week—he has not enough for his own wants," he wrote to Ross.

Suddenly, in the thick of the clouds closing all about him, he caught a faint gleam for his temporary salvation. Douglas was his debtor. Before he went to prison there had been a certain "debt of honor" of five hundred pounds which Bosie, under the guarantee of his brother Percy, had pledged himself to pay him as part of the expenses of the trial that he had so disastrously undertaken. Bosie might leave him at Lady Queensberry's bidding, but he must first discharge, at least in part, that debt owing to him. His need was beyond niceties. "To tilt with Death is worse than to tilt with windmills . . ." Quixotic chivalry was out of the question. Once more the ill-starred friendship was strained to the breaking point. Before the two men parted, however, Lady Queensberry had sent two hundred pounds for Oscar and funds enough to carry Bosie to Paris.[2]

Wilde stayed on alone at the Villa Giudice, a wreck of nerves after the last storm. He could neither eat nor sleep, and lived almost entirely on cigarettes. His letters overflowed with bitterness. No one was spared now as he lumped together guilty and guiltless alike in the abyss of his despair. "I never came across anyone in whom the moral sense was dominant," he unburdened himself to Smithers, "who was not heartless, cruel, vindictive, log-stupid and entirely lacking in the smallest sense of humanity. Moral people as they are termed, are simple beasts. I would sooner have fifty unnatural vices than one unnatural virtue." Threats of suicide occurred repeatedly. "But I want to see my poem out before I take steps."

[2] In his latest utterance, the preface to the play *Oscar Wilde* by Leslie and Sewell Stokes, Lord Alfred Douglas dismisses the subject by saying he left Wilde at the villa "after giving him a sum of money." He is a little more explicit about that money in his *Without Apology* (London, 1938) though his reason for giving him so large a sum is still withheld. However, Lord Alfred quotes a letter addressed to Lady Queensberry on December 7, 1897, in which he says in part: "It was for you to force me to go, and to give me the means of going by accepting my terms. This you have done, and you *must* fulfil them to the letter. You must pay this £200 at once. . . . I have given myself away to you so completely now that if you fail me I shall be utterly powerless. . . . Also if you possibly can, pay him the rest of the £500. . . . If you do that I am *quitte*." Lord Alfred glosses the letter with the footnote: "I cannot now, after all these years, give any explanation of this reference to 'the £500.' I can only assume that I had asked her originally to give him £500, and that she had told me that it was impossible, but that she could manage £200." There is a letter, however, written by Wilde to Ross shortly after he received the two hundred pounds in which he hotly denies that the money was given to him by Lady Queensberry on condition that he and Bosie part. Bosie, Wilde insists, owed him five hundred pounds, a debt of honor formally guaranteed by his brother. He had received two hundred pounds, less than half of what was owed to him. It is conceivable that Lord Alfred has not seen this letter, although it has been published.

The publication of the ballad no longer held any pleasure. Smithers' extreme caution in bringing it out as if it had been some under-the-counter pamphlet, and the smallness of the edition whereby he sought to feel the pulse of the public, exasperated the already overwrought man. "He is so fond of suppressed books that he suppresses his own," he broke out.

Smithers himself took no delight in it. The one for whose work he would have sacrificed everyone else had ceased wandering in a search to prolong his days and waited for death at Mentone, in a little room dominated by a crucifix and the candlesticks with which he would never part. In March of 1897 Beardsley had been received into the Catholic Church. Now, in the same month, a year later, he made himself ready to leave the world. "Jesus is my Lord and Judge," he headed his dying note to his friend. "I implore you to destroy all copies of Lysistrata and bad drawings . . . By all that is holy *all* obscene drawings." He signed it "Aubrey Beardsley—In my death agony." On the 16th of March, 1898 "the wonderful boy" of the 1890's died as many of his immediate contemporaries were to die—in the bosom of the Catholic Church, on foreign soil. Smithers, however, for all his devotion, destroyed none of the illustrations whose existence had darkened the last hours of the repentant Catholic. The bookseller had proved stronger than the friend.

The Ballad of Reading Gaol came out as the work of C.3.3. from Smithers' Royal Arcade shop on the 13th of February with scarcely any advertisement and that little almost in a whisper. What was his surprise when, as he was mourning the loss of Beardsley, he found himself called upon to print edition after edition of the poem, ushered out like a penitent in cinnamon-colored linen boards. More astonishing still, the press received it with nearly unanimous acclaim but for the dissentient voice of W. E. Henley in his magazine, *The Outlook*. As the article was fuller of personalities than of balanced judgment it did good rather than harm by rousing sympathy where it would have stirred up the old animosity. With the printing of the seventh edition, Oscar Wilde's name was inserted between sheltering brackets on the title page. It was the last time it appeared on any new book of his. Too literally had the gods interpreted his prison wish, "If I can produce only one beautiful work of art. . . ."

Chapter XVI: In the Circle of the Boulevards

WILDE wrote no more. With the last great effort whereby the pagan born out of his time came to terms with the Christian world against which his life had been an unremitting struggle, he exhausted his creative reserve. He had to face it: he was intellectually impotent. On first coming out of prison he had endeavored to drive out of his mind the fixation that only in England could he produce great things. He needed the excitement of London and in his ears the sound of that English which he had raised from the dead level of his age to a new distinction. England was the soil wherein his imagination had taken root; transplanted, it could only die.

Out of patience with him for throwing away the good will of his sympathizers by returning to the relation which they blamed for his ruin, Robbie Ross when the last break came, did not respond as gently as he might have done to the laments for which alone Wilde now took up his pen. The printing of the *Ballad* had brought him little money despite its success. There was small prospect after the wreck of his recent emotional readjustment, of his settling down to the play which would have opened to him the doors of Paris.

Like a too faithful hound calamity pursued him. On the 7th of April, 1898, Constance died far from home. Under the low hills of Genoa she was buried, those who had the care of her monument raising above her a simple cross of marble entwined with bronze ivy leaves, symbolic of the enduring sorrow her gentle and beautiful nature had been too frail to bear. Her husband's name still infamously known, was not carved on the grave—only her own. Thus the passersby who read the stone of "Constance Mary, daughter of Horace Lloyd, Q.C." would not have occasion to disturb with their thoughts the peace of the dead.

It was some days before Wilde heard of her death, and then he could only turn to Robbie on whom he now depended for everything, with a despairing telegram, begging him to come to him. There was one comfort. As if knowing her days were numbered, Constance had appointed a guardian for the two boys. Wilde was to know yet another loss when Robbie broke to him the news of his brother Willie's death—poor, delightful, weak, superficial Willie whose life had been like one great zero, encompassing no great good, yet also no great evil in the circle of its nullity.

Desperately, in spite of the inner knowledge of his impotency, Wilde forced himself to write, to no avail. "My writing has gone to bits, like my character," he groaned. "I am simply a self-conscious nerve in pain." Again he would confess his fears to Robbie: "I don't think I shall ever really write again. Something is killed in me. I feel no desire to write—I am unconscious of power. Of course my first year in prison destroyed me, body and soul." His return to society completed his destruction.

From now on, together with his complaints, came prayers, rather, demands for money. Ross and Adey, drawing upon the funds they had collected for Wilde's rehabilitation, doled it out to him in small sums to make it last as long as possible. Perhaps, they deluded themselves, he might still write a successful play, for the very managers who had erased his name from the theatre placards indicated their willingness to reopen their box offices to new prosperity. Wilde, however, was more concerned with the problem of making two hundred and fifty francs a month provide him with food, shelter, clothing and the bock and cigarettes that made existence bearable, than with the writing of plays. Many a time he came face to face with real want, when he walked the streets without a penny in his pocket, consumed with a wild longing for something to deaden the acuteness of hunger. "It was really like journeying through Hell," he told Robbie. "I was in the Circle of the Boulevards—one of the worst in the Inferno."

Alas, Paris had proved quite other than the city of refuge his friends had hoped it would be. Not that Wilde had failed to forewarn them. When, during his first weeks in Berneval, they had suggested the capital he had refused with the horror of one who sees again the noose that had nearly strangled him. "If I live in Paris I may be doomed to things I don't desire . . ."

His stay in Italy had paved the way. However, the old literary circle that had once courted him would have nothing more to do with him now. With the exception of André Gide, Bauër and one or two others, the French *littérateurs* revealed themselves as vulnerable in their prejudices as the least intelligent English Philistine. *"Je ne fréquente pas les forçats,"*[1] one of them flung out. The fact that after the publication of the *Ballad* he wrote another letter in *The Daily Chronicle* renewing his plea for prison reform wrought as little with them as it did with the English reader, except perhaps to act as a reminder that he was writing from experience.

But the young gathered round him. In the cheap little cafés on the Left Bank where the *soucoupes* piled up all night keeping the reckoning for the drinks when all had lost count, he became a figure like poor Lélian, long taken by death from a sordid environment which, with the blessed simplicity of a Fra Angelico he had in his last months tried to transmute to beauty with a brush and cheap gold paint. But Wilde had much more to give than the childlike Verlaine whose words, when he did not sing, had a sense rather below than above human understanding. There was nothing that Wilde, talking, could not accomplish. The beautiful prose poems, each word of which fit into the pattern of language like a well-cut jewel, still marked him the meticulous artist. The plays which he could not get himself to write enacted themselves before his listeners, scene following scene, as Wilde took now one part, now the other, his face and voice changing in masterly mimicry in the scintillating dialogue he had not the will power to set down. Stories of Christ, imagined events that the Gospels might well have recorded, sounded above the clatter of the *garçons* busy with their trays and glasses. Sometimes he expounded some original exegesis of Dante who was now frequently on his lips in an identification that had its

[1] "I do not associate with convicts."

convincing parallels; but they were adventures of his own sojourn in Hell that he told.

As time passed with no change in his condition except the occasional windfalls from Bosie who kept prize-winning horses at Chantilly and ran them regularly at the races, his face froze to lines of weariness. He was past joy and sorrow although when people he loved were near the old light illumined his face. Then Sebastian Melmoth was forgotten and he became Oscar Wilde, wearing briefly the mantle of his glory, till some terrible memory shattered the illusion. His hand, at such moments, passed tremblingly over his face, and with outthrust arm he warded off the past that had not died, whatever might have happened to the players in the tragedy. He showed no emotion on learning of Queensberry's death. Too well the old Marquis had played his part, like some over-realistic actor who used for murder the knife that had been put into his hand for play. With a bitter smile he learned that the dying man had toward the end confused the roles. He was being persecuted by "Oscar Wilders" he cried out in his delusions, rambling into mad tales of how he had been driven out of hotels by their vengeance, and of how they woke him out of his sleep by shouting opprobrious names. Before he died the Catholic Church had received the repentant atheist.

Sometimes old friends who were not ashamed to be seen in his company sought out Sebastian Melmoth in some fifth-rate hotel on the Left Bank where he could get lodgings for eighty francs a month. They would take him to the luxurious places he loved where for a day, for the space of a dinner, perhaps, he could put aside the assumed self and be what he really was. "Call me Oscar Wilde," he would plead after the first few awkward moments. And like a conjuration the name obliterated things as they were. Then no one had ever talked as he could talk, not even the Wilde of the splendid years. Words poured out of him with the rush of a cataract, as if eternity were not enough for all that he had to say. Sunlit by his undimmed imagination, they dazzled and astounded. Wilde by ceasing to write had not ceased to work. With wisdom beyond the ken of those who re-

356

proved, he knew that what he set down was but the shadow of his luminous thought, and he refrained, in a weakness of body that was daily becoming more pronounced, from making the exertion.

"You must not be angry with one who has been crushed," he said with ineffable sadness to André Gide who would have taunted his genius to activity. Frank Harris, always the soul of practicality, turned Wilde's inaction to his advantage. There was a scenario for a play that Wilde had worked out in detail without setting pen to paper. Would Wilde sell it to him? With less confidence of Harris's ability than he deserved, Wilde sold it and gave him full consent to use it as he saw fit. When Harris's *Mr. and Mrs. Daventry* was finally produced with some success Wilde became unreasonably angry. Harris had no right, he said, to use his scenario and so deprive him of a source of income—for as Harris found out before his play reached the boards, Wilde had already made the same deal with four or five other purchasers. There was no concealing the unpleasant fact: Wilde's morale like his genius and everything else that had made him the vital representative of his age, had fallen to ruin.

He now lived entirely on the generosity of his friends, a precarious life, alternating between joyous weeks on the Riviera and the weary trudging round the Circle of the Boulevards waiting for some chance acquaintance to relieve his thirst at a cheap American bar. Manhattans and whisky sodas and deadly absinthe—what better way to make one forget for a few blessed hours?

The months of his exile added into years; but the hope grew dimmer that he would ever throw off the slow death creeping upon him, body and soul. Gradually even those who had come to him for the sake of the past avoided him. He had grown unhealthily fat, a bloated caricature of the once handsome Oscar. He was getting deaf. The smile that used to light up his face with the radiance of his inner joy was now marred by the gold of his artificial teeth—provided also by the charity of friends. Heartbroken, Ross watched the gradual disintegration, knowing that nothing, not even a miracle, could restore the

357

wonderful man he had known. A miracle? Wilde laughed at the idea. "I fear that if I went before the Holy Father with a blossoming rod it would turn at once into an umbrella or something dreadful of that kind." But in his laughter there was the grimace of anguish.

In despair Ross ceased trying to reach him through his conscience. "What can you want to lecture me about except my past and my present—which you expressly exclude?" Wilde answered. "I have no future, my dear Robbie." Worse, he lived as if he believed he had none.

Long since he had fallen into his old way of living which he had had no illusions of ever overcoming. Indeed, even before he left Reading Gaol he warned Robbie of possible consequences: "It would be bestial infamy to again send me to prison for offences that in all civilized countries are questions of pathology and medical treatment. . . ." In his thinking he was far in advance of his time, though four decades of psychological research have done little since then toward bridging the differences between pathology and the law. To Will Rothenstein his justification took a more arrogant tone. "I have still difficulty in understanding why the frequentation of Sporus should be considered so much more criminal than the frequentation of Messalina."

After his stay at Posilipo he frankly took the offensive, blaming Ross for his severity because he had gone to join Bosie. He advanced specious arguments. A patriot, imprisoned because he loved his country, he said, will still love his country; a poet, imprisoned because he loved youth, will still love youth. Had he changed his manner of life, he equivocated, it would have meant his admission that such love was ignoble, whereas he maintained that it was not only noble, but more exalted than all other forms. Many who saw some of the company he frequented admired the power of his imagination.

The spring of 1900 he spent traveling in Rome and Sicily, a holiday made possible by Lord Alfred. Wilde had been ailing. Nothing serious, he thought—a case of poisoning brought about by his having eaten mussels. Nevertheless, months of treatment in Paris had done nothing to alleviate his condition. In Italy, however, he felt so much better that he was certain that at last a miracle had been accomplished when, on Easter Sunday, he received the blessing of the Holy Father. "By the way, did I tell you that . . . I was completely cured of my mussel poisoning? It is true, and I always knew it would be . . . The blessing of the Vicar of Christ made me whole." Ross knew that Wilde believed it even though in the next paragraph he wrote with levity that one of his friends, an artist, had offered to paint a votive tablet in celebration. "The only difficulty is the treatment of the mussels—they are not decorative, except the shells, and I didn't eat the shells." Ross, however, had learned to read between the lines. Time and again of late Wilde had expressed the wish to become a Catholic.

In Rome the wish became a fixation, centered about the person of the Pope whom he took every opportunity of seeing at each public appearance. On a Sunday, disregarding the objections of the Papal officers, he worked his way to the front rank of a band of pilgrims in the Vatican, and stood there waiting for the Holy Father to be carried past on his throne. "I have seen nothing like the extraordinary grace of his gesture, as he rose from moment to moment to bless—possibly the pilgrims, but certainly me." In that blessing he saw a sign that God had not cast him out. It was the sign he needed. From then on he haunted the vicinity of the Vatican and its gardens hoping for a vision of that "white soul robed in white" passing through those waste, somber avenues where the screams of the peacocks alone shattered the quiet. The tragic melancholy of the scene brought his own state vividly to mind. If only he could find refuge for his last years in some holy retreat . . . "The cloister or the café—there is my future. I tried the hearth, but it was a failure."

It was to be the café, as Ross too well realized. Back in Paris, his money spent, Wilde once again fell into the easiest mode. For that matter Paris had nothing better to offer. Between American bars and the mean little holes where few took the trouble to notice him, he swung the pendulum of his purposeless life.

One wet day, as he was making his way from one *bistro* to another, his mind fogged with drink, he had a strange meeting, hazy and indistinct like an image in moving water. A tall man, uncertain of feature in the rain, was about to cross the street near him when suddenly, to avoid a passing fiacre, he lurched back quickly and knocked him down. As the man helped him to his feet and made his apologies, Wilde detected a familiar ring in the voice, and an unmistakable Irish accent. The Queensberry trial flashed before his mind, suddenly become the theatre of that dreadful scene when that voice spat at him the questions that broke him. His eyes met Carson's and they knew each other, but neither spoke. When Carson, shuddering, walked away, he thought of that other meeting in a London street the day that Wilde's carriage had almost run him down. How triumphant the man had been that day—and how low he had sunk!

One by one even Wilde's young disciples fell away. Every day was like another and all were full of nothingness. In the dingy Hôtel d'Alsace whose proprietor, J. Dupoirier, had more than once befriended that poor lonely Monsieur Melmoth who had a way of arranging and rearranging every object in his room like a prisoner in a cell, Wilde found the only corner he could call home. Number 13 Rue de Beaux Arts was but a two-minute walk from the Hôtel Voltaire where he had first donned the gown of an artist; but how much water had flowed in the Seine, under the eyes of Voltaire, smiling his saturnine smile, between that dawn of brilliant promise and the present dark! No fresh-cut flowers on his table now, and no gold-tipped cigarettes in their cloisonné box. Bare and unbeautiful essentials were all that M. Dupoirier could offer, besides the pride of his heart, the much advertised electric call bell, newly installed. Wilde's dark little bedroom over the noisy French courtyard was but another cell in the vast prison of life. Four paces and the bed overhung with curtains of a faded burgundy, matching the upholstery of the rickety sofa opposite the mantelpiece where time, in marble, was guarded by a crouching lion in brass

—six paces, and one looked out on the small patch of courtyard with its shrill green grass. Even the sky overhead showed like that tent of blue on which Wooldridge had looked so wistfully.

Wilde seldom rose before midafternoon. Why hasten to meet a day that no longer held anything for him? A lassitude, like a chain of iron, deadened his body, carried ponderously from café to café till his money or his credit gave out and he was forced to return to his cheerless room. He hardly touched food any more and then only when weakened from hunger. As he made no alteration in his life the rash which he had attributed to mussel poisoning broke out again over his body in spite of the Pope's blessing, and what was worse, he began to suffer from recurrent headaches that made him cry out in a delirium of pain. On the 10th of October, with no one to tend him but the kind M. Dupoirier, he underwent an operation. A wire to Robbie who was then traveling with his mother brought him to Oscar at once. He was appalled at the transformation that had come over him even though when he arrived Wilde had begun to rally. Monsieur Melmoth had suffered terribly, Dupoirier told him, so terribly that even after morphine injections the sick man kept raising his hands to his head as he tossed from side to side. He had lost a great deal of weight, and the pale flesh hung loosely from his cheekbones. Buried in the depths of their sockets, even his eyes seemed dead.

The nearness of Ross, however, and the friends he brought to cheer the sickroom had a most wonderful effect. Surrounded by affection, Wilde revived. As he sat there among them he had pathetic flashes of the old splendor; the joyousness and gaiety of his spirit bubbled up in laughter till the room rang with the absurdity of his sallies and even death turned away. "I'm more like a great ape than ever," he said to Robbie one day, apologizing for scratching himself. "But I hope you'll give me lunch, Robbie, and not a nut." At times as if to deceive them on what they saw too clearly, he plunged into a pyrotechnic of talk, flashing from one subject to another, interrupting himself breathlessly and then, with a desperate energy, forcing himself to go on. But disease had damped the once perfect design, allowing but a flare here and there, some beautiful spurt of color, to indicate the broken pattern.

On the 30th of October Ross took Wilde out for a drive to the Bois. If the sick man had looked ghastly in his bed he resembled a corpse in the clothes that hung limply from his great skeleton. They had scarcely been out a few minutes when at the first café they passed Wilde stopped the fiacre and insisted on drinking absinthe. Robbie humored him, reminding him, however, that the doctors had strictly forbidden him alcohol. Wilde waved the warning aside. At the next café the same scene was repeated, and again at the third.

"Oscar, you are killing yourself!" Robbie remonstrated.

Wilde turned to him sadly and laid his hand on his to mitigate the words. "And what have I to live for, Robbie?"

At the look in those spent eyes Ross averted his own in silence. It was the last time the sick man was ever to leave his room.

For another month he lingered between life and death, the doctors disagreeing in their diagnosis. Too late they discovered it was a cerebral meningitis complicated by another more terrible disease. Ross now had Reggie Turner take turns with him in staying with the dying man, Dupoirier relieving them with a devotion that ennobled the horror of the services he was called upon to perform. Yet even in the nearness of death Wilde's brilliance was not quenched. When to please him one night they brought him the iced champagne he loved, he said with a glimmer of the irresistible Oscar, "I am dying beyond my means." How little it took to light the old spark! Only once they found him depressed after a dream wherein he had been supping with the dead. "My dear Oscar, you were probably the life and soul of the party," Reggie Turner flashed brightly, whereupon Oscar's spirits revived till he became almost hysterical with the mirth he created.

But as November neared its end, the friends realized that Wilde's life, too, was drawing to a close. He had periods of delirium followed by coma from which they despaired of his ever waking. On the 29th Ross saw he had no time to lose to fulfill a promise exacted by the dying man, so that night Father

Cuthbert Dunn of the Passionists administered baptism and extreme unction; Oscar was too weak to receive the Eucharist. The following day, toward two in the afternoon, when Ross and Turner had left the room for a moment after a weary watch, Wilde died in Dupoirier's arms.

Ross was completely crushed. He had grown to feel a personal responsibility for the unfortunate man as for everything connected with him except his genius. "He had become for me a sort of adopted prodigal baby. I began to love the very faults which I would never have forgiven in anyone else." Such fervid selfless devotion forgave the dead man much in the sight of God.

Before the funeral Ross and Turner sent telegrams to Lord Alfred, Frank Harris and others of Wilde's friends who might wish to be present, and then busied themselves, to deaden their grief, sorting the few belongings he had left. Among his papers they found a receipted bill for two suits at seventy francs each and a pawnshop ticket, constantly renewed, for the Berkeley Gold Medal won by the youthful classical scholar at Trinity.

Le Petit Parisien printed an obituary notice of a few lines, and the following day many literary men called upon Wilde, dead, who had avoided him, living. But as he lay in his coffin in the grave humility of death, a rosary round his neck and on his breast a medal of St. Francis placed there by one of the nuns who had kept watch through the night, he was beyond their belated pity.

Monday morning, the 3rd of December, so early that the shopkeepers along the Rue Bonaparte had not yet taken down their blinds, the funeral cortege filed through from the Rue des Beaux Arts toward the beautiful old church of St. Germain des Prés whose bells had marked the empty hours for the exile. But the bells were silent this morning, and only the side chapel of the Sacred Heart, bare of all funeral pomp, was opened to the sinner. A low mass without music was said by the Vicar of St. Germain assisted by two priests; then Father Dunn read the burial service over the remains of Oscar Wilde.

A crowd had gathered on the square before the church. As the coffin was being lifted into the hearse draped in silver and black, a captain of the guard who was standing by lifted his hand in a salute of magnificent dignity. The mourners Ross, Reggie Turner, Lord Alfred Douglas, Dupoirier and Jules the servant of the hotel, the doctors who had attended Wilde, Father Dunn and the acolytes, together with three or four others entered the funeral coaches and the cortege drove to the cemetery of Bagneaux, an hour and a half away.

The place was a barren desert of the dead. Not a tree shaded the vast graveyard whose tombs bore the haggard, weatherbeaten remains of artificial wreaths. After Wilde's coffin had been lowered into the ground the place blossomed with the masses of roses, lilies, orchids and laurels that affirmed the devotion of those whose love was stronger than prejudice. But the most eloquent tribute of all was a pathetic bead trophy inscribed, *"À mon locataire,"* from the humble Dupoirier who in the pariah had loved him who had sinned much, but also suffered much.

The remains of Oscar Wilde now lie in the Paris cemetery of Père Lachaise under a monument by Epstein. Against a massive mausoleum a virile angel, Sphinx-like of face, struggles upward on lifted wing, only to be weighed down by a too earthly body. The symbolism is clear and beautiful. But the Philistine vandal, pursuing even beyond death his puny rancor, has mutilated the stone.

FINIS

Bibliography

Any bibliography is necessarily incomplete. At the very time it is being prepared someone is at work adding to the list. Again, as in the present case, the limitations of space forbid the inclusion of literally hundreds of newspapers and fugitive magazines which have been consulted for even the least ray on the subject. The author has contented herself, therefore, with listing only a negligible fraction of such source material which has passed through her hands. It is her grateful duty, however, to give special thanks to Dr. Asa Don Dickinson, Librarian of Brooklyn College, for his *open sesame* to otherwise obdurate doors; to Miss Belle da Costa Greene of the Pierpont Morgan Library for her ever gracious and cheerful assistance with the precious manuscripts in her care; and to Dr. A. S. W. Rosenbach for his generosity in permitting the use of his invaluable holograph and rare book collection. The author also remembers with pleasure the courtesy of the attendants of the British Museum Reading Room, the Reference Room of the New York Public Library and the Montague Branch of the Brooklyn Public Library. To the Columbia Law Library goes a special tribute for allowing the use of an otherwise inaccessible book.

ABBOTT, EVELYN and LEWIS CAMPBELL, *Life and Letters of Benjamin Jowett*. London, 1897.

Academy. London, July 4, 1891.

ANONYMOUS, *Oscar Wilde, Three Times Tried*. (Privately printed in an edition of 999 copies.) Paris, n.d.

ARCHER, WILLIAM, *Poets of the Younger Generation*. London, 1902.

ARNOLD, MATTHEW, *Essays Literary and Critical*. London, 1909.

Poetical Works. New York, 1897.

Athenaeum. Reviews of Oscar Wilde's works. London, July 23, 1881; September 1, 1888; June 6, 1891; June 27, 1891.

ATKINSON, G. T., "Oscar Wilde at Oxford," in *The Cornhill Magazine*. May, 1929.

BALZAC, HONORÉ DE, *La fille aux yeux d'or*.

Melmoth réconcilié.

Peau de chagrin.

Séraphita. (In *Oeuvres complètes*. 24 volumes. Paris, 1875-1892.)

BARBEY D'AUREVILLY, J. A., *Ce qui ne meurt pas*.

Les diaboliques.

Memoranda. (In *Oeuvres complètes*. 17 volumes. Paris, 1926-1927.)

BARRES, CLARA, *Life and Letters of John Burroughs*. 2 volumes. Boston, 1925.

BAUDELAIRE, CHARLES, *Les fleurs du mal*. Paris, 1857.

BAZILE, CECIL G., "Les derniers jours d'Oscar Wilde," in *Revue Hebdomadaire*. November 28, 1925.

BEARDSLEY, AUBREY, *Letters from Aubrey Beardsley to Leonard Smithers*. London, 1937.

BEER, THOMAS, *The Mauve Decade*. Garden City, 1926.

BEERBOHM, MAX, *A Peep into the Past*. London, 1923.

"Notes on Oscar Wilde," in *Saturday Review*. Volume 90.

BENDZ, ERNEST, *Oscar Wilde, a Retrospect*. Vienna, 1921.

BENSON, E. F., *As We Were: a Victorian Peep Show*. London, 1930.

BERNHARDT, SARAH, *Memoirs*. London, 1907.

BERRICHON, PATERNE, *La vie de Jean-Arthur Rimbaud*. Paris, 1897.

BIRNBAUM, MARTIN, *Oscar Wilde; Fragments and Memories*. London, 1920.

BLAIR, D. O. H., "Oscar Wilde as I knew him," in *The Dublin Review*. July, 1938.

BLOY, LÉON, *Un brelan d'excommuniés*. Paris, 1889.

BLUNT, WILFRID SCAWEN, *My Diaries*. 2 volumes. London, 1919-1920.

BOCK, E. J., *Oscar Wildes persönliche und frühste literarische Beziehungen zu Walter Pater*. Bonn, 1913.

Bookman. Pater's review of *Dorian Gray*. November, 1891.

BOYD, ERNEST, *Ireland's Literary Renaissance*. New York, 1916.

BRASOL, BORIS, *Oscar Wilde; the Man, the Artist, the Martyr*. New York, 1938.

BRAYBROOKE, PATRICK, *Oscar Wilde, A Study*. London, 1929.

BRÉGY, KATHARINE, *Poets and Pilgrims*. New York, Cincinnati, etc., 1925.

The Poet's Chantry. St. Louis, Mo., 1913.

BRÉMONT, ANNA, COMTESSE DE, *Oscar Wilde and His Mother*. London, 1911.

BROPHY, LIAM, "Ernest Dowson, Poet of Despair—and Faith," in *The Irish Monthly*. Volume 61.

BROWNING, MRS. E. B., *Letters*. 2 volumes. London, 1897.

BURDETT, OSBERT, *The Beardsley Period*. London, 1925.

BURNE-JONES, LADY G., *Memorials of Edward Burne-Jones*. 2 volumes. London, 1904.

CELLIER, F. A., *Gilbert, Sullivan and D'Oyly Carte*. London, 1914.

CHARASSON, HENRIETTE, "Ernest Dowson," in *Mercure de France*. Volume 107.

CHESTERTON, G. K., *The Victorian Age in Literature*. London, 1925.

"Writing Finis to Decadence," in *Independent*. January 15, 1917.

CHURCH, E. W., *The Oxford Movement*. London, 1909.

COLERIDGE, GILBERT, "Oscar Wilde," in *The Nineteenth Century and After*. April, 1922.

COLLINGWOOD, W. G., *Life and Work of John Ruskin*. 2 volumes. Boston, 1893.

CORVO, FREDERICK, BARON, *Hadrian the Seventh*. New York, 1925.

In His Own Image. New York, 1925.

COWAN, ROBERT E. and WILLIAM ANDREWS CLARK, JR., *The Library of William Andrews Clark, Jr.* 5 volumes. 1922-.

CREW, ALBERT, *The Old Bailey*. London, 1933.

CROCE, BENEDETTO, "Studii su poesie antiche e moderne: un Gesuita inglese poeta," in *Critica*. Napoli, 1937.

CROSLAND, T. W. H., *The First Stone*. (Pamphlet, privately printed.) London, 1912.

Daily Chronicle. For letter of Wilde on prison reform. London, May 28, 1897.

DANEL, JOSEPH, *Les idées économiques et sociales de Ruskin*. Paris, 1912.

DAVRAY, HENRY, *Oscar Wilde; la tragédie finale*. Paris, 1928.

DENNISON, ARTHUR JR. and HARRISON POST, editors; introductory essay by DR. A. S. W. ROSENBACH, *Some Letters from Oscar Wilde and Alfred Douglas, 1892-1897*. (Privately Printed.) San Francisco, 1924.

DOUGLAS, LORD ALFRED, *City of the Soul*. London, 1911.

My Friendship with Oscar Wilde: Being the Autobiography of Lord Alfred Douglas. New York, 1932.

Without Apology. London, 1938.

DOWSON, ERNEST, *Poetical Works*. (With introduction by Desmond Flower.) London, 1934.

DULAU CATALOGUE, Number 161. *A Collection of Original Manuscripts, Letters and Books of Oscar Wilde*.

ELLIS, HAVELOCK, *Studies in the Psychology of Sex*. Philadelphia, 1901-1910.

ESDAILE, ARUNDELL, "The New Hellenism," in *The Fortnightly Review*. October, 1910.

FITZ-GERALD, S. J. A., *The Story of the Savoy Opera*. New York, 1925.

FLAUBERT, GUSTAVE, *Correspondance*.

Madame Bovary.

Hérodias.

Salammbô.

Notes de Voyages. (In *Oeuvres complètes*. 18 volumes. Paris, 1910.)

FLETCHER, J. G., "Gerard Manley Hopkins—priest or poet?" in *American Review*. Volume 6.

FORD, JULIA ELLSWORTH, *Simeon Solomon, an Appreciation*. New York, 1908.

FOSTER, JOSEPH, *Alumni Oxonienses, 1715-1886*. Oxford, 1886.

FRY, JOHN H., *The Revolt against Beauty*. New York, 1934.

GAUTIER, THÉOPHILE, *Charles Baudelaire*. (English.) London, 1915.

Honoré de Balzac. Paris, 1859.

Histoire du Romantisme. Second edition. Paris, 1874.

Mademoiselle de Maupin. Paris, 1835.

GIDE, ANDRÉ, *Oscar Wilde, a Study.* Oxford, 1905.

Si le grain ne meurt. Paris, 1928.

GILBERT, W. S., *The "Bab" Ballads.* London, 1869.

Complete Plays of Gilbert and Sullivan. Garden City, 1938.

GONCOURT, E., *Journals des Goncourts: Mémoires de la vie littéraire.* 9 volumes. Paris, 1851-1895.

GORCE, AGNÈS DE LA, *Francis Thompson et les poètes catholiques d'Angleterre.* Paris, 1932.

GOWSWORTH, JOHN, "The Dowson Legend" in *Transactions of the Royal Society of Literature of the United Kingdom.* Volume 17.

GRISEWOOD, H., "Gerard Manley Hopkins," in *Dublin Review.* Volume 189.

HAGEMANN, CARL, *Oscar Wilde: Sein Leben und sein Werk.* Stuttgart, 1925.

HAMILTON, WALTER, *The Aesthetic Movement in England.* London, 1892.

HARRIS, FRANK, *Contemporary Portraits.* New York, 1915.

Second Series, 1919.

Third Series, 1920.

Oscar Wilde; His Life and Confessions. (With *Memories of Oscar Wilde* by Bernard Shaw.) Published by the author. New York, 1918.

HICHENS, ROBERT, *The Green Carnation.* New York, 1894.

HIRSCHBERG, DR. M., *Die Homosexualität.* Berlin, 1914.

HOPKINS, GERARD MANLEY, *A vision of the mermaids.* London, 1929.

Further Letters. London, 1938.

Letters. London, 1935.

Note-books and Papers. London, 1937.

Poems. (Edited by Robert Bridges.) London, 1918.

HOPKINS, O. T., *Oscar Wilde; a Study of the Man and His Work.* London, 1916.

HOUSMAN, A. E., *A Shropshire Lad.* London, 1896.

Last Poems. New York, 1922.

More Poems. London, 1936.

HOUSMAN, LAURENCE, *A. E. H.* London, 1937.

Echo de Paris. London, 1923.

Selected Poems. London, 1908.

HUNEKER, J. G., *Essays.* New York, 1929.

HUNT, W. HOLMAN, *Pre-Raphaelitism and the Pre-Raphaelite Brotherhood.* 2 volumes. London, 1905.

HUYSMANS, J. K., *Certains.* Paris, 1908.

Oeuvres Complètes. 18 volumes. Paris, 1928-1934.

INGLEBY, L. C., *Oscar Wilde; Some Reminiscences.* London, 1912.

In Memoriam Oscar Wilde. Leipzig, 1911.

JACKSON, HOLBROOK, *The Eighteen Nineties.* London, 1913.

JOHNSON, LIONEL, *Poetical Works.* New York and London, 1915.

Post Liminium. New York, 1912.

JOWETT, B. (translator), *The Dialogues of Plato.* 5 volumes. Third edition, Oxford, 1924.

JUNG, C. G., *Psychological Types.* New York, 1924.

KAHN, GUSTAVE, *Symbolistes et Décadents.* Paris, 1902.

KELLY, B. W., *The Mind and Poetry of Gerard Manley Hopkins, S. J.* London, 1935.

KELSHALL, T. M., *Robert Bridges.* London, 1924.

KENILWORTH, W. W., *A Study of Oscar Wilde.* New York, 1912.

KENNEDY, J. M., *English Literature, 1880-1905.* London, 1907.

KERNAHAN, COULSON, *In Good Company.* London, 1917.

KITCHIN, GEORGE, D. D., *Ruskin in Oxford and Other Studies.* London, 1904.

LAHEY, G. F., S. J., *Gerard Manley Hopkins.* London, 1930.

LA JEUNESSE, ERNEST, "Oscar Wilde," in *La Revue Blanche.* December, 1900.

LANGTRY, LILY, *The Days I Knew.* New York, 1925.

LA SIZERANNE, R. DE, *Ruskin et la religion de la beauté.* Paris, 1898.

LE GALLIENNE, RICHARD, *The Romantic '90s.* Garden City, 1925.

LEMONNIER, LÉON, *La vie d'Oscar Wilde.* Paris, 1931.

LEWIS, LLOYD and HENRY JUSTIN SMITH, *Oscar Wilde Discovers America.* New York, 1936.

LYTTON, HENRY A., *Secrets of a Savoyard.* London, 1922.

MACFALL, HALDANE, *Aubrey Beardsley.* New York, 1927.

MAETERLINCK, MAURICE, *Les Aveugles.* Bruxelles, 1892.

Les Sept Princesses. Bruxelles, 1891.

MAHAFFY, JOHN PENTLAND, *Social Life in Greece from Homer to Menander.* London, 1874.

MARJORIBANKS, E., *The Life of Lord Carson.* 2 volumes, the first by Marjoribanks. London, 1932.

MASON, A. E. W., *Sir George Alexander and the St. James Theatre,* London, 1925.

MASON, STUART (pseudonym of CHRISTOPHER MILLARD), *Bibliography of Oscar Wilde,* London, 1914.

Introduction to *The Priest and the Acolyte.* London, 1907.

MATURIN, REV. CHARLES ROBERT, *Melmoth the Wanderer.* Edinburgh, 1820.

MÉGROZ, R. L., *Francis Thompson.* London, 1926.

MENPES, MORTIMER, *Whistler as I Knew Him.* New York, 1904.

MELMOTH, SEBASTIAN (Oscar Wilde? Trans.), *What Never Dies.* Boston, 1909.

MEYNELL, EVERARD, *The Life of Francis Thompson.* New York, 1913.

MEYNELL, VIOLA, *Alice Meynell, a Memoir.* New York, 1929.

MILLAIS, JOHN GULLE, *The Life and Letters of Sir John Everett Millais.* 2 volumes. London, 1899.

MITHOUARD, A., *Paul Verlaine ou le scrupule de la beauté.* Paris, 1897.

MORE, PAUL ELMER, *Shelburne Essays,* 10th Series. Boston, 1919.

MORRIS, WILLIAM, *Art and Socialism.* London, 1884.

NEWMAN, J. H., *Apologia pro vita sua.* London, 1864.

New York Daily Graphic, January 19, 1882.

NORDAU, MAX, *Degeneration.* New York, 1895.

O'SULLIVAN, VINCENT, *Aspects of Wilde.* New York, 1936.

PACQ, H., *Le Procès d'Oscar Wilde.* Paris, 1933.

PATER, WALTER, *Marius the Epicurean.* New edition. 2 volumes. London, 1913.

The Renaissance. London, 1877.

PEARSON, HESKETH, *Labby; the Life and Character of Henry Labouchère.* London, 1936.

POE, EDGAR ALLAN, *Complete Works.* 17 volumes. New York, 1902.

PENNELL, JOSEPH and E. R., *The Life of J. A. M. Whistler.* Philadelphia, 1908.

Ed. *The Whistler Journal.* Philadelphia, 1921.

Philadelphia Press, January 17, 1882; January 19, 1882.

Philadelphia Record, January, 1882.

PLARR, VICTOR, *Ernest Dowson, 1888-1897.* London, 1914.

PRAZ, MARIO, *La carne, la morte e il diavolo nella letteratura romantica.* Milano, 1930.

Punch, June 17, 1880; January 15, 1881; February 12, 1881; June 25, 1881; December 10, 1881; July 19, 1890.

RANSOME, ARTHUR, *Oscar Wilde, a Critical Study.* London, 1912.

RAYMOND, E. T., *Portraits of the Nineties.* London, 1921.

RAYNAUD, ERNEST, "Souvenirs sur le Symbolisme," in *Minerve Française.* Volume 6.

Reading Mercury, July 10, 1896. (For the execution of Wooldridge.)

RENIER, G. J., *Oscar Wilde.* New York, 1933.

RETTÉ, ADOLPHE, *Le Symbolisme.* Paris, 1903.

RHYMERS' CLUB, *First Book.* London, 1892.

Second Book. London, 1894.

RICKETTS, CHARLES S., *Oscar Wilde—Recollections.* Bloomsbury, 1932.

RIMBAUD, ARTHUR, *Les Illuminations.* Paris, 1886.

Lettres. Paris, 1899.

Poésies complètes. (With a preface by Paul Verlaine.) Paris, 1895.

Une Saison en Enfer. Bruxelles, 1873.

RODD, RENNELL, *Rose Leaf and Apple Leaf.* Philadelphia, 1882.

ROSS, ROBERT, *Aubrey Beardsley.* London, 1909.

"Simeon Solomon" in *Bibelot.* Volume 17.

ROTHENSTEIN, J. K. M., *Artists of the 1890's.* London, 1928.

Life and Death of Conder. London, 1938.

Ed. *Sixteen Letters from Oscar Wilde to W. Rothenstein.* London, 1930.

ROTHENSTEIN, WILLIAM (SIR), *Men and Memories.* 2 volumes. London, 1931, 1932.

RUSKIN, JOHN, *Complete Works*. New York, 1894.

SAVOY, THE. London, 1896, 1897.

SEARLE, TOWNLEY, *Sir William Schwenk Gilbert*. London, 1931.

SHERARD, ROBERT H., *Bernard Shaw, Frank Harris, and Oscar Wilde*. New York, 1937.

Life of Oscar Wilde. New York, 1928.

Oscar Wilde, "Drunkard and Swindler." (Pamphlet) Calvi, 1933.

Oscar Wilde: the Story of an Unhappy Friendship. London, 1902.

The Real Oscar Wilde. London, 1915.

Twenty Years in Paris. London, 1905.

SHORTER, C. K., *Lionel Johnson*. London, 1908.

SMOLLETT, TOBIAS, *The Adventures of Roderick Random*. New edition. London, 1930.

SQUIRE, J. C., *Essays on Poetry*. London, 1923.

STARKIE, ENID, *Arthur Rimbaud*. London, 1938.

Arthur Rimbaud in Abyssinia. Oxford, 1937.

STOKES, LESLIE and SEWELL, *Oscar Wilde*. (A drama in three acts, with an introduction by Lord Alfred Douglas.) London, 1937.

STURGEON, MARY, *Michael Field*. London, 1922.

SULLIVAN, HERBERT and NEWMAN FLOWER, *Sir Arthur Sullivan; His Life, Letters and Diaries*. New York, 1927.

SWINBURNE, ALGERNON C., *Complete Works*. 20 volumes. London, 1925-1927.

SYMONDS, JOHN ADDINGTON, *A Problem in Greek Ethics*. (Privately printed in an edition of 100 copies.) London, 1901.

A Problem in Modern Ethics. (Privately printed in an edition of 100 copies.) London, 1896.

SYMONS, ARTHUR, *A Study of Oscar Wilde*. London, 1930.

Aubrey Beardsley. London, 1898.

"Ballad of Reading Gaol" in *The Saturday Review*. March 12, 1898.

Collected Works. London, 1924.

Dramatis Personae. Indianapolis, 1925.

From Toulouse-Lautrec to Rodin. London, 1929.

Studies in Prose and Verse. London, 1904.

The Symbolist Movement in Literature. London, 1899.

THOMPSON, FRANCIS, *Selected Poems*. (With an introduction by Wilfrid Meynell.) Revised edition. New York, 1929.

Works. 3 volumes. London, 1913.

TOBIN, A. and E. GERTZ, *Frank Harris, a Study in Black and White*. Chicago, 1931.

TYNAN, KATHERINE, *Twenty-Five Years' Reminiscences*. London, 1913.

VERLAINE, PAUL, *Arthur Rimbaud*. Paris, n.d.

Oeuvres complètes. 5 volumes. Paris 1899-1900.

Oeuvres posthumes. Paris, 1903.

VINCIGUERRA, MARIO, *Romantici e decadenti inglesi*. Foligno, 1926.

WEISZ, E., *Psychologische Streifzüge über Oscar Wilde.* Leipzig, 1908.

WELBY, T. EARLE, *Arthur Symons,* a Critical Study. London, 1925.

WHISTLER, J. A. M., *Ten O'Clock.* London, 1888.

    The Gentle Art of Making Enemies. New York, 1890.

WILDE, LADY FRANCESCA ELGEE (SPERANZA), *Ancient Legends . . . of Ireland.* Boston, 1888.

WILDE, OSCAR, *After Berneval: Letters of Oscar Wilde to Robert Ross.* Beaumont Press, 1922.

    After Reading: Letters of Oscar Wilde to Robert Ross. Beaumont Press, 1921.

    Complete Works. 12 volumes. Garden City, 1933.

    De Profundis. London, 1905.

    Epistola in Carcere et Vinculis. (A translation into German of the complete prison letter, by Dr. Max Meyerfeld.) Berlin, 1925.

    Letters to the Sphinx. (With reminiscences of the author by Ada Leverson.) London, 1930.

    Letters to Sarah Bernhardt. Haldeman-Julius, 1924.

WILSON, EDMUND, "Axel and Rimbaud," in *New Republic.* February 26, 1930, and March 5, 1930.

    Axel's Castle. New York, 1931.

WINWAR, FRANCES, *Poor Splendid Wings; the Rossettis and Their Circle.* Boston, 1933.

WYNDHAM, H. S., *The Savoy Operas and Their Composer.* London, 190-.

YEATS, W. B., *Autobiographies: Reveries over Childhood and Youth, the Trembling of the Veil.* New York, 1916.

YELLOW BOOK, THE. London, 1894-1897.

ZANCO, EMILIO, *Oscar Wilde.* Genoa. 1934.

Index